CW00740696

2013

THE BEDFORDSHIRE
HISTORICAL RECORD SOCIETY

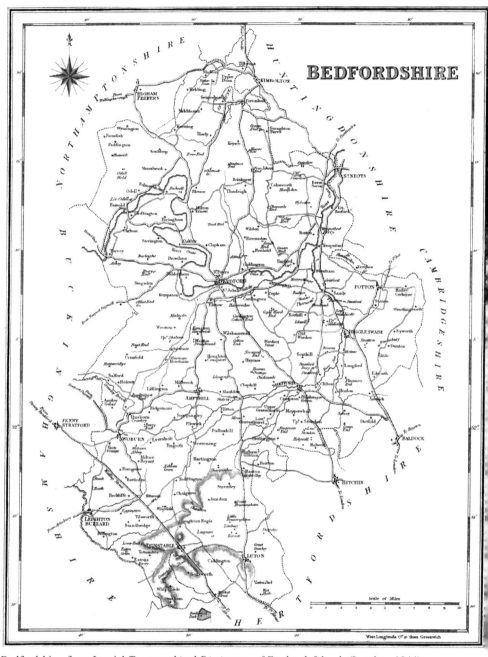

Bedfordshire, from Lewis' *Topographical Dictionary of England*, 5th ed. (London, 1844)

THE PUBLICATIONS OF THE BEDFORDSHIRE
HISTORICAL RECORD SOCIETY
VOLUME 92

THE RISE OF METHODISM
A STUDY OF BEDFORDSHIRE, 1736–1851

Jonathan Rodell

Mike,

Love, like death, hath all destroyed,
Rendered all distinctions void;
Names and sects and parties fall;
Thou, O Christ, art all in all!   C.W.

With very best wishes.

[signature]

2. viii. '16.

THE BEDFORDSHIRE HISTORICAL RECORD SOCIETY

THE BOYDELL PRESS

First published 2014

A publication of
Bedfordshire Historical Record Society
published by The Boydell Press
an imprint of Boydell & Brewer Ltd
PO Box 9, Woodbridge, Suffolk IP12 3DF, UK
and of Boydell & Brewer Inc.
668 Mt Hope Avenue, Rochester, NY 14620–2371, USA
website: www.boydellandbrewer.com

ISBN 978–0–85155–079–4

ISSN 0067–4826

The Society is most grateful for financial support from the
Simon Whitbread Charitable Trust; the Beds, Essex and
Herts Methodist District; and other donors who have
helped make the publication of this volume possible

Details of previous volumes are available from
Boydell and Brewer Ltd

A CIP catalogue record for this book is available
from the British Library

The publisher has no responsibility for the continued existence or accuracy of
URLs for external or third-party internet websites referred to in this book,
and does not guarantee that any content on such websites is,
or will remain, accurate or appropriate.

This publication is printed on acid-free paper

Contents

Obituaries of Bedfordshire Wesleyan and Primitive Methodists; Wesleyan and Primitive Methodist Societies in Bedfordshire before 1852; and Itinerant Wesleyan and Primitive Methodist preachers stationed to Bedfordshire circuits 1763–1851 appear on the website of the Bedfordshire Historical Record Society.

Maps and Tables

Illustrations

Picture acknowledgements:

Cover: Private collection, Bridgeman Art Library

The author: frontispiece, Plates 5, 13, 18, 19, 22, 27, 28, 29, 30 and 31

Bedford Library Services: Plate 8 and 12

Bedfordshire and Luton Archives and Records Service (BLARS): Plates 1, 2, 16, 17, 20, 21, 23, 24, 25, 26

Centre for Buckinghamshire Studies: Plate 32

Englesea Brook Chapel and Museum: Plates 14 and 15

The Oxford Centre for Methodism and Church History: Plates 3, 4, 6, 7, 9, 11 and 20

Stephanie McCurdy: Plate 10

Photography Plates 16 and 20 Martin Deacon; Plates 22, 27–30 Colin Dunn, Scriptura; frontispiece and Plate 31 Mikhail Hounslow

Preface

This book began life as a doctoral thesis and still contains some traces of that earlier existence but let me reassure the reader, whose spirits are already sinking at that news, that it has been thoroughly revised, re-structured and expanded for publication. There is probably more local detail here now than a strictly academic readership might appreciate and perhaps still too much information on the historiography of Methodism for the more general reader. I can only crave your patience and suggest you skip to the bits that are of more interest to you.

The bulk of the material is arranged chronologically in three chapters that relate to the three main periods of Methodist growth. Each chapter begins with a narrative and then moves on to an analysis of a series of themes – the social constituency of Methodism, the internal life of the movement, its impact on local politics and the reaction of the wider community. A fourth chapter considers how this picture of Methodism in Bedfordshire squares with the existing historiography of Methodism and a final essay offers a critical evaluation of the main sources for Methodist history.

My purpose from the outset has been to produce a piece of history that views its subject matter from the bottom up, rather than the top down. It aspires to be a history of the involvement of ordinary people in Methodism, rather than of the movement's institutions (though they will make their appearance) or its official doctrines. Ordinary people, in the eighteenth and nineteenth centuries, did not leave vast paper trails in their wake and I have had to draw on hundreds of often tiny fragments of evidence to build up this picture of their activities. Everything that I have tracked down has found its place here. If the final account is partial in some respects, then it is at least shaped by the priorities of those who produced the original documents, and the accidents of history that decided which ones would survive, rather than by the selections of my own prejudices.

Most religious history has been written by religious people and most Methodist history has certainly been written by Methodists. Perspectives have often been shaped by apologetic considerations and there has been a pronounced tendency to hagiography. I hope that this intense study of one, relatively small, area will help to dismantle some of those misleading myths, provide a new evidential benchmark for discussions about Methodist history, and help to establish a more accurate meta-narrative of the movement's contribution to British society; a contribution that is at present too easily overlooked.

Even after thirty years of searching, new sources continue to crop up and will no doubt continue to do so, probably just after the publication of this book. With this in mind, a number of webpages are being posted on the BHRS site that will sit alongside the printed volume. They will provide an opportunity to share new material with the reader as it comes to light, as well as access to some of the data collections that were created as part of the original research. I hope too that they will carry an extended collection of illustrations, and a selection of Methodist music, that will help readers to enter more imaginatively into the world we are about to explore.

Acknowledgements

The gestation of an elephant takes approximately two years. The gestation of this book has taken just short of thirty. Inevitably, over such a length of time, not everyone who helped to knit matinee jackets for this baby is still around to celebrate its birth.

I am, however, able to thank my doctoral supervisor, Professor David Thompson, both for his extraordinary patience and for trying to teach me to balance a naturally cavalier approach to history with some roundhead rigour. I am grateful also to John Walsh, Boyd Hilton and David Bebbington, all of whom read and commented on the doctoral thesis.

Peter Forsaith at the Oxford Centre for Methodism and Church History; Peter Nockles at the Methodist Archives and Research Centre; Susan J. Chapman of the Church of Jesus Christ of Latter-day Saints, and the staff at the Bedfordshire and Luton Archives and Records Service, the Centre for Buckinghamshire Studies, Hertfordshire Archives and Local Studies and the Bridwell Library, Southern Methodist University, Dallas, who have all gone out of their way to help me track down the mountain of often obscure documents on which this study is built.

I would particularly like to acknowledge those who have given permission for me to publish extracts from their own work or documents in their care:
Extracts from NM 100/5/1A, NM 114/3/6/26, NMP 100/7/1 and Q/W/G are published by permission of the Centre for Buckinghamshire Studies;
Extracts from Jones 39.B.24 are published by permission of the Trustees of Dr Williams's Library, London;
Extracts from Job Smith's Diary are made by permission of the Tom Perry Special Collections, Harold B. Lee Library, Brigham Young University, Provo, Utah;
Extracts from HFMC/5 are published by permission of Northamptonshire Record Office;
Use of the analysis in 'The Social Structure of English Methodism: Eighteenth-Twentieth Centuries', *BJSoc* 28 (1977), pp. 199–225 is made with permission of the author, Dr Clive Field.

The Bedfordshire, Essex and Hertfordshire district of the Methodist Church in Great Britain have kindly made a grant towards the cost of including illustrations in this volume and I would additionally like to thank BLARS, the Wesley Historical Society, the Bridgeman Art Library, Englesea Brook Chapel and Museum, and Stephanie McCurdy for permission to use particular images. I also owe a debt to Michael Athanson, of the Bodleian Library, Oxford, who prepared the maps and to Martin Deacon of BLARS and Colin Dunn of Scriptura who took photographs.

Barbara Tearle, the editor of the BHRS, has made an enormous contribution to the book. She has helped to bring clarity from confusion and, more than anyone, has born the frustration of getting this project to the press.

It has been a long haul but I have received unflagging encouragement and assistance from a band of fellow enthusiasts. Chris Mesley (who has been working on the history of Methodism in Leighton Buzzard) and Nigel Pibworth (whose knowledge of John Berridge is unrivalled) have both been more than generous in sharing the fruits of their own research. Roger Thorne has been a great support for many years now and his unparalleled knowledge of West Country Methodism has provided an important point of reference.

Above all, I should like to express thanks to my family for their patience over many years; particularly to my father who has continued to ask 'How is the book going?' long after others lost interest, and who has always been ready to get on his bike and cycle down to the Centre for Buckinghamshire Studies to double check some detail for me at a moment's notice.

Thank you all. If, despite all your efforts, there are still mistakes and shortcomings in what follows, then the responsibility is entirely my own.

Abbreviations

AM	*Arminian Magazine*
BHRS	Bedfordshire Historical Record Society publications
BJSoc	*British Journal of Sociology*
BLARS	Bedfordshire and Luton Archives and Records Service
Br., Bro.	Brother
Bucks	Buckinghamshire
Cambs	Cambridgeshire
CBS	Centre for Buckinghamshire Studies
col.	column
comp.	compiler
HALS	Hertfordshire Archives and Local Studies
HCP	House of Commons Papers
HCPP	House of Commons Parliamentary Publications
Herts	Hertfordshire
Hunts	Huntingdonshire
JEH	*Journal of Ecclesiastical History*
jun.	junior
MARC	Methodist Archives and Research Centre, University of Manchester
MM	*Methodist Magazine*
nd	no date
Northants	Northamptonshire
np	no place
p., pp.	page, pages
PMM	*Primitive Methodist Magazine*
PWHS	*Proceedings of the Wesley Historical Society*
Rev. Revs, Revd, Revds	Reverend, Reverends
RO	Record Office
RS	Record Society
Sr	Sister
WMM	*Wesleyan Methodist Magazine*

Mr. Hague … had been brought up in the manufacturing district on the borders of Lancashire, Cheshire, Derbyshire, and Yorkshire, among lively Methodists. His first appointment [as a preacher] was Ampthill circuit, a great way from Yorkshire, and the good man thought that "so far south there was no Methodism." But when he saw the Methodist chapel in Ampthill, with an ascent of twenty steps to go up to it; and when he entered it, and saw a high pulpit, a large congregation, and a large choir of singers, with instruments of music, "to praise the Lord withal," his courage failed him; and when he had proceeded a little way in his sermon, his memory and his strength forsook him, he turned pale, fainted, and fell back in the pulpit.

Coles, *Youthful days*, 153–4.

Introduction

> Too much writing on Methodism commences with the assumption that
> we all know what Methodism was.[1]

In Search of a Lost Culture

When a DVD on the history of Luton was produced in 2006, its sleeve notes explained that some subjects covered in detail in earlier printed histories were not included in the film.[2] Two redundant topics specifically mentioned were the development of educational provision in the town and the history of Methodism. It is easy to see why the story of, what is today, a small Christian denomination should seem a rather uninteresting byway, not only of Luton's story but also of history generally. To venture into the world of religious nonconformity in the eighteenth or nineteenth centuries is certainly to make a journey into a landscape quite unfamiliar to the twenty-first century mind. The pious language in which these people expressed themselves is now foreign to modern ears and the basic experience of their lives, spartan, hard and uncertain, was quite different from today's. Even more challengingly, it requires an act of imagination to understand the thinking of people who made sense of their world using a mental framework alien to current presumptions. To make such a venture is not, however, to disappear into the backwaters of English history but rather to explore what was once a significant moral, cultural and political influence on society.

The emergence in Bedfordshire during the late 1730s of the movement called Methodism forms part of far wider religious developments that occurred not only across England and Wales, but also across the North Atlantic world in the early eighteenth century. From the small Protestant communities in the Habsburg territories of central Europe to the Puritan settlements of New England, a shift is discernable away from the cerebral acceptance of doctrinal systems to a new emphasis on the spiritual authenticity of emotion and personal experience. (Indeed, this shift was not confined to Protestant Christianity but was mirrored in eastern European Judaism by the simultaneous rise of the Hasidic movement.) The first manifestation of this new religious spirit is generally acknowledged to be 'the revolt of the children' in Silesia, in 1707, when young Protestants, whose churches had been confiscated and closed by the Catholic authorities, began to hold open-air meetings for prayer and hymn-singing.[3] Fifteen years later, in the face of renewed persecution, Protestants from Silesia and Moravia sought refuge in Lutheran Saxony and founded a community at Herrnhut under the patronage of a local aristocrat, Count Nikolaus von Zinzendorf. In 1727 the Herrnhutters established a formal religious organisation, the Unitas Fratrum (Unity of the Brethren), better known as the

---

1   Thompson, *Making of the English working class*, 918.
2   *The story of Luton* (DVD, Amazon Events, 2006); Dyer and Dony, *Story of Luton*.
3   Ward, *Protestant Evangelical awakening*, 71–3.

Moravian Church, and began to send missionaries and emigrants out to form new communities in other parts of Germany, in Switzerland and in the British colonies of North America. Even before the Moravians reached North America, however, a movement towards heart-religion, apparently independent of events in Europe, was already evident among both English and Dutch settlers.[4]

It was inevitable that London, the gateway between Europe and Britain's American colonies, would soon be exposed to these developments. An account of a 'New Light' revival at Northampton, Massachusetts was published there in 1737, and a small Moravian society was established in May 1738 by Peter Böhler, a German pastor in transit to Georgia. Once again, however, an indigenous movement seems to have pre-existed these international contacts. A number of individuals, including Howell Harris, Daniel Rowland and George Whitefield, had, quite independently of each other, already undergone dramatic conversion experiences and begun to preach the need for a 'new birth' as early as 1735. The diverse followers of the rapidly expanding movement which resulted from the cross-fertilisation of these native and continental developments are the people whom contemporaries labelled as 'Methodists'. Over time, the word has gradually come to have a considerably narrower meaning, referring only to those groups that trace their descent in some way from John Wesley and, among them, to those that joined the modern Methodist Church in 1932. Throughout the period, however, the broader meaning continued to hold and in 1851 the census of religious worship still recognised two major categories of Methodist denominations – Arminian and Calvinistic. The Methodists of this book include everyone who used that name of themselves or who would have been described as such by their contemporaries.[5]

Methodism and Bedfordshire

The first use of the word Methodist in relation to people in Bedfordshire appears to have occurred in February 1739, when the poet John Byrom wrote in his diary 'Thence I went to Abington's, where they were talking about the Methodists, and a Bedfordshire attorney violently against Mr. Ingham, who had spoiled his clerks.'[6]

The next three chapters trace the history of the movement in the county over the next century or more. The first deals with the initial period of Methodist enthusiasm in the mid-eighteenth century. The second considers the transformation which the movement underwent during a quarter century of extraordinary growth from about 1790 onwards, a period once referred to by Methodist historians as 'The Middle Age'.[7] The third looks at the final episode of significant Methodist growth, in the 1830s. Each of the chapters tries to uncover what actually attracted people to Methodism; what being a Methodist entailed; how Methodists were perceived; and what

---

4   Butler, *New World faiths,* 119–23.
5   In the late 1740s the rector of St Peter's, Bedford noted several 'Methodists' in his burial and baptismal registers. These were people associated with the town's Moravian congregation. By modern definitions they were not Methodists, but the rector reflects contemporary usage rather than confusion as to the group's identity (Anderson, *Early Methodism in Bedford,* 7).
6   *WMM* (1863), 911.
7   George Smith divided the history of Wesleyan Methodism into 'Wesley and His Times' (to 1791), 'The Middle Age' (1791–1816) and 'Modern Methodism' (1817 onwards) (Smith, *History of Wesleyan Methodism*). C. H. Crookshank's history of Irish Methodism subsequently followed the same structure, extending the Middle Age to 1820 (Crookshank, *History of Methodism in Ireland*).

impact Methodism may have had on the wider community. A fourth chapter looks at some of what has previously been written about the early history of English Methodism and assesses how well it fits the Bedfordshire evidence.

Bedfordshire might, at first sight, seem an unlikely choice for a micro-study of this kind. An agricultural county in southern England, it is not the kind of district that has previously featured prominently in Methodist historiography. It was not affected in any dramatic way by the processes of industrialisation before 1851 or by the introduction of powered machinery; its communities, with the exception of Luton which did experience rapid population growth, were largely settled. There were no miners or fishermen here, no forest areas and few widely-scattered settlements. According to the generally accepted interpretation of Methodist growth this should have been a Methodist wilderness and yet by 1851 Methodism was stronger in Bedfordshire than in any county in England except Cornwall. In fact, Methodism was stronger in many southern counties than has been generally acknowledged, with Methodists forming a larger proportion of the population in Norfolk, Suffolk, Cambridgeshire, Huntingdonshire, Northamptonshire, Buckinghamshire, Dorset and Wiltshire than in much-studied Lancashire.[8]

The strength of Methodism in Bedfordshire is all the more intriguing because this was a county in which both the Church of England and Dissent were also strong.[9] The cumulative effect was to give Bedfordshire the highest church attendance rates of any English county in 1851 and to make it the buckle on Victorian England's very own Bible Belt, a string of counties that included Suffolk, Cambridgeshire, Huntingdonshire, Northamptonshire and Buckinghamshire. Despite the fact that these counties represent the very apogee of the nineteenth-century phenomenon of mass church attendance, they have received very little attention from historians. Yet it is perhaps here that the life, appeal and distinctiveness of all the various religious communities (church, meeting-house and chapel), are exposed most clearly to scrutiny. Bedfordshire was scattered with Methodist congregations, not because Church of England provision was overwhelmed nor because there was any lack of an alternative to the parish church but, it would seem, because nearly a third of the population made a conscious choice to join them.

Bedfordshire in the Eighteenth and Nineteenth Centuries[10]

> BEDFORDSHIRE, an inland county, bounded on the north and north-east by Huntingdonshire, on the east by the county of Cambridge, on the south-east and south by that of Hertford, on the south-west and west by that of Buckingham, and on the north-west by that of Northampton. It ... includes four hundred and sixty-three square miles.... The population, in 1821, amounted to 83,716.[11]

Situated at the point where East Anglia, the Midlands and the south-east all meet and merge, even though it measures only thirty-five miles by twenty-seven,

---

8   Gay, *Geography of religion*, 320.
9   Church of England attendances in Bedfordshire in 1851 were broadly in line with the rest of southern England. The Baptist index of attendances was one of the four highest in an English county (Gay, *Geography of religion*, 292).
10 For background on Bedfordshire see Godber, *History of Bedfordshire* and Bigmore, *Bedfordshire and Huntingdonshire landscape*.
11 Lewis, *Topographical dictionary of England*, I, 127.

Bedfordshire's complex geology gave the county a varied agricultural economy. Across the middle of the county stretches a greensand ridge which was dominated by a handful of great estates: the Dukes of Bedford at Woburn, the Earls of Ossory at Ampthill and the Grey family at Wrest. For much of the eighteenth century this poor soil was mostly abandoned to sheep but in the early nineteenth century it began to be brought under the plough. The population increased dramatically, by something like 60% between 1801 and 1851, and this growth was not without social cost.[12] Across the north of the county lies a belt of heavy Midland clay. This too was dominated by large estates, including those of the Dukes of Bedford, the Orlebar family at Hinwick and the St Johns at Melchbourne. The heavy soil was hard to work and the farms, which were generally quite small, were increasingly given over to pastoral farming. In the south, on the chalk uplands of the Chilterns, the story was rather different. The straw grown on this soil was peculiarly suited to making plait and plaiting was a significant cottage industry from the seventeenth century. During the Napoleonic wars, when it was impossible to import Italian plait, demand soared. After the war, plait production was protected by tariff from cheaper foreign imports until 1842.[13] By then, many farms were in any case moving across first to raising meat and then to dairy production for the growing London market. Over to the east, on the alluvial soil along the banks of the river Ivel, a tradition of market gardening had existed in the parish of Sandy from the seventeenth century. Improvements to the Great North Road, in the early eighteenth century, and later works to enable boats to navigate the Ivel as far as Biggleswade, made possible a great expansion of gardening along the banks of both the Ivel and the Ouse to exploit the demand for vegetables in London. Here landholdings were often extremely small and the work was labour intensive.

The county town, Bedford, developed steadily throughout the period, its population rising from 3,948 inhabitants at the first census in 1801 to 11,693 by 1851. The growing population found employment in a number of agriculturally-based industries that flourished in the town, particularly brewing and the manufacturing of farm machinery. About twenty miles to the south the small market town of Luton, which in 1801 had a population of 1,794, mushroomed into something akin to an industrial town. When the chalk uplands replaced Tuscany as the principal source of straw plait, Luton emerged both as a major centre of production and the main plait market. By the 1820s factories were opening and London hat manufacturers were relocating to Luton to be closer to their suppliers. The county's other market towns, Biggleswade, Dunstable and Leighton Buzzard, followed a less spectacular course of development. Situated on Watling Street, Dunstable was a major coaching stop in the eighteenth century, and shared in the prosperity of the growing trade in straw-plait and hats. Biggleswade, likewise, benefited from its location on the Great North Road, and from the fact that the Ivel navigation gave it access to the sea. Leighton Buzzard, by contrast, had poor communications in the eighteenth century but from 1800 was linked to London and the Midlands by the Grand Junction canal and from

---

[12]   The figure is based on the average for the six parishes of Eversholt, Houghton Conquest, Lidlington, Marston Moretaine, Silsoe and Wilstead.
[13]   Dyer and Dony, *Story of Luton*, 103–6.

1838 by the London and Birmingham railway. None of these towns was large and even in 1851 their populations were still only 3,589, 4,460 and 4,465 respectively. Information about the social make-up of the population in the eighteenth century is scarce but one valuable piece of evidence is a survey of the village of Cardington, south of Bedford, which was carried out in 1782. It records a community in which the genders were almost equally balanced (51:49 female to male); in which 40% of the population were under fourteen; and in which, of those over fourteen, 25% were single, 62% were married and 13% were widowed.[14] Subsequent data from the censuses carried out from 1801 onwards seems both to confirm that general demography and to suggest that it continued largely unchanged throughout the period.[15] There was some local variation; the female majority in Bedford, and later Luton as well, was larger than in the surrounding villages and was particularly pronounced in the fifteen to thirty age range, presumably as a result of girls working in domestic service and the straw hat trade.[16]

In fact, large numbers of women in paid employment appear to have been another constant feature of the local social landscape. The Cardington survey found a community in which most married women had paid occupations and in 1851 the county had the highest percentage of economically active adult women in England.[17] Recent work on baptism registers from about fifty parishes has also provided a picture of the pattern of male employment. It suggests that in the early eighteenth century about 9% of adult males were farmers, 50% were farm workers, 32% craftsmen and 9% tradesmen and professionals. In the early nineteenth century the proportion of farm workers increased, perhaps reaching 60% by the 1820s, but declined steadily after that and was down to 43% by 1851.[18]

In religion, Bedfordshire had a strong Puritan tradition. Archbishop Laud's metropolitan visitation of 1633 had found the county 'the most tainted of any part of the diocese' of Lincoln and full of 'the sort of people that run from their own parishes after affected preachers.'[19] Dissent from the Restoration settlement was deep-rooted and tenacious. In 1720 all but six very small parishes contained some Dissenters and there were even a few places – St Cuthbert's parish in Bedford, Stevington and Keysoe – where they were in the majority.[20] In the south, Particular Baptists predominated with meeting-houses at Dunstable, Luton, Markyate and Thorn (all offshoots of the Kensworth church in Hertfordshire).[21] In the north, the legacy of John Bunyan was a network of mixed communion churches in which Independents,

---

14 Baker, *Inhabitants of Cardington*, 36.
15 The overall ratio of women to men was 52:48 in 1801, 53:47 in 1811, 52:48 in 1821, 51:49 in 1831, 52:48 in 1841 and 51:49 in 1851. There is no information on the age of the population until 1821 when 40% were under 15; in 1841 and 1851 the figure was 38%. In 1851, of those 15 years of age and over 39% were single, 53% were married and 8% were widowed.
16 In 1821 women formed 54% of the population of Bedford, 60% in the 20–30 age range. In 1841 they formed 54%, including 58% in the 20–25 age range, and 57% in Luton, including 67% of the 15–20 age range.
17 This seems to have been especially true of the Luton district where 70–80% of adult women were economically active (Shaw-Taylor and Wrigley, 'Occupational structure of England').
18 Kitson, 'Male occupational structure of Bedfordshire.'
19 Quoted in Godber, *History of Bedfordshire*, 228.
20 The villages in which no Dissent was recorded were Eyeworth, Farndish, Lower Gravenhurst, Knotting, Melchbourne and Upper Stondon (Bell, *Episcopal visitations in Bedfordshire*).
21 The Bedfordshire section of the Evans List (of Dissenting congregations in 1715) appears in Wigfield,

Presbyterians and Baptists worshipped together. There was little sign of decline in these communities in the early eighteenth century, with a new church being formed at Blunham in 1724 and new meeting-houses erected at Stevington in 1721 and Keysoe in 1741.[22] Other denominations were also present in the county. At Southill and Carlton, the meeting-houses were described as 'Davisite', after Richard Davis the pastor of Rothwell Independent Church in Northamptonshire.[23] At Leighton Buzzard and Sundon there were General Baptist churches.[24] Earlier, in 1658 the first national meeting of Quakers had been held in Bedfordshire, at Beckerings Park, and in the early eighteenth century there were meetings at Ampthill, Clifton, Cranfield, Dunstable, Langford, Leighton Buzzard, Luton, Markyate, Pulloxhill, Sewell and Stotfold.[25]

The majority of people, of course, continued in their loyalty to the Church of England, the local parish structure of which appears to have been well-resourced and fully-functioning when Methodism made its first appearance in the county. The bishop of Lincoln's visitation of 1720 found a resident clergyman in three-quarters of Bedfordshire parishes and prayers being read both morning and afternoon on Sundays in more than half. There does, however, seem to have been a lack of energy. Evidence for Sunday preaching is almost entirely lacking, with only eight returns making any reference to it, including Bedford St Cuthbert's where 'Publick service is read in this Church every Lord's day at five aclock in the afternoon, except on every 3rd Sunday that I preach there betwixt the hours of one and three in the afternoon.'[26]

Only ten parishes celebrated communion more than once a quarter and nearly half did so only at Christmas, Easter and Whitsun. Even then, just one in ten adults participated. Indeed, there appears to have been little appetite for devotions that went beyond the social duty of Sunday attendance. At Dunton the vicar noted that 'I formerly tried to bring them to Prayers on Wednesdyes, Frydayes and all Holydayes but could not obtain my desire.' It was the same at Milton Bryan 'on Good Friday and Ash-Wednesday my Congregation is very small, there being a Market in one neighbouring Town and a Fair in another on those days.' Many clergy referred to the negligence of parents in sending their children to church for catechising, and many young people, it appears, refused to attend. At Potsgrove 'There have been none chatechized this year. The youth are all servants, and they too wise (as they think)

'Recusancy and Nonconformity in Bedfordshire', 207–8. See also Baker, *For the generation following* and Fisher, *People of the meeting house.*

[22] Tibbutt, *Bunyan Meeting Bedford*; Tibbutt and Hart, *Keysoe Brook End and Keysoe Row Baptist Churches*; Tibbutt, *Stevington Baptist Meeting.*

[23] Relations between Davis's followers and other Independents were clearly very strained. The Davisite congregations in Bedford (which later migrated to Southill), Wellingborough, Olney and Northampton were established in opposition to existing Independent churches and the Carlton church was formed by secession from Stevington. The precise nature of the differences between the two camps is harder to establish. One element may have been that Davis gave a greater role to the laity, both in the ordination of ministers and in preaching, than was the practice among other local Independents. See Streather, *Memorials of the Independent Chapel at Rothwell* and Nuttall, 'Baptists and Independents in Olney', 26–37.

[24] Champion, *General Baptist Church of Berkhamsted, Chesham and Tring*, 18, 65, 68 and 133; Brittain, *Theological Remembrancer.*

[25] Godber, *Friends in Bedfordshire and West Hertfordshire*, 36–9.

[26] Bell, *Episcopal visitations in Bedfordshire*, 189.

to be chatechized.' At Riseley the incumbent confessed to the bishop that there were families in his parish that 'go neither to Church nor meeting.'[27]

Finally, it should be noted that Methodist geography rarely coincided with civil or ecclesiastical boundaries. A glance at Edwin Tindall's *Wesleyan Methodist Atlas of England and Wales*, published in 1874, instantly reveals how the structures of Methodist organisations mapped the English landscape in a unique way.[28] Preaching circuits, quarterly meetings, gatherings for love-feasts and anniversaries all created their own links and loyalties, catchments and watersheds. The Wesleyan 'Bedfordshire circuit', for instance, at one point embraced parts of Hertfordshire, Buckinghamshire, Northamptonshire, Huntingdonshire, Cambridgeshire and even Warwickshire. In the same way the Primitive Methodists of Luton began as an outpost of a circuit based on the village of Shefford in Berkshire. This study, while focused on the county of Bedfordshire, does not impose arbitrary limitations on the more complex and evolving network of relationships which constituted 'Methodist Bedfordshire'. Rather, it encompasses all the societies and congregations which were linked to Methodist communities in Bedfordshire at any particular period.

---

[27] Bell, *Episcopal visitations in Bedfordshire*, 205, 225, 230, 232.
[28] For a discussion of the way in which their organisational structures created its own mental map for Methodists, see Richey, *Methodist Conference in America*, 27–35.

Chapter One

Pious societies: the first rise of Methodism 1736–1790

Part 1 Narrative

The First Methodists

The first green shoots of the Methodist revival appeared early in Bedfordshire. When Francis Okely formed a society in Bedford in the summer of 1736 'to pursue Religion in the greatest Strictness and Purity', news of the 'second Pentecost' in Saxony and of 'the surprising work of God' in Massachusetts had not even reached England.[1] A few individuals in other parts of Britain, including Howell Harris, Daniel Rowland and George Whitefield, had already experienced their own religious awakenings during the previous twelve months but even John Wesley's iconic experience, of feeling his heart 'strangely warmed,' lay a full two years in the future. Societies like Okely's had, of course, been a feature of Anglican devotional life since the 1670s, but this one was unusual, and in ways that pointed to the future rather than the past, in that it was lay-led and mixed gender.[2] Okely went up to Cambridge later that same year but the Bedford society continued without him, possibly under the leadership of his mother, Ann, and then later of Jacob Rogers, the newly appointed curate of St Paul's, Bedford.[3]

At Cambridge, Okely met with a number of other young men whose religious ideas and experience were developing in a similar direction, and through them he, and the Bedford society, were brought into contact with other emerging evangelical groups. In particular, in the autumn of 1738, he became friends with William Delamotte, whose older brother Charles had belonged to John Wesley's Holy Club at Oxford and had accompanied the Wesley brothers to the fledgling American colony of Georgia where he had had a profound religious experience, possibly under Moravian influence. It was probably through the Delamottes that the Cambridge circle made contact with Benjamin Ingham, another former Holy Club member, who had been preaching the need for conversion since his own awakening, in Yorkshire, in September 1738. A nineteenth-century manuscript history of Ingham's work, based on diaries that have since been lost, records that he met Okely and Delamotte in Cambridge on 16 December.[4] A fuller account of the visit is preserved in a manuscript life of Ann Okely:

---

[1] Welch, *Bedford Moravian Church*, 219.
[2] Rack, 'Religious societies and the origins of Methodism', 587.
[3] Rogers graduated from Cambridge in 1737 and worked first as an usher at Bedford Grammar School before securing ordination and appointment as curate to the vicar of St Paul's.
[4] William Batty 'Church history collected from the memoirs and journals of Mr. Ingham and the labourers in connection with him', MARC, MAM P11B quoted in Pickles, *Benjamin Ingham,* 17.

It happened that Mr Ingham in his Way to Yorkshire called at Cambridge to visit William Delamotte, and was by him introduced to the whole Society of serious and awakened Students. When Bedford and Mr Rogers were mentioned in the Course of Conversation [Rogers had been at school with Ingham], and in particular that Mr Rogers had said, he should be glad to see Mr Ingham, He and Mr William Delamotte immediately formed a Resolution to go over thither, to see what could be done farther for the Lord ... When Mr Ingham and William Delamotte came to Bedford they lodged of course at Mother Okely's, who had been lately recovered of the Small Pox, which had raged in so Melancholy a Manner that all the Town and Country were divinely prepared to be serious. Mr Ingham by preaching in the Churches in and about Bedford, and William Delamotte by expounding the holy Scriptures in private Houses, made a great Stir and general Awakening both in Town and Country; and Societies were gathered together, where Preaching and Expounding went forward as often as Opportunity served, but every Evening regularly in Bedford. The Difficulty at first was to find a proper Place there for the great Numbers who came to hear. But a Remedy was soon found for this Inconvenience by William Delamotte's proposing to Mother O. to fit up a Barn in her Yard for this Purpose.[5]

At the beginning, the society was closely associated with the Church of England; its members, having held their own meetings during the week, apparently followed Rogers from church to church on a Sunday as he provided cover for various non-resident incumbents. This arrangement, however, lasted only a few months. Early in 1739, having denounced the local clergy in a sermon on the text 'His watchmen are blind: they are all ignorant, they are all dumb dogs, they cannot bark; sleeping, lying down, loving to slumber', Rogers was dismissed from his curacy.[6] He took to the open air and the society followed him. When George Whitefield visited the town in May 1739, he preached to an audience that he reckoned to number about three thousand from the stairs of a windmill, 'the pulpit of my dear brother and fellow labourer, Mr. Rogers.'[7]

Encouraged by Whitefield, Rogers seems to have left Bedford in the summer of 1739 to preach around Donnington Park, the Leicestershire home of the Earl and Countess of Huntingdon, and in Nottingham.[8] The following spring he joined Benjamin Ingham and William Delamotte for a preaching tour in Yorkshire.[9]

There is some evidence that during this period Rogers, like many of the first Methodists in the Midlands, came to adopt Baptist views and it is clear that the society which he left behind in Bedford moved in that direction.[10] On 10 October 1740 Francis Okely, now back in Bedford, was baptised by Thomas Craner, the recently appointed minister of Blunham Meeting, a congregation which had originally been an outpost of the mixed-communion Bedford Meeting but had been

5   Welch, *Bedford Moravian Church*, 219–20.
6   The text is from Isaiah 56: 10–11. The occasion is thought to have been the funeral of Francis Hunt, Rector of St Paul's and of St Cuthbert's, Bedford. Hunt died on 22 February 1739.
7   Murray, *Whitefield's journals*, 274. Whitefield also preached at Hertford, Hitchin, St Albans, Olney and Northampton on this tour. See also 'Mary Collier's Relation' in Welch, *Bedford Moravian Church*, 210.
8   Houghton, *Letters of George Whitefield*, 92.
9   *Weekly Miscellany* (London), 26 July 1740.
10   Welch, *Bedford Moravian Church*, 8; Welch, 'The Origins of the New Connexion of General Baptists in Leicestershire', 59–70.

constituted as a distinct Baptist church in 1724.[11] Six days later Craner obtained a licence for the barn in Mrs Okely's yard to be a preaching place for Dissenters and on 31 October 'our beloved Brother Okely was solemnly sent forth' by the Blunham church 'and set apart for the work of the ministry according to the Holy Ghost's direction in such cases agreeable to Acts 13.1, 2, 3.'[12]

The new Methodist wine could not long be contained in an old Dissenting wineskin and the relationship between the Bedford society and the Blunham church lasted little more than eighteen months. When Francis Okely's younger brother, John, introduced him to a number of the Moravians he had met at the Fetter Lane society in London, Okely was immediately drawn both to their pietistic spirituality and to their church discipline. For consorting with such 'seducers and broachers of heresy', he was solemnly excommunicated by the Blunham Baptists in April 1742. Rogers and the rest of the Bedford society, who numbered 40 in the town itself, with another 112 in the surrounding villages, followed Okely's lead and over the next three years sought increasing Moravian supervision of their life together.[13] They were not, of course, the only Methodists to take such a step. The early days of the revival were a period of excitement and confusion; no clear organisational structures existed nor even any clear doctrinal framework. Relationships between the leading preachers were often stormy and those who co-operated closely one minute might easily be found denouncing each other the next. Whitefield's long absences in America prevented him from exercising any clear leadership and Wesley had yet to emerge as a serious player on the evangelical scene. The Moravians by contrast, although recently arrived in England, were well established in Germany and seemed to offer solid ground amid the shifting sands. Benjamin Ingham had led his societies in Yorkshire into the calm security of the Moravian fold in May 1742 and John Cennick would bring his Wiltshire societies over at the end of 1745.[14] Moravian tutelage certainly seems to have secured the continuing prosperity of the Bedford society, for by December 1744 its membership had risen to 259, with 52 in the town and the remainder spread across thirty-eight towns and villages in five counties.

On 17 January 1745 the Moravian society at Bedford was recognised as a full congregation of the Unitas Fratrum (a congregation being a group entitled to celebrate the sacraments) and began to acquire property for a settlement (that is a place where members could live communally).[15] By 1745 houses had been hired for the Married Brethren and Sisters, the Single Brethren and the Single Sisters and by early 1751 an estate had been purchased on the edge of the town where a purpose-built settlement could be created. Here, in June of that year, a burying ground was consecrated and the foundation stone of a new chapel laid; in August, a new Brethren's house was begun on the site; and in May 1757 a new Sisters' house, Ministers' house and

---

[11] Craner was set apart to the pastoral office on 31 August 1739 (Tibbutt, *Old Meeting, Blunham*, 6).
[12] Church book of Blunham Baptist meeting 1724–1891, BLARS, X525/1; Welch, *Bedfordshire chapels*, 26.
[13] Podmore, *Moravian Church in England*, 105.
[14] Podmore, *Moravian Church in England*, 88–95 and 170.
[15] A brief account of the celebration of the centenary anniversary at Bedford, January 17th 1845, BLARS, MO 672.

Table 1. Membership of the Okely's Society, 1744

Bedfordshire	no.			Buckinghamshire	no.
Bedford	52	Old Warden	6	Astwood	
Biddenham	13	Over Dean		Olney	3
Biggleswade	6	Ravensden	7		
Cardington	1	Renhold	1	*Cambridgeshire*	
Elstow	8	Ridgmont	12	Cambridge	3
Eversholt	2	Riseley	9	Little Shalford	11
Fenlake	3	Sharnbrook	2		
Goldington	3	Southill	3	*Huntingdonshire*	
Haynes	7	Stevington	6	Swineshead	1
Houghton [?Conquest]	5	Sutton	1		
Husborne Crawley	2	Thurleigh	14	*Northamptonshire*	
Kempston	10	Tilbrook	8	Higham Ferrers	2
Lidlington	15	Wilden	2	Kimbolton	
Milbrook	1	Woburn	2	Northampton	14
Milton	2	Wootton	7	Raunds	1
Nether Dean	3	Wootton Pillinge	3		
Odell	8				
				Total	259

Places listed without members may have received preaching, but no-one had yet committed to membership.

Source: Society members: Bedford and District 1744, BLARS, MO 3.

Congregation Hall.[16] By 1759 there were 365 people in the Moravian community at Bedford, including children, and another 60 to 80 at Riseley, a village about nine miles to the north.[17] Five labourers (or ministers) travelled some three hundred miles a week visiting outlying societies which included Riseley (where a chapel was built in 1759), Lidlington, Haynes, Ridgmont and Shefford, Northampton and Culworth in Northamptonshire, and Emberton in Buckinghamshire.[18] The significance of the Bedford community can perhaps best be judged by comparing its numbers with those of its London counterpart. In 1753 the Moravian community at Fetter Lane had 300 congregation members, a further 200 society members, 100 children and numerous regular hearers.[19] Given the comparative populations of London and Bedford, the strength of the Bedford settlement is remarkable and underscores its importance in the early Methodist landscape.

[16] *Short sketches of the work carried on by the ... Moravian Church in Lancashire*, 36–7; Welch, *Bedford Moravian Church*, 31. William Parker's account of the Moravians' building programme is recorded in Wesley's Journal (*Works of Wesley*, XX, 477–8).
[17] Podmore, *Moravian Church in England*, 105.
[18] *Short sketches of the work carried on by the ... Moravian Church in Lancashire*, 37. A chapel was built at Northampton in 1770. Later in the century services would also be held at Cardington, Silsoe and Wilden.
[19] Podmore, *Fetter Lane Moravian Congregation*, 12.

Elsewhere in the county, other religious societies, more on Okely's original lines, were beginning to appear. Some such group may have existed in the little market town of Potton, in the east of the county, by 1747, for in February of that year John Wesley responded to an invitation to preach there and found 'a serious congregation'; two years later he preached there again, in the Market Square.[20] Further south, the 'new enthusiasm' apparently reached Luton, another market town, in about 1750. The earliest account of the origins of Methodism in the town is contained in a letter dated 24 January 1839 and written by George Spilsbury, who claimed that his mother was one of the first members. According to Spilsbury, the Luton society was begun by a Mr Bull, a rush basket maker, who was already a Methodist when he came to the town. The first meeting place was in Castle Street but the society migrated from there to the Bull Barn, which had been used as a preaching place by John Bunyan, and then to Cawdell's harness shop which William Cole fitted up as a meeting room.[21]

Over to the west, Olney in Buckinghamshire, was an early centre of Calvinistic Methodism. Whitefield visited the town twice in May 1739, a society was formed, a preaching-house built, and by 1744 it was the base for a preaching circuit of Whitefield's connexion.[22] Thomas Lewis wrote to *The Christian History*, a Whitefieldite periodical, in October 1744 that he had preached for an entire week in the Tabernacle at Olney, and also at Northampton.[23] Three years later Joseph Smith mentions preaching not only at Olney but also at Emberton, Towcester, Sherington and in Northampton 'at the College-Lane Meeting-House.'[24] The records of the connexion are extremely scant and it is unclear how widely this circuit stretched, but it is hard to imagine that it did not include parts of Bedfordshire at some stage at least. One of the Cambridge Methodists, William Hammond who preached at Bedford in 1738, was on the circuit before he defected to the Moravians in 1745. Howell Harris spent three days in Olney in July 1748 during which he preached, met the society, and divided it into bands; and Whitefield himself returned in 1748, 1750 and again in 1753, when he also preached in Bedford.[25] The circuit, however, was given up that year when Moses Browne, a former curate of James Hervey and

---

20 *Works of Wesley*, XX, 155 and 295.
21 George Spilsbury's account of the beginnings of Methodism in Luton, 1839, MARC. Samuel Vincent, in the *Luton Reporter* 7 November 1885, says that the society began with a George Bull and nine others in 1750 but offers no authority. Balch, *Souvenir of a century of Wesleyan Methodism in Luton*, 3 repeats the reference to 1750 and identifies an upper room in the Market Place as the first meeting place. Tearle, *Our Heritage*, 11 repeats the reference to an upper room and identifies it as being in a house on Market Hill belonging to a harness-maker called Cawdell. No record of any licence survives before 1798, and neither Bull nor Cawdell appear in the circuit book's list of members in 1781. Before any of this, in 1742, a Luton man, William Peter Knolton, a fan-maker by trade and a Baptist by persuasion, had been a member of the Fetter Lane society in London (Benham, *Memoirs of James Hutton*, 90).
22 Hindmarsh, *John Newton and the English evangelical tradition*, 183–4.
23 Letter from Lewis to *The Christian History*, quoted in Tyerman, *Life of George Whitefield*, II, 112. For an account of *The Christian History* see Jones, 'A glorious work in the world', 82–5.
24 *The Christian History* (1847), 168.
25 Beynon, *Howell Harris's visits to London*, 206; Tyerman, *Life of George Whitefield*, II, 315 and 410. Apart from *The Christian History* the principle source for the Olney circuit are the minutes of the English Calvinistic Methodist Association 1744–9 published in Welch, *Two Calvinistic Methodist chapels*. There are also references in the records of the Bedford Moravian congregation (Welch, *Bedford Moravian Church*, 22, 23, 30, 37, 42, 65 and 236).

protégé of the Countess of Huntingdon, was presented to the living of Olney by its patron Lord Dartmouth, himself a leading Methodist sympathiser.[26]

Mr Wesley's People

William Parker, a grocer in Angel Street, Bedford, was one of those who were affected by the preaching of Ingham and Delamotte in 1739 and who, by 1741, had joined the Moravians.[27] It was to be a troubled relationship. When, early in 1742, the Moravians began to hold their services at the same time as the parish church, he wrote to John Wesley (who had withdrawn from the Moravian-inspired society in Fetter Lane about eighteen months previously), asking him to visit but was quickly persuaded to write again withdrawing the invitation. Four years later Parker was in dispute with the Moravian leadership over his involvement in borough politics and in 1750 was arguing with them about a property deal that had fallen through. Finally, in December 1752, he was expelled for allowing his daughter to marry without the permission of the elders.

Nothing daunted, Parker seems to have formed his own society and issued a fresh invitation to John Wesley to come and visit.[28] A significant part of the letter is preserved in Wesley's *Journals*. It appears that John's first response was to ask his brother Charles to go on his behalf but that Charles declined to do so. In a letter to Charles, dated 20 October 1753, John wrote: 'I came back from Bedford last night ... I am sure it was God's will for you to call there.'[29] Despite this initial complication, the first visit seems to have been a success. John had travelled out to Bedford from London on 15 October and 'In the evening ... met the little society, just escaped with the skin of their teeth'.[30] The following day he preached twice in the open air on St Peter's Green and spent two more days in the town before returning to the capital. Other visits followed and gradually the new society was integrated into Wesley's connexion. In 1754 Wesley spent two days in the town on his way back to London from Norwich.[31] In April 1757 he stayed with Parker on his way from London to Leicester and in November of that year spent time in the town talking to disaffected Moravians.[32] In February 1758 Parker, in his turn, journeyed down to London to preach at the Foundry, Wesley's London headquarters. 'A more artless preacher I never heard' Wesley observed, 'but not destitute of pathos. I doubt not, he may be of much use among honest, simple-hearted people.'[33]

---

[26] James Hervey, a one-time member of Wesley's Holy Club, was a leading Calvinistic Methodist. Curate to his father, the rector of Collingtree and Weston Favell in Northamptonshire, from 1743 to 1752, he succeeded to the two livings and died in 1758. Selina Hastings, Countess of Huntingdon, was an early Methodist convert. After Whitefield's death she emerged as the central figure in English Calvinistic Methodism and a remnant of her connexion still exists (Hindmarsh, *John Newton and the English evangelical tradition*, 184).

[27] *Works of Wesley*, XX, 476–9.

[28] *Works of Wesley*, XX, 476.

[29] *Works of Wesley*, XXVI, 526.

[30] *Works of Wesley*, XX, 479.

[31] *Works of Wesley*, XX, 489.

[32] *Works of Wesley*, XXI, 91 and 131. It is possible that the conversation recorded on 1 August 1757 also took place in the town.

[33] *Works of Wesley*, XXI, 135.

From 1756 Bedford was included on the round of Wesley's London-based preachers, along with Portsmouth, Norwich, Leigh and Canterbury.[34]

There are records of two such visits, in 1760 and 1762, both by John Murlin, a Cornishman known as the Weeping Prophet. From these, it appears that the preachers spent a month at a time in Bedford. Given that there were only four preachers stationed in London in 1755, and the scale of their other commitments, it seems very likely that there were long gaps between the visits.[35] The fact that both Murlin's visits took place in April/May raises the possibility that they were no more than annual visitations.[36]

The preachers' visits may have contributed to the formation of a number of other Wesleyan societies that begin to appear at about this time. Wesley preached at Great Barford when he visited Bedford in 1757, and again in 1761, and Murlin writes of his second visit, that 'While we were in those parts I visited Towcester, Whittlebury and some other places, and found a blessing among those simple, honest-hearted people.' One of these other places was presumably Clifton, where Parker applied for a licence for a labourer's cottage to be a preaching place in 1761.[37] Another may well have been Sundon, about twelve miles south of Bedford. On the death of Lord Sundon, in 1752, his estate had passed into the hands of four nieces, one of whom was married to William Cole, the son of a member of Wesley's London society.[38] Wesley travelled with Mrs Cole to Sundon in April 1754 and later commented in his journal that it would be a miracle if such wealth did not 'drown her soul in everlasting perdition.'[39]

Whatever his concerns about the effect of such luxury on Mrs Cole's soul, Wesley seems not to have harboured too many about its effect on his own. Over the next twelve years he stayed at Sundon on at least eight other occasions, often for several days at a time.[40] On some of these visits Wesley mentions preaching, the first being in September 1759 when 'a considerable number of people' gathered to hear him, and in his account of a visit in 1764 he seems to suggest that Sundon was the scene of regular preaching by others.

Parker's society seems, nevertheless, to have struggled to make progress. Although Wesley's occasional visits drew a reasonable congregation, numbers seem to have dwindled.[41] A visitor to Bedford, in 1758, found the society renting a room

---

[34] Letter from John Wesley to Thomas Olivers, 10 July 1756, Telford, *Letters of Wesley*, III, 183–4.
[35] *Works of Wesley*, X, 273.
[36] 'I left London in April [1760], and on the 26th I arrived at Bedford. ... On 28th May I returned to London' (*The experience of several eminent Methodist preachers*, 60–1). 'On the 10th of April [1762] we [Murlin had just married] set off in the stage for Bedford. ... We returned to London again on 3rd May' (Ibid., 61–2).
[37] Welch, *Bedfordshire chapels*, 54.
[38] There is a John Cole listed among the married band-leaders at the Foundry in 1744, an Anne Cole among the married sisters and an Elizabeth Cole among the single sisters (Stevenson, *City Road Chapel, London*, 33–8).
[39] *Works of Wesley* XX, 485–6.
[40] *Works of Wesley*, XX, 485–6. The other recorded visits were: 17–20 June 1754; 6–9 March 1758; 22–23 November 1759; 9–10 January 1761; 6–7 February 1761; 23–27 January 1764; 17–18 February 1766; and 10–14 November 1766.
[41] On 27 August 1759 his congregation was 'numerous' and on 23 November 1759 it was 'pretty large' (*Works of Wesley*, XXI, 225 and 234).

in the yard of the George Inn but their numbers were greatly diminished.[42] He offered thirty guineas towards the cost of a chapel:

> Mr Pearson, of Bedford, was glad to hear my proposal, and said he should endeavour to help it forward. Alderman Walker was very glad, and no doubt will assist, but as the Society in Bedford is poor in general, little can be expected from it.[43]

It was another four years before a property was purchased, in Angel Street. This was apparently a large spinning room and was probably the new room mentioned by Wesley in 1763 when he felt that 'we at last see some fruit of our labour.'[44]

John Berridge's Circuit

Methodism had by now also made an appearance on the Cambridgeshire side of the county, but here it was to take a different direction. John Berridge, the vicar of Everton, had been born at Kingston, Nottinghamshire in 1716 and had entered Clare Hall, Cambridge in 1734. He had proceeded to a college fellowship, which required ordination, even though he held Socinian views. In 1749, he had taken on the curacy of Stapleford, which he had served from college, and in 1755 had been admitted to the vicarage of Everton, a college living, which he held until his death. In December 1757, overwhelmed by a sense that his preaching was achieving nothing, he 'fled to Jesus alone for refuge' and began to preach a new message of sin, repentance and faith.[45] Soon people were coming from up to fourteen miles away to attend the services at Everton each Sunday. News clearly reached Bedford, and in early June 1758 John Walsh, a London Methodist who was visiting the town, walked across to Everton, with a Brother Tansley, to hear Berridge for himself. He wrote to John Wesley that the vicar:

> meets little companies of his Converts from several towns and villages, at his own house. He was once ashamed of the word Methodist, but takes it to himself as freely as I do. The country seems to kindle around him.[46]

Later that month, Berridge began to preach in neighbouring parishes, alienating many of his clerical neighbours but winning the support of Samuel Hicks, rector of Wrestlingworth. Hicks had known Berridge from his days at Cambridge, and may also have had some prior contact with Methodism.[47] By the end of July Whitefield himself had visited Everton and in November Wesley included the village in a visit to Bedford. On that occasion, Berridge and Wesley proceeded together to Wrestlingworth, where Wesley preached that evening in Hicks's church and then again the next morning, when

---

[42] John Walsh to John Wesley dated 21 June 1758 and published in *AM* (1780), 104.

[43] *AM* (1780), 104.

[44] *Works of Wesley*, XXI, 433; *WMM* (1833), 51–2; Anderson, *Early Methodism in Bedford*, 15.

[45] Pibworth, *Gospel pedlar*, 23 and 34. For a full account of Berridge's life see also Whittingham, *Works of Berridge*, ix–lviii.

[46] John Walsh to John Wesley, 21 June 1758, *AM* (1780), 103–5.

[47] Samuel Hicks (not William Hicks, as given in *Works of Wesley*, XXI, 171), rector of Wrestlingworth from the day after his ordination in 1744 until the day of his death in 1796.

In the middle of the sermon a woman before me dropped down as dead, as one had done the night before. In a short time she came to herself and remained deeply sensible of her want of Christ.[48]

Over the coming months these dramatic, sometimes violent, expressions of religious excitement were to become considerably more pronounced.

The following summer, in May 1759, John Walsh was back at Everton in company with a Mr B-ll.[49] Walsh forwarded to Wesley a lengthy and detailed account of the extraordinary scenes that they witnessed. On the Sunday B-ll attended an early morning preaching service at the vicarage, and they both went to matins and even-song in the church. On all three occasions they witnessed people crying out and fainting, the description of the afternoon service recording that

When the power of religion began to be spoke of, the presence of God really filled the place. And while poor sinners felt the sentence of death in their souls, what sounds of distress did I hear! This occasioned a mixture of various sounds; some shrieking, some roaring aloud. The most general was a loud breathing, like that of people half-strangled and gasping for life. And indeed almost all the cries were like those of human creatures dying in a bitter anguish. Great numbers wept without any noise; others fell down as dead; some sinking in silence; some with extreme noise and violent agitation.[50]

After evensong Berridge's house was full of penitents and the scenes of anguish and joy continued long after Berridge himself had retired to bed:

Mr Berridge about this time retired ... We continued, praising God with all our might, and his work went on as when Mr. B[erridg]e was exhorting. I had for some time observed a young woman all in tears, but now her countenance changed. The unspeakable joy appeared in her face, which quick as lightning was filled with smiles and became of a crimson colour. About the same time John Keeling of Potton fell into an agony. But he grew calm in about quarter of an hour, though without a clear sense of pardon.[51]

It was the same at Wrestlingworth, where, on the Thursday evening, the visitors saw fifteen or sixteen people drop down during Hicks' sermon, and even more dramatic scenes in the parsonage house after the service. People 'either lay as dead, or struggled with all their might' and 'their cries increased beyond measure, so that the loudest singing could scarce be heard'.[52]

---

[48] *Works of Wesley*, XXI, 171.

[49] Mr B-ll has usually been identified with the London banker Ebenezer Blackwell and it has been presumed that the author of this account was his wife ('Revival at Everton', 22–4 and *Works of Wesley*, XXI, 195). A careful review of the evidence, however, points to the author of the journal quoted here being John Walsh. Walsh is known (from internal evidence and from a letter from Berridge to Wesley of 16 July 1759) to be the author of a second journal extract regarding Everton that is quoted in Wesley's *Journal* under the date 29 July 1759 and it is clear from the opening lines of that passage that the author was also present during the earlier visit. One of the main reasons for ascribing the first extract to Mrs Blackwell was apparently that it mentions the author's difficulty getting up in the morning, a problem mentioned in relation to Mrs Blackwell in other sources, but the second extract, which is known to be from Walsh, refers to the writer suffering from the same complaint. Indeed, Mr B-ll may, in fact, have been George Bell, a London Methodist lay preacher who is known to have visited Berridge several times (Whittingham, *Works of Berridge*, li).

[50] Journal of John Walsh, 20 May 1759, *Works of Wesley*, XXI, 195–6.

[51] *Works of Wesley*, XXI, 197.

[52] *Works of Wesley*, XXI, 198.

In mid-June 1759 Berridge and Hicks began preaching in the open air. As Berridge records it:

> On Monday se'nnight Mr. Hicks accompanied me to Meldreth. On the way we called at a farmer's house. After dinner I went into the yard, and seeing nearly an hundred and fifty people, I called for a table and preached, for the first time, in the open air. ... We then went to Meldreth, where I preached in a field, to about four thousand people. In the morning at five Mr. Hicks preached in the same field to about a thousand. And now the presence of the Lord was wonderfully among us. ... And, I trust, beside many that were slightly wounded, nearly thirty received true heartfelt conviction.[53]

Growing in confidence, the two men agreed to extend their labours into Hertfordshire and 'to separate, and go round the neighbourhood, preaching in the fields, wherever a door is opened, three or four days in every week.'[54]

By mid-July they already had more work than they could cope with and were concentrating their efforts on the most promising locations:

> Mr H. and myself have been preaching in the fields for this month past. ... We have been casting the gospel-net in the neighbourhood; but success at present only, or chiefly attends us in the Eastern parts: and there we now direct the whole of our endeavours. Near twenty towns have received the gospel in a greater or lesser degree; and we continually receive fresh invitations.[55]

John Walsh, back in Everton on another visit, sent Wesley a second report covering a two-week period in which he heard Hicks preach at Cockayne Hatley and followed Berridge through a string of Cambridgeshire villages. The crowds at the mid-week, open-air services were now very large – Walsh estimated 1,500 at Stapleford and perhaps 2,000 at Triplow – and stories were reaching Everton of conversions taking place in-between the preachers' visits. One visitor 'brought good tidings to Mr. Berridge from Grantchester, that God had there *broken down* seventeen persons last week by the singing of hymns only'.[56] Everywhere it seems the dramatic, physical expressions of grief and joy continued:

> One woman tore up the ground with her hands, filling them with dust and with the hard-trodden grass, on which I saw her lie with her hands clinched, as one dead, when the multitude dispersed. Another roared and screamed in a more dreadful agony than ever I heard before. I omitted the rejoicing of believers because of their number and the frequency thereof; though the manner was strange, some of them being quite overpowered with divine love and only showing enough of natural life to let us know they were overwhelmed with joy and life eternal. Some continued long as if they were dead, but with a calm sweetness in their looks. I saw one who lay two or three hours in the open air, and being then carried into the house, continued insensible another hour, as if actually dead. The first sign of life she showed was a rapture of praise, intermixed with a small joyous laughter.[57]

---

[53] Berridge to John Wesley, nd, quoted in Wesley's journal (*Works of Wesley,* XXI, 199). A second letter, dated 16 July 1759 (*AM* (1780), 611), recounts that Berridge and Hicks had been preaching in the fields 'this month past' which suggests that the field-preaching began in the middle of June and that this letter should be dated late June.
[54] *Works of Wesley,* XXI, 200.
[55] Berridge to John Wesley 16 July 1759, *AM* (1780), 611.
[56] Journal of John Walsh, 14 July 1759, quoted in Wesley's journal, *Works of Wesley,* XXI, 213.
[57] *Works of Wesley,* XXI, 214.

Hicks is said to have reckoned the total number of converts in the first twelve months of itinerating to have reached two thousand.

The events at Everton attracted considerable interest amongst prominent Methodists. The Revds Martin Madan and William Romaine, who were closely associated with the Countess of Huntingdon, were among the visitors in July and although initially sceptical were apparently won over by what they saw. John Wesley arrived in early August, but by then the manifestations of intense emotion were already diminishing:

> I preached at eight on 'The wicked shall be turned into hell, and all the people that forget God.' The whole congregation was earnestly attentive. But not above one or two cried out. And I did not observe any that fainted away, either then or in the morning. ... Those whom it pleases God to employ in his work ought to be quite passive in this respect. They should *choose* nothing, but leave entirely to him all the circumstances of his own work.[58]

He returned at the end of the month, and was rewarded with a small taste of the heady days of July:

> I preached on those words in the Second Lesson, 'We know that we are of God.' One sunk down, and another, and another. Some cried aloud in agony of prayer. I would willingly have spent some time in prayer with them. But my voice failed, so that I was obliged to conclude the service, leaving many in the church crying and praying, but unable either to walk or stand.[59]

The excitement seems to have tailed off somewhat towards the end of the year and when Wesley visited in November 1759, he 'observed a remarkable difference since I was here before as to the *manner* of the work. None now were in trances, none cried out, none fell down or were convulsed'.[60]

Even now, however, huge numbers were still attending Berridge's preaching. When the Countess of Huntingdon arrived, in March 1760, with an entourage of clergy in tow, the church in Everton was said to have been 'unable to contain a fifth of the people.' News of the visit spread rapidly through the locality and by the third day 'it was judged *ten thousand* at least assembled to hear.'[61] Nor had the manifestations of intense excitement completely disappeared. When Howell Harris heard Berridge preach at Everton in 1763 he witnessed 'the uncommon glory and power on him and the people; some crying out and he affected all the while.'[62]

At first, the links between Berridge and Wesley's connexion were strong. Wesley described Berridge to the Countess of Huntingdon as 'one of the most simple, as well as most sensible, men of all whom it pleased God to employ in reviving primitive Christianity.'[63] He preached several times at Everton, and at Wrestlingworth, and seems to have sent preachers to help on Berridge's circuit.[64] Berridge, for his part, made his loyalties very clear in the preface to the hymn-book which he produced in 1760, attacking first the Calvinistic Methodists and then the Moravians:

58 *Works of Wesley*, XXI, 223.
59 *Works of Wesley*, XXI, 225–6.
60 *Works of Wesley*, XXI, 234.
61 Seymour, *Life of Countess of Huntingdon*, I, 399 and 400.
62 Beynon, *Howell Harris, reformer and soldier*, 204.
63 Wesley to the Countess of Huntingdon, 1 March 1759, Tyerman, *Life of Wesley,* II, 324.
64 Whittingham, *Works of Berridge*, li.

we would not have you be tost about, like a Wave of the Sea, with every Wind of Doctrine: Among which, that of unconditional Election is remarkably strange to us with whom you are now joined in Society, or at least assemble your-selves to hear the Gospel. ... Another caution I must give you, concerning some Foreigners, who have entered our Land under the Name of Moravians. I shall speak of these with more Freedom, because a Nest of them is at Bedford. ... I have had a private circumstantial Account of their Proceedings, from a person of well-known Integrity; who was drawn in among them, remained some Years in their Den, and escaped at last with only the Skin of his Teeth. This Person, who is yet alive, and living where Satan's Seat is, made me acquainted with the covetous Artifices, detestable Lewdness and Popish Superstitions, that are found amongst them; ... Deliver us, O Lord, from these Locusts![65]

Berridge's hostility to the Moravians was also apparent in a letter to a friend, written in July 1758 and published, without his consent, in 1760:

If you had lived in this Neighbourhood, you would have known that I am utterly detested and continually reviled by the Moravians. And no Wonder: For I warn all my Hearers against them both in public and private. Nay, I have been to Bedford, where there is a Nest of them, to bear a preaching Testimony against their corrupt Principles and Practices.'[66]

The stage seemed set for Berridge's circuit to be accommodated within Wesley's connexion much as William Grimshaw's round, which was similarly based on a parish ministry, at Haworth in Yorkshire, had been.[67] Wesley, however, was not an easy man to work with and there were personal tensions almost from the outset. The first glimpse of such difficulties comes in April 1760 when Wesley took exception to Berridge's hymn-book, writing from Dublin:

After we had been once singing an hymn at Everton, I was just going to say, 'I wish Mr. Whitefield would not try to mend my brother's hymns. He cannot do it. How vilely he has murdered that hymn, weakening the sense as well as marring the poetry!' But how was I afterwards surprised to hear it was not Mr. Whitefield, but Mr. B.! In very deed it is not easy to mend his hymns any more than to imitate them.[68]

Some of Berridge's emendations may have been motivated by a desire to offer hymns in a more vernacular and less literary vocabulary, so Charles Wesley's line 'The Æthiop then shall change his skin' appears in Berridge's version as 'The Black-moor, too, shall change his skin.' Others are rather harder to explain, such as the recasting of two other lines in the same hymn:

Wesley's Hymns	*Berridge's Divine Songs*
He speaks, and, listening to His voice,	When Jesus speaks, we know His voice,
New life the dead receive.	The dead new life receive.[69]

Given that Wesley too was given to revising other men's words, this scolding over artistic integrity seems rather self-regarding. It was not Wesley's only complaint, however, and he went on to write:

[65] Berridge, *Collection of divine songs*, xvi, xix, xx–xxi. The preface is reproduced in Whittingham, *Works of Berridge*, xxxiii–xxxv.
[66] *Fragment of the true religion*, 24.
[67] The parallels between Berridge and Grimshaw are noted in passing in Baker, *William Grimshaw*, 103.
[68] Wesley to Berridge, 18 April 1760, Telford, *Letters of Wesley*, IV, 93.
[69] Stelfox, 'Mr Wesley's Preface to the Hymn-Book', *WMM* (1876), 531.

Has not this aptness to find fault frequently shown itself in abundance of other instances? Sometimes with regard to Mr. Parker or Mr. Hicks, sometimes with regard to me? And this may be one reason why you take one step which was scarce ever before taken in Christendom: I mean, the discouraging the new converts from reading – at least, from reading anything but the Bible. ... I can hardly imagine that you discourage reading even our little tracts, out of jealousy lest we should undermine you or steal away the affections of the people.[70]

Berridge's response, which he delayed writing 'that I might not write in a spirit unbecoming the Gospel', emphasises his desire to continue working closely with Wesley:

I discourage the reading of any books, except the Bible and the Homilies, not because of the jealousy mentioned by you, but because I find that they who read many books, usually neglect the Bible, and soon become eager disputants, and in the end turn out Predestinarians. At least this has happened so with me. If my sentiments do not yet altogether harmonize with yours, they differ the least from yours of any others. And as there is nothing catching or cankering in those senti-ments of yours which are contrary to mine, I am not only willing but desirous you should preach at Everton, as often as you can favour us with your company. Last week I was at Bedford, and preached to your society; from whom I heard, that you was returned out of the West, and purposed to come amongst us soon. Will you call at Everton ...? You will be welcome. My invitation is sincere and friendly: accept of it.[71]

Wesley did accept the invitation, visiting Everton a few weeks later, and the co-operation continued.[72] Berridge assisted Wesley at the covenant service in Spital-fields on 1 January 1762 and Wesley set out the next day to supply Berridge's circuit for over a week, preaching at Rood Farm, near Biggleswade, and Potton, among other places.[73] Berridge, however, also began to co-operate with Whitefield, preaching for him in London in March 1761 and again in January 1762; indeed, it was the latter of these engagements that created the need for Wesley to supply at Everton.[74] In February 1763 it was Whitefield's turn to preach at Everton, which he did on his way to Scotland, and Berridge was, once again, one of those who supplied his London pulpits in his absence.[75]

It was at this juncture that another incident did permanent damage to the rela-tionship between Wesley and Berridge. George Bell, one of Wesley's preachers and a visitor at one point to Everton, inspired by Wesley's teaching on Christian perfection, gathered around him a group who believed themselves to be restored to the purity of Adam and Eve and incapable of sin. When he prophesied that the world would end on 28 February 1763 he caused panic in London and was arrested, bringing the whole Methodist movement into disrepute.[76] Berridge was one among

---

[70] Wesley to Berridge, 18 April 1760, Telford, *Letters of Wesley*, IV, 93.
[71] Berridge to John Wesley, 22 November 1760, *AM* (1797), 305.
[72] Wesley's journal records visits to Everton, after receipt of this letter, on 11–12 January and 2–5 February 1761 and on 2–10 January 1762 (*Works of Wesley*, XXI, 299, 302, 347, 349).
[73] *Works of Wesley*, XXI, 347–9.
[74] 'One Mr. Berridge, late Moderator of Cambridge, has been preaching here with great flame': Whitefield to John Gillies, 14 March 1761. 'Mr. Berridge is here, and preaches with power': Whitefield to unknown correspondent, 8 January 1762 (Tyerman, *Life of George Whitefield*, II, 441 and 452).
[75] Tyerman, *Life of George Whitefield*, II, 462.
[76] Rack, *Reasonable enthusiast*, 338–9.

many who blamed Wesley for Bell's excesses. Howell Harris, on a visit to Everton in October 1763, records that 'He was full against the Moravians and Mr John Wesley's Perfection.'[77] Wesley, who refused to accept any responsibility for what had happened, clearly felt that he was being treated unfairly, and wrote to the Countess of Huntingdon:

> My Lady – By the mercy of God, I am still alive, and following the work to which He has called me, although without any help, even in the most trying times, from those of whom I might have expected it. Their voice seemed to be rather, '*Down with him, down with him; even to the ground.*' I mean (for I use no ceremony or circumlocution) Mr. Madan, Mr. Haweis, Mr. Berridge, and (I am sorry to say it) Mr. Whitefield.[78]

He wrote 'an angry letter' to Whitefield, to which Whitefield thought it best to make no reply, and it may well be that something similar was sent to Everton.[79] Wesley never visited Everton again, even when Berridge wrote in 1768 seeking reconciliation:

> I see no reason why we should keep at a distance, whilst we continue servants of the same Master; ... Though my hand has been mute, my heart is kindly affected towards you. I trust we agree in Essentials, and therefore should leave each other at rest with his circumstantials. ... When I saw you in town, I gave you an invitation to Everton; and I now repeat it, offering you very kindly the use of my house and church.[80]

Wesley publicly distanced himself that year from Berridge in a printed response to criticism made of Methodism by Dr Thomas Rutherforth:

> In your first charge you undertake to prove that 'Christianity does not reject the aid of human learning.' Mr. B[erridge] thinks it does. But I am not accountable for him, from whom in this I totally differ.[81]

It was a grudge that time did little to defuse. Twelve years later, in a letter to Brian Bury Collins, a young clergyman who had preached for Wesley the previous year but was currently assisting at Everton, Wesley pointedly made no reference to Berridge, but wrote:

> A few years ago the people at and around Everton were deeply alive to God and as simple as little children. It is well if you *find* them so now. Perhaps you may by the help of God *make* them so now. Mr. Hicks in particular *was* a burning and a shining light, full of love and zeal for God. I hope you will see him as often as you can, and (if need be) lift up the hands that hang down, and encourage him to set out anew in the great work.[82]

---

[77] Beynon, *Howell Harris, reformer and soldier*, 204. According to Whittingham, *Works of Berridge*, li-lii, Berridge sarcastically asked Bell for a ride in the chariot of fire that Bell claimed would be taking him to heaven.

[78] Wesley to the Countess of Huntingdon, 20 March 1763, Tyerman, *Life of Wesley,* II, 463.

[79] Whitefield to Charles Wesley, 17 March 1763, Bridwell Library, Southern Methodist University.

[80] Berridge to John Wesley, 1 January 1768, *AM* (1783), 616. Wesley was, however, reconciled to Hicks and records visits to Wrestlingworth on 4–5 December 1783; 21 December 1784; 17–18 October 1786; 31 October 1787; 18 November 1788; 3 November 1789; and 26 November 1790.

[81] Wesley, *Letter to the Rev. Dr. Rutherforth*, (1767); *Works of Wesley*, IX, 376.

[82] Wesley to Brian Bury Collins, 14 June 1780, Telford, *Letters of Wesley*, VII, 23.

Berridge continued to preach regularly at the London chapels built by George Whitefield, at Moorfields and in Tottenham Court Road; usually taking up residence there from just after Christmas to just before Easter. A long period of illness in the late 1760s brought a change in his theological outlook and in 1773 he published *The Christian world unmasked: pray come and peep*, a critique of Arminianism from a Calvinistic standpoint. It signalled the end of any co-operation with Wesley's connexion, as Berridge noted in a letter to John Newton in September that year, 'my midway preaching in Bedford seems to be foreclosed by the stench which my pamphlet has occasioned.'[83]

Even then, he maintained good relations with John Fletcher, one of Wesley's chief apologists who had published works attacking *The Christian world unmasked*, warmly welcoming him to Everton in 1776.[84]

So, instead of a circuit within Wesley's connexion, Berridge's societies became part of the rather looser network of Calvinistic Methodism. John Thornton, one of the trustees of the Tabernacle, gave continual financial assistance and the Countess of Huntingdon helped Berridge find preachers. With this help, despite continuing bouts of ill health which prevented his itinerating, Berridge sustained what was clearly a substantial circuit. In 1773 it apparently consisted of about 40 places and was served by two paid lay preachers, who 'ride from town to town, preaching morning and evening every day' and six 'Sunday preachers'.[85] Some 386 hymn-books were distributed that year; a further 200 in 1774, when Berridge reported that his 'cathedral barns are much crowded'; and no fewer than 1,000 in 1778.[86] An extraordinary figure when illiteracy was still widespread. It is hard to recreate the geography of the circuit but it certainly included Potton, Biggleswade, and probably Stotfold, in Bedfordshire; stretched as far to the north-east as Ely; and to the south-east as Steeple Bumpstead. Berridge may have been in contact with the Unwins and William Cowper at Huntingdon, who by 1766 had 'acquired the name of Method-ists', and he certainly worked in concert with Henry Venn, who from 1771 was vicar of Yelling.[87]

Berridge was also in contact with developments on the other side of Bedford-shire. He was in regular correspondence with John Newton, who became curate of Olney in 1764 when the vicar, Moses Browne, moved to Morden College.[88] There was even an exchange of pulpits between the two men, although Berridge's poor health seems to have meant Newton was a more regular visitor at Everton than he at Olney.

---

[83] Berridge to John Newton, 20 September 1773, Whittingham, *Works of Berridge*, 377.

[84] *WMM* (1825), 607.

[85] Berridge to John Thornton, 3 May 1773, *Congregational Magazine* (1842), 221.

[86] Berridge to John Thornton, 25 September 1773, 10 August 1774 and 12 June 1778, Whittingham, *Works of Berridge*, 377, 384 and 391.

[87] William Cowper to Maria Cowper, 20 October 1766, King and Ryskamp, *Letters and prose writings of William Cowper*, I, 152. It is possible that there were other sympathetic clergy. Smith refers to John Jones at Alconbury and to two clergymen at Huntingdon called Hodgson and Nicholson (Smith, 'Early Methodism in Huntingdonshire', *WMM* (1881), 586).

[88] Francis Okely had originally been proposed for the post but the bishop of Lincoln had refused to recognise his Moravian ordination (Podmore, *Moravian Church in England*, 287).

I entreat you not to pass by Everton without warming a bed, and a pulpit. If the Lord gives me strength, I will pay off all my debts; but if I am forced to be insolvent, do you act like a generous Christian, and continue your loans.[89]

At Olney Newton preached in the church on Thursday evenings as well as Sundays, and used the empty Great House, belonging to Lord Dartmouth, for children's meetings, prayer meetings and a ticketed Sunday evening meeting for hymn-singing. Although claiming to eschew itinerancy, he also conducted pastoral visits and parlour preaching across a wide area of north Buckinghamshire, southern Northamptonshire and western Bedfordshire, including in Turvey and Bedford itself.[90] With support from John Thornton, Berridge's financial backer, he also helped to found, in 1782, a 'dissenting methodistical academy', at Newport Pagnell, to train preachers under the tutorship of William Bull, minister of Newport Pagnell Independent Church.[91] Nor was Newton the only Methodist clergyman in the area; David Simpson was curate at Buckingham in 1771, until his Methodist preaching led to his dismissal the following year; and Thomas Jones, who had been expelled from St Edmund's Hall, Oxford, in 1768 for holding Methodist tenets, was curate of Clifton Reynes from 1772. Itinerant preachers supported by the Countess of Huntingdon were also active, both around Berkhamsted to the south and Raunds to the north, and Calvinistic Methodists were beginning to appear in the pulpits of some of the local Dissenting meeting-houses.[92] The Independent churches at Cheese Lane, Wellingborough, and at Olney had both appointed Whitefieldites to their pulpits by 1776.[93] At New Mill, near Tring, a Particular Baptist meeting-house which had been redundant for some time was re-opened in the early 1770s for a minister and congregation who, although formally constituted as a Baptist church, were in reality Calvinistic Methodists.[94]

Wesley's Bedfordshire Circuit

At the height of the Perfectionist debacle in 1763, and perhaps to ensure that Parker's society in Bedford did not throw in its lot with Berridge, Wesley made the town a permanent base for one of his itinerant preachers.[95] At some point around this date there was also a significant capital investment in the Bedford society with the building of a small chapel on the site of the old spinning room. In 1767 the adjacent workhouse was purchased for £71 13s 0d, and made into cottages, with the house formerly occupied by the master of the workhouse becoming the preacher's residence.[96] The first real glimpse of the circuit which the Bedford preacher travelled comes in October 1766 when Wesley was taken on a tour of six preaching places by

---

89   Berridge to John Newton, 20 September 1773, Whittingham, *Works of Berridge*, 377.
90   Hindmarsh, *John Newton and the English evangelical tradition*, 196–203, 207–11.
91   John Newton to William Bull, 20 June 1782, quoted in *Congregational Magazine* (1831), 394.
92   Sidney, *Life of Rowland Hill*, 102; Seymour, *Life of Countess of Huntingdon*, II, 474–5; Urwick, *Nonconformity in Herts*, 378; *MM* (1816), 23.
93   Nuttall, 'Baptists and Independents in Olney', 36–7. In the 1780s Cotton End Meeting was supplied for a time by Mr Walker, the minister of the Countess of Huntingdon's chapel at Berkhamsted (Tibbutt, *Cotton End Old Meeting*, 15).
94   *WMM* (1834), 321; Urwick, *Nonconformity in Herts*, 466; Champion, *General Baptist Church of Berkhamsted, Chesham and Tring*, 154.
95   *Works of Wesley*, X, 866.
96   *WMM* (1833), 52; Anderson, *Early Methodism in Bedford*, 15.

James Glasbrook, who had been stationed to Bedford at the preceding conference. One of the places, Sundon, had clearly been a Wesleyan preaching venue for some time, and Cople is mentioned in connection with a visit earlier in the year but this is the first occasion on which Wesleyan preaching is recorded at the other four.[97] Wootton, Milbrook and Lidlington had a history, however, of Moravian activity and as already recounted there is a strong tradition that a religious society had existed in Luton from about 1750.[98] The first years of the circuit, it would seem, were spent drawing together existing Methodists under Wesleyan leadership rather than in missioning new ground. Although officially described as the Bedfordshire circuit, from the outset the preacher's round also covered several neighbouring counties.[99] Whittlebury and Towcester were almost certainly part of the circuit from the beginning, as was Hertford.[100] Northampton was added to the circuit in the autumn of 1766. Jonathan Scott, a cavalry officer who had been converted in Sussex after hearing a sermon by William Romaine, had arrived in Northampton with his regiment in the spring of that year.[101] He seems to have found an existing non-Wesleyan Methodist society and to have been instrumental in securing for them a visit from Richard Blackwell, one of the Wesleyan preachers stationed in London. A London preacher and men in uniform proved to be a crowd-drawer, and Scott wrote to Wesley in August that 'all denominations flock to hear the Word. The desire of the people to hear the Gospel from Mr. Blackwell was so great that they would not part with him till after Sunday.'[102] Blackwell returned to Northampton in October and on the following Sunday exchanged with Glasbrook, the preacher at Bedford whose sermon, it was claimed, drew nearly two thousand hearers.[103] The following day, Scott was ordered to Leicester and wrote to Wesley asking him to ensure that the work at Northampton would continue:

> As soon as it was known at Northampton [that I was leaving], some persons came to me under great concern, fearing it would cause the Preacher to go away, for want of a place to preach in. They added rather than that should be the case, they were willing to contribute something towards getting one. But as long as our Regiment stays at Northampton, this will be unnecessary; as we can contrive to let them have our Riding-house. ... I therefore trust you will take this affair into serious consideration, and send another Preacher into the Bedford Circuit,

97   Wesley had preached a funeral sermon at Cople for Glasbrook's wife on 19 February 1766. On this second visit he described Cople as 'the most lively of all the little societies in Bedfordshire' (*Works of Wesley*, XXII, 30, 67–8).
98   Webb, *To serve the present age*, 3, attributes the founding of the Lidlington society to Thomas Bigg, a travelling blacksmith, some time after 1786 but this contradicts the circuit book which shows the society existing in 1781 and Bigg joining it in 1792.
99   Hartley, *Hall's Circuits and Ministers,* 37; Rodell, 'Francis Asbury's first circuit: Bedfordshire, 1767', 110–21.
100   A Methodist society may have existed in Hertford from May 1739 when Whitefield preached to four or five thousand people, by his own estimate. Wesley preached in the town in 1763, 1766, 1768, 1769, 1770, 1772 and 1773 as part of his regular tour of the Bedfordshire circuit.
101   Saul, 'Methodism in Northants'.
102   Scott to Wesley, 24 August 1766, quoted in Saul, 'Methodism in Northants'. This was not the first Methodist preaching in the town. Whitefield had preached in Northampton in 1739, 1743, 1750, 1753, 1758 and 1767 and the town had been on the Calvinistic Methodist Olney circuit until it was given up in 1753.
103   Scott to Wesley, 15 October 1766, *AM* (1783), 441.

who can take Northampton and two or three other villages in, that I know would receive you.[104]

Less than a month later, Wesley set out for Northampton himself but was diverted into Bedfordshire by Glasbrook and had to make do with sending Blackwell again.[105] Despite not getting to see the situation first hand, and having denied a request for assistance from the Bedfordshire circuit only the year before, at the conference of 1767 he complied with Scott's request and sent Francis Asbury, a junior preacher, to Bedford to work under Glasbrook.[106] Despite this intervention, the large congregations at Northampton proved short-lived. By October 1767 services had been moved from the riding school to the society's own room and, although a disused Baptist meeting-house was acquired in 1770, it was described as being 'very small'.[107] Scott's prediction, that Wesley's preachers would find groups or individuals willing to receive them in some of the villages around Northampton, seems to have been entirely accurate. In October 1767, and again in 1768, Wesley mentions preaching at Weedon, during a tour through Northamptonshire and Bedfordshire; and in 1769 at Ashton, Brington, Haddon and Harpole.[108] Indeed, such was the expansion of the circuit in Northamptonshire that it seems that from 1769 the second preacher was actually based at Northampton.[109] Other additions to the circuit by then included Cranfield in Bedfordshire, Pirton in Hertfordshire, and perhaps even Coventry.[110] Membership rose from 167 in 1766 to 260 in 1769, 'a glorious increase' according to Wesley, but it then levelled out and was only 282 in 1773.

In the mid-1770s, again in the aftermath of a crisis in relations with Berridge, there appears to have been a concerted attempt to extend the circuit into the area already worked by Berridge's preachers. Wesley himself preached at Godmanchester in November 1774 in a large barn which had, until that point, been used by Berridge and Venn. The obituary of his hostess, Sarah Reeve, written forty years later, records that Berridge, Hicks and Venn

104 *AM* (1783), 441–2. 'The Riding School was used for various purposes in addition to that from which it took its name. Sales were held there, and various performances took place in it. It had a pit, gallery and upper gallery' (Saul, 'Methodism in Northants').

105 *Works of Wesley*, XXII, 67.

106 *Works of Wesley*, X, 344.

107 Wesley records that on 26 October 1767, 'we rode to Northampton, where, in the evening (our own room being far too small), I preached in the riding-school to a large and deeply serious congregation' and on 24 October 1770 that 'We had now a more commodious place to preach in, formerly used by the Presbyterians' (*Works of Wesley*, XXII, 107 and 257).

108 *Works of Wesley*, XXII, 107, 163 and 209.

109 Asbury describes himself as having been appointed assistant in Northamptonshire in 1769, when the minutes record him as junior preacher on the Bedfordshire circuit for the second time. It seems quite possible that on this occasion his role was more autonomous, that he was based in Northamptonshire (his two surviving letters from this period were both sent from Towcester) and that he and the Bedford preacher interchanged rounds periodically rather than travelling the same round. In 1774 there is an explicit reference to the Northampton preacher in the minutes of the annual conference (*Works of Wesley*, X, 432).

110 Wesley preached to a 'serious congregation' at Cranfield on 27 October 1769 (*Works of Wesley*, XXII, 209). Francis Asbury, who was on the circuit in 1767/8, and again in 1769/70, was remembered as having preached in the home of the Hudson family at Pirton (*WMM* (1829), 289). There was a Wesleyan society at Coventry in 1760, which was then part of the Staffordshire circuit (Jackson, *Lives of early Methodist preachers*, II, 181). By the late 1780s it was part of the Northampton circuit (Saul, 'Methodism in Northants'). It is not clear when the transfer took place but Saul suggests that the society was part of the Bedfordshire circuit in Asbury's time.

used occasionally to visit her, and preach in her house; but as these excellent men embraced the doctrines of unconditional election and reprobation, she did not enjoy their preaching as she had done prior to their change of sentiment, (particularly with regard to Mr. Berridge); she was therefore anxious to become acquainted with Mr. Wesley ... whose sentiments on these points were congenial with her own.[111]

She met Wesley in Bedford in about 1774 and Wesley seems to have given high priority to the opportunity that her invitation created, following up his initial visit with a second six weeks later and a third less than twelve months after that. On this third visit he also preached at St Neots, seven miles from Everton, which seems to have led to the formation of a Wesleyan society in that town and it appears that Wesleyan preachers began visiting Huntingdon at about the same time.[112] At the conference of 1775 the number of preachers allocated to the Bedfordshire circuit was increased from two to three, despite the fact that only the previous year the circuit had needed a £30 subsidy to maintain its existing staffing.[113] At Hertford, a society which may, like Bedford, have previously been receiving both Wesley's and Berridge's preachers, collapsed for a time during 1773 because 'the servants of God quarrelled among themselves.'[114] Despite that particular loss, the invasion of Berridge's territory and what appears to have been a simultaneous expansion into some of the villages in Northamptonshire missioned by the Countess of Huntingdon's preachers seem to have yielded a fair haul for the Wesleyan circuit.[115] The minutes of Wesley's annual conferences show membership of the Bedfordshire circuit growing from 282 in 1773 to 550 in 1778, and the division of the circuit the following year, on an east-west basis, with two preachers appointed to both Bedford and Northampton.[116] Viewed through that lens, Methodism might appear to have been growing rapidly in the south Midlands but the expansion of the Wesleyan connexion at the expense of its rivals was perhaps a feature of wider Methodist decline.

Stagnation and decline

Looking over these earliest decades of Methodist activity in Bedfordshire several things are perhaps striking. The first is the scale of the initial response to Methodist preaching. Even allowing for some exaggeration in Whitefield's claim that three thousand came to hear him at Bedford in 1739, it is clear that within months of

---

111 *MM* (1818), 447.

112 *WMM* (1881), 587–8.

113 *Works of Wesley* X, 441.

114 *Works of Wesley*, XXII, 357.

115 In 1781 the Bedfordshire Wesleyan circuit book lists several societies whose geography suggests that they may have originally been part of Berridge's circuit, including not only Godmanchester, Huntingdon and St Neots but Buckden and Stevenage. It also lists eight previously unmentioned societies on the border of Northamptonshire and Huntingdonshire – at Raunds, Rushden, Hargrave, Old Weston, Molesworth, Great Gidding, Buckworth and Hamerton.

116 See Appendix B for the sub-divisions of the Bedfordshire Wesleyan circuit 1763 to 1851. There is no list of the societies that went with Northampton to form the new circuit but they presumably included Whittlebury (formed 1760), Towcester (c.1760), Northampton (1766), Brackley (1770), Hanslope (before 1775), Maids Moreton (before 1777), Stony Stratford (before 1777), Coventry (before 1779) Hinckley (before 1779) and Foleshill (before 1779). The circuit may also have included some of the Northamptonshire villages mentioned by Wesley in the late 1760s - Weedon, Ashton, Brington, Haddon and Harpole.

the first Methodist preaching in the town the movement was able to attract huge audiences. Twenty years later, Berridge too was reporting crowds of up to ten thousand at some of his first open-air services in western Cambridgeshire. Only a small minority, of course, of those who gathered to witness the spectacle of field-preaching went on to join a Methodist society but even their numbers were impressive. By 1744 the members of Okely's society outnumbered the members of the town's long established and politically powerful Dissenting Meeting; and by the late 1760s even in a village like Waterbeach, more than twenty miles from Everton, the new curate found his parish 'above half full of Methodists, made so by Mr Berridge of Clare Hall.'[117] A second striking feature of early Methodism in Bedfordshire is the extent of its geographic penetration. By 1744 Okely's society had members not only in the borough itself but in twenty-nine of the other 120 parishes in the county. Twenty years later, the work of Berridge and his preachers probably meant that at least half the villages in the county had had some experience of Methodism. Halévy's claim, that Methodism saved England from revolution in 1739, has generally been dismissed on the grounds that the movement could not possibly have influenced anything like the numbers of people necessary to have had such an impact at such an early date. It may be, however, that the scale of the initial response to Methodism has been underestimated by historians, partly because they have been blind to non-Wesleyan varieties of Methodism and partly because they have presumed that the first published membership statistics for Wesley's connexion, in 1765, must represent the pinnacle of twenty-five years steady advance. In fact, the evidence from Bedfordshire, and surrounding counties, suggests that by 1765 the Methodist movement as a whole was, if anything, on the wane. The day of huge crowds had long passed at Bedford and was disappearing into memory at Everton, while at Northampton, where Whitefield had preached to about two thousand in 1750, the Methodist presence was negligible and although there would be a resurgence of interest in 1766 it would prove equally temporary. Recruitment into actual society membership seems to have slowed considerably; the register of the Bedford Moravian congregation shows that while there were 112 admissions between 1750 and 1759 there were only 47 between 1760 and 1769; and in some places Methodism seems to have disappeared altogether. In the late 1760s Francis Okely could find little trace of the work done by James Hervey, the Methodist rector of Weston Favell who had died in 1758.[118]

The decline seems to have continued through the 1770s. Moravian recruitment fell to thirty-nine people between 1770 and 1779 and Berridge too was clearly having difficulty attracting new recruits. In 1782 he wrote to John Newton that 'church-work goes on heavily here; many of the old sheep are called home, and few lambs drop into the fold' and to another correspondent that 'My church at present is in decline, and seems consumptive … my hearers are dwindling away.'[119] The Wesleyan societies appear to have fared no better. Alexander McNab, who was sent to the Bedfordshire circuit in 1766, remembered later that 'Here he was tempted to

[117]   Stokes, *Blecheley diary*, 249.
[118]   Saul, 'Methodism in Northants'.
[119]   Berridge to John Newton, 17 September 1782, Whittingham, *Works of Berridge,* 408; Berridge to Benjamin Mills, 24 September 1782, *Congregational Magazine* (1845), 273.

give up the work'; Francis Asbury, who was stationed to Bedford in 1767 and again in 1769, wrote to his mother 'I am in trying circumstances about the people and places; but sometimes I please myself that I shall go hence and leave these parts.'[120] John McEvoy, who was sent to the circuit in 1771 did give up during his second year.[121] Wesley himself recognised the circuit's problems, acceding to a request, in 1767, that James Glasbrook be allowed to stay on the circuit a second year 'considering the present distress' and writing rather wistfully to Thomas Hanson, the senior preacher in 1773, that there had been growth before 'So there may be again ... Perhaps the hour is at hand.'[122] The society at Bedford was a continuing disappointment. In 1766 Wesley expressed himself exasperated by 'these drowsy people.' In 1767 he found them a 'civil, heavy congregation' and in 1768 he felt moved to preach to them on the text 'Awake thou that sleepest', commenting 'for a more sleepy audience I have not often seen.'[123] The village societies fared even worse. By 1781, when the circuit book commences, the previously mentioned societies at Great Barford, Clifton, Cranfield, Milbrook, Sundon, Wootton Pillinge and Cople had all disappeared, as had a short-lived society at Woburn.[124] Only two of the Bedfordshire village societies mentioned in the 1760s were still in existence, Luton and Lidlington. There were three new societies, Markyate, Leagrave and Stanbridge, all probably offshoots of the Luton society, but that still made only six societies with a total of 115 members in the whole of Bedfordshire.[125] Other losses, beyond the county boundary, included Hertford, with its purpose-built preaching-room and school.[126] Nor, it seems, were such losses confined to the Bedfordshire circuit. In 1777 the question was asked at the annual conference of Wesley's preachers 'Are the societies in general more dead or more alive to God, than they were some years ago?' and, although Wesley insisted that his societies were 'not a fallen people', he had to tell his own preachers '*You*, and *you* can judge no farther than you see. You cannot judge one part by another ... none but myself has an opportunity of seeing them throughout the three kingdoms.'[127]

An astonishingly similar conversation had taken place at the Moravian Provincial conference in 1771, when it had been recognised that the movement was losing ground both numerically and in terms of vitality.[128] In fact the decline was not even confined to Methodism. Across Bedfordshire Dissent was also in retreat. At Blunham, membership of the Baptist church fell from 38 in 1739 to 29 in 1778; at

[120] Atmore, *Methodist memorial*, (1801), 293; Potts, *Journal and letters of Francis Asbury*, III, 8.

[121] *Works of Wesley*, X, 416–18.

[122] Wesley to Abraham Andrews, 18 August 1767, Bridwell Library, Southern Methodist University; Wesley to Thomas Hanson, 13 February 1773, Rodell, 'A new Wesley letter', 228.

[123] *Works of Wesley*, XXII, 68, 107 and 163.

[124] Woburn Congregational Church Book 1791–1837, BLARS, CRPu 4/16.

[125] The society at Leagrave, a hamlet of Luton, had presumably arisen out of the Luton society and Stanbridge may, in turn, have been an offshoot of Leagrave as Richard Partridge, the class leader at Leagrave, seems to have had family links with Stanbridge (Genealogical notes on Richard Partridge, BLARS, CRT 180/183). The Bedfordshire circuit also included 8 societies in Huntingdonshire, 3 in Northamptonshire, 2 in Hertfordshire and 2 in Buckinghamshire.

[126] There may have been a brief attempt to re-launch the Hertford society in 1788 when the house of Abraham Andrews, of East End Green, in the parish of Hertingfordbury, was registered by Andrews, Thomas Wyment, William Cole and William Wooding.

[127] *Works of Wesley*, XXIII, 64–5.

[128] Stead, *Exotic plant*, 75.

Southill the membership of the Independent church dropped from 69 in 1756 to 46 in 1778 and it is reported that the congregation had also decreased significantly.'[129] The General Baptist church at Sundon, the Particular Baptist church at Eversholt and the Independent church at Goldington were all dissolved. The Church of England, too, appears to have experienced a quite dramatic falling away. At St Neots, in 1782, Henry Venn reported that:

> The church having long been deserted, and all worship of God given up, that even curiosity will not bring them to hear, and in a morning not more than one hundred out of a population of sixteen hundred are to be seen at church.[130]

The 1780s seem to have brought little reprieve. Of the twenty-one societies listed in the Bedfordshire Wesleyan circuit book when it begins in 1781 no fewer than ten had disappeared by the end of the decade, including Huntingdon, where a purpose-built preaching room had been erected in 1780.[131] Membership fell from 274 to 237. One preacher's comment was almost despairing: 'I earnestly pray that whoever come into this Circuet [sic] next year, may have more comfort than I have had.'[132] The Bedford society, whose membership fell from 45 to 34 in 1785, seems to have been plagued with internal disputes. Charles Wesley received a letter in 1781 about a Mrs B. who 'has lived many years at Milton near Bedford, and well known in the society there, tho lately separated from it, not by her own choice but I fear by the workings of a spirit in some in that society straightened in their own bowels but not in hers.'[133] In February 1787, John Pawson wrote to 'The Rev. Barnabas Thomas at the Methodist Chapel, Bedford' commiserating that he had been sent to such a difficult appointment:

> Bad work, very bad work indeed when we fall by the way. I was heartily sorry to hear of what was done in Bedford Circuit last year. But how it came to pass that you was sent there I really do not know. However, who so likely to quench that bad fire as a man of your good temper. They who are able to bear all things, you know, must often have all things to bear. I hope that the Lord will help you and enable you so to act as to regain what those lost who went before you.'[134]

Even an optimistic reference to Bedford in John Wesley's journal late in 1788 underscores the society's history of difficulties: 'as all disputes are at an end, there is great reason to hope that the work of God will increase here also.'[135] Not that the situation was any better in the Northampton circuit where the Northampton society had only fifty members in 1790; at Buckingham 'the work of God was very low'; and at Brixworth the preacher noted: 'I cannot get this class to meet unless the preacher meets them.'[136]

---

[129]   Wildman, 'Changes in membership recruitment', 332–46.
[130]   Henry Venn to James Stillingfleet, 24 December 1782, *WMM* (1881), 592.
[131]   The Huntingdon society may have lost out to Godmanchester General Baptist church which was formed about this time.
[132]   The preacher was Joseph Pescod and the comment was written in the circuit book in 1784; see Plate 23.
[133]   John Barham to Charles Wesley, 4 December 1781, MARC, DDPr 1/9.
[134]   Bowmer and Vickers, *Letters of John Pawson*, I, 44. The nature of the problem the previous year remains obscure but the junior preacher, John Ingham, and a supernumerary, John Watson, jun., both disappear from the roll of preachers.
[135]   *Works of Wesley*, XXIV, 114.
[136]   Saul, 'Methodism in Northants'.

There were, of course, some successes. Moravian recruitment picked up slightly and the congregation register shows fifty-six new members being admitted between 1780 and 1789 (still only half the number in the 1750s) while Berridge was able to report of Everton that 'My church is usually very full in afternoons, and the people are awake and attentive.'[137] Among the Wesleyan societies Luton appears to have been the most thriving, Wesley commenting 'How long did we seem to be ploughing upon the sand here! But it seems there will be some fruit at last.'[138]

In 1778 he noted that Mr Cole, who had moved from Sundon Hall to rent the empty vicarage in Luton, had 'fitted up a very neat and commodious Room' for the society.[139] Two years later Cole presented the society with a new preaching-house built at his own expense. Several times Wesley refers to this building as being thoroughly filled.[140] Thomas Taylor, one of Wesley's preachers, also preached in Luton, on his way from York to the conference of 1781. Having complained about the pitifully small congregations in Lincolnshire, he too found that the Luton preaching-house, though not large was well filled.[141] The numbers, however, were still probably quite modest. Seventy years later it was estimated that the building held 250 people but it is very likely that its original capacity would have been much less and the number of members was certainly not more than thirty.[142]

Part 2 About the People

Age and Marital Status
The first glimpse of the demographics of the early Methodist community in Bedfordshire come from a list of the members of Francis Okely's society, dated December 1744, which survives among the records of the Moravian congregation.[143] In it the members are described simply by marital status – single, married, widowed. Well over half the membership were single and the married members were outnumbered even by the widows. Given the average age at marriage in the eighteenth century (around 25 for women and 27 for men) it looks as if the majority of members were quite young.[144] When Ingham preached in Bedford in 1738 many of them may have been in their teens; Okely himself was only 19 and Jacob Rogers, 24. This broadly mirrors the situation in other very early Moravian societies, such as Lamb's Hill in Yorkshire and Fetter Lane in London, where young people also formed a disproportionate element of the first recruits. Unmarried adults continued to provide an

137 Berridge to John Thornton, 13 July 1785, Whittingham, *Works of Berridge*, 416.
138 *Works of Wesley*, XXIII, 111.
139 *Works of Wesley*, XXIII, 111.
140 29 October 1778, 6 December 1781, 3 December 1784, 31 October 1785, *Works of Wesley*, XXIII, 111, 228, 338 and 379.
141 Jackson, *Lives of early Methodist preachers*, V, 57.
142 Bushby, 'Ecclesiastical census, Bedfordshire', 183; Bedfordshire Wesleyan circuit book, BLARS, MB 1.
143 List of society members, Bedford and district, December 1744, BLARS, MO 3.
144 Wrigley and Schofield, *Population history of England*, 255. Later Moravian lists also record date of birth and confirm a very strong correlation between age and marital status. Of the 66 people who joined the Bedford Moravian congregation between 1780 and 1789, 33 were single, 29 were married and 4 were widowed. Of the 62 recruits whose date of birth is given, 29 were twenty-five or under, 27 were between twenty-six and fifty, and 6 were fifty-one or over.

absolute majority of Moravian recruits in Bedfordshire throughout this period.[145] As recruitment declined, however, the overall age profile of the congregation rose steadily; by 1752 nearly two-thirds of the members were aged between 30 and 49 and by 1780 the same proportion were over 41.[146]

Table 2. Marital status of early Moravian members

Place and date	Single		Married		Widowed		Total
	no.	%	no.	%	no.	%	
Okely's society, Bedfordshire, 1744	30	59%	9	18%	12	23%	51
Lamb's Hill, Pudsey, Yorkshire, 1743	72	59%	48	39%	3	2%	123
Fetter Lane, London, 1742	30	42%	34	47%	8	11%	72

Source: Society members, Bedford and district, 1744, BLARS, MO 3; Benham, *Memoirs of James Hutton*, 89–96 and 231–3.

The great crowds drawn by John Berridge's preaching in the late 1750s also seem to have included a high proportion of young people and even children. John Walsh noted in 1759 that:

> many cry out, especially children, whose agonies were amazing. One of the eldest, a girl ten or twelve years old, was full in my view, in violent contortions of body ... And several much younger children were in Mr. B-ll's view, agonizing as this did.[147]

At the close of the service he noted that 1 man, 2 women, and 3 children had been justified and observed how few elderly people were involved: 'Upon the whole I remark that few ancient people experience anything of this work of God.'[148] After this initial influx of young recruits, the available evidence suggests that the average age of Berridge's following rose steadily as recruitment dried up and this original cohort of converts grew older. Looking at his congregation in the 1780s, more than two decades after the initial outburst of excitement, Berridge noticed that 'grey hairs are sprinkled upon us' and that 'Many old sheep are housed in the upper fold.'[149]

Wesleyan recruits also seem to have been young. At Whittlebury, in 1774, a 'work of God' brought in six new recruits, all of whom were aged between 11 and 14 but that was probably unusually young. Some insight into the age of Wesleyan recruits during the 1770s and 1780s may be gained from the obituary pages of the *Arminian Magazine* and its successors. Those memorialised in this way were not, of course, a representative sample, women are very clearly underrepresented, but their stories nevertheless suggest at least some common themes that are noteworthy. Of the 27 people whose memorials record the age at which they became a

---

[145] Between 1750 and 1759, 55% of those admitted into membership were single at the time and between 1780 and 1789 the figure was 50%.
[146] Catalogue of Bedford Moravian congregation, BLARS, MO 4.
[147] *Works of Wesley*, XXI, 195.
[148] *Works of Wesley*, XXI, 198.
[149] Berridge to John Newton, 12 December 1780 and. Berridge to John Thornton, 13 July 1785, Whittingham, *Works of Berridge*, 402 and 416.

Methodist, 19 were under thirty when they joined, suggesting a pattern similar to that of the Moravians. As with the Moravians, however, by the 1780s those young recruits were joining an ageing community. In 1781, across the circuit as a whole, unmarried Wesleyans were almost outnumbered by the widows and widowers.[150] At Lidlington, Leagrave and Breachwood Green, Hertfordshire, half the members of the societies were widowed, while at neighbouring Northampton it was now thought noteworthy that several young people were attending the preaching.[151] Indeed, the average age of the membership may have become an obstacle to recruitment. Mary Gilbert, apparently, attended for a while as a girl but 'the serious society of the aged' proved much less attractive than that of her own age group and she fell away again for several years.[152]

Gender

Although men dominate the narrative of early Methodism in Bedfordshire, as else-where, a glance at the membership list of Okely's society reveals that the over-whelming majority of the first recruits were women. In 1744 women outnumbered men by almost 3:1.[153] This is in striking contrast to other early Moravian congrega-tions where men were in the majority and perhaps reflects the fact that the Mora-vians drew heavily on existing religious societies and, while these were generally all-male affairs, Okely's society had been open to women from the outset.[154] Over the next four decades the gender imbalance among recruits to the Bedford Moravian congregation fluctuated but never fell below 3:2 in favour of women and in the 1770s, when recruitment was at a very low level, rose to 9:1.[155] The membership of the Wesleyan circuit in 1781 shows a similar bias, with women outnumbering men again by a ratio of 3:2.[156] There was even one society, Godmanchester, which was entirely composed of women. Studies of early Methodism in other parts of the country have suggested that the gender balance of members varied between rural and urban areas and it has been argued that 'urbanization brought a "feminization" of the churches.'[157] Here, however, in a very rural district, both the Wesleyan and Moravian communities were clearly highly feminised. One explanation may be that the deciding factor was not urbanisation but rather the existence of employment opportunities for women and therefore the financial independence to take on the cost of membership. Bedfordshire had high rates of female employment, much of it at this point connected with a domestic industry in lace-making, and working women figure prominently in the membership lists. Among the first 40 women admitted to the Moravian congregation, 21 were described as lace-makers and there was also

---

150   There were 45 single members (16%), 193 married (70%) and 38 widowed (14%) (Bedfordshire Wesleyan circuit book, BLARS, MB 1).
151   *AM* (1788), 494.
152   *MM* (1816), 211.
153   In 1744 the Bedford society consisted of 14 men and 38 women.
154   The membership at Fetter Lane in 1742 consisted of 40 men and 32 women; at Lamb's Hill in 1743 there were 64 men and 59 women, although there were also 10 girls (Benham, *Memoirs of James Hutton*, 89–96 and 231–3).
155   Moravian recruits: 1750–59: 41 men, 71 women; 1760–69: 18 men, 43 women; 1770–79: 3 men, 27 women; 1780–89: 24 men, 42 women (Catalogue of Bedford Moravian congregation, BLARS, MO 4).
156   In 1781 the membership of the Bedfordshire Wesleyan circuit consisted of 122 men and 181 women.
157   Malmgreen, 'Domestic discords', 60.

a nurse, a linen-draper, a mantua-maker and a dairy-woman. Of the 181 female members listed in 1781 in the Wesleyan circuit book, no fewer than 79 were credited with their own occupation, including lace-makers, seamstresses, servants, mantua-makers, washerwomen, shopkeepers, straw-platters, woolspinners, farmers and a publican.[158]

Women were not only more likely to become Methodists than men, they were also more likely to join at a young age. Nearly two-thirds of the women who joined the Bedford Moravian congregation between 1760 and 1789 were under 25 at the time but less than half of the men. They were also much more likely to join when they were unmarried: spinsters and widows accounting for four-fifths of female recruits but bachelors and widowers for little more than a third of male recruits.

Table 3. Age of recruits to the Bedford Moravian congregation, 1760–1789

Gender	Under 25		25–40		Over 40		Total
	no.	%	no.	%	no.	%	
Male	17	46%	9	24%	11	30%	37
Female	64	61%	24	23%	17	16%	105

Source: Catalogue of the Bedford Moravian congregation, 1744–1812, BLARS, MO 4.

The surviving Wesleyan records do not, unfortunately, provide similar information about age and marital status at the time of recruitment but the membership list for 1781 reveals gender discrepancies which are likely to have been created by differences in the pattern of recruitment between men and women. Again, the indications are that women tended to join while still unmarried, or perhaps in widowhood, while men were more likely to be married when they joined.

Table 4. Marital status of recruits to the Bedford Moravian congregation, 1760–1789, and of members of the Bedfordshire Wesleyan circuit, 1781

Denomination and gender	Single		Married		Widowed		Total
	no.	%	no.	%	no.	%	
Moravian men	19	51%	17	46%	1	3%	37
Moravian women	76	72%	23	22%	6	6%	105
Wesleyan men	12	11%	91	80%	10	9%	113
Wesleyan women	34	21%	102	62%	28	17%	164

The marital status of 9 Wesleyan men and 17 Wesleyan women is not recorded.

Sources: Catalogue of the Bedford Moravian congregation, 1744–1812, and Bedfordshire Wesleyan circuit book, BLARS, MO 4 and MB 1.

[158] Catalogue of Bedford Moravian congregation, and Bedfordshire Wesleyan circuit book, BLARS, MO 4 and MB1.

Commenting on a similar imbalance in the Wesleyan membership lists for east Cheshire, Gail Malmgreen has argued that the different patterns of male and female recruitment suggest that men and women tended to join Methodist societies for different reasons. For women, joining either before or after marriage, membership was an expression of independence while for men, joining at about the same time that they married, it was part of the process of settling down. She also noted that the majority of men who attended class meetings in east Cheshire did so with a female relative, but that the majority of women, whether married or not, did so without their husband, father or brothers. The participation of men in Methodism, she concluded, was largely dependent on the involvement of the women in their lives.[159]

Without piecing together the entire family tree of each member it is not possible to say definitively that any of the male members were attending without a female relative but it is clear that only half of the men who belonged to Okely's society in 1744 shared a surname with a female member, and that among the Wesleyans in Bedfordshire in 1781, 12 out of thirty-four married men (35%) were not attending with their wives and 8 out of the other eleven men (73%) were not attending with a woman who shared their surname.[160] Wives, mothers, sisters and, no doubt, sweethearts brought men to Methodist meetings, but early Methodism evidently had an appeal for men independent of this. There is evidence that in some places, and at some stages, men were in the majority. The society at Luton may have begun as an all-male affair, for certainly the only names remembered by a later generation were those of men.[161] This may, of course, be an example of selective memory but given the tradition of all-male religious societies it is clearly possible. Men appear to have been in the majority at Everton in the early days of Berridge's Methodist ministry: John Walsh thought that there were three times more men than women present at the service he attended.[162] Thirty years later, at Bluntisham in Huntingdonshire, when the Calvinistic Methodist society re-constituted itself as an Independent church, more than half the founding members were men.[163] Men also outnumbered women in a few of the Wesleyan societies in the 1780s. Even when they were in the minority, men were at least as well represented in Methodist gatherings as in the congregations of some of the existing religious communities.[164]

The Rich, the Poor and the Middling Sorts

A third feature of the various early Methodist societies in Bedfordshire is that they appear to have drawn support from quite varied economic and social constituencies.

Of the fifty-three men received into membership of the Bedford Moravian congregation between 1745 and the end of 1752, 41% were labourers and 38%

---

[159] Malmgreen, 'Domestic discords', 60.
[160] Society members, Bedford and district, 1744, and Bedfordshire Wesleyan circuit book, BLARS, MO 3 and MB 1.
[161] The names remembered in 1885 were George Bull, Thomas Rotherham, Thomas Spilsbury, Crawley and Thrussell (*Luton Reporter*, 7 November 1885).
[162] *Works of Wesley*, XXI, 195.
[163] Dixon, *Century of village nonconformity*, 151–5.
[164] Women constituted 62.8% of the membership of Baptist and Independent churches in Bedfordshire between 1651 and 1750 (Field, 'Adam and Eve: gender in the English Free Church constituency', 67).

were artisans, which was probably a fair reflection of the local population.[165] As the congregation became more established, however, it appears that it underwent a process of gentrification. As early as the 1750s there appear to have been a significant number of wealthy members. Writing about the congregation's financial affairs in 1753, William Parker noted that eight members had guaranteed a loan to the community of £800, two members a further loan of £100, and another member had given credit to the community that totalled £700.[166] These men were clearly not labourers or even artisans but people of considerable property. One result of this, or perhaps reason for it, was that life in the settlement became much more comfortable. The first inhabitants of the single sisters' house had lived together 'in great poverty' but by 1761 conditions were sufficiently tempting that the Countess of Huntingdon, Lord Rawdon, the sister of Sir Charles Hotham and an entourage of servants stayed for more than a week.[167] Catherine Edwin, a very wealthy widow, had moved in permanently by 1758, and Mr Barham, who had made a fortune in the West Indies, by 1757. Between 1753 and 1762 the proportion of men joining the congregation who made their living by labouring fell to 11%, while gentry, professionals and farmers grew to account for 32%. Okely's description, in 1769, of the Northampton Moravian congregation, an early offshoot of Bedford, seems to reinforce this impression of affluent gentility for he boasts of it containing 'several of the magistrates, and other considerable persons of the town.'[168]

The early Calvinistic Methodists also attracted some well-heeled support. At Hertford Whitefield was given hospitality by an unnamed gentlewoman and spent the night in great comfort; and at Northampton 'a gentleman of great worth and rank in the town invited us [Whitefield and Hervey] to his house, and gave us an elegant treat.'[169] At Olney the Whitefieldite circuit had forty subscribers to *The Christian History* in 1747 and Methodist clergy were appointed to the parish because the patron, Lord Dartmouth, was sympathetic.[170] The following that John Berridge was building up in the east of the county seems to have come very much from the opposite end of the social spectrum. Although many members of the university are reported to have attended one of his open-air services, it was noted that 'scarce any of the rich' were affected by the outbursts of fits and fainting. Wesley's correspondent, John Walsh, clearly thought that the presence of two or three well-dressed young women in the congregation at Everton was worthy of comment; from which it may be concluded that they stood out.[171] Of course, villages were not likely to have the kind of professional and business people resident in them that inhabited the county town but Berridge's letters certainly give the impression that, even within the limited social range present in a rural community, his congregations were

---

165   The recruits consisted of 1 clergyman, 3 farmers, 3 shopkeepers, 1 butcher, 1 dancing master, 1 grocer, 1 ironmonger; 4 carpenters, 4 wool combers, 3 breeches makers, 3 smiths, 2 tailors, 1 bricklayer, 1 shoemaker, 1 turner, 1 weaver, 17 husbandmen, 2 dairyman, 1 shepherd, 1 waterman, 1 widower.
166   *Works of Wesley*, XX, 477–8.
167   Welch, *Bedford Moravian Church*, 211.
168   *Supplement to the short sketch of the work carried on by the Moravian Church in Northampton*, (1888), 3.
169   Murray, *Whitefield's journals*, 272; Tyerman, *Oxford Methodists*, 259.
170   Jones, '*A glorious work in the world*', 90.
171   *Works of Wesley*, XXI, 198 and 197.

drawn primarily from the lower levels. Writing to the Countess of Huntingdon, he described the homes in which he stayed while travelling his circuit:

> Cold houses to sit in, with very moderate fuel, and three or four children roaring or rocking about you! Coarse food and meagre liquor; lumpy beds to lie on, and too short for the feet; stiff blankets, like boards, for a covering; and live cattle in plenty to feed upon you![172]

Some years later, in a letter to John Thornton, soliciting donations for the victims of the great fire at Biggleswade, he observed that:

> The wealthy sufferers had insured three-fourths of their substance. This loss, therefore, will not break their backs, nor does it seem to humble their hearts; but the little tradesmen and poor labourers have lost their all ... among whom are several of the Lord's dear children, begotten under my ministry.[173]

This may, however, have been less than the full picture. The society at Blunt-isham certainly included seven farmers and at Godmanchester Sarah Reeve, whose house was used for preaching, was apparently wealthy enough to have a chaise. It also seems unlikely that the poor labourers would have had much use for the many hundreds of books which Berridge's letters record him distributing among his auditors:

> Your three hundred and fifty Alleines are dispersed about the country, thirty miles round. The Lord attend them with a blessing. I have lately received two hundred hymn-books, and a dozen of Omicron's letters, for which I return you hearty thanks.[174]

Most of Berridge's followers were, no doubt, poor, most people were; but he certainly drew support from a wider constituency and the number of readers in his societies suggests a disproportionately literate body.

Wesleyan writers too were prone to emphasis the poverty of their membership. In 1758, when John Walsh visited Bedford, he found the society 'poor in general' and John Wesley described the congregation at Lidlington as 'plain, country people.'[175] The circuit book, however, shows that the 116 men attending class meetings in 1781 included farmers, tradesmen and artisans, as well as labourers, in numbers that broadly reflected the occupational structure of the local community as a whole.[176] What was absent was any representative of the gentry or the professions, and the fragmentary evidence we have for the female members suggests that even these classes were not wholly unrepresented, with at least two members described as gentlewomen and another as a governess. Nevertheless a comparison with records of other Wesleyan circuits suggests that Bedfordshire's membership was unusually plebeian. This may, in part, reflect the fact that more affluent and educated

---

[172] Berridge to the Countess of Huntingdon, 26 December 1767, Whittingham, *Works of Berridge*, 453.

[173] Berridge to John Thornton, 2 July 1785, Whittingham, *Works of Berridge*, 414.

[174] Berridge to John Thornton, 10 August 1774, Whittingham, *Works of Berridge*, 385. 'Alleines' probably refers to Joseph Alleine's *An alarme to unconverted sinners* (1672) which went through numerous editions in the eighteenth century; and 'Omicron's letters' to *Twenty six letters on religious subjects, to which are added hymns etc. by Omicron*, a volume written by John Newton but published anonymously in 1774.

[175] John Walsh to John Wesley, 21 June 1758, *AM* (1780), 103; John Wesley to Thomas Hanson, 13 February 1773, Rodell, 'New Wesley letter', 229–30.

[176] Bedfordshire Wesleyan circuit book, BLARS, MB 1.

Methodists were drawn off to the Moravians but it also reflects the poverty of the local economy in comparison with the mill towns of Yorkshire and Lancashire and with a fashionable spa such as Brighton. It is a reminder that the profile of Methodist membership was shaped by its setting rather than any universal appeal to particular social groups.

Table 5. Occupations of male Wesleyans

Circuit and date	Percentage of occupations in each circuit					
	Gentry	Professions	Farmers	Tradesmen	Artisans	Labourers
Manchester 1759	1.7	2.1	11.9	3.8	61.7	18.7
Keighley 1763	0.3	1	19.3	4.5	65.1	9.8
Sussex 1777	5	1	14	8	35	36
Bedfordshire 1781	0	0	14	8	35	43
General population, 1760	1.2	4.4	24.8	12.1	20.9	36.6

Sources: For Manchester, Keighley and the general population: Clive Field, 'The social structure of English Methodism', 201–2; for Sussex: Sussex Wesleyan circuit book, East Sussex RO, NMA/4/1/1; for Bedfordshire: Bedfordshire Wesleyan circuit book, BLARS, MB 1.

The contrast between the social background of the Wesleyans and the Moravians may not have been quite as sharp as at first appears. For it is clear that there were wealthy Wesleyans: mention has already been made of William Cole, the High Sheriff in 1758, but there was also John Hill, owner of The Rose Inn, with whom Wesley lodged when in Bedford, George Gorham, who inherited £30,000 and was Wesley's host at St Neots, and Elizabeth Harvey, another host, who in the 1790s would build and endow Wesleyan preaching houses at Biggleswade, Baldock and Stevenage.[177] What was different about the Wesleyan community was that it operated at two distinct and separate social levels. At one level was the circuit recorded in the Bedfordshire circuit book, with its class meetings made up of ordinary folk; at another, was Wesley's personal circuit of affluent sympathisers. In the 1760s the two parts were held together by Wesley himself who, while staying with the Coles and preaching for them, would also visit the villages on his preachers' circuit and speak to their congregations of 'plain, country people.' By the mid-1780s, age was taking its toll and while he was still regularly preaching for Miss Harvey and Samuel Hicks, the only society officially in his connexion with which he had any contact was that at Bedford. One factor in this was undoubtedly the increasing reluctance of an old man to accept the kind of hospitality that was available in most places. After the death of William Cole he visited the thriving society at Luton only once, noting that 'For many years, I had lodged at Mr. Cole's in Luton, but he was now gone to his long home. The room prepared for me now was very large and very cold and had no fireplace in it.' Of Miss Harvey's, by contrast, he wrote 'Adjoining to

177   Anderson, *Early Methodism in Bedford*, 11; *WMM* (1901), 923; *Works of Wesley*, XXIII, 337; *WMM* (1835), 212.

Miss Harvey's house is a pleasant garden. And she has made a shady walk round the neighbouring meadows. How gladly could I repose awhile here!'[178]

Even the later visits to Bedford may have owed more to the hospitality of George Livius, one of the wealthy Moravians, than to the fact that it was the head of a circuit. Livius' house was apparently 'a palace, the best house by far in the town.'[179] Many of these wealthy patrons no doubt shared to some degree in the religious sentiment of the Methodist movement, but the fact that the names of so many of John Wesley's affluent hosts do not appear on any class list strongly suggests that they viewed the local Wesleyan circuit as something to patronise rather than participate in.

It is possible, of course that this suited the ordinary members very well and that the washerwoman and the farm labourer were much more comfortable sitting in a class meeting with their own social class than in a Moravian choir meeting with Catherine Edwin and Mr Barham. William Parker, who founded and dominated the Bedford Wesleyan society until his death in 1785, also had reason to prefer the social distinction of the Wesleyan connexion. A successful grocer and alderman, even he was not in the same league as some of the people who had begun to join the Moravians and it is clear from his own account of his disenchantment with the Moravians that he bridled at being told what to do.[180] The arm's length support of William Cole and Miss Harvey may have suited him well.

A Puritan Legacy

Young, single and female, the average Methodist recruit was also likely to have had a religious background. Although Methodist publications gave great prominence to cases in which godless sinners were converted – there are accounts of four condemned men repenting while awaiting execution in Bedford alone – these were hardly typical.[181] Existing churchgoers were by far the most important source of recruits. At Northampton the Moravian congregation was formed largely of people drawn away from Castle Hill meeting-house, and the huge crowds that attended the first Wesleyan sermons in the town were said to be composed of 'multitudes of all denominations.'[182] The membership register of the Bedford Moravian congregation, likewise, notes previous religious affiliations for all but two of the people who joined before the end of 1750 and while that may not necessarily have reflected a deep religious commitment, the surviving narratives of individual Methodists suggest that they had often been highly religious before their encounter with Methodism. Thomas Pierson, for example, who was received into the Bedford Moravian

---

[178] *Works of Wesley*, XXIII, 379 and 247.

[179] *Works of Wesley*, XXIV, 114. For a more detailed treatment of this point see Rodell, '"The best house by far in the town"', 111–22.

[180] *Works of Wesley*, XX, 477–8.

[181] John Wynn executed at Bedford in 1785 (*AM* (1788), 69, Tattershall, *Account of Tobias Smith* (1792); Richard Crosby and Samuel Rhodes executed at Bedford in 1794 (*AM* (1795), 391). There is also a tradition that John Wesley accompanied a condemned man to the gallows in Northampton in 1770 and an account of a gallows conversion in the town in 1813 (Lawton, 'Notes on early Methodism in Northampton', 91; Davies, '*A brand plucked out of the fire!*'). Nor was this interest in prisoners confined to Wesleyans. Okely visited two condemned highwaymen in Northampton gaol in 1770 (*Supplement to the short sketch of the work carried on by the Moravian Church in Northampton*, 10). See also p. 53 below.

[182] Deacon, *Philip Doddridge*, 138; Saul, 'Methodism in Northants'; *Short sketch of the work carried on by the ... Moravian church in Northamptonshire* (1886), 10.

congregation in 1748, had been taught prayers and hymns as a child by his parents and grandfather, and as an adult was among the tiny minority of churchgoers who took communion.[183]

A pious home had prepared William Cumberland for his life as a Wesleyan:

> [His mother] was, it appears, a woman of genuine piety: her affectionate tenderness, her maternal admonitions, her fervent ejaculations on his behalf (often placing him before her, stroking his hair, and exclaiming:- 'May the Lord bless you, my child!') made an indelible impression upon his mind; and the circumstance of his conversion to God was considered by him to be one reward of her believing and incessant prayers.[184]

Of thirty Wesleyans whose stories are known from obituaries, twenty are described as having been religious before joining the Methodists and none as having been without religion. It is possible that this was simply part of the narrative to which lives were made to conform by obituary writers, but the fact that it recurs in obituaries written over eight decades, and that it fits poorly with Methodists' claim to be an agency for calling sinners to repentance, seems to lend weight to its veracity.[185]

One of the legacies of a religious upbringing was evidently a deep and distressing sense of God's inescapable judgement. Francis Hews, who went on to become a Calvinistic Methodist, described how, as a child in the 1770s, he had had repeated panic attacks:

> At another time, being at play on the Lord's day, all on a sudden, I thought a fireball was coming down from the clouds upon me, and I stood with my shoulders drawn up and my back bent, when one of my companions giving me a push, said, 'what do you stand so for?' all my reply was 'O dear!' I then looked up, to see if I could see God, who I expected was looking all the while upon me with great anger: when I found he was not to be seen, I took to my heels, and ran home as fast as possible, not daring to look up, for fear I should see the frowning face of God; and when I entered my father's house, durst not venture out any more that evening, but was glad to think I had escaped so well.[186]

William Cumberland's experience was strikingly similar:

> From a child I had had repeated convictions, and often promised to be good; but I broke my resolutions as often as I made them. ... I felt afraid that the earth would open and swallow me up; and that God would make me a monument of His displeasure: that I had committed the unpardonable sin against the Holy Ghost, and that there was no mercy for me.[187]

Even allowing for the fact that these stories probably follow some kind of literary convention (perhaps one based on Bunyan), there is evidence here that Methodism drew on a tradition of popular Puritanism that had largely disappeared from parish churches. Another story from this period relates to Patty Tompkins of Thrapston, Northamptonshire. Brought up in a church-going family who read the Bible on

---

183 'Life of Thomas Pierson', Welch, *Bedford Moravian Church*, 225.
184 Greeves, *Memorials of Wm Cumberland*, 2.
185 Michael Watts looked at a sample of 362 conversion experiences from the *Methodist Magazine* between 1780 and 1850 and found that 307 referred to the subject's religious upbringing (Watts, *Dissenters*, II, 51–3).
186 Hews, S*poils won in the day of battle*, 2.
187 Greeves, *Memorials of Wm Cumberland*, 10–11. See also *AM* (1784), 642 and (1790), 465.

Sunday evenings, Patty had burnt her dancing slippers and cut off her long curls before she had ever met a Methodist.[188] It was a common charge among contemporary critics that Methodism was nothing more than Puritanism revived but it might be more accurate to say that Methodism provided some relief for the cultural and emotional tensions left unresolved by the demise of Puritanism.

A Lifelong Commitment?

What is also clear, from both Wesleyan and Moravian membership lists, is that those who joined Methodist societies in the eighteenth century generally maintained that commitment thereafter. The membership register of Bedford's Moravian congregation records the names of 103 people who were admitted between 1745 and 1750 and gives details of the subsequent stories of all but two. Sixty-eight continued in membership until their death and only 33 lapsed or were expelled. The degree of continuity is all the more impressive when it is considered that 13 of the members who left were later re-admitted and among the others were those who seceded to form the Wesleyan society. Despite generally joining at a younger age, women appear to have been better at maintaining their commitment than their male counterparts: 5 out of 6 were members until their death compared with fewer than half the men. The information recorded in the Wesleyan circuit book does not allow the history of individuals to be followed in anything like the same detail and the custom of women changing their surnames on marriage makes it particularly difficult to trace their membership careers. What can be said is that of the 46 men who are known to have belonged to Wesleyan societies in Bedfordshire in 1781, 23 were still members in 1792. From other sources it is known that one of the men whose names had disappeared from the roll, Bletsoe Allen of Bedford, had gone over to the Moravians and that two other Bedford men, William Parker and Sam Goodman, had died; given what is known about the ageing profile of the membership, it seems quite likely deaths may have accounted for quite a few of the losses. The Wesleyan circuit book, however, suggests that by the 1780s this pattern of lifelong commitment was breaking down and that Methodism was beginning to have difficulty retaining recruits. Of the 28 men who joined societies across the whole circuit in 1782 only 8 were still members three years later.

Part 3   Being a Methodist

So what did being a Methodist in the eighteenth century involve? John Wesley's *Directions given to the Band Societies*, issued in 1744, set out quite clearly what he expected of his own early followers. They were instructed 'carefully to abstain from evil' and 'zealously to maintain good works', but also 'constantly to attend on the ordinances of God' and in particular:

> 1. To be at church, and at the Lord's Table, every week, and at every public meeting of the bands.

---

[188] Pope, *Finedon Methodism*, 5.

2. To attend the ministry of the Word every morning, unless distance, business, or sickness prevent.

3. To use private prayer every day, and family prayer if you are the head of a family.

4. To read the Scriptures, and meditate thereon, at every vacant hour. And,

5. To observe as days of fasting or abstinence all *Fridays* in the year.[189]

In other words, for Wesley being a Methodist involved attending the services of the Church of England and supplementing that spiritual diet with a number of Methodist meetings, including a preaching service at 5.00am every morning, a rigorous pattern of personal devotions, and a strict moral code.[190] While all of those elements find some echo in the records of Methodist life in Bedfordshire, the reality of Methodist practice, even among Wesley's own people, seems to have been rather more varied.

The Parish Church

It has generally been accepted, largely on Wesley's testimony, that Methodists were regular attendants at their parish churches until the 1780s but that from then on they were progressively thrust out of the Church by clerical harassment.[191] More recently there has been a tendency to argue that Church Methodism remained widespread for much longer. Frances Knight, in her study of the Lincoln diocese, claims that it was usual amongst the early Methodists to attend Sunday morning service at their parish church and that this practice continued well into the nineteenth century.[192] While Edward Royle has quoted an example of such practice, in Yorkshire, from as late as 1894, the evidence from Bedfordshire, however, suggests quite the opposite.[193]

Moves towards separation from the established church began almost from the very beginning. Even though Okely's society was founded with the stated purpose of pursuing religion 'according to the best Devotional Tracts of the Church of England', within four years it had become an avowedly Dissenting congregation and within six, as a Moravian society, it was holding services 'at the same hour we used to go to church'.[194] In 1747 three female members were actually censured for attending St Paul's, Bedford.[195] Sixteen years later, it is true, Howell Harris records that 'Mr. Rogers gave an account of his persuading the people (near Bedford) to continue in the Church of England' but this almost certainly refers to his discouraging would-be converts, in line with the Moravian policy of only accepting those with a clear call into membership, rather than to his encouraging Moravian members to attend their parish church.[196]

Berridge's followers too, despite his position as vicar of Everton, seem to have separated from the Church of England both naturally and swiftly. It began, as in Bedford, with people abandoning their own parish churches in order to attend one

[189] 'Directions given to the Band Societies Dec. 25, 1744', *Works of Wesley*, IX, 79.
[190] John Wesley to John Grace, 25 October 1789, Telford, *Letters of Wesley*, VIII, 177.
[191] Gilbert, *Religion and society*, 78.
[192] Knight, *Nineteenth-Century church and English society*, 27.
[193] Royle, 'When did Methodists stop attending their Parish Churches?', 290.
[194] 'Life of Ann Okely' in Welch, *Bedford Moravian Church*, 219; *Works of Wesley*, XX, 477.
[195] Welch, *Bedford Moravian Church*, 93.
[196] Beynon, *Howell Harris, reformer and soldier*, 154.

where there was Methodist preaching, among them Samuel Bennett of Tempsford who 'as he unhappily could not have what he desired in his own parish church, ... for some time sat under the ministry of the Rev. John Berridge.'[197] From the outset, the cottages and barns where Berridge held his mid-week meetings were licensed under the Toleration Act.[198] He seems to have accepted that his congregations would become Dissenting churches, writing to the Countess of Huntingdon in 1777:

> What has become of Mr. Venn's Yorkshire flock? What will become of his Yelling flock, or of my flocks at our decease? Or what will become of your students at your removal? They are virtual dissenters now, and will be settled dissenters then.

He appears to have been completely sanguine about the prospect, telling the Countess, in the same letter, that two of his lay assistants had already become Dissenting ministers:

> Some years ago, two of my lay-preachers deserted their ranks, and joined the dissenters. This threw me into a violent fit of the spleen, and set me a coughing and barking exceedingly; but when the phlegm was come up, and leisure allowed for calm thought, I did humbly conceive the Lord Jesus might be wiser than the old Vicar; and I did well in sending some preachers from the old Methodist mint among the dissenters, to revive a drooping cause ...[199]

Indeed, he seems to have seen it as a positive development, telling the Revd Benjamin Mills, a fellow Methodist, that where a parish clergyman did not preach the gospel: 'of course his flock must become Dissenters to get food, for awakened sinners cannot live upon chaff.'[200] It is quite conceivable that Berridge is the unnamed person in John Wesley's report of a visit to St Neots in 1775, that 'almost all the Methodists, by the advice of Mr. –, had left the Church.'[201] By 1785 Berridge noted that even many of those who had previously travelled to Everton on a Sunday now attended local meeting-houses instead, and on his death many of his remaining societies formally constituted themselves as Dissenting churches.[202]

The evidence relating to the local Wesleyan societies is slightly more ambiguous. There is certainly some evidence of Wesleyans participating in the services of their parish church. One of William Parker's stated reasons for leaving the Moravians in 1752 was that they held their services at the same hour as the church and at Luton, in the 1790s, Sarah Hill still regularly attended the services of the parish church, although perhaps significantly only 'in the intervals of the [Methodist] Preachers' visits.'[203] Other pieces of evidence point to Wesleyans abandoning their parish churches at an early date. At St Neots, in the 1780s, John Marlow, rather than attend his parish church between the visits of the preachers, walked many miles

197 *WMM* (1841), 707.
198 A series of licences for what appear to be Berridge's followers in Potton begins with one issued in 1758 (Welch, *Bedfordshire chapels*, 134).
199 Berridge to Countess of Huntingdon, 26 April 1777, Whittingham, *Works of Berridge*, 515–16.
200 Berridge to Benjamin Mills, 20 November 1784, *Congregational Magazine* (1838), 163–4.
201 *Works of Wesley*, XXII, 479.
202 Berridge to John Thornton, 13 July 1785, Whittingham, *Works of Berridge*, 416.
203 *Works of Wesley*, XX, 477; *WMM* (1846), 614. In fact, several of the curate's own children were members of the Methodist society (*WMM* (1834), 237; *AM* (1791), 360–5; and *WMM* (1835), 804).

to hear Methodist preaching.[204] James Durley, of Bierton in Buckinghamshire, did much the same and when he became a Methodist, in 1783, resigned his position as parish clerk 'in order that I might have full liberty to attend to the sound of gospel grace.'[205] By 1790 the society at Irchester was holding a morning preaching service, which in all likelihood clashed with matins at the parish church, and elsewhere on the Bedfordshire circuit societies were using Sunday mornings for prayer and class meetings.[206] Even William Parker's loyalty to the Church of England seems not to have lasted, for as early as 1761 he obtained a license for a house in Clifton under the Toleration Act, abandoning what would remain the official Wesleyan position for the next twenty-five years, that such a move was unnecessary as Methodists were part of the Church of England and their meetings therefore not liable to the penalties of the Conventicle Act.[207]

To characterise what happened as Methodists withdrawing from the Church of England presumes, of course, that they had previously belonged to it. This was not always the case and it is clear that early Methodism drew significant support from those who already stood outside the state church. At Hertford, in 1739, it was Dissenters and Quakers who entertained George Whitefield and it was Dissenters again who both invited him to preach at Hitchin and provided the bulk of his audience.[208] Even Coriolanus Copleston, the curate whose preaching was so appreciated by Wesleyans at Luton, had originally been ordained as a Presbyterian.[209] Far from being a society within the Church of England, Methodism was seen as a movement that transcended the divisions between the Church and Dissent. As early as 1738 Philip Doddridge had written to Whitefield:

> A truly generous and catholic spirit is prevailing in different denominations and I trust will still prevail till we come all to the unity of the Spirit and the stature of a perfect man. Oh what little things are those that divide us, with those many strong, endearing bands which will bind us close to Christ and one another for every Christians glorious title! Oh that every sectarian name were lost in that![210]

Twelve years later, when Whitefield preached at Northampton in 1750, he did so with Doddridge on his right and two clergymen, Hervey and Hartley, on his left.[211]

---

204   *MM* (1810), 481.
205   *MM* (1816), 119.
206   *WMM* (1828), 362. The Bedford membership list for 1794 refers to the Bedford Sunday morning class. James Durley recorded in his journal in 1796 that 'My Sunday mornings are taken up in meeting *Aston* and *Aylesbury* alternately' (Durley, *Centenary annals*, 11). At Stewkley, in 1803, there was a prayer meeting on Sunday morning from 7 to 8, class meeting from 9 until 10, then preaching at 10.30, 2 and 6 (Coles, *Youthful days*, 82).
207   Welch, *Bedfordshire chapels*, 54.
208   Murray, *Whitefield's journals*, 272 and 290; *Weekly Miscellany* 2 June 1739 quoted in Tyerman, *George Whitefield*, I, 232.
209   Copleston, born in Bideford in 1718, was a student at Doddridge's academy from 1736–40 on a scholarship from the Coward Trust. He assisted at Norwich and was ordained minister of the Presbyterian congregation at Princes Risborough in 1743. He conformed and was ordained deacon by the Bishop of Carlisle in 1761. In 1775 he was licensed as curate to the absentee vicar of Luton on a stipend of 50 guineas. He died in 1800.
210   Doddridge to Whitefield, 23 December 1738, Jones, '*A glorious work in the world*', 113.
211   James Hervey was curate of Weston Favell and Thomas Hartley vicar of Winwick (Tyerman, *Oxford Methodists*, 259).

It was a tradition continued by Berridge who, until his death, happily shared the pulpits of Whitefield's London chapels with Dissenting ministers.

The Lord's Table

Wesley's expectation that his followers would attend the Lord's Table every week was never a realistic one outside London and a few major cities. Across southern England the overwhelming majority of parishes only celebrated communion three or four times a year – at Christmas, Easter, Whitsun and, perhaps, Michaelmas – and this was certainly the case in Bedfordshire.[212] In fact, communion was not a central feature of the life of any of the early Methodist groups and perhaps the Wesleyans least of all. Even those members of Okely's society who had been communicants at their parish churches almost certainly ceased to be so during 1739. Those who followed Okely into membership of Blunham Baptist church would have been expected to attend its monthly communion service but, distrusting outward forms as suggesting some kind of salvation by works, they appear to have been reluctant to do so. Indeed, one of the charges brought against Okely by the Baptists was that he despised the ordinances of their church. From 1744 some of the Bedford society were chosen to attend communion with the Moravian congregation at Fetter Lane in London and in June 1745 the first Moravian communion was held in Bedford itself. Attendance was extremely tightly guarded with those who had been received into membership of the congregation having to wait until chosen, again by lot, for admission to communion, a process that quite commonly took several years. At Fulneck, in Yorkshire, communion services were held once a month and the pattern at Bedford was probably the same.[213] It was a solemn and powerful occasion and, as the congregation diary records, after receiving the bread and wine the recipients quite literally prostrated themselves on the chapel floor:

> We had the Lord's Supper with melted and ashamed Hearts indeed, and our Saviour gave us new Strength and Courage to our future Race by feeding us with his Flesh and Blood. All that came to this blessed Feast for the first Time were blessed or consecrated thereto by Br Dober and Sr Hutton. We adored our dear Lamb upon our Faces for this new and amazing Grace.[214]

At Everton Berridge too seems to have introduced a monthly communion service, although probably influenced by the practice of Dissenting churches rather than the Moravians or any High Church tradition. On one occasion there were said to have been 270 communicants, a vast number when, even at Easter, well over half the parishes in Bedfordshire reported fewer than twenty communicants, the supposed minimum for holding a service.[215] Even so this would have been a fraction of his following, most of whom lived too far from Everton to attend. There is no record of any communion services being held by local Wesleyan societies but it is known that Wesley himself celebrated communion in some of his preaching-rooms, for instance

---

[212]   In 1720 in Bedfordshire 90% of parishes held four or fewer communions a year; in Essex and Hertfordshire it was 84%; and in Oxfordshire over 80% (Bell, *Episcopal visitations*, 185–248; Mather, 'Georgian churchmanship reconsidered', 255).

[213]   Stead, *Moravian settlement at Fulneck*, 66.

[214]   Welch, *Bedford Moravian Church*, 33.

[215]   Folder of papers concerning John Berridge prepared by Revd John Jones, vicar of Bolnurst, c.1760, Dr Williams's Library, Jones 39.B.24; Bell, *Episcopal visitations*.

at Dorking in Surrey, and it is not impossible that he did so at Bedford.[216] There is also no record of Wesleyans attending their parish church for communion but Joseph Pescod, Wesley's assistant on the Bedfordshire circuit from 1783 to 1785, received communion from a Church of England clergyman, apparently without comment, while visiting a condemned man in Bedford gaol, which may suggest that some Wesleyans at least were in the habit of doing so.[217]

Early Methodist Preaching

The importance of preaching to the experience of the very first Methodists comes across strongly from their reminiscences and obituaries. More than fifty years after the event, Mary Collier could still remember how Jacob Rogers 'preached with astonishing power' both in Bedford and the surrounding villages and Virtue Kingham remembered to her death-bed in 1828 the text of a sermon she heard Wesley preach in Luton in 1770.[218] Why Methodist preaching had this impact is a complex question and to answer it not only its content and style but its setting and social function need to be considered.[219]

The very first Methodist sermons were delivered in Bedford's parish churches, and the parish churches at Everton and Wrestlingworth continued to provide pulpits for Methodist preachers until the 1790s. George Whitefield's journal records that on a visit to Bedfordshire in 1758 four clergyman lent him their churches on a single day and John Wesley appears to have preached at least once both at St Paul's, Bedford and at Luton parish church.[220] Rather more surprisingly, Dissenting meeting-houses also provided the setting for some early Methodist sermons. Francis Okely preached in Blunham Baptist meeting-house in 1740 and George Whitefield in the Bedford meeting-house in July 1758, in Castle Hill meeting-house, Northampton in 1743 and 1767, and in Doddridge's academy in 1750 and 1753.[221] John Wesley also 'expounded' to the students in Doddridge's academy, in 1745, preached in 'Presbyterian' meeting-houses at Weedon in 1767 and at Northampton in 1785 and 1788, and in a 'Dissenting' meeting-house at Towcester in 1789.[222] Even taken

---

[216]   Although Wesley's published *Journals* make no reference to it, his manuscript diaries reveal that he celebrated communion in the Dorking preaching-house on his annual visits in 1784, 1785, 1786, 1787, 1789, 1790 and 1791. Diaries have not survived, however, for long periods of his career.

[217]   *AM* (1788), 124–5.

[218]   Welch, *Bedford Moravian Church*, 210; *WMM* (1828), 215.

[219]   Surprisingly little has been written about this central aspect of Methodist life, with most books on Methodist worship, such as Trevor Dearing's *Wesleyan and Tractarian Worship* and David Chapman's *Born in Song*, choosing to focus instead on the textual minutiae of the officially produced, but largely unused, liturgies. The one exception is Adrian Burdon's pamphlet, *The Preaching Service* and even this is largely given over to a discussion about the sequence in which sermon, prayers and hymns may have been arranged.

[220]   Gillies, *Works of Whitefield*, III, 238; *Works of Wesley*, XXI, 137 and XXII, 304. It is possible that Wesley preached at St Paul's a second time: the obituary of Daniel Pressland, written in 1845, claims that he heard Wesley preach in St Paul's church from 1 Cor. 1:30 and met him afterwards. The claim receives partial corroboration from an entry in Wesley's diary which records his preaching at Bedford, on 27 October 1790, from 1 Cor. 1:3 and meeting the society afterwards. The venue of the sermon is not mentioned and its timing, at 6.30pm, makes the parish church an unlikely choice (*WMM* (1845), 841). It is clear from the diary entries relating to other visits that a more usual venue for such sermons would have been the society's own room.

[221]   Church book of Blunham Baptist meeting 1724–1891, BLARS, X525/1; Lawton, 'Notes on Early Methodism in Northampton', 89.

[222]   Gillies, *Works of Whitefield,* III, 238; *Works of Wesley*, XXII, 107. In fact, Weedon was a Davisite

together, however, the sermons delivered in churches and meeting-houses can have represented only a small proportion of the totality of Methodist preaching.[223]

One alternative venue for Methodist preachers was to 'take to the field' and the image of that has powerfully shaped many assumptions about early Methodism.[224] Bedfordshire certainly witnessed some open-air Methodist preaching in the eighteenth century, with Jacob Rogers again taking the lead. There are accounts of John Wesley preaching on St Peter's Green in Bedford in 1753, 1754 and 1759 and in Potton market place in 1749.[225] Berridge and Hicks too preached in the open air in the late 1750s.[226] These were great occasions that caused a considerable stir and lingered in the memory as a result but it is highly unlikely that they were ever commonplace either in Bedfordshire or more generally. The journal entry for Wesley's 1754 sermon is instructive in its admission that he had 'never preached abroad since I was here before': that is nine months previously.[227] Whitefield's journal also, having detailed a whole week of preaching engagements across Buckinghamshire, Bedfordshire and Northamptonshire in July 1758, concludes with the comment, 'and at Northampton I took the field', presumably not having done so at any other location.[228] After the 1750s there is little evidence of open-air preaching, and where it did occur it appears not to have been by choice. At Kislingbury, on the Northamptonshire side of the circuit, Wesley was 'obliged by the largeness of the congregation to stand in the open air' in 1770 and in 1778, at John Farey's farm in Sheep Lane: 'I designed to preach in the house, but the number of people obliged me to preach abroad in spite of the keen east winds.'[229]

Given the English climate, and that many sermons were preached at the end of the working day, the most common setting for Methodist preaching in the eighteenth century was, in all probability, a cottage or barn. Ann Okely's barn was fitted up for preaching in 1739, but it was not the only place that the Bedford society used.[230] When Moravian preachers from London began to visit the society in 1742, they used Mr Eston's house as their venue, 'The Minister stood In the passage between

---

Independent church and Towcester a mixed gathering of Baptists and Independents. Wesley also calls the property in Northampton which his society bought a Presbyterian meeting-house when it was in fact built for Particular Baptists. It is hard to believe that he was ignorant of these distinctions and seems quite likely that he was carefully managing the public presentation of his connexion's relationship with Dissent.

[223] Of the forty or so towns and villages that are known to have been part of the Bedfordshire Wesleyan circuit at some point or other, only two ever witnessed Methodist preaching in a parish church and three in a meeting-house.

[224] George Dolbey's study of Methodist architecture paints an idyllic picture: 'The architectural setting of most early Methodist worship was that of nature itself – the grass for its floor, the trees its columns, the sky its roof, and a rock or hillock its pulpit'(Dolbey, *Architectural expression of Methodism*, 22). Even Adrian Burdon's pamphlet on the Methodist preaching service has on its cover an early twentieth century image of John Wesley preaching from the steps of a market cross.

[225] *Works of Wesley*, XX, 295, 479 and 489.

[226] Letter from Berridge, probably to John Walsh, quoted in *Works of Wesley*, XXI, 200; Letter from Berridge to John Wesley, 16 July 1759, *AM* (1780), 611.

[227] *Works of Wesley*, XX, 489.

[228] Gillies, *Works of Whitefield*, III, 238.

[229] *Works of Wesley*, XXII, 257 and XXIII, 110. The obituary of John Wingrave in 1858 says that he could remember hearing Wesley preach on the Moor at Luton when he was four, in 1784. Wesley did preach in Luton in 1784 but on 3 December at 6.00pm which makes an open-air sermon seem quite unlikely.

[230] 'Life of Ann Okely' in Welch, *Bedford Moravian Church*, 220.

the House and parlour The women were in the Parlour the men In the first Room or House.'[231]

John Berridge preached in his vicarage as well as his church and fitted up a number of barns in other villages as what, with characteristic eccentricity, he referred to as 'preaching shops.' He wrote to a friend in 1773:

> It would delight you to see how crowded my cathedrals are, and what abundance of hearers they contain, when the grain is threshed out. I believe more children have been born of God in any one of these despised barns, than in St Paul's Church or Westminster Abbey.[232]

Wesley preached in the homes of several of his wealthy hosts, as in 1782 when 'many of the villagers flocked together, so that her [Miss Harvey's] great hall was well filled', but also in a barn, a malt room, a riding school and, as time went on, in purpose built structures described as preaching-rooms or preaching-houses.[233] The first purpose-built Methodist meeting place in the area appears to have been the Tabernacle at Olney, built by Whitefield's connexion around 1744; it was followed by Moravian chapels at Bedford (1751), Riseley (1759) and Northampton (1770); by Wesleyan preaching-rooms at Bedford (by 1767), Hertford (1768), Luton (1778) and Huntingdon (1780); and by Miss Harvey's chapel at Hinxworth (1784).[234]

None of these buildings appear to have survived, and images exist for only two of them, the Moravian chapel at Northampton and the Wesleyan preaching-room at Luton. The Northampton chapel, situated discreetly in an alley way, was nevertheless a stylish, classical structure, broader than it was deep, with separate entrances for men and women (as indeed there were at the Bedford Moravian chapel).[235] The Luton preaching-room, hidden in a yard behind two cottages was equally discreet but much less dignified, with a double-ridged roof and windowless frontage. If it followed Wesley's stipulations it would have had 'no tub-pulpit, but a square projection with a long seat behind' and the seating would have consisted of simple forms, for there should have been 'no pews and no backs to the seats, which should have aisles on each side, and be parted in the middle by a rail running all along, to divide the men from the women.'[236] Whether men and women really sat apart is unclear. There is certainly evidence that they did so at Stewkley and a tradition of them doing so at Lidlington but Wesley's repeated re-iteration of the rule suggests that it was not universally observed.[237] The story that William Cole built a pew for himself

---

231   'Life of Thomas Pierson' in Welch, *Bedford Moravian Church*, 226.
232   Letter from Berridge to John Thornton, 3 May 1773, *Congregational Magazine* (1842), 221.
233   *Works of Wesley*, XXIII, 247.
234   It is sometimes claimed that a chapel was built at Whittlebury in 1763, when the society was part of the Bedfordshire circuit. However, the new preaching-house mentioned in Wesley's journal for that year (*Works of Wesley*, XXI, 419) appears, in this case, to have been a house in which preaching took place rather than a purpose-built structure. A preaching-house, in the sense of a chapel, was built in the village in 1783, but Whittlebury was by then part of the Northamptonshire circuit (*Methodist Recorder* 29 June 1883).
235   The Bedford Moravian chapel seems also to have been a stylish structure. There were long discussions about the kind of hedging to be used in the burying ground (someone was sent to Barnet to look at yew trees) and the interior may have been hung with paintings (Welch, *Bedford Moravian Church*, 96–143 and 186; Podmore, *Moravian Church in England*, 152).
236   *Works of Wesley*, X, 930.
237   Coles, *Youthful days*, p. 68; Telford, *Letters of John Wesley,* VII, p. 32.

and his family (flouting another prohibition in the process) certainly suggests that at least some men and women sat together at Luton.[238]

However varied its setting, the message of most Methodist sermons appears to have followed a common theme: the 'three capital and distinguishing Doctrines of the Methodists, viz. Original Sin, Justification by Faith, and the New Birth.'[239] That was certainly pretty much what John Spangenberg had to say in 1742:

> he shew'd the very state we are in by Nature, And then set forth the Ritches, and Grace of Our Dear Saviour in Becoming a man and Giving himself a Sacrifice for our Sins. It Quite melted my heart Especially when he said Our Lord was Ready and Willing to Receive us Just as we are.[240]

It was also what John Berridge encouraged preachers to concentrate on:

> Acquaint them with the searching eye of God, watching us continually, spying out every thought, word, and action, noting them down in the book of his remembrance. ... When your hearers are deeply affected with these things (which is seen by the hanging down of their heads), preach Christ. ... Let them know that ... he is full of love as well as power.[241]

And it is essentially the theme of John Wesley's assizes sermon at Bedford in 1758, which concluded:

> Hath he not bought you with his own blood, that ye might 'not perish, but have everlasting life'? O make proof of his mercy rather than his justice! Of his love rather than the thunder of his power![242]

Spangenberg, Berridge and Wesley were, of course, all educated and leading men. What the foot soldiers of the Methodist movement preached is even harder to establish.[243]

The richest vein of evidence comes from Bierton in Buckinghamshire, just outside the boundaries of the Bedfordshire circuit. It consists of a notebook belonging to James Durley in which he recorded summaries of 11 sermons he heard preached in the autumn of 1787 and the texts of some 94 others he attended between 1789 and 1791.[244] The texts bear no relation to the lectionary of the Book of Common Prayer and suggest that the preachers largely followed their own inclination in choosing what to speak on.[245] Nevertheless, the 11 sermons for which there are fairly full notes, preached by four different preachers, all essentially conform to the basic evangelical theme: God's judgement on sinners, Christ's atoning sacrifice, and the promise that if you believe with all your heart you will be happy when you die. Old Testament

---

238   George Spilsbury's account of the beginnings of Methodism in Luton, 1839, MARC.
239   'Life of Ann Okely' in Welch, *Bedford Moravian Church*, 219.
240   'Life of Thomas Pierson' in Welch, *Bedford Moravian Church*, 226.
241   Letter from John Berridge, nd, Whittingham, *Works of Berridge*, 440. The recipient was identified as Charles Simeon in *AM* (1794), 496.
242   *Works of Wesley*, I, 375.
243   The texts of quite a few sermons by both itinerant and local preachers are known (see, for example *AM* (1785), 625; *MM* (1798), 272 and 273; *MM* (1816), 286–7; Coles, *Youthful days,* 73–4) but it would be dangerous to imagine that they tell much about the content or style of the preaching that flowed from them.
244   Notebook of James Durley, CBS, DX 544/1.
245   This appears to be confirmed by the preaching records of individual preachers, for while more than half of William Horner's twenty-nine sermons were based on Old Testament texts another colleague, whom Durley heard preach seventeen times, never once preached on an Old Testament passage.

texts, like Psalm 92:12 'The righteous shall flourish like the palm tree; he shall grow like the cedar in Lebanon', and texts that might appear to offer moral themes, such as Matthew 23:35 'I was a stranger, and you took me in', were all used to introduce the same message. There is no mention of particular sins, such as sabbath-breaking, swearing or fornicating, nor any mention of good works, except attending preaching and private prayer. What was said of one Moravian preacher could, it seems, have been said about most Methodist preachers: 'he always preaches the same Thing.'[246]

Most witnesses seem to agree that the style of Methodist preaching was very plain.[247] William Cumberland never forgot the simplicity of a sermon preached by John Wesley nor the conversational language: '"Now don't you see the force of this?" – "'Tis as plain as that two and two make four." – "'Tis as easy as easy."'[248] Mary Collier, likewise, remembered Jacob Rogers' preaching for 'his manner simple and unaffected.'[249] The effect of this plain style was that members of the congregation felt that the preacher 'spoke as If he had spoke to me'.[250] There appears to be an implied contrast here with the preaching styles prevalent in both parish churches and Dissenting meeting-houses and it was certainly a conscious strategy. Henry Venn, vicar of Yelling and a Methodist sympathiser, wrote in the 1770s 'I am under necessity of labouring to be very plain … I find, therefore, it is very profitable to tell them stories.'[251] John Berridge too 'was remarkably careful to preach with great plainness of speech; so much so, that if possible, there might not be uttered a word but the meanest of his hearers might understand.'[252]

It is possible, however, that there was more to the impact of Methodist preaching than either its content or its style. John Walsh's detailed account of his visit to Everton in 1759 is full of observations about what was happening in the congregation during a series of services taken by both Berridge and Hicks but his only comment on the actual sermons was that 'neither of these gentlemen have much eloquence.'[253] Something of the power of early Methodist preaching clearly lay not in what was said, nor even the way it was said, but in the occasion of a sermon.

Most early Methodist preaching in Bedfordshire seems to have involved travelling. Sometimes the congregation had travelled, as when members of Okely's society walked out to Lidlington or Ridgmont to hear Jacob Rogers preach, or when crowds travelled to Everton to hear Berridge.[254] William Cumberland and a friend went so far as to walk to London to hear John Wesley, and on their return 'delighted and edified the pious household to which they belonged with a copious detail of all that they had seen, and heard, and felt.'[255] Other times it was the preacher who had travelled: Ingham and Delamotte came down to Bedford from Cambridge; White-

246 Welch, *Bedford Moravian Church*, 92.
247 'I talked of preaching, and of the great success which those called Methodists have. JOHNSON: "Sir, it is owing to their expressing themselves in a plain and familiar manner, which is the only way to do good to the common people."' Boswell, *Life of Johnson*, I, 306.
248 Greeves, *Memorials of Wm Cumberland* (1834), 24.
249 'Mary Collier's Relation' in Welch, *Bedford Moravian Church*, 210; *Works of Wesley*, XXI, 135.
250 'Life of Thomas Pierson' in Welch, *Bedford Moravian Church*, 226.
251 Venn, *Life and letters*, 176.
252 Whittingham, *Works of Berridge*, xlvii.
253 *Works of Wesley*, XXI, 198.
254 'Mary Collier's Relation' in Welch, *Bedford Moravian Church*, 210.
255 Greeves, *Memorials of Wm Cumberland*, 24.

field and Wesley passed through on their grand tours; Berridge travelled a circuit of up to a hundred miles a week.[256] The novelty of listening to strangers and the sheer effort involved in bringing people and preacher together probably created a real sense of occasion. When William Goodson gave it out in the Buckinghamshire village of Waddesdon that a new preacher would be visiting, more people came to hear than the house would contain and at Whittlebury a sermon was sufficient of an event to attract the young and 'giddy' as well as the serious.[257]

Nor were Methodist preachers coy about exploiting significant events to lend their sermons greater moment and drama. Benjamin Ingham's preaching in Bedford in 1739 seems to have made use of the fact that the town had suffered an outbreak of smallpox.[258] Jacob Rogers took as his text in December 1745 'When ye hear of wars, and rumour of wars, see that ye be not troubled' and when John Wynn was executed at Bedford in 1785, Joseph Pescod 'preached upon the occasion at the Methodist chapel at seven, to a very crowded audience, from 1 Cor. 1:9 – But we had the sentence of death in ourselves, that we should not trust in ourselves, but in God which raiseth the dead.'[259]

It was probably quite some time before the sense of occasion was diluted by familiarity. Although the Moravian congregation in Bedford enjoyed regular weekly preaching from perhaps 1742, elsewhere visits from preachers were very rare events. Whitefield paid only three visits to the county between 1739 and 1760, and Wesley perhaps ten.[260] As time went on opportunities to hear Methodist preaching became more numerous but it was a very slow process. Everton and Wrestlingworth clearly had weekly preaching from 1758 and by the 1760s Berridge was employing 2 or 3 full-time lay preachers. Wesley stationed 1 preacher to Bedford in 1765, increasing that to 2 in 1767 and 3 in 1775; but those preachers, like Berridge's, were not used to provide weekly preaching in one place, rather they were sent on vast circuits preaching regularly but infrequently in dozens of towns and villages.[261]

In most places such preaching happened mid-week. Berridge's routine was to preach in Everton on a Sunday and then set off on Monday on a round of preaching in neighbouring villages before returning home on Saturday ready for his Sunday duties. On the Monday he would then set off on a different round, apparently following a six-week cycle.[262] Wesleyan circuits also seem to have followed a six-week cycle, though the preacher was not necessarily itinerating on all of them.[263] Where two preachers were stationed in the same circuit they appear to have followed the same round, so that societies might expect a visit once every three weeks and,

---

256 Pibworth, *Gospel pedlar*, 80–1.
257 Diary of William Goodson, quoted in Durley, *Centenary annals*, 6; *AM* (1790), 465.
258 'Life of Ann Okely' in Welch, *Bedford Moravian Church*, 219.
259 'Congregation Diary' in Welch, *Bedford Moravian Church*, 47; *AM* (1788), 127.
260 Whitefield is known to have visited Bedford in May 1739, October 1753 and July 1758 (Tyerman, *Life of George Whitefield*, I, 231; II, 315 and 410).
261 Hartley, *Hall's Circuits and Ministers*, 37.
262 Pibworth, *Gospel Pedlar*, 81; Baker, 'Polity', 233.
263 Evidence of this is provided by Joseph Pescod, who was at Bedford from 1782 to 1785, and John Hickling, who was there from 1793 to 1795. Both men have left glimpses into the pattern of their itinerancy in the accounts they give of their ministrations to condemned men in Bedford gaol. Although sometimes away from home for up to a fortnight at a stretch, equally there were weeks when they were able to visit the prisoners every day; presumably preaching in the evening for societies within easy reach of Bedford (*AM* (1788), 70 and (1795), 390–5).

where there were three preachers, once a fortnight.[264] As late as the 1790s, however, not every Methodist society was able to have even mid-week preaching regularly.[265]

Mid-week preaching meant that services generally had to be fitted around the working day and held either early in the morning or in the evening. Whitefield preached at 7.00am on his visit to Bedford in 1739, as did Wesley on his first visit to the town fourteen years later.[266] This, however, seems to have been an unusually late hour that made some allowance for the celebrity status of the preachers and the more normal time appears to have been 5.00am.[267] In the evening, the preaching took place at around 6.00pm.[268] During the harvest even these timings interfered with the working day and preaching was probably suspended.[269] By the late 1760s the practice of morning preaching seems to have fallen into general decline. Wesley certainly felt the need to instruct his preachers in 1768: 'Let the preaching at five in the morning be constantly kept up, wherever you have twenty hearers. This is the glory of the Methodists. Whenever this is dropped, they will dwindle away into nothing.'[270] Mid-week morning preaching had completely disappeared from Berridge's circuit by the early 1770s, when Walter Shirley came to help out at Everton, and by the 1780s even Wesley himself preached only infrequently in the early morning on his visits to Bedfordshire.[271] The problem with morning preaching may well have been that even at 5.00am it was simply too late in the day for farm workers.

> Mr Wesley preached one week night in that old chapel [Luton], and one of his hearers was old Mr Davis, the farmer of Couridge End. At the close of the sermon, Mr Wesley announced that he would preach there again the next morning at 5 o'clock, adding "doubtless many of you will be in bed then." Mr Davis thought to himself, "*I* shall not be in bed, but shall be unable to come to hear you."[272]

It was a hard life for the itinerant preachers. John Berridge warned the Countess of Huntingdon that any assistant that she sent him would have to be able to bear 'Long rides and miry roads in sharp weather!'; and John Pritchard, Wesley's assistant on the Bedfordshire circuit in 1778, would later record:

264 Durley, *Centenary annals*, 7.
265 James Durley's diary records that in 1791 the society at Wendover declined 'taking the preacher at present, so *Oving* gets the privilege' and that in 1796 the preachers themselves declined to go 'to Aylesbury for the present, as one place must be left or the others neglected' (Durley, *Centenary annals*, 8 and 10). As has already been noted, even a relatively large society like Luton, with a purpose-built preaching house, still experienced intervals between the preachers' visits (*WMM* (1846), 614).
266 Gregory, *Autobiographical recollections*, 10–11.
267 Murray, *Whitefield's journals*, 274; *Works of Wesley*, XX, 479.
268 Whittingham, *Works of Berridge*, 533.
269 Whittingham, *Works of Berridge*, 384.
270 *Works of Wesley*, X, 361.
271 Whittingham, *Works of Berridge*, 533. Compare this with what appears to be an earlier set of instructions which detail arrangements for both morning and evening preaching (Ibid., 440–1). Between December 1782 and February 1791 (the final period covered by his surviving manuscript diaries) Wesley preached 52 times in the Bedfordshire circuit. Eleven of these sermons were given in the early morning, 33 in the evening and 8 during the working day.
272 Hawkes, *Rise of Wesleyan Sunday schools*, 10.

In the winter my horse fell ill; and I being poor, (for a Methodist preacher is likely to be so as long as he lives,) and the people poor also, I travelled the winter and spring quarters on foot, about twelve hundred miles.[273]

In some places, volunteers supplemented the work of the paid preachers and the contribution of these lay, or local, preachers has often been seen as vital to the expansion of early Methodism.[274] That does not, however, seem to have been the case in Bedfordshire. Preaching among the Moravians was restricted to ordained clergy and most of the work on both Wesley's and Berridge's circuits was carried out by men who, although often not ordained, were nevertheless paid, full-time professionals. Berridge did make some use of 'Sunday preachers', including it seems the rather unreliable John Miller of Potton, but only two such preachers are recorded among the Wesleyans before 1796.[275]

When no preacher was available, some societies seem to have organized their own public worship. According to the obituary of John Marlow, in the 1780s preachers made only rare visits to St Neots but in between times he held his own meetings. What happened at these particular gatherings is not recorded, but at Bierton, at about the same time, on a Sunday evening James Durley 'prayed, and read a sermon, or expounded a chapter in my own house, as well as I could, to all who were willing to hear me.'[276] Durley went on to become a local preacher, but he appears to have been careful to distinguish, as were others, between expounding and that later role. Technically the difference lay in whether or not the speaker took a particular verse of scripture as their starting point, but expounding was also probably a much shorter and less formal affair.[277]

Hymn Singing

Singing also clearly played a significant part in the experience of early Methodist worship. The preface of a twentieth-century Methodist hymn-book claimed that 'Methodism was born in song' but, while there has been much textual analysis of hymns, little has been written about Methodist singing. In truth, the role of music had already begun to grow both in the worship of parish churches and Dissenting meeting-houses before the arrival of Methodism. Although hymns were prohibited in the Church of England, it was legal to sing metrical psalms and there is evidence of this being done in several Bedfordshire parishes in the early eighteenth century. At Everton and at Ampthill there are references in the 1720s to people being paid to teach psalm-singing and there was a choir at Dunstable by 1726.[278] From around

273 Whittingham, *Works of Berridge*, 503. Jackson, *Lives of early Methodist preachers*, VI, 267.
274 Milburn and Batty, *Workaday preachers*, 18.
275 For John Miller see Whittingham, *Works of Berridge*, 430–1. The two Wesleyans were Aldermen Parker and Walker. Walker is mentioned once in relation to preaching at Sundon (*WMM* (1886), 595). Parker's career is well-recorded. He was sufficiently distinguished to preach at the Foundry in 1758; was responsible for the conversion of Hannah Course in about 1766; was preaching as far afield as Towcester in 1769; and in 1782 the Bedford preaching-house was identified in a will as the one 'whereof Mr William Parker is now one of the ministers or preachers' (*Works of Wesley*, XXI, 135; *AM* (1785), 624–6; *WMM* (1827), 134–5; *Supplement to the short sketch of the work carried on by the Moravian Church in Northampton*, 7; Anderson, *Early Methodism in Bedford*, 22; *MM* (1810), 481).
276 *MM* (1816), 120.
277 Milburn and Batty, *Workaday preachers*, 15.
278 Godber, *History of Bedfordshire*, 343.

1690 local Dissenting congregations also began to sing. The Bedford meeting appears to have led the way:

> Our brethren have determined that those that are perswaded in there consciences that publick singing is an ordinance of God, shall practice it on the Lord's Day in our meeting in Bedford. Those that are of differing judgment have there liberty whether they will sing, ye or noe, or whether they will be presant whilst we sing.[279]

Stevington followed in 1713 when 'it was agred upon by this Church of Christ that wee should sing at the Lord's Tabol in imataishion of Christ and his Church.'[280] The quality of much of this singing seems to have left much to be desired. Berridge was scathing: 'This tax of praise is collected chiefly from an organ, or a solitary clerk, or some bawling voices in a singing loft. The congregation may listen if they please, or talk in whispers, or take a gentle nap.'[281] One of the reasons was that women were required either to sing quietly or not to sing at all, so that there was no question of them usurping men in the leading of worship.[282] All the Methodist groups, by contrast, encouraged everyone to participate and, although the melody was generally sung by the men, it was not uncommon to use tunes that created antiphonal dialogues in which one sex sang first and then the other responded.[283]

Nothing, however, that had gone before compared with the musical outpouring that accompanied the introduction of Moravianism. The diary of the Bedford congregation is full of references to singing, usually of single verses, rather than whole hymns, and sometimes written by members of the congregation. At a baptism service singing interspersed the prayers:

> we sung that Verse, Sanctify thy Congregation etc. during which Br Heck. set a Chair just before the Table, spread a fine clean Cloth upon it, and brought in the Water and set it down upon the Table; and just as we were singing that Line, Bless ev'ry little one, Mother Okely Brought in Br Roger's little Son … Then Br R. spoke very short … Then we all rose up, singing that Verse, The Water spouting from thy Side etc. … he took the little Heart into his Arms, and said Jacob I baptize thee … Upon which he gave out that Verse, Sacred anointing Oil etc. … and we went on singing that Hymn to the End, which Br Rog. alter'd very prettily into a Prayer for his Son.[284]

At other times the whole service consisted of singing. These carefully structured 'singing hours' drew on verses from different hymns to explore a particular theme. They were emotionally powerful occasions and one, on the blood and wounds of Christ, was apparently 'very much blest.'[285] The singing of the original Bedford society was probably unaccompanied but as it came under more direct Moravian supervision musical instruments appear to have been introduced in line with continental Moravian practice. A minute of September 1745 records the decision 'to have Musick in our singing Hours, which would make them more sweet and

279 Tibbutt, *Minutes of the Bunyan Meeting Bedford*, 93.
280 Tibbutt, *Some early Nonconformist Church Books*, 43.
281 Whittingham, *Works of Berridge*, cc.
282 Temperley and Banfield, *Music and the Wesleys*, 6.
283 Temperley, 'Methodist Church Music', *New Grove Dictionary of Music and Musicians*, XVI, 521–2.
284 Welch, *Bedford Moravian Church*, 53–4.
285 Welch, *Bedford Moravian Church*, 31 and 49. See also Podmore, *Moravian Church in England*, 149.

Churchlike.'[286] Two years later it was resolved to build a special gallery for the musicians where they could not only play but keep their instruments.[287] By 1754 there was an organ and the congregation were even providing hymn-books for visitors to use during the services.[288] Over time the Bedford congregation achieved quite a reputation for its music, but this was not true of all Moravian congregations and at Riseley the singing was apparently dreadful.[289]

Singing was also much in evidence at Everton from the outset of Methodist preaching. Berridge noted that his new converts did nothing but sing in their meetings, and that it was only as time went on that they began to read the Bible and pray as well, while John Walsh's journal recounts walking over to Cockayne Hatley 'sixteen in number, singing to the Lord as we went.'[290] Hymns also formed a part of the week-day preaching services on Berridge's circuit 'the Method with us is, first to sing a hymn, then pray, then preach, then sing another hymn, then pray again, then conclude with "Praise God from whom," &c.'[291] If the Moravian hymn-singing was sweet and musical, the singing at Berridge's services seems to have been hearty and loud and he had to warn them 'Aim not to make as great a noise as you can in singing.'[292] Berridge published *A Collection of divine songs* for his followers in 1760 and twenty-five years later produced a second hymn-book containing some 342 hymns of his own composition. His correspondence with John Thornton also records him distributing hundreds of copies of other hymn-books, including Newton and Cowper's *Olney Hymns* and collections by Isaac Watts.

> I have received twelve dozen of small Bibles, nine dozen of small Testaments, and one thousand Hymns for children, which I will distribute as carefully as I can. ... I gave thirty of Watts' small Hymns to the neighbouring Baptist minister ...[293]

The range of hymn-books Berridge was giving away suggests that their function was not to facilitate congregational singing, for which the words were, in any case, read out a few lines at a time. Rather, their principle purpose would seem to have been to provide popular devotional reading for private meditation, family prayers and cottage meetings.

There was surprisingly little hymn-singing at Wesleyan Methodist preaching services. A contemporary account of John Wesley's preaching records that he began his services with a short prayer, then led the singing of a hymn, preached for about half an hour, led the singing of a few verses from another hymn and closed with another prayer.[294] What singing there was almost certainly did not develop to the sophisticated level of the Moravian congregation but remained monophonic and

[286] Welch, *Bedford Moravian Church*, 40.
[287] Bunney, *Bedford St Luke's*, 71.
[288] Welch, *Bedford Moravian Church,* 102 and 104.
[289] Britton and Brayley, *Beauties of England and Wales*, I, 8; Welch, *Bedford Moravian Church*, 158.
[290] Letter from John Berridge to John Wesley, 16 July 1759, *AM* (1780), 611; John Walsh's journal, quoted in Wesley's (*Works of Wesley*, XXI, 212).
[291] Berridge to Walter Shirley, nd, Whittingham, *Works of Berridge*, 533–4.
[292] Pibworth, *Gospel pedlar*, 235.
[293] Berridge to John Thornton, 27 July 1779 [incorrectly dated 1775] and 12 June 1778, Whittingham, *Works of Berridge*, 395 and 391.
[294] *AM* (1787), 101. See also Burdon, *The Preaching service*, 22.

unaccompanied. Yet the obituaries and memoirs of early Wesleyans attest to the enormous power which hymns exercised over their imaginations. On his death-bed Thomas Harris 'entreated the friends to sing'; John Wynn sang 'And am I born to die', standing under the gallows awaiting his execution, apparently with great cheerfulness. Samuel Newman even had a musical vision of heaven: 'When one asked what he heard, he answered, "The sweetest music I ever heard in my life: did you not hear it?" His brother answered, "No: it is not for us, it is for your encouragement. The angels wait to conduct you safe to the heavenly mansions."'[295]

Methodist Meetings

Although public preaching was undoubtedly the most visible element of Methodist communal life, it was certainly not the only kind of Methodist gathering or indeed the most frequent. Okely's religious society was meeting for mutual improvement before the first Methodist sermon had been preached in the county and domestic meetings for religious conversation, prayer and hymn singing continued to be the most common form of Methodist gathering throughout the eighteenth century.

Many of these meetings were informal. George Gorham, the St Neots' banker, would recall in later life that when John Fletcher, the Methodist vicar of Madeley in Shropshire, had preached at the parish church on a visit to the town in 1776 'After service, several persons came to my father's house, desirous of an introduction to the Preacher. As there yet remained some time before the afternoon service, it was proposed to Mr. Fletcher, that he should give a short exhortation to the persons who had assembled. About thirty individuals were present.'[296] At Everton, people gathered in Berridge's vicarage both before and after the services in the church on Sundays and when it was known that some prominent Methodist had arrived on a visit.[297] At Whittlebury, people gathered for religious conversation before the preaching began.[298] The obituaries in the *Arminian Magazine* also talk frequently of Methodists coming together in the homes of the sick and dying to pray and sing and keep vigil.

Methodism not only created new opportunities for social interaction, it also colonised everyday social intercourse, turning a wide range of activities into religious occasions. Family meals were a time of prayer, manual labour was an occasion for hymn singing, and the shop counter was potentially a pulpit.[299] William Cumberland kept his Bible on the counter of his shoemaker's shop: 'Was a Christian friend the visitor? After giving him his customary benediction, he would say, – "Here's a blessed passage; here's food for the soul" and would then read it, and delightfully comment upon it.'[300] At Everton vicarage visitors were the cause for an impromptu prayer meeting: '"Brother," said MR. BERRIDGE, "we must not part without your praying with us." The servants being called in, Mr. FLETCHER offered up a prayer. ... MR. BERRIDGE then began, and was equally warm in prayer.'[301] In the

[295] *MM* (1798), 274; *AM* (1788), 69; *AM* (1790), 473–4.
[296] *WMM* (1825), 608.
[297] *Works of Wesley*, XXI, 198 and 234.
[298] *AM* (1788), 492.
[299] Coles, *Youthful days*, 71 and 92.
[300] Greeves, *Memorials of Wm Cumberland*, 47.
[301] *WMM* (1825), 607.

Moravian settlement even birthdays were celebrated with a love-feast.[302] For the committed Methodist, work, home and leisure time were potentially a seamless robe of religious interaction. The whole of life was a Methodist meeting.

Among Berridge's followers this impulse to religious socialising was left to find its own way but among the Moravians it was carefully channelled into more structured forms.[303] The diary of the Bedford congregation records a pattern of life shaped by a myriad of meetings that punctuated each day, each week, each month and each year. There were meetings which the public could attend, meetings for the society (everyone who put themselves under Moravian tutelage) and meetings for the congregation (those admitted into formal membership of the Moravian church), There were separate choir meetings (devotional rather than musical gatherings) for single women, single men, married couples and widows. There were meetings for listening to readings from the Bible and for listening to readings from letters sent by other Moravian communities. There were meetings for singing, for prayer and for sharing spiritual experiences, quite apart from several kinds of business meeting.[304]

The economy of the Wesleyan connexion was more modest. The earliest gatherings were society meetings. These began as a weekly occasion for all the members to meet together in private.[305] Wesley's account of his first visit to Bedford, in 1753, recalls that having travelled up from London 'in the evening I met the little society.'[306] As time went on and other meetings began to be held for various purposes the society meeting seems to have become more exclusively a private devotional gathering for members led by the preacher. Wesley's diaries refer to his meeting the societies in Bedford, Luton and St Neots.[307] All of these meetings seem to have taken place either before or after he preached in public and his assistants seem to have followed a similar approach, for Sarah Hill was converted in Luton in 1794 when she was persuaded to stay behind after a sermon while the preacher met the society.[308] What happened in the meetings is not clear from local sources but it appears to have included a second, shorter sermon specifically for the society members. John Murlin's sermon register contains a discrete collection of exhortations to be used on such occasions, which appear to have more practical themes 'Walk outwardly circumspect before men ... Use the means of grace ... Let wives

---

[302] '20th April 1756. Bro Foster gave all the Chilldren a Love Feast it being his birthday today' (Welch, *Bedford Moravian Church*, 151).

[303] Benyon, *Howell Harris, reformer and soldier*, 204. The Countess of Huntingdon seems to have followed a similar approach with her chapel at Berkhamsted (Seymour, *Life of Countess of Huntingdon*, II, 474–5).

[304] Welch, *Bedford Moravian Church*, 22–54. Geoffrey Stead's study of the Moravian settlement at Fulneck in Yorkshire uncovered a pattern of such meetings that filled each Sunday and extended over every day of the week; the Bedford settlement seems to have offered much the same (Stead, *Moravian settlement at Fulneck*, 64–9). See also Benham, *Memoirs of James Hutton*, 194–6.

[305] Baker, 'Polity', 213–18.

[306] *Works of Wesley*, XX, 479.

[307] Bedford, 30 November 1784, 19 November 1788 and 27 October 1790; Luton, 31 October 1785 and 1 November 1785; St Neots, 28 October 1790. He also met Miss Harvey's society at Hinxworth several times (4 December 1783, 29 November 1784, 21 December 1784 and 2 November 1789). The Hinxworth society does not appear in the Bedfordshire circuit book and seems to have been a private venture of Miss Harvey's.

[308] *WMM* (1846), 614. There is a clue in the minutes of the Wesleyan conference for 1779 which record, '*Q.26* Preachers hasten home to their wives after preaching. Ought this to be done? *A*. Never, till they have met the society' (*Works of Wesley*, X, 494).

be subject to their own husbands in everything … Order thy conversation aright … Why is it that so many make no more progress in the way to heaven?'[309]

The most common Wesleyan gathering was almost certainly the class meeting. Classes, or divisions, of about a dozen members and with an appointed leader, had been formed in the Bristol society in 1742 as part of a penny-a-week fundraising scheme (twelve members produced a shilling). The leaders were soon given pastoral responsibility for the members on their list and instead of calling on them each week were instructed to gather them together for a weekly class meeting. In this meeting 'advice or reproof was given as need required, quarrels made up, [and] misunderstandings removed.'[310] By 1781, when the circuit book begins, the Bedford society was already divided into three classes and the Luton society into two. At Leagrave, Lidlington and Stanbridge, although the small societies were not sub-divided into classes, the fact that one of the members is identified as the leader suggests that a class was operating. Indeed, that leaders are identified but society stewards are not can perhaps be taken as an indication of the way in which the class meeting had become the pre-eminent meeting among the Wesleyans. Where a society was capable of sustaining more than one class there was clearly an opportunity to separate men and women but this seems to have been acted on only rarely. In 1792 one of the classes at Luton became exclusively female, and in 1798 the other became exclusively male. Interestingly, the classes at Eaton Bray became exclusively male and female the same year, suggesting perhaps that these moves were at the initiative of one of the itinerant preachers appointed to the circuit that year. The classes at Bedford remained resolutely mixed, perhaps in reaction to the strict gender separation practised by their Moravian neighbours.[311]

An extract from Letitia Norris' diary in the 1790s, quoted in her obituary, appears to confirm that local class meetings followed the approved format and provided an opportunity for confession and mutual encouragement that created a strong bond of attachment between the members:[312]

> Through unwatchfulness I was again brought into sorrow; for having been hurried in business so much before Easter, I had omitted some opportunities of secret prayer: these omissions so distressed me, that I went to my class one day in such an uncomfortable state of mind as to grieve the minds of my friends … Such was our affection for each other, that we never had rest if one of us was miserable.[313]

Another passing reference, to William Cumberland's first experience of meeting in class in the 1780s, suggests that there may also have been an educational element to the meeting, for William apparently made 'rapid advances in knowledge and in piety.'[314]

Regular attendance at the class meeting was a condition of membership and was supposed to be strictly enforced. A note from the outgoing superintendent of the Bedford circuit to his successor in 1797 suggests that the situation was never quite

309   John Murlin's sermon register, MARC.
310   Baker, 'Polity', 222–3.
311   Podmore, *Moravian Church in England*, 31–2.
312   Watson, *Early Methodist class meeting*, 95–7.
313   *MM* (1816), 288.
314   Greeves, *Memorials of Wm Cumberland*, 18.

as straightforward as Wesley's directives implied: 'If you find persons in the class Papers who have met but poorly I wish you to believe I have taken pains to persuade them to meet and have consulted with the Leaders if there is any and have not left any a member who I think ought to have been put out.'[315]

A third kind of meeting among the Wesleyans was the band. Band meetings had originally provided a voluntary precursor to the class meeting and John Wesley had published rules to govern them as early as 1738.[316] With the introduction of compulsory class attendance as a condition of society membership the continued existence of bands might have seemed superfluous but they remained an optional, additional discipline well into the nineteenth century. Unlike the class meeting, the accountability in the band was mutual rather than hierarchical, but the questions to be asked, and answered, were very similar.[317] The attraction of the band seems to have lain in the increased intimacy of a smaller gathering, perhaps only three or four members, and one in which the members were apparently always of the same sex. Going the extra mile of belonging to a band may also have given some spiritual status to those involved. Band members were certainly issued with special membership tickets distinct from those of class members. How common bands were, particular in a rural circuit where the classes were already generally quite small, is hard to judge. Passing references record a female band at Whittlebury in 1774 and another at St Neots in 1789, but there is no mention of bands in the circuit book until 1796.[318] In that year details of two bands are given at the end of the list of classes, both connected with the Bedford society and both all female; one comprised of 3 members and the other of 4. Three years later a third band meeting is listed, this time at Eaton Bray and all male.

A quite different kind of gathering was the quarterly meeting. At one level this was simply a gathering of preachers and stewards to handle the business of a circuit but, as Russell Richey's studies of early American Methodism have shown, it was also an important occasion for fellowship, including opportunities for hospitality, conversation, and preaching.[319] Assistants were required to hold quarterly meetings from 1749 and a quarterly preachers' meeting from 1796. With people coming from such distances, meals and accommodation were undoubtedly provided and the whole event would have had a social air. By the end of the eighteenth century a pattern seems to have become firmly established by which there would be a meeting in the morning for preachers, travelling and local, followed by lunch and then the quarterly meeting in the afternoon. There is even some local evidence that these gatherings were used, as in America, as an occasion for preaching. A note in the Bedfordshire circuit book, written by Joseph Harper to the preacher who would succeed him in 1799, explained that 'Mickelmass and midsummer Quarter meetings are at Bedford. The Quarter meeting at Christmas is at Luton and the Quarter meeting at Ladyday is at Eaton Bray. But for the time to come, as they have got a

---

[315] Bedfordshire Wesleyan circuit book 1781–1806, BLARS, MB 1.
[316] Baker, 'Polity', 218–20.
[317] '1. What known Sin have you committed since our last Meeting? 2. What Temptations have you met with? 3. How was you delivered? 4. What have you thought, said or done, of which you doubt whether it be a Sin or not?' (Baker, 'Polity', 219.)
[318] *AM* (1788), 493. John Wesley to Sarah Rutter, 29 July 1789, Telford, *Letters of Wesley*, VIII, 156.
[319] Richey, *Early American Methodism*, 21–32.

Chapel at Stuckley, I think it would be best to take one of the Quarter meetings from Bedford to Stuckley as these will be the largest congregation.'[320]

Private Devotions

Not all the ordinances to which Wesleyans were expected to attend were communal. Members were also expected 'to use private prayer every day.'[321] Coriolanus Copleston was one who 'often used to retire to his chamber and pour out his soul to God.'[322] It is impossible to say how widely this was observed but there is certainly evidence that it happened. Members were also meant to use 'family prayer if you are head of a family' and again there are local examples. In the 1780s one Methodist farmer regularly held a prayer meeting every morning at five o'clock for his workers; and when George Coles' brother became a Methodist in about 1800 the family began to pray together both in the morning and evening.[323]

Wesleyans were also expected to 'read the Scriptures, and meditate thereon, at every vacant hour.' Mary Gilbert apparently 'spent hours together in the profitable exercise of reading and praying over the sacred records' and it is evident that some people read more widely as well.[324] It is worth recalling, however, that not everyone was able to read; in fact, Bedfordshire had unusually low literacy rates.

Wesley's final ordinance was fasting, and he required that members 'observe as days of fasting or abstinence all Fridays in the year.' One Methodist family for whom William Cumberland worked in the 1780s, certainly kept the Friday fast but how typical they were is not known.[325]

Methodist Morality

There was more to being a Methodist, however, than attending meetings and saying prayers before going to bed. The Moravians observed a strict discipline: at Fulneck there were rules against gossiping and joking, wearing showy clothes, spending money unnecessarily and making loans; and at Bedford the supervision appears to have been similarly close.[326] In September and October 1745 the Labourers upbraided Martha Claggett for breaking the rule that all personal correspondence must be read by the minister before it was sent; told Ann Eagles to be more diligent in her spinning; and agreed that Brother Heckenwälder should speak 'quite plain and hearty' to Sister Odell who 'visits at the married brethren's house very often and sits there for hours.'[327] The motivation for this was not to make members' lives conform to some understanding of divine law: indeed the Moravians explicitly rejected everything that obscured humanity's utter dependence on the saviour's love.[328] The purpose of Moravian discipline seems to have been much more functional. At Fulneck the role

---

320   Bedfordshire Wesleyan circuit book 1781–1806, BLARS, MB 1.
321   'Directions given to the Band Societies Dec. 25, 1744', *Works of Wesley*, IX, 79.
322   *AM* (1791), 360.
323   Greeves, *Memorials of Wm Cumberland*, 22; Coles, *Youthful days*, 71.
324   *MM* (1816), 211.
325   Greeves, *Memorials of Wm Cumberland*, 22.
326   Stead, *Moravian settlement at Fulneck*, 37–9.
327   Welch, *Bedford Moravian Church*, 82–4.
328   When Blunham Baptist church accused Okely of despising the ordinances and daily family prayers he told them that they were 'quite dead and settled upon your Law' (Welch, *Bedford Moravian Church*, 8).

of the overseers was to 'remove any cause of disharmony' and to preserve the peace of the congregation; while at Bedford records show that several people were spoken to because their conduct was 'offensive to the World.'[329]

The Wesleyans, by contrast, believed that both 'doing no harm' and actively 'doing good' were outward signs of inward faith.[330] Wesley developed a talmudic interpretation of his original injunction 'carefully to abstain from doing evil', prohibiting members from buying and selling on the Lord's Day, pawning goods, wearing jewellery, drinking spirituous liquors and smoking tobacco.[331] There is evidence that at least one of those prohibitions was observed locally. Sarah Thorpe, a shopkeeper at Buckingham, ceased trading on a Sunday, under the influence of the Methodist curate, and resolutely refused to answer when would-be customers banged on her door.[332] On the other prohibitions, however, the record is silent.

Wesley similarly elaborated on the meaning of 'doing good', his 'Directions given to the Band Societies' requiring members 'to give alms ... to reprove all that sin in your sight ... to be patterns of diligence and frugality.'[333] Reproving sin was certainly an activity in which local Wesleyans engaged. Susannah Spencer of Whittlebury, who was converted in 1760 and died in 1774, 'was particularly exact in reproving sin and lost no opportunity of doing it.' Even the Wesleyan children at Whittlebury in 1774 spent their time 'in prayer and singing, and in reproving all that sinned in their hearing, both young and old.'[334] There is much less evidence in relation to almsgiving. Both the Moravians and Berridge gave some support to the poor within their own communities but while a great deal has been made in recent years of John Wesley's efforts at poor relief there is no evidence that the Wesleyans in Bedfordshire were active in this regard.[335] Although there is evidence of members visiting the sick and prisoners in Bedford gaol, it is quite clear that the focus of concern was missionary rather than humanitarian. When the preacher Joseph Harper visited a dying woman it was to take the opportunity 'of asking her many questions' and of establishing that her religious experience was to his 'entire satisfaction'.[336] Similarly, while other people in the town were engaged in trying to secure a reprieve for Richard Crosby and Samuel Rhodes, the purpose of John Hickling's visits was to bring them to the point where, with the noose around their necks, they could say 'This is the happiest hour I ever knew in my life; I hope in a few minutes we shall be in Paradise.'[337] Whether, in their context, these limited acts of concern for the sick and the condemned should be judged more generously is, of course, a matter of interpretation. What is a matter of fact is that in the hagiographical obituaries of the early Bedfordshire Wesleyans, a concern for the material and social well-being

---

[329] Stead, *Moravian settlement at Fulneck*, 39; Welch, *Bedford Moravian Church*, 155.

[330] See, for instance, Wesley's sermon 'On visiting the sick' (*Works of Wesley*, III, 385).

[331] *Works of Wesley*, IX, 79.

[332] *MM* (1816), 116. Mary Lawley and her husband likewise ceased to trade on a Sunday when they joined the Leighton Buzzard society in 1802 (*WMM* (1847), 409).

[333] *Works of Wesley*, IX, 79.

[334] *AM* (1788), 492.

[335] Welch, *Bedford Moravian Church*, 100, 116, 120 and 132; Berridge to John Thornton, 3 May 1773, *Congregational Magazine* (1842), 221; Jennings, *Good news to the poor*; Heitzenrater, *The poor and the people called Methodists*; Valenze, 'Charity, custom and humanity', 59–78.

[336] *Works of Wesley*, XXII, 434.

[337] *AM* (1795), 394.

of their neighbours is almost entirely absent. It was not a trait which they valued or esteemed.

Where members failed to maintain the standards of behaviour to which the local Methodist community attached importance, the leadership was evidently quite prepared to exercise discipline. The catalogue of the Moravian congregation shows that about 20% of male recruits and 10% of female were subsequently excluded for moral failures of one kind or another.[338] There are not, unfortunately, comparable records for the Wesleyans but at Lidlington in the 1790s 'some old professors, who walked disorderly, ... After they had been repeatedly reproved and long borne with, ... were excluded.'[339] Keeping a society pure seems to have been considered more important than its numerical growth.

The Spiritual Experience of Early Methodists

Being a Methodist involved more, however, than simply participating in all these various meetings and activities. Indeed, at its root, if the records are to be believed, was a shared spiritual or psychological experience celebrated in many Methodist hymns, including Charles Wesley's 'And can it be?'

> Long my imprisoned spirit lay,
> Fast bound in sin and nature's night.
> Thine eye diffused a quick'ning ray;
> I woke; the dungeon flamed with light.
> My chains fell off, my heart was free,
> I rose, went forth, and followed thee.[340]

This was certainly very close to the experience which Ann Simpson, a sixteen-year-old from Orwell in Cambridgeshire, described undergoing in 1759. Overwhelmed by distress during one of Samuel Hicks's sermons,

> I thought myself at that time on a little island and saw Satan in a hideous form, just ready to devour me, hell all round open to receive me, and myself ready to drop in, while no help appeared, nor any way to escape. But just as I was dropping in, the Lord appeared between me and the great gulf, and would not let me fall into it. As soon as I saw him, all my trouble was gone and all the pain I felt before. And ever since I have been light and joyful and filled with the love of God.[341]

Sometimes these experiences, like Ann's, took place within the context of intensely emotional communal events. During the early days of Methodist preaching at Everton, congregations were swept up in a frenzy of fainting and contortions, shouting and weeping, involuntary laughter, trances and visions. Many people were overwhelmed by an impending sense of doom and destruction that suddenly broke into joy and confidence. Extraordinary moments of this kind were not, in fact, common features of Methodist life but they were certainly not unique to Everton; they had accompanied Wesley's preaching in Bristol nineteen years earlier, and would be mirrored in Yorkshire in the 1790s. Indeed, in some localities, such as Cornwall and

---

[338]   Catalogue of Bedford Moravian congregation 1744–1812, BLARS, MO 4.
[339]   *MM* (1816), 288.
[340]   From Charles Wesley's hymn 'And can it be', *Works of Wesley*, VII, 322.
[341]   *Works of Wesley*, XXI, 212–13.

Newfoundland, they would continue to break out at intervals, apparently spontane-ously, well into the nineteenth century.[342] At Everton the manifestations continued for at least four years but local Methodists were very soon divided in their attitude to them. As early as 1761 John Wesley found that some people no longer interpreted trances and visions as signs of deep faith but had come to believe that 'whoever had anything of this kind had no faith.'[343] The appetite for free, emotional expression did not completely disappear, however, and more than ten years later, in 1775, a visit to Everton by the Newfoundland missionary Lawrence Coughlan prompted a brief resurgence of the phenomena. Berridge was furious, describing his congregation as having been 'cast into a spiritual lunacy' and denouncing Coughlan as 'a light-spirited, vain glorious, and Canterbury Tales' man' before launching into a diatribe against uncontrollable laughing during services: 'Laughter is not found in heaven … it is a disease of fallen nature.'[344] Many Bedfordshire Methodists would have agreed. Their spiritual experience was very different and laughter had no part in it.

This other kind of Methodist experience can most easily be traced in the obitu-aries published by the *Arminian Magazine*. Here, instead of sudden and dramatic epiphanies, the stories are of individuals engaged in long, often lonely, searches for some assurance about their eternal fate, of prolonged periods of doubt and despond-ency, and of a peace found only on their death-bed. William Parker had been the 'nursing father' of the Bedford society for more than thirty years when he died in 1785, but the published account of his last days says that when he was asked 'if he felt his evidence for heaven clear' he replied 'Yes, blessed be God! I have not had the least doubt of my acceptance for more than half a year.'[345] The journal of Miss Barham, a Bedford Moravian, records a veritable rollercoaster ride of doubt and enthusiasm:

> March 18, 1781 … I received Jesus into my heart, as my Saviour, and gave myself entirely to him. Since that blessed event took place, I neither have nor can doubt for one moment of the reality of that precious truth, *My beloved is mine and I am his* …
> Aug. 8, 1781. Having been for some time in a very barren state of heart …
> Sept. 4, 1781. After much prayer, I ventured to taste of his supper, which was to me a divine repast. But before two days were elapsed, my Beloved had again withdrawn himself.[346]

The differences between these two kinds of experience should not, however, obscure their similarities. Miss Barham's journal describes an experience every bit as emotionally intense as Ann Simpson's. Jesus was 'my Beloved', 'my Love' whom she longed 'to be with for ever' and when she did something she considered a sin, she described herself as 'an adulteress.'[347] William Burton, a Wesleyan, cried out on his sick bed 'I love every body; and if my arms were long enough, I could

[342] *Works of Wesley* XIX, 49–62; Baxter, 'The great Yorkshire revival', 46–76; Luker 'Revivalism in theory and practice: the case of Cornish Methodism', 603–19; Rule, 'Explaining revivalism: the case of Cornish Methodism', 168–88; Hollett, *Shouting, embracing, and dancing with ecstasy*.
[343] *Works of Wesley*, XXI, 234.
[344] Whittingham, *Works of Berridge*, 391–2.
[345] *AM* (1785), 624–5.
[346] *AM* (1786), 603–4.
[347] *AM* (1786), 604.

embrace all the world!'; and Richard Crosby wrote from the condemned cell that 'My desire is so much for Christ ... that I could always be talking of him and praying to him ... I feel such love to your souls, that I know not how to leave off writing.'[348] The erotic language in which these experiences were expressed has been noted by a number of historians, and it may be that part of the actual attraction of Methodism was that it provided this surrogate channel for sexual feelings, allowing them to be vented without breaching established moral standards.[349]

A second common feature of early Methodist spirituality was its dependence on a community of mutual encouragement. The ecstasy of those caught up in the events in Everton parish church was clearly inconceivable outside the context of a crowded and expectant gathering. But the lifelong pilgrimages and the death-bed scenes recounted in the *Arminian Magazine* were equally dependent on the support and nurture of fellow believers. On his death-bed, William Parker exhorted the members of his class to 'cleave to God: cleave to the Preachers, and to the Society.'[350] Outside the Methodist community the spiritual experience of the individual would fade and grow dim, it required a collective context in which to blossom and flourish. Thomas Harris of Northampton almost lost faith because 'he thought none experienced the like, and therefore deemed it needless to relate his sorrow' but when he joined a Wesleyan society he 'derived much comfort from the conversation of Christian friends, as he found that they enjoyed the same happiness.'[351] In this respect, class and band meetings were as important in shaping and sustaining the inner, spiritual life of Methodists as they were in shaping and policing their outward behaviour.

Perhaps the most important feature uniting the various spiritual experiences of eighteenth-century Methodists in Bedfordshire, however, was that they were all rooted in a profound fear of death. At Everton, Berridge's sermons actively set out to provoke anxiety among his listeners. He advised a colleague,

> When you open your commission, begin with laying open the innumerable corruptions of the hearts of your audience ... Declare the evil of sin in its effects, bringing all our sickness, pains, and sorrows ... with death close to these present sorrows, and hell afterwards to receive all that die in sin.[352]

Elsewhere, subtler cultural legacies worked on people's minds. Martha Padbury's involvement with Methodism began in 1788, when 'her conscience was greatly alarmed by a violent disorder; – she thought it would end in death' and Samuel Newman's in 1789 when 'it pleased the Lord to visit him with affliction of body.'[353] In fact, death or illness is pinpointed as the catalyst to faith in all but two of the Bedfordshire obituaries that appeared in the *Arminian Magazine* before 1800. According to those obituaries, thoughts of mortality unleashed a deep fear of hell and damnation. William Burton is described as being very afraid 'there is no mercy

---

[348] *AM* (1784), 643; *AM* (1795), 395.
[349] Abelove, *Evangelist of desire*, 49–73. Thompson, by contrast, argued that the erotic imagery was a by-product of Methodism's obsessively repressive attitude to sexuality (Thompson, *Making of the English working class,* 407).
[350] *AM* (1785), 625.
[351] *MM* (1798), 272, 273.
[352] Berridge to unidentified clergyman, nd, Whittingham, *Works of Berridge*, 439–40.
[353] *AM* (1790), 465; *MM* (1801), 477.

for such a wretch as I am' and Samuel Newman's illness caused him 'awful apprehensions of death and judgment.'[354]

Not that death was the only anxiety that fed Methodist recruitment. The movement also tapped in to a vigorous folk-culture of deep fears about dark supernatural powers that constantly threatened to visit disease, disaster and misfortune on the unwary. While rationalist ideas may have been gaining ground amongst the educated élite, fears of witchcraft and a desperate faith in amulets and charms to ward off the evil eye remained widespread.[355] Methodism fully embraced this trepidation and local Methodist records abound with references not simply to evil as a general concept but to specific incidents of supernatural malignance. In 1745 the Bedford Moravians, noting that John Braybrooks had been taken ill, concluded that 'There seems to be a searching Time, and the Devil is trying what he can do against us by his Instruments, but we believe, he will not get his Aim.'[356] Some fifty years later Patty Tompkins blamed the Devil for her fire going out while she was at the Sunday morning service, seeing in it a plan to prevent her attending a love-feast in a neighbouring village that afternoon.[357] John Smith was almost certainly speaking literally, rather than figuratively, when he advised Wesley in 1768 that 'No man is of use to this round but such as neither fears man or devils.'[358]

In the face of these threats Methodism offered its devotees access to a range of protective supernatural powers. Methodists believed that they were able to communicate directly with a God who routinely intervened in their everyday lives and that he, in turn, communicated with them. Dreams, in particular, were subject to close analysis as messages from the Almighty. There were numerous articles in the *Arminian Magazine* on the subject and David Simpson, the one-time curate of Buckingham and close ally of John Wesley, published *A discourse on dreams and night-visions* in 1791. At Luton, William Burton was told that a 'remarkable dream' he had had was a warning from God and John Walsh, the benefactor of the Bedford Wesleyan society, appears to have kept a record of his dreams in his journal.[359] It was not, however, necessary to wait for such divine guidance for there were several ways actively to elicit God's advice. The Moravians submitted many of their decisions, including admissions to church membership and the allocation of preachers, to the lot (usually offering providence three options – yes, no and blank).[360] Berridge, for his part, appears to have preferred bibliomancy, the process of opening a Bible and pointing to a verse at random as means of divining God's will. In a letter to Lady Huntingdon in 1770 he records using this method to establish whether he should seek a wife:

> I besought the Lord to give me a direction; then, letting the Bible fall open of itself, I fixed my eyes on these words, 'When my son was entered into his wedding chamber, he fell down and died.' 2 Esdras x. 1. This frightened me

---

354 *AM* (1784), 642 and (1790), 465.
355 Thomas, *Religion and the decline of magic*, 196 and 276.
356 Welch, *Bedford Moravian Church*, 36.
357 Pope, *Finedon Methodism*, 11.
358 Saul, 'Methodism in Northants'.
359 *AM* (1784), 643; Walsh to Charles Wesley, 11 August 1762, Webster, *Methodism and the miraculous*, 209–25.
360 Welch, *Bedford Moravian Church*, 12–13 and 77–80.

heartily, you may easily think; but Satan, who stood peeping at my elbow, not liking the heavenly caution, presently suggested a scruple, that the book was Apocryphal ... I requested a second sign, and from the Canonical Scriptures; then letting my Bible fall open as before, I fixed my eyes directly on this passage, 'Thou shalt not take thee a wife ...' Jer. xvi. 2.[361]

God not only warned and advised, he miraculously shielded Methodists from many dangers. At Whittlebury it was claimed that a stone, thrown through a window into the house where the Methodist preachers stayed, fell on the pillow between Thomas Padbury and his wife, John Wesley observing that 'The devil sent the stone, but God directed it.'[362] Later, when fire destroyed much of Potton in 1783, Berridge claimed that the homes of most Methodists were preserved.[363]

By contrast, Methodists believed that those who opposed them were exposing themselves to the risk of divine retribution. At Weedon, in Northamptonshire, John Wesley was told of a local man who had been swearing when 'he began vomiting blood and in ten minutes was stone-dead.'[364] At Everton, John Walsh, noted that:

There were three farmers, in three several villages, who violently set themselves to oppose [Berridge's preaching]. And for a time they kept many from going to hear. But all three died in about a month. One of them owned the hand of the Lord was upon him, and besought Him, in the bitterness of his soul to prolong his life, vowing to hear Mr. B[erridge] himself. But the Lord would not be entreated.[365]

The belief that it was unlucky, even dangerous, to cross Methodists may have actually gained some popular currency. When the Tempsford Wesleyan society were looking for land on which to build a chapel in 1804 no one was initially prepared to part with any. Then an old man turned up at the home of Samuel Bennett, the leading Wesleyan, and announced:

I am come about that ground you wanted for the chapel. I count you must have it after all. I have not been easy in my mind since I said 'No' to you. You are like to have it; and the sooner the better.[366]

Being a Methodist was, for some at least, a source of confidence and courage. Twelve-year-old Molly Raymond thought nothing of walking home alone in the dark after meetings, for 'neither she nor the other justified children were afraid of anything.'[367] Indeed, Methodists not only felt safe but powerful. James Currie, a member of the Northampton Wesleyan society, appears to have written to John Wesley in 1788 about casting out evil spirits and a detailed account survives of a Methodist exorcism at Waddesdon, in Buckinghamshire, in 1805.[368] Here the local Methodists acted on the entreaties of the mother of the 'possessed' children, suggesting that people outside the society may also have seen them as having

[361] Berridge to the Countess of Huntingdon, 23 March 1770, Whittingham, *Works of Berridge*, 508.
[362] Saul, 'Methodism in Northants'.
[363] Berridge to John Thornton, 30 December 1788, Whittingham, *Works of Berridge*, 430.
[364] *Works of Wesley*, XXII, 257.
[365] *Works of Wesley*, XXI, 198–9.
[366] *WMM* (1841), 711.
[367] *Works of Wesley*, XXI, 214.
[368] Telford, *Letters of Wesley*, VIII, 37 and 280; Account of diabolical possession at Waddesdon, CBS, NM 100/9/2.

extraordinary powers. At Whittlebury too, it was to the Methodists that local people turned when John Weston, an eleven-year-old, 'dreamed that Satan was coming.'[369]

Part 4 Methodists and Politics

The opportunities for anyone, whether Methodist, Dissenter or loyal supporter of the Church of England, to play a part in political life during this period were highly circumscribed. About 10% of adult males in Bedfordshire were enfranchised to elect the two members that the county sent to Parliament, and in Bedford itself about 40% of the men were entitled to vote for the two members that the borough returned.[370] Even those who were qualified to vote were seldom called upon to do so: the county was polled only twice between 1740 and 1790 and the borough only four times.[371] Likewise, although Bedford's corporation was theoretically elected by the freemen of the borough, the fact that the right to nominate rested exclusively with the existing members of the corporation meant that it was largely a self-sustaining oligarchy.[372] It would be wrong, however, to confuse a lack of opportunity for mass democratic decision-making with a lack of interest in politics. Great events, such as foreign wars, and local concerns, such as the poor state of the postal service to Ampthill, both excited strong feelings and these found expression through a variety of means from petitioning the powerful to rioting but also including religious affiliation.[373] Dissent was openly allied with Whig and radical politics and the nonjurors with Jacobitism. All of which begs the question, was there a political facet to eighteenth-century Methodism?

Political Activity amongst the Methodists
Eighteenth-century Methodism has traditionally been thought of as a movement that inculcated an attitude of isolation from politics but, even at first glance, the evidence from Bedfordshire challenges that picture.[374] Many of the local Methodist leaders were politically active. No fewer than six Methodists held office as mayor of Bedford before 1790 and at least one other was a member of the corporation. Indeed, local politics played a significant role in shaping the early history of the movement in the county.[375] Control of the borough corporation was, at this point, the subject of an ongoing power struggle between the Duke of Bedford, a Whig grandee,

---

[369] *AM* (1788), 491.

[370] According to Namier and Brooke, *House of Commons 1754–90* the county electorate in the late eighteenth-century numbered about 2,500 and the borough electorate about 1,000 (but perhaps five hundred of the latter were non-resident freemen). The total population of the county was less than 60,000 and of the borough about 3,000, of whom perhaps 30% were adult males (Godber, *History of Bedfordshire*, 414 and *Story of Bedford*, 91).

[371] The county was polled in 1774 and 1784; and the borough in 1747, 1768, 1774 and 1780.

[372] Godber, S*tory of Bedford*, 86.

[373] Twenty-seven of the 'Principall inhabitants' of Ampthill petitioned the Duke of Bedford to secure an improvement to the town's postal service in 1755 (Collett-White, *How Bedfordshire voted,* 108). The passing of the Militia Act in 1757 was met with rioting (Godber, *History of Bedfordshire*, 365).

[374] Taylor, *Methodism and politics*, 11.

[375] William Parker, a Wesleyan, was mayor in 1756 and 1771; John Heaven, a Moravian, in 1768. Francis Walker had already been mayor in 1734 and Edward Chapman was mayor in 1772, after he had left the Moravians. John Hill, one of John Wesley's hosts in Bedford, was mayor in 1746 and 1759. John

and a coterie of the town's tradesmen who jealously guarded their privileges and independence. The ducal party enjoyed the support of the town's large Dissenting congregation and the tradesmen, the backing of the county's Tory gentry. With most of the town's parishes in Whig patronage, a new religious community may have had attractions for the anti-ducal party and it is certainly interesting that two of its leading members, Francis Walker and William Parker, were early supporters of Okely's society. Evidence that Walker, at least, saw the political potential of the new congregation can be found in the minutes of the Moravian Labourers' conference. In November 1745 they asked Walker, in his capacity as an alderman, to help a Brother Smith become a freeman of the borough, a necessary pre-requisite to setting up in business in the town. Walker made it clear that, in return, he expected Smith to promise his vote to the anti-ducal party. The deal was apparently done. A subsequent minute records that Walker had assured the Labourers that Smith could now 'work in Bedford without fear of being disturbed' and they in turn resolved that 'As to Voting in any Case, Every Brother is quite at his Liberty, those who can, may.'[376]

A political alliance with a faction that included Tories, some of whom were suspected of being Jacobites, was poorly timed in 1745 and a month later had repercussions for the Moravians. Early in December 1745 'a great Alarm' swept Bedford when it was rumoured that the Young Pretender's army had reached Stamford. The Moravian minutes record that 'we heard that People take Offence at us, and are even suspicious about us, because we are cheerful in these Times.' The situation was clearly volatile and Jacob Rogers evidently felt it necessary to pray publicly that same day for the royal family and for 'the Confusion of all their Enemies.' A few days later the congregation went out of its way to hold two services to mark the public fast day. Nearly a year later, however, concern that they were seen as Jacobite sympathisers seems to have still haunted the congregation. There were 'great Rejoicings etc.' to mark the Thanksgiving Day for the crushing of the rebellion and Count Zinzendorf's pronouncement that it was 'a Matter out of Doubt with him that King George was the right and lawful King ... and that none have greater Cause to rejoice on this Occasion than we' was written in to the church minutes.[377] The Moravian leadership also, apparently, took another step, as William Parker later explained to John Wesley, 'In 1746 Heckenwälder, the chief labourer, insisted upon my putting myself out of the corporation. I was much in doubt whether it was right to do so. But he commanded, and I obeyed.'[378]

In the borough election of 1747 Parker and Walker both cast their votes for the Tory candidates, Sir Boteler Chernocke and John Cotton, but at least three other Moravians, William King, William Nottingham and Thomas Pierson, gave their votes to the Duke of Bedford's nominees. Nottingham canvassed for the duke and both he and the matriarch of the Moravian congregation, Ann Okely, were reimbursed by the duke's agent for expenses they incurred during the election. This was not chance; it was policy. In order to support its growing population the settlement

---

Pheasant, mayor in 1783, became a Wesleyan some time later. William Parker's son, William Hornbuckle Parker, was a councilman in 1768.

376   Welch, *Bedford Moravian Church*, 85.
377   Welch, *Bedford Moravian Church*, 48, 50, 70, 83.
378   *Works of Wesley*, XX, 477.

needed to develop economically but its business ventures were viewed with suspicion and hostility by the tradesmen who dominated the corporation. The Moravians needed the duke to patronise their ventures, like the coal merchant's run by Jacob Rogers, and to protect them from the corporation.[379] If they expected support from the duke the brethren knew he expected support from them. A letter from Rogers to the duke's agent in 1748 assured him that pressure was being brought to bear on Walker to switch his political allegiance to the duke's party.[380] Walker and Parker, however, appear to have remained obdurate. Parker rejoined the common council in 1747 as a Tory nominee and, although politics was not the stated reason for his subsequent expulsion from the Moravian congregation in 1752, it clearly played a significant part in the breakdown in relations.[381] It probably also explains Walker's decision to join the Wesleyan society Parker formed. Relations between the Moravian congregation and the corporation were, not surprisingly, chill and a request for permission to dig for stones during the building of the chapel, in 1750, was declined.[382]

Parker's subsequent political career saw him elected mayor in 1756 and again in 1771. In office he appears to have followed a traditional Tory policy of using secular power to impose religious standards, winning praise from John Wesley for his zeal in suppressing vice:

> There is no cursing or swearing heard in these streets, no work done on the Lord's Day. Indeed there is no open wickedness of any kind now to be seen in Bedford. O what may not one magistrate do who has a single eye and a confidence in God![383]

He was also instrumental, in 1757, in making William Pitt the elder, the leading opposition politician, a freeman of the borough.[384] In fact, the whole Wesleyan community seem to have been united in its political loyalties. In 1774 Parker, his son and William Cole, the only known Wesleyans to vote in the county election, all plumped for the unsuccessful candidate, Thomas Hampden, a Wilkesite with Tory backing.[385] Ten years later, six Wesleyan voters are identifiable and all of them voted for Tory candidates, as did John Hill, the innkeeper who was Wesley's host in Bedford.[386]

The alliance between the Moravians and the duke's interest did not prove to be long standing. In 1767 William Vowell, a prominent member of the Moravian congregation, was the principal instigator of a petition to the duke, signed by 200 voters, objecting to his choice of candidates for the borough. Two years later another

---

379   Wellenreuther, 'Politische Patronage', 85–93.
380   Collett-White, *How Bedfordshire voted*, 67.
381   Anderson, *Early Methodism in Bedford*, 9–10.
382   Welch, *Bedford Moravian Church*, 97.
383   *Works of Wesley*, XXI, 91.
384   Collett-White, *How Bedfordshire voted*, 107.
385   John Wilkes (1725–97), editor of the *North Briton* and a radical MP, first for Aylesbury and later Middlesex, owned land at Totternhoe.
386   The duke had reached an arrangement by which his candidate, the Earl of Ossory, and the Hon. St Andrew St John, a member of one of the county's leading Tory families, would stand for the two seats. Parker, John Dickens, William Balls and William Cole all voted for this arrangement. Another Tory, Lord Ongley, also stood and received the votes of William Mingay and Joseph Emmerton. John Hill split his vote between the two Tories.

Moravian, John Heaven, was at the centre of a major coup against the duke's influence in the borough. It began with Heaven's election as mayor in 1768. He had, in fact, lost the election to the duke's nominee by 95 votes to 18 but it was ruled that his opponent's nomination had been defective (on the grounds that the duke's representative, the deputy-recorder, did not have the right to nominate) and he was declared the winner. During the course of his year in office a bill was presented to Parliament that would have amended the terms of the Harpur Trust to the benefit of the corporation. The bill failed and the duke seems to have been suspected of playing a part in its defeat. Heaven's response was to create an additional five hundred freemen of the borough, the great majority of them tenants of the wealthy Wilkesite Sir Robert Barnard of Brampton Park near Huntingdon. In one swoop the duke's electoral influence in the borough was nullified. At the next mayoral election the Moravian chapel became the gathering place for many of these new, non-resident freemen, rather to the concern of the Moravian leadership:

> the chapel was extraordinary crowded, but as the strangers were of those who are come to Town on account of the Election of a Mayor and all full of party spirit, no agreeable feeling attended it. And in general this present commotion in the Town put us today and chiefly [on the] 4th under some apprehension.[387]

The apprehension proved misplaced and although 'Some Persons cast bitter Reflections on the Brethren probably because of Mr. Heaven's having been among us' there was no riot. Where Heaven led, other Moravians gradually followed. At the next county election, in 1774, the Moravian voters were split almost evenly between the duke's nominees and the corporation's candidate, and by 1784 all but one voted against the duke.[388]

Less is known about the politics of the Calvinistic Methodists, not least because they had no presence in Bedford itself, where the scope for political expression was greatest. Despite having the strongest religious links with Dissent of any of the Methodist groupings there is no evidence that either Berridge or his followers shared the meeting-house's political allegiance to the Whigs. The only record of Berridge voting appears to be in the county election of 1784 when he plumped for Lord Ongley, the independent Tory candidate, as did the three Potton voters identifiable as Calvinistic Methodists.[389] He was certainly no radical. He bitterly opposed the Act, passed in 1778, to remove some of the disabilities imposed on Roman Catholics and was pleased when Tom Paine was burnt in effigy at St Neots in 1793.[390]

Much has been made, by some writers, of the doctrinaire High Church Toryism found in the writings of John Wesley, or of the radicalism inherent in George Whitefield's message. The political activity of Bedfordshire Methodists, however, appears

---

[387] Gilmore, 'Alderman Heaven,' 135–46, 139.

[388] In 1774 Thomas Pierson and Negus Eston voted for both candidates on the duke's slate; Joseph Foster Barham and Henry Brandon only voted for the duke's brother-in-law. Joseph Inskip, Thomas Sykes, John Giles and Francis Ambridge all voted against the duke.

[389] John Keeling of Potton is named as one of Berridge's converts in Wesley's journal (*Works of Wesley*, XXI, 211). George Emery and Edmund Bunbury were among the signatories of an application to licence a barn in Potton in 1788 (Welch, *Bedford Moravian Church*, 134).

[390] Berridge to John Thornton, 12 March 1779, *Congregational Magazine* (1845), 29; Whittingham, *Works of Berridge*, xlvi.

to have been rooted not in the theologies of the various forms of Methodism but rather in the complex networks of local economic patronage.

Part 5 Contemporary Responses to Methodism

There has been significant scholarly interest in the response to Methodism in eighteenth-century England both in terms of the arguments of pamphleteers and the actions of the wider community. Much has been made of the violent opposition which Methodism provoked in some places and this has often been interpreted as underlining the essentially progressive nature of Methodism.[391] The very first glimpse of local reaction to Methodism appears to conform to all these expectations. The angry Bedford attorney whom John Byrom met in February 1739 was furious that Methodists had spoilt his clerks and Byrom goes on to record that 'He said many ridiculous things about them; and that he would drive them away, and prosecute them. [He alleged] that they made William Law's 'Christian Perfection' the bottom of their scheme.'[392]

Confusion about the nature of the movement, fears about its corrupting effect on deferential relationships, suspicions about its political tendencies (Law was a prominent nonjuror), a belief that its activities were in some way illegal, and a willingness to contemplate responding to it with violence – the conversation overheard by Byrom, the first comment on Methodism in Bedfordshire, beautifully encapsulates what is generally understood to be the public reaction to the movement in the early 1740s. Whether that response was really typical is rather more doubtful and in trying to piece together how people were thinking and behaving locally it is necessary to proceed cautiously, not least because much of the evidence comes from Methodist sources.

There is no doubt that nineteenth-century Methodists looking back on the eighteenth century saw it as an era of persecution and mini-martyrdoms over which their forebears had triumphed with apostolic faith and endurance. The gathering which marked the centenary of the Bedford Moravian congregation, in 1845, was told that its founders:

> when going to and returning from their first temporary place of worship [had] to 'run the gauntlet' (to use their own expression) between the rows of the rude populace, hooting, yelling and loading them with abuse and imprecations.[393]

The Wesleyans of Luton were similarly informed in 1839 by George Spilsbury, the son of two of their earliest members, that in the early years the society had been:

> very few, very poor and very much Despised, disturbed in their meetings and much persecuted for righteousness sake ... Mr MacNabb once stood upon the Market Hill where a dead cat was thrown at him and hit him on the side of his

---

[391] See Walsh, 'Methodism and the mob', 213–27; Walsh, 'Methodism and the local community', 141–53; Snape, 'Anti-Methodism in Eighteenth-Century England', 257–81.

[392] *WMM* (1863), 911. William Law's *Practical treatise upon Christian perfection* was a popular devotional text among early Methodists.

[393] A brief account of the celebration of the centenary anniversary at Bedford, January 17th 1845, BLARS, MO 672.

head. His text was 'Hear me patiently while I speak after that mock on.' …The boys in the street thought they had liberty to knock me about because they said it was no harm to kill a Methodist and what a Methodist was at that time I did not know … I began to think it was high time I did know what it was upon Inquiry I found it was those that went to chapel I knew my Father and Mother did and took me with them and found that was the reason I was used so ill by the Boys; I began to think my Father and Mother were the greatest Fools in the World and actually thought (at one time) they went to Chapel on purpose so that the Boys might kick me about.[394]

It is very tempting to take these accounts as evidence of the kind of rough music, or popular social control, that is often said to have greeted the introduction of Methodism into local communities. There are, however, several reasons to doubt their veracity.

The first is that although contemporary eighteenth-century sources give evidence of hostility towards Methodism very little of it suggests communal opposition. The second is that it can clearly be seen how, from a very early date, the way in which Methodists told stories about their early history was subject to a process of mythologizing. To take one example, in 1783 John Wesley wrote to Elizabeth Padbury, a member at Whittlebury:

I love to see anything that comes from you, although it be upon a melancholy occasion. Nothing can be done in the Court of the King's Bench till the later end of the next week at the soonest, and till then I am trying all milder means which may avail. If nothing can be done this way, we can but fight at sharps. But prayer and fasting are excellent uses; for if God be with us, who can be against us.[395]

Nothing in the letter provides any clue as to the nature of the dispute but by 1883 it was stated as a matter of fact that Wesley was responding to a situation in which 'the parish minister, with the help of a mob, would tear down by night' the chapel that the Methodists were building by day.[396] There is no evidence to support this account and the similarities to a story told in relation to Hinde Street Wesleyan chapel in London at about the same time suggest that a stereotype may have been shaping how clues about the past were interpreted.[397]

So what is the evidence of hostility to early Methodism in Bedfordshire?

Opposition to Okely's Society
Local opposition to Methodism in the months that followed the visit by Ingham and Delamotte to Bedford in December 1738 is mentioned in two letters written by London Methodists in April 1739 to William Seward, a friend of both George Whitefield and Charles Wesley.[398] One asks for details of the opposition which the writer has heard that Methodists are experiencing in Bedford and the other refers to a particular incident in which Okely and Rogers were imprisoned while on a visit to Cambridge but managed to preach through a grate to a crowd gathered in the

---

394   George Spilsbury's account of the beginnings of Methodism in Luton, 1839, MARC.
395   Wesley to Elizabeth Padbury, 29 October 1783, Telford, *Letters of Wesley*, VII, 193–4.
396   *Methodist Recorder* 29 June 1883.
397   Telford, *Two West-End chapels*, 108.
398   Letters of William Seward (21 and 24 April 1739), MARC, DDSe 37 and 39. Seward himself was killed by a mob in Hay-on-Wye in October 1740.

street. What is probably the same incident is also recorded, some years later, in the recollections of an eyewitness, Mary Collier:

> He [Rogers] preached likewise when he could to the prisoners. Once he begged the turnkey to let him into the jail, and preached from 9 to 12 in the forenoon to them. His voice was so loud, that the great multitudes, that gather'd in the Street (among whom was Mary Collier) could hear ev'ry word. When he had finish'd, the turnkey refused to let him and his friends, who had gone in with him, out, till he was releas'd by some respectable friends interfering.[399]

There are also two accounts of an incident a few months later, in the summer of 1739. Zachary Grey, the rector of Houghton Conquest, wrote the following year that:

> [George Whitefield's] *dear Brother,* and *Fellow Labourer,* Mr. *R---rs,* at the Bishop of *Lincoln's* Visitation, at *Bedford,* the last Summer, did not behave with common Decency: For when the *learned Preacher,* with great Candour and Judgment, was exposing the *Follies of this upstart Sect,* and exhorting the People to beware of him, this *Gentleman* called out, loud enough to be heard by more than one or two, *that's a Lye, that's a notorious Lye, that's a villainous Lye*; with other Expressions to the same Purpose. I am at a Loss to know under which of the *Fruits* of the *Spirit* he will rank this Kind of Behaviour. Sure I am, it is contrary to the *Laws of the Land.*[400]

Mary Collier's recollection of events was that:

> The irregularities, and probably his submitting to adult baptism, occasioned the bishop on his visitation in Bedford in 174[blank] to take his gown and cassock from him. Br Faldo, who was present with him, fell about his neck and said; Never mind it, my Brother; they can't take the Spirit of God from you, bearing witness with your testimony. M. Coll was present at St Paul's, when this was done.[401]

A gaoler keeping prison visitors waiting before letting them out is not the same as people being imprisoned for their religious beliefs; and a bishop publicly warning his flock against a former curate who had joined a Baptist church might well be said to have been simply doing his job. Nor do either of these incidents amount to any kind of mob or popular opposition to the first Methodists. The nearest thing to that in contemporary records is an attempt made, on 4 December 1745, at the height of the alarm about the Jacobite rebellion, to disrupt a Moravian meeting. According to the congregation diary, 'This evening some Gentlemen's Servants came to disturb us in our Quarter of an Hour' but it seems to have been a fairly half-hearted attempt for they 'were disappointed in their Aim' by Jacob Rogers who 'gave them a pretty rough Reception.' Two years later, there is also an account of a very crowded evening service on 16 February 1747 at which several people 'appear'd disorderly but after speaking to them they behav'd pretty well.'[402] References to violence and intimidation are equally rare in relation to the first Wesleyan societies and although Wesley refers to a 'stupid and senseless mob' at Hertford in 1772 the words seem to mean little more than a crowd of common people. Indeed,

399   Welch, *Bedford Moravian Church,* 210.
400   Grey, *Quaker and Methodist compared,* 96.
401   Welch, *Bedford Moravian Church,* 210.
402   Welch, *Bedford Moravian Church,* 48, 91.

far from causing trouble, even by his own account, they listened quite attentively to him.[403] The absence of any violent response to the appearance of Methodism in Bedfordshire is all the more striking because communal violence was not unknown and two people were killed by a mob in 1751 when a witch-hunting craze swept through Hertfordshire and southern Bedfordshire.[404] Methodism, it seems, simply did not provoke that kind of passion.

The secular authorities also seem to have been quite relaxed about Okely's society. When the Moravian preacher John Wade came to Bedford in 1745 and set up home in a property belonging to Mrs Okely without producing a Poor Law settlement certificate, the parish overseers initially threatened to sue her unless she evicted him. However, the matter was quickly and amicably settled 'Br Hutton went to speak with Mr Russel, the Mayor of the Town, and he behaved very friendly, and said that he would speak to the Overseers, that they might be easy.'[405]

This apparently relaxed attitude is all the more remarkable given that there clearly was potential grounds for concern about the threat which Methodism posed to the social order. A few weeks after leaving Bedford, Benjamin Ingham sparked a riot in Yorkshire by his preaching; mills were attacked, flour seized and magistrates threatened by a large crowd which included some of Ingham's followers. In his published account of the incident the vicar of Dewsbury claimed:

> I can prove by the incontestable evidence of great numbers, both of his constant and accidental hearers, that a *community of goods* is a common topic of discourse with him, in his sermons, in his expositions, and in his private conversation also. I know, that, he has endeavoured to persuade several of his followers to sell their estates and possessions, as the first Christians did, for the relief of their poor brethren; and that he has declared over and over, *That private property was inconsistent with Christianity; and that as long as anyone had anything of his own, he could not enter into the kingdom of heaven.*[406]

Ingham, for his part, insisted that he had been misunderstood but he may have said something similar in Bedford for it is known that at least one local man thought that the Bedford society lived 'in Common like the Apostles.'[407] Methodist preachers certainly seem to have railed against the clergy. Jacob Rogers' attack on his then colleagues as 'dumb dogs' has already been noted and it was clearly a theme in his preaching for he struck a similar note while on a visit to Wakefield:

> Mr. Rogers, in preaching from 'Beware of dogs,' advised his hearers to beware of ministers of the present age; for all the ministers now-a-days preach false doctrine to tickle their carnal ears, that they may fill their coffers with money.[408]

George Whitefield may have said much the same when he visited Bedford in May 1739, for the message of his field-preaching a few days later was a fierce denunciation of the clergy:

---

[403]   *Works of Wesley*, XXII, 357.
[404]   Blaydes, *Bedfordshire Notes and Queries* I, 43.
[405]   Benham, *Memoirs of James Hutton*, 176; Welch, *Bedford Moravian Church*, 36.
[406]   Tyerman, *Oxford Methodists*, 117.
[407]   Welch, *Bedford Moravian Church*, 92. See Walsh 'John Wesley and the community of goods', 25–50.
[408]   *Weekly Miscellany* 26 July 1740 quoted in Tyerman, *Oxford Methodists*, 115–16.

I could not help exposing the impiety of those letter-learned teachers, who say, we are not now to receive the Holy Ghost, and who count the doctrine of the new birth, enthusiasm. Out of your own mouths will I condemn you. Did you not, at the time of ordination, tell the bishop, that you were inwardly moved by the Holy Ghost, to take upon you the administration of the Church? ... You lied, not unto man, but unto God.[409]

Benjamin Ingham seems to have gone even further and to have described the Church of England as 'the scarlet whore prophesied of in the Revelation.'[410]

Not surprisingly perhaps, the fiercest criticism of Methodism came in return from local clergy. The rector of Houghton Conquest, in a pamphlet entitled *The Quaker and Methodist compared*, tried to draw a parallel between Methodist claims to special inspiration and those of the radical sects of the civil war, raising the spectre of a return to the anarchy of the seventeenth century:

the *Extemporary Spirit of Prayer*, hath been the Cause of much Mischief to the Church, and of much Dishonor to the Name of God – By this, the People of these Kingdoms have been led into the most unnatural *Schism* and *Rebellion* that ever was.[411]

This was clearly a serious charge but the fact that in the next breath the rector also implied that Methodism was a Jesuit plot suggests that even he saw it as an exercise in name-calling.[412] Certainly when Talbot Williamson, squire of Husborne Crawley, passed on the Jesuit theory to his brother, the Revd Edmund Williamson, it was as an amusing satire rather than a cause for concern:

[Bath] is full of good company, many of your cloth; the Archbishops of York, and Cashel in Ireland; Bishop of Carlisle, Bishop of Exeter, Dr. Lavington. This last a few years ago put out two excellent little books against the pest of Methodism, entitled 'The enthusiasm of Methodists and Papists compared', in which he finds parallels from all the legends old and modern, enthusiasts, saints and hypocrites in their feelings, ecstasies, visions, inspiration, communication, assurances, combats, temptations, infidelities, despairings, torments and pangs of the new birth; in their leaders deceiving and deceived; false pretensions to miracles and cures subsequent to their intercessions; divisions, strife, backbitings, puffings up, spiritual pride, vain glory, Jesuitism, Popery. There is a proper sharpness of wit exerted and much learning on these topics, so that it entertains as well as displays the character of these Pharisaical saintlings. I hope one day to send it to you. ... There is another of the same against Zinzendorf and his Moravians, a society as bad and filthy as the Gnostics of old.[413]

Opposition to Berridge

The surviving evidence does not suggest that Berridge's Methodist ministry met with any greater degree of popular hostility than Okely's society, despite the extraor-

---

[409] Murray, *Whitefield's journals*, 276.
[410] Tyerman, *Oxford Methodists*, 112.
[411] Grey, *Quaker and Methodist compared*, 83.
[412] Grey quotes from Bishop Burnet '*Jesuits* were sent into *Scotland* about the same Time, that they begun to Field Conventicle' (Grey, *Quaker and Methodist compared*, 96).
[413] Talbot Williamson to Edmund Williamson, 12 May 1761, Manning, *The Williamson letters*, 79. The accusation of Popery was not without danger and at the time of the Gordon riots the Bedford Moravian congregation took down their paintings for fear of being thought Roman Catholics (Welch, *Bedford Moravian Church*, 186).

dinary scenes at Everton and elsewhere. In 1759 there was almost an incident at Stapleford, in Cambridgeshire, when over a thousand people descended on the small village to hear Berridge preach. John Walsh records that 'those who rejoiced in God gave great offence to some stern-looking men, who vehemently demanded to have those wretches horse-whipped out of the close.'[414] Even here, however, everything passed off peacefully.

Like Rogers before him, Berridge attracted the active hostility of a number of his clerical colleagues, twelve of whom are said to have petitioned the bishop to deprive him of his living. However, removing a vicar from his freehold was an altogether different matter from dismissing a curate and although Berridge was called to an interview with the bishop no action was taken against him. Berridge believed he was saved by the intervention of powerful friends but papers belonging to one of his critics, John Jones the vicar of Bolnhurst, record that 'The Diocesan [Bishop John Thomas] … judges it best not to meddle, and thinks, with many more, that putting the laws in execution against him, will but make bad worse.'[415] Interestingly, Thomas's successor gave similar advise to the vicar of Newport Pagnell, when he complained about the Methodist-sympathising Dissenter William Bull, encouraging him to adopt 'a moderate way with those People, who are never gained by Persecution.'[416]

Unlike the Moravians, Berridge also appears to have provoked an intense reaction from local landowners who are said to have given notice to tenant farmers that attended his preaching.[417] Moreover, this imposition of economic sanctions against Berridge's followers seems to have been sustained over many years for as late as 1773 Berridge was reporting that 'Labouring men have been turned out of work; and some, who are unable to work, through sickness, lameness, or old age, have been deprived of parish collection, or received a very scant one, because they are Methodists.'[418] Berridge himself suggests that employers were concerned that late night prayer meetings and long excursions to hear sermons were a cover for shirking. Among the hymns in *Sion's songs* is one 'To be read, but not sung' that contains the following verses:

> When Israel's grieving tribes complain'd
> Of Pharoah's hard oppressive hand;
> 'Idle ye are,' the tyrant cries,
> 'And therefore would go sacrifice.'

> And now when sinners flock to hear,
> The tidings of salvation dear;
> 'Idle ye are,' task-masters say,
> 'And therefore would go sing and pray.'[419]

Hostility to Methodism among the landed élite may, however, have been rooted in rather deeper concerns. It is not hard to imagine that the crowds which attended Berridge's preaching, and the uncontrolled emotion they displayed, seemed to

---

414   *Works of Wesley*, XXI, 216.
415   Dr Williams's Library, Jones 39.B.24.
416   Stokes, *Blecheley Diary*, 109.
417   Martin Madan to John Wesley, 29 April 1758, *AM* (1797), 613.
418   Berridge to John Thornton, 3 May 1773, *Congregational Magazine* (1842), 221.
419   Whittingham, *Works of Berridge*, 327.

threaten large scale communal disorder. Barely twelve months earlier a crowd of about one thousand five hundred men had gathered in nearby Biggleswade to protest against the new Militia Act and had then descended on Sutton Park, refusing to leave until Sir Roger Burgoyne had handed over the muster lists, distributed beer, and given each man five shillings for his troubles.[420] In 1761 *Lloyd's Evening Post* even carried a story that a landowner at Steeple Bumpstead, a town on Berridge's circuit, had received a threatening note:

> On the Recept of this goo and Tell Hemsted Pickett and Milleway and all the Rest of your Heaverill Gang of the Bandity that so Vilinously oppoose the Gorspell being Preeched that if we meet with any more affronts or abuse when we Come again as we Intend to Doo on the 17th Instant we are Resolved to Reveng itt on your Parssons or Houses for as wee have listed under the Baner of Christ our Captain we are on and all determin'd to stand by on another our Number is Larg and our Caus good therefore we sett all your Mallis att Desians Dont say You had no Notis or worning for Wee are so prepar'd that we fear you not therefor tak Care what you doo I am order'd by my Brethren in the Lord to Sighne for the Rest your Friendly Moneter five Hundred or the Gospel Legion.[421]

The threat to social order created by Berridge's preaching was one of the themes taken up by John Green, the Dean of Lincoln, in a substantial pamphlet published in 1760. Earlier that year Berridge had been mocked as a man 'sadly out at the Elbows' but Green warned that his foolishness might have serious consequences:

> As it may be difficult to abstract low and groveling minds from the grossness of material things, it may be and has often been dangerous to the publick peace, to raise in the vulgar too high notions of their favour and interest in heaven; for whatever description of spiritual rewards or images of celestial happiness you may set before them, I much doubt whether they will not direct their thoughts to meer objects of sense, will not swell with the expectation of earthly blessings, and plume themselves on the value of those reversionary possessions, which will fall to their share, *when the saints come to inherit the earth.*

He even reported an incident in which Methodists had been involved in a seditious conspiracy:

> The history of Enthusiasm abounds with instances of this kind; a very remarkable one is said to have happened lately in the neighbourhood of Nottingham. The Elect were taught to expect some extraordinary acknowledgment of their cause, and visible interposition in their favour. Swords were to come from heaven, with which, like Joshua, they should conquer the devoted people, and divide their land. By some management a day was inadvertently fixed upon for the accomplishment of these great things. The day came, but no heavenly weapons were sent, no supernatural appearances seemed to favour the attempt. It past and nothing was done.[422]

---

[420] Godber, *History of Bedfordshire*, 365.

[421] *Lloyd's Evening Post and British Chronicle*, 8–10 June 1761, p. 548, col. 1. Wesley rode through Haverhill in January 1762 while standing in for Berridge at Everton. He records that as he did so 'we were saluted with one huzza, the mob of that town having no kindness for Methodists' (*Works of Wesley*, XXI, 347).

[422] [Green], *Principles and practices of the Methodists considered*, 24–5.

Just how serious Green thought the threat of Methodist violence to be is hard to say. This particular accusation is tucked away in the middle of a compendium of charges against Berridge that includes: attacking university learning while continuing to benefit from university emoluments; encouraging his servant to preach; displacing the Bible as the rule of faith; claiming visions, like a Romanist; making everything he did 'the Lord's doing'; seeking popularity by making fun of the clergy; enlivening his 'popular harangues with occasional digressions and strokes of humour'; encouraging people to scream, faint and fall during preaching; and telling people that they did not need to do anything to be saved as Christ had done it all already. Even more tellingly perhaps, when he became bishop the following year Green continued in the policy of his predecessor and took no steps against Berridge.

Domestic Discords

Much more common than any persecution by mobs or magistrates, were problems that arose from domestic disputes over religion. In 1758 John Walsh found that Parker's society were much disturbed by the fact that 'hogs were kept under the [preaching] room; and Alderman Parker's own nephew took care to have them fed, (that the noise as well as stench might interrupt his uncle) at the stated hour of preaching.'[423] Likewise, when Sarah Rutter joined the Wesleyan society at St Neots in 1778 it was her brother George who 'made my way very rough.'[424] One reason for discord was, of course, the duty which Methodists felt to reprove sin. James Cumberland found that 'His strictness of deportment and warmth of piety frequently subjected him to the taunts and ridicule of his less scrupulous brother.'[425] Another source of tension was that the dramatic mood swings, between despair and elation, that were encouraged in Methodist spirituality were often seen as signs of madness. Anna Cordeux's 'union with the Methodists and decided attachment to them, exposed her to trials of no ordinary kind from her parents and relations.' In fact, her parents were Dissenters who 'often spoke of divine things' but who believed that an assurance of salvation was something that evolved slowly over time and was enjoyed by 'some *aged* Christians' not by young girls. When Anna prayed and wept her mother 'overhearing me, thought I was ill, and sent me to bed.'[426] Thomas Fowler was nineteen years old when he became a Wesleyan, in 1789, and he converted his sister shortly after. 'She mightily wrestled with the Lord in prayer, insomuch that the whole family were greatly alarmed, being afraid (as has often been the case) that they were both gone mad together.'[427] Rumours clearly abounded that Berridge's converts were driven to total despair:

> Within these 8 or 9 weeks past (I am well assured) no fewer than eight of his auditors have, on the account of his doctrines, destroyed themselves. Four persons of that number deprived themselves of life, on the same day and in the same hour.[428]

423   John Walsh to John Wesley, 21 June 1758, *AM* (1780), 103. A year later, Wesley too found 'the stench from the swine under the room was scarce supportable' (*Works of Wesley*, XXI, 234).
424   *AM* (1792), 238.
425   Greeves, *Memorials of Wm Cumberland*, 7.
426   *WMM* (1825), 294–5.
427   *AM* (1797), 290.
428   Dr Williams's Library, Jones 39.B.24; O'Connor, *St Mary's Church Everton cum Tetworth*, 30.

Little wonder that families felt anxious.

Another concern was that Methodists were charlatans who fleeced the unsuspecting. In 1746 the father of John Peacock, a young Moravian convert at Riseley, accused David Heckenwälder in the street of being a pickpocket.[429] It is easy to see the grounds for his concern, for a few years later Peacock was bearing the entire expense of entertaining other Moravians who came to Riseley for meetings. Not surprisingly perhaps, given their ambitious building programme and extensive business interests, the Moravians seem to have been particularly vulnerable to this kind of allegation. It was claimed that 'they have got what they call the *Saviour's chest*; which will not only contain your whole house and land, but all the houses, and all the lands, of all the simple folks in England.'[430]

Even Berridge, who made no collections among his followers specifically to 'stoppeth the world's clamour', was still considered suspect on this point:

> This gentleman has, I think, a much more sincere Regard for his Countrymen, than Dr. Mount-stage, whatever he may pretend. The Doctor, to be sure, does a World of Good, and sells a vast deal of useful Medecines for a little Money. Mr B. is at as much Pains, does as much Good, and takes no Money. I have often thought it would be very clever for both of them, if they could contrive to carry on Business in some kind of Partnership.[431]

Methodist life also created bonds of attachment and figures of authority that challenged those of the family. This was particularly obvious in respect of the Moravians who often lived together, called each other brother and sister, celebrated each others birthdays and were governed by their leaders in key life choices, particularly about marriage and occupation. It was also true of other kinds of Methodism in which classes, bands and societies forged intense relationships and claimed a jurisdiction over members' lives that trumped the opinion of parents and husbands. This was perhaps the point at which Methodism pressed most provocatively on its neighbours, that prompted Mrs Cranfield to attend the Bedford Moravian congregation without her husband's knowledge, that led to a Riseley woman being beaten by her husband and that drove Ann Sone's family to try and kidnap her from the Bedford Moravian settlement in 1754:

> Nanny Sone's Aunt came down to Bedford in order to get her out of the Choir House away with her and as she cou'd not by Persuasion and Enticement she Endeavour'd to do it by Force and as she was going along the Street they thrust her into Presland's House in Order to take her away by Force, but Priscilla being with her they together made their Way out again. They urg'd to her for Argument that if she wou'd come away from those German Devils she shou'd have gold enough etc. etc. etc.[432]

---

[429]   Welch, *Bedford Moravian Church*, 85.
[430]   Whittingham, *Works of Berridge*, xxxiv. Wesley, likewise, quotes William Parker as saying, 'It is a general observation in Bedford that the Brethren are the worst paymasters in the town. They contract debts and take no care or thought about discharging them' (*Works of Wesley* XX, 478).
[431]   John Berridge to John Thornton, 3 May 1773. *Congregational Magazine* (1842), 221; *Fragment of the true religion*, iv.
[432]   Welch, *Bedford Moravian Church*, 90, 38 and 104.

Curiosity and Indifference

If Methodists provoked hostility in some of their neighbours, they provoked curiosity in many more. In 1739, and again in 1759, huge crowds converged on Methodist preaching, not to defend their communities from this intrusion, but for a bit of entertainment. John Green, in 1760, was sure that what drew the crowds to Berridge's preaching was not the power of the gospel but the power of novelty:

> Did you never once think, that the power of novelty was a circumstance, which might co-operate a little with your own endeavours, and have its share in drawing this numerous crowd after you? One who has duely attended to the common course of events, must have observed, in a variety of instances the wonderful force of this passion for what appears new.[433]

Open-air sermons by visiting celebrity preachers, and the emotional scenes which sometimes accompanied them, were, for a short season, the best show in town. William Cumberland 'walked on a Sunday to Everton, to hear Mr Berridge; more, indeed, out of curiosity than with any better motive.'[434] It made for a lively crowd and not necessarily a respectful one. John Walsh reckoned that the majority of those who gathered to hear Berridge at Stapleford in 1759 were 'laughers and mockers' but they were there to enjoy the occasion, not to drive the Methodists way.[435] Eighteenth-century English life has often been characterised as parochial and xenophobic but far from being frightened or threatened by things that were new or different or strange, like the German accents of many of the Moravian preachers, most people in Bedfordshire were evidently attracted to them.[436] When a Methodist preacher visited Raunds for the first time, William Ekins went to hear him, as did many others apparently, because it was 'some new thing.'[437]

Nothing remains new for long, and it would probably be fair to characterise the attitude towards Methodism of most people for most of the eighteenth century to be one of complete indifference. No local clergymen published angry pamphlets against the Bedford society after 1740 nor against Berridge after 1760. Even William Cole, who when he first settled in Waterbeach had written in his diary that he would never have taken the curacy if he had realised the parish was full of Methodists, was soon on normal neighbourly terms with their leader:

> My Neighbour Baxter the Methodist Teacher agreed to let me put my Tonkin Sow in his Yard & to use a Lodge for Straw for my Horses, which will be much more convenient for me than to build a new Lodge in the most dirty Yard imaginable.[438]

When, for the bishop's visitation in 1788, all the local clergy were asked, in addition to the usual questions about Dissenters and Papists, to make a return of Methodists, many failed to register the existence of any in their parish and none who did appear to have expressed any concern about it.[439] Attendance at Methodist

---

433   [Green], *Principles and practices of the Methodists considered*, 21–2.
434   Greeves, *Memorials of Wm Cumberland*, 5.
435   Letter from John Walsh quoted in Wesley's journal (*Works of Wesley* XXI, 216).
436   See, for example, 'The culture of local xenophobia', in Snell's *Parish and belonging*, 28–80.
437   *MM* (1816), 45.
438   Stokes, *Blecheley Diary*, 299.
439   The Wesleyan societies at Luton, Leagrave, Lidlington, Markyate and Stanbridge all escaped notice

preaching was left to those who had a serious interest in such things so that Berridge could write, in 1774, that he was met everywhere with silence and attention.[440] When Methodists intruded into the public space, as when John Fletcher preached in the parish church at St Neots in 1776, the worst that happened was that 'an old lady left her seat, and abruptly quitted the church.'[441]

By 1789 it was even possible for a member of the aristocracy to write about Methodists as having a useful social function. The Hon. John Byng, brother of Viscount Torrington of Southill and not a religious man himself, thought they kept the clergy on their toes:

> Thence over The Sandy Hills to near Everden Church (whence were many people returning from the Evening-Service) where a famous Preacher has been renowned in his Pulpit for many years. His Face appears to me abundant of Honesty, Zeal, and good works, ... To his Church does the County flock for Instructions, and Consolation: But He is generally term'd a Methodist: and as such held out by the Clergy, as a stumbling Block, and a dangerous Character. Now what the Title of Methodist is meant to signify I know not: but if these Preachers do restore attention, and congregations within the Churches, and do preach the Work of God, They appear to me as men most commendable; and as useful to the Nation, by their Opposition to the Church Ministry, as in an opposition of The Minister of the Country, in Parliament: Active Orators keeping vigilant Observation, and Preventing any Idleness in, or abuse of their authority; and so tending as effectually to the Preservation of our Rights, as these Methodistical Preachers do to the conservation of Religion. They are like military Martinets, who are scoff'd at by the Ignorant, and Indolent, but who preserve the Army from Ruin.[442]

Indeed, some employers, like Mrs Hatton, were now actively encouraging Methodism among their servants. Before trying to preach in Harpenden the Wesleyans had called at her house, the largest in the village, and sought permission to do so:

> The Colonel was not at home; but his worthy lady, pleased with the respectable bearing of her visiter, desired him to preach near her house, and gave directions to her servants to attend and hear him. Her own maid and coachman were deeply impressed under the sermon.[443]

Methodists and Dissenters

There is one specific group within the local community whose relationship with Methodism seems to have had its own dynamic, the Dissenters. It has generally been accepted that their response to Methodism was initially one of suspicion but warmed, gradually, in the 1770s and 1780s as Dissent began to benefit numerically from Methodist evangelism.[444] The evidence from Bedfordshire, however, paints a quite different picture. First reactions were unequivocally positive. Thomas Brittain, a leading General Baptist, thought Jacob Rogers preached the gospel 'truly & realy' when he heard him in 1739. Three years later he was even more impressed, during

---

and in Bedford only twenty Methodists were reported, all of them in St Paul's parish (Returns of Bishop of Lincoln's visitation, 1788, Lincolnshire Archives DIOC/SPE/4).

[440]   Berridge to John Thornton, 10 August 1774, Whittingham, *Works of Berridge*, 384.
[441]   *WMM* (1825), 608.
[442]   Andrews, *Torrington diaries*, IV, 105.
[443]   *WMM* (1858), 378.
[444]   Watts, *Dissenters*, I, 450–4.

a visit to London, by a sermon of George Whitefield's 'the Prince of Methodists a Zealous Affectionate Awakening Preacher'.[445]

He was not the only one taken with Whitefield, as Dissenters were said to have formed the principal part of his audience when he preached at Hitchin in 1739, the *Weekly Miscellany* reporting that 'Mr. Whitefield called at Hitchin, on his way to Bedford, and, at the desire of several Dissenters, was prevailed on to return there on Friday last, at which time several hundred Dissenters of that parish, and the neighbouring Dissenters, attended him.'[446]

The church at Hitchin followed a policy of mixed communion, on the Bunyan model, but even Particular Baptists, like the church at Blunham and Anne Dutton, wife of the minister at Great Gransden in Huntingdonshire, responded enthusiastically to the first appearance of Methodism.[447] Dissenters were, perhaps, more attuned to theological distinctions between the various Methodist groupings than their Church of England neighbours and it was not long before particular kinds of Methodism were beginning to attract criticism from specific sections of Dissent. The Moravians were the first to attract hostile comment and it was soon coming from all quarters. Okely's attack on the religion of the Blunham Baptists as being no more than 'sound doctrines, and church order, reformation from a grossly wicked life, and something of a legal working' seems to have left a bitter legacy.[448] In 1743 the Bedford church formally warned Mr Nottingham about attending Moravian services and a few years later we find members talking sharply with Mrs Stokes for doing the same (she was eventually excommunicated).[449] In 1746 Anne Dutton published her *Thoughts on some of the Mistakes of the Moravian Brethren*: 'you might well say, Sir, that I had wrote against *some* of ye errors of ye Moravians; for like evil men and seducers, alas for them! they was worse and worse.'[450] Even that most catholic-spirited of Dissenters, Philip Doddridge, minister of Castle Hill meeting in Northampton, turned against them and by 1748 had 'dropped that intimacy of correspondence which I once had with them.'[451] Against this must be set, of course, the fact that other kinds of Methodists became extremely hostile to the Moravians as well. It was John Berridge who wrote:

> You charge me with being a Moravian. Credulous mortal! Why do you not charge me with being a Murderer? You have just as much Reason to call me one as the other. If you lived in this Neighbourhood, you would have known that I am utterly detested and continually reviled by the Moravians. And no Wonder: For I warn all my Hearers against them both in public and private.[452]

John Wesley's Arminianism also came in for criticism. Anne Dutton, again, produced a series of pamphlets beginning in 1742 with *A letter to the Reverend*

[445] Brittain, *Theological remembrancer*, 12 and 13.
[446] Tyerman, *Life of George Whitefield*, I, 232.
[447] Wallington, 'Wesley and Anne Dutton', 43–8. See also Watson, *Selected spiritual writings of Anne Dutton*.
[448] Walsh, 'The Cambridge Methodists', 273.
[449] Welch, *Bedford Moravian Church*, 91; Tibbutt, *Minutes of the Bunyan Meeting*, 175 and 178. By the same token, the Moravians upbraided six female members who attended a funeral at the 'great meeting' (Welch, *Bedford Moravian Church*).
[450] Anne Dutton to Philip Doddridge, nd, Bridwell Library, Southern Methodist University.
[451] Deacon, *Philip Doddridge*, 133.
[452] *Fragment of the true religion*, 24.

Mr. John Wesley in Vindication of the Doctrines of Absolute Election, Particular Redemption, Special Vocation, and Final Perseverance, although it should be said that her tone remained respectful and amicable. One letter concluded, 'Wishing you all Joy and Peace in Believing and all Assistance, Success and Defence in our Dear Lord's work'.[453]

Concerns about Wesley seem to have been chiefly among the Particular Baptists. In 1773 John Ryland, son of the minister of the College Lane church in Northampton, wrote to Rowland Hill about one young man who 'went to Wesley's out of curiosity and has been half in despair for a while through their falling away doctrine.'[454] The objection was not to Methodism itself, Ryland was friends not only with Hill but John Newton and James Hervey, the issue was specifically with Wesley. In 1781 the annual circular letter of the Northamptonshire Baptist churches (which included churches in Bedfordshire and Buckinghamshire) attacked not only Wesley's theology but his personal integrity:

> It is somewhat singular that this notion of faith, as consisting in an assurance of personal interest in Christ, which was in the last age reckoned a distinguished tenet of those that were then called *Antinomians*, should be principally maintained by the most zealous *Arminians* of the present day.
> The well known leader of the *Arminian Methodists* has been frequently charged with duplicity and ungenerous artifice, but perhaps one instance which has been hitherto unnoticed, will be found, upon examination, to exceed those for which he has been most severely censured – We refer to his most *partial* and *mutilated* abridgement of *President Edwards's account of the life of David Brainerd*; the original of which we so warmly recommended in our last annual letter. We should apprehend that whoever compares the genuine account with Mr Wesley's extract ... would be unable to forbear suspecting that his grand design in this performance was under pretence of giving his people the substance of Mr Brainerd's experience, to keep them from perusing a book replete with the most striking evidence of the holy tendency of the doctrine of grace. No publication we ever yet saw is better calculated to sap the foundation of Mr Wesley's erroneous principles.[455]

Other Dissenters, however, seem to have been more relaxed about Wesley's eccentricities and, as has already been mentioned, he was lent a number of Independent, Presbyterian and mixed communion and Presbyterian pulpits during his preaching tours of the district.

Calvinistic Methodism raised far fewer problems. Anne Dutton was in regular correspondence with Whitefield, who visited her at Great Gransden in 1741 and encouraged other Methodists to correspond with her.[456] Philip Doddridge and Samuel Saunderson, minister of the Bedford Meeting, both welcomed Whitefield into their pulpits; and Joshua Symonds, Saunderson's successor, and John Sutcliffe, minister of Olney Baptist church, were both on friendly terms with Berridge. William Bull, minister of Newport Pagnell Independent church, was, like Berridge, a regular preacher at Moorfields Tabernacle and Tottenham Court Road chapel, the London headquarters of Calvinistic Methodism; and, as already noted, some Dissenting

453 Wallington, 'Wesley and Anne Dutton', 45.
454 Sidney, *Life of Rowland Hill*, 97.
455 Hall, *Nature of faith*, 11.
456 Gillies, *Works of Whitefield* I, 91, 102, 250, 277, 328, 449 and II, 31, 32, 39–40.

churches issued calls to former Calvinistic Methodist preachers to be their ministers. It is evident that these warm relations were not universal, that there were Dissenters who were suspicious even of Calvinistic Methodism and that by the 1770s they may even have represented a significant majority. At Carlton, in 1779, the church book records that the members were unanimous in rejecting a potential minister who had trained at the Countess of Huntingdon's college:

> We received Intelligence from Mr. Ryland of Northampton, that there Was one Mark Wilkes at Liberty ... to Whom we made Application for two Months on Approbation, to Which request he Complied, and Came to, and Supplied us two Sabbaths in Feby. 1779, A rank Methodist Indeed Who refused All rule, Order or Dicipline in the Church of God ... We was all Unanimous in refusing and rejecting him for the above reason. And he Left us to our great joy the 21st of Feby. 1779.[457]

Ryland's own congregation in Northampton was suspect to some, and one young man was encouraged by his family to attend Castle Hill meeting instead because they thought that at College Lane there was 'too much predestination, too much water, too much methodism' and too many lay preachers.[458] The last point may have been particularly significant for the very same year, 1773, ten of the fifteen Dissenting ministers in Bedfordshire were among the signatories of a petition to Parliament for legislation that would not only have ended the requirement for them to subscribe to the Church of England's Thirty-Nine Articles but would have placed serious obstacles in the way of itinerant preachers on the Methodist model.[459] As churchgoing declined in the 1770s and 1780s, many Dissenters, it seems, were retreating behind the barricades of their distinct identity and not only in relation to Methodism. At Ridgmont, the Baptist church closed its communion table to Independents in 1770 and at Bedford in 1772 Independents withdrew from the mixed communion meeting.

Part 6 Eighteenth-century Methodism

After 1790 Methodism in Bedfordshire was to undergo such a dramatic transformation that it is perhaps worth pausing at this point to reflect on the overall character of the movement in its first fifty years. Stepping back from the detail to consider the larger picture, two features emerge from the local records that are immediately striking.

The first is the chaotic diversity of the movement. Contrary to popular mythology, it is clear that not all Methodists were Wesleyans. Indeed, even in the 1780s when Wesley's connexion was engaged in a fairly aggressive acquisitions strategy, the societies who looked to him for leadership were probably still in the minority. Most societies were the products of local initiatives, by parish clergy or pious lay men and

---

[457] Typed transcript of the Church book of Carlton Baptist church made by F. W. P. Harris, BLARS. Wilks went on to be minister of a Calvinistic Methodist congregation in Norwich which under his leadership became a Baptist church.
[458] Sidney, *Life of Rowland Hill*, 97.
[459] Brown and Prothero, *Bedfordshire Union of Christians*, 31. See also Coles, *Opposition opposed*.

women. They were independent, initially at least, of any of the national connexions and even when they did establish a relationship with one of these networks it was often an open marriage. In 1773 three of the most important societies in Wesley's Bedfordshire circuit were all receiving regular visits from preachers of whom he disapproved.[460] Co-operation between the local societies was marred by rivalries and disputes. The Bedford Moravians refused to provide preachers for the Methodist society at Northampton in 1745 because the Northampton society wanted to continue to receive preachers from elsewhere as well.[461] Fifteen years later neither the Bedford Moravians nor Wesleyans would invite Howell Harris to address them when he visited the town, though members of both watched while he preached in the open air.[462] Even Berridge, who dismissed the dispute between Arminian and Calvinistic Methodists as a struggle between Pope John and Pope Joan, was scathing in his denunciation of Moravians and advised one correspondent that while he might attend Wesleyan preaching if none else was available, he should refrain from joining their society.[463]

The second surprise is that after the initial bursts of enthusiasm, first around Bedford itself in 1738 and then around Everton in 1758, Methodism quickly ceased to be an actively proselytising movement in Bedfordshire and retreated out of the limelight into its own closed world of small, private meetings. This withdrawal from the world was most obvious amongst the Moravians. Village preaching was progressively abandoned until only two outposts were maintained and members were encouraged to move into the settlement at Bedford. By 1759 fifty people had done so from Riseley alone.[464] Links with those outside the Moravian community were reduced to a minimum. Employment was arranged for members either in businesses owned by the church itself or by other members. No one was allowed to leave the settlement without permission from the elders, even to visit family; there was a distinctive dress code (which went as far as different coloured ribbons for married and single sisters); and everyone was required to choose their marriage partners from within the fellowship. Moravians often spoke of their community as a protective sheepfold and the minutes of the Bedford elders' conference reveal just how carefully the walls of that fold were maintained.[465] What they sought and craved was not a general religious awakening but simply 'a still, inward and solid blessing' for themselves.[466]

While other Methodist groupings may not have gone as far as to build their own village in which to live together, they too sought to minimise contact with

---

460 Bedford and Hertford, as already noted, were receiving visits from Berridge. Towcester was receiving visits from 'that [po]or creature Flynn' (Rodell, 'A New Wesley letter', 228).
461 Welch, *Bedford Moravian Church*, 38.
462 Benyon, *Howell Harris, reformer and soldier*, 75.
463 The reference being to John Wesley and Selina, Countess of Huntingdon., quoted in Sidney, *Life of Rowland Hill*, 398. Berridge to unidentified recipient, 20 September 1776, *Congregational Magazine* (1845), 272.
464 Podmore, *Moravian Church in England*, 105–6.
465 Entries for April–June 1758 include: 'The soap boiling Business may be given up to Pierson, and Skangel may stay ¼ of a Year to teach some body to carry it on, for which Pierson is to allow him 20 or 25£. … A Marriage between the younger Sams in Bocking and Patty Pierson was talk'd of and liked. … Sister Lorel goes to see her people at Risely tomorrow'(Welch, *Bedford Moravian Church*, 163–4).
466 Welch, *Bedford Moravian Church*, 46.

their unawakened neighbours and to withdraw into a separate Methodist community. Old companions were abandoned, secular social gatherings were shunned, employment and accommodation were arranged, where possible, with other Methodists and marriage partners were preferred from within the society.[467] Meetings were held, by and large, in private homes and it is telling that, among the Wesleyans, it was the members-only class meeting, rather than public preaching, which provided the community's heartbeat. The ethos of eighteenth-century Methodism can perhaps best be caught in the words of one of their long-forgotten hymns, from the section in Wesley's hymn-book headed 'For the Society, Praying':

> Never let the world break in,
> Fix a mighty gulf between,
> Keep us little and unknown,
> Prized and loved by God alone.[468]

It was a prayer that was in large measure answered and by the 1780s, when the original cohort of young converts were reaching the end of their lives, it was actually a movement in numerical decline.

---

[467] James Durley 'came out from among the ungodly' when he joined in 1786 and Miss Barham resolved to turn 'a deaf ear to the voice of every stranger' (*MM* (1816), 120 and *AM* (1786), 606). John Field refused to attend a family gathering where there would be card games (*WMM* (1829), 289). Durley hired Robert Bull as his journeyman on the recommendation of the travelling preacher (*MM* (1816), 120); William Cumberland left the employment of the ungodly Mr Purser and went to work for fellow Wesleyan Mr Anderson (Greeves, *Memorials of Wm Cumberland*, 21–2); and the young recruit, George Coles, was apprenticed as a shoemaker to the local preacher Richard Harris (Coles, *Youthful days*, 98–9). William Cumberland broke off his engagement to a girl who did not wish to become a member and married an older woman who was a Wesleyan of long standing instead (Greeves, *Memorials of Wm Cumberland*, 20–1).

[468] *Works of Wesley*, VII, 683.

Chapter Two

Respectable congregations: the second rise of Methodism 1791–1830

Part 1 Narrative

War and growth 1790–1815

In 1790, a visitor to Everton broke the news to John Berridge that the Countess of Huntingdon had died: "'Ah!' said the good man, "is she dead? Then another pillar is gone to glory. Mr Whitfield is gone, Mr Wesley and his brother are gone, and I shall go soon."'[1] Less than two years later, on 22 January 1793, he 'fell asleep in Christ'. An era was ending, and not only for the little world of English Methodism. The whole of Europe was changing; the same year that John Berridge died peacefully in his bed, the King and Queen of France died violently under the guillotine. The fire of revolution flared out of control and none of the *anciens régimes* of Europe would sleep easily in their beds again until 1815. For Britain as a whole, the decades following 1790 would prove to be years of political anxiety. For Methodism they were to be no less significant.

By the 1790s the term Methodist was becoming increasingly appropriated, in England, to the group who, a generation earlier, would have been described as Mr Wesley's people. This was certainly the case in Bedfordshire where the self-limiting policy of the Moravians ensured that they remained a small, enclosed community, and Berridge's death deprived Calvinistic Methodism of any focal point or organisation. Neither tradition disappeared, and their story will be picked up again in due course, but there is no doubt that it was the Wesleyans who now took centre stage and, after decades of decline, launched Methodism into a new era of dramatic expansion. Nationally, the Wesleyan connexion saw its membership rise from 54,359 in 1789 to 171,179 in 1815 but the rate of growth in and around Bedfordshire was even greater.[2] In 1789 the Bedford circuit, which included societies in Hertfordshire, Buckinghamshire, Northamptonshire and Huntingdonshire, had 237 members. By 1815 membership of the circuits covering the same ground totalled in excess of 3,675, a growth rate of over 1,500%, five times the national average (see Table 15).

The growth came in a series of distinct pulses. The first, between midsummer 1789 and midsummer 1793, saw the Bedford circuit's membership rise from 237 to 660. The growth was almost entirely the result of a flood of new societies, the existing Wesleyan societies appearing to have experienced only marginal increases in membership, and was largely the achievement of one man, William Jenkins, the

---

[1] Whittingham, *Works of Berridge*, liii.
[2] Currie, Gilbert and Horsley, *Churches and churchgoers*, 139–40.

senior preacher on the circuit from 1789 until 1791. Local obituaries remember Jenkins as the first Methodist preacher to visit a string of towns and villages but his real achievement appears to have been to bring into the Wesleyan fold a network of cottage meetings in Northamptonshire which had been formed in the 1780s by Daniel Pressland, a local shopkeeper.[3] In this respect what Jenkins did was nothing new, the cannibalisation of rival Methodist groups being a long-standing Wesleyan strategy. What pointed to the future, however, was the way in which he built on these windfalls. When he went to the conference of 1790, at the end of his first year on the circuit, he was able to report an increase of 139 members and returned having secured an additional preacher. The following year he was able to report an increase of 124 members and secured a fourth preacher for the circuit. In 1792, a year after Jenkins left the circuit, a fifth preacher was appointed and the year after that the circuit was divided into three – based on Bedford, Higham Ferrers and St Ives - with a total allocation of six preachers.

Six years later the new Bedford circuit experienced another growth spasm, its membership soaring from 349 in midsummer 1799 to 847 in midsummer 1804 according to the Bedford circuit book (see Table 16). Geographic expansion again played its part. Thirteen new societies accounted for 238 members but this time they were in the south of the county, and in adjacent parishes in Buckinghamshire and Hertfordshire.[4] This multiplication of societies appears to have been carefully planned. In 1798 the circuit was granted an increase in its complement of itinerant preachers and in 1801 the decision was taken to base one of them in the south of the county, at Markyate. At that point the village had no Wesleyan society but it was chosen, presumably, because its location on Watling Street offered ready access to a wide area.[5] At the same time several members were persuaded to re-locate to Leighton Buzzard to provide the nucleus of a new society there.[6] This was only

---

[3] Pressland apparently held meetings in various cottages at which he read a chapter of the Bible, explained it and prayed (*WMM* (1845), 836–8). Jenkins was clearly an extraordinary man. Trained as an architect, he was appointed senior preacher on the Bedford circuit in his very first year as an itinerant. In addition to drawing Daniel Pressland's societies into the circuit, he re-introduced Wesleyan Methodism into St Ives and Raunds and introduced it into Wellingborough, Harpenden, Dunstable and Eaton Socon (*WMM* (1881), 588; *MM* (1816), 24; *WMM* (1828), 362–4; *WMM* (1858), 378; Welch, *Bedfordshire chapels*, 61 and 70). He retired from the ministry in 1810 on grounds of ill-health and practised as an architect, designing chapels in the classical style for societies in London, Exeter, Bath, Hull and Sheffield. He was certainly responsible for the Biggleswade chapel of 1834 (Plate 19) and may have had a hand in other building projects in the county.

[4] In 1799 there were twenty societies on the circuit; in 1804 there were twenty-nine. The societies at Biddenham and Toddington in Bedfordshire and Redborn in Hertfordshire had disappeared and the society at Great Barford had been transferred to the St Neots circuit. The new societies were at Chalton, Greenfield, Heath, Leighton Buzzard, Markyate, Silsoe and Willington; Great Brickhill, Stoke Hammond, Wavendon and Wing in Buckinghamshire; and Colney Heath and How Green in Hertfordshire.

[5] *City Road Magazine* (1874), 505. There had been a society in the village in the early 1780s but it had failed by 1792. A new society was formed during 1801/2. In 1802 Joseph Hallam is described as 'a preacher then labouring at Eaton Bray' but it is unclear whether this means he was based there or simply that it was on his round (Church book of Northall Baptist church, in the possession of the church).

[6] Letitia Norris of Lidlington wrote 'At Midsummer Quarter, 1803, I was strongly solicited to come over to Leighton, and help the little society there; at that time there were but few members, and they had preaching only occasionally. I thought if there was a place in the world in which I might be made more useful in another, I would willingly go thither when given to see it was my duty to do so' (*MM* (1816), 289). Samuel Copleston, the leader of the Leighton society from its founding in 1801 was involved in launching several societies. He was originally a member of the society in Luton, where his

part of the story, for the additional members produced by these new societies were more than matched by a dramatic growth in the membership of some of the existing societies. At Bedford, Lidlington, Luton, Stanbridge and Tilsworth in Bedfordshire, at Stewkley in Buckinghamshire, and at Harpenden and St Albans in Hertfordshire, membership either doubled, or came very close to doing so, adding 283 members to the circuit. Something new was happening: the Wesleyans were beginning not just to extend their reach but somehow to broaden their appeal.

For the next five years membership remained fairly constant. Then in 1808 the circuit was again successful in securing additional staffing. The societies in the south of the county were separated into their own circuit, based on Luton. It was served by two itinerant preachers and one of the new home missionaries, a class of preacher created in 1805, largely at the instigation of Thomas Coke, and supported from central funds.[7] The missionary's commission was to extend Wesleyan work further south into Hertfordshire. Other organisational developments followed with almost bewildering speed. In 1810 the Hertfordshire Mission became a distinct circuit from Luton and in 1811 the society at Barnet, formerly part of the London circuit, was joined to it.[8] In 1812 it was the turn of the societies around Leighton Buzzard to be hived off from the Bedford circuit and formed into another new circuit. In 1813 a home missionary was attached to the Bedford circuit and, perhaps as a result of his work, the following year a group of societies around Ampthill were detached to create their own circuit and a number of other societies, along with societies from the Leighton Buzzard and Northampton circuits, to form yet another new circuit, based on Newport Pagnell. In 1815 four out of the ten home missionaries employed by the Wesleyan conference in England were working in Bedfordshire.[9]

The story of the Bedford circuit was mirrored by the St Ives and Higham Ferrers circuits. Higham Ferrers expanded its territory northwards, spawning circuits based on Kettering, Stamford, Market Harborough and Wellingborough; while the St Ives circuit (which was quickly re-designated St Neots) similarly colonised eastern Bedfordshire, northern Hertfordshire, Cambridgeshire and Huntingdonshire with circuits based on Biggleswade and Huntingdon. The cumulative effect of all these sub-divisions was that where there had been one circuit served by 2 preachers in 1789, by 1815 there were no fewer than twelve circuits served by 30 preachers.

The creation of circuits that were geographically more compact and the increase in the number of professional preachers appear to have had a direct impact on Wesleyan growth. Within a year of its formation in 1808 the Luton circuit had increased its membership by nearly a fifth (from 366 to 435); Leighton Buzzard's first year, 1812/13, saw membership increase by a quarter (from 350 to 435); and the appointment of two extra preachers to the Bedford circuit in 1813 led to an increase

---

father, Coriolanus Copleston, was curate. In the membership list for 1792 he appears as leader of the newly formed Harpenden society and in 1793 as the first leader of the St Albans society.

7   Vickers, *Thomas Coke*, 304–6; see Appendix B for the sub-division of the Bedfordshire circuit.

8   The Barnet circuit included societies at Watford, St Albans and South Mimms (Luton and Barnet Circuit (Wesleyan Methodist): Baptisms, TNA, RG 8/1). When the circuit was dissolved in 1813 Barnet returned to the London circuit and these societies, together with a missionary, were transferred to the Luton circuit. In 1814/15 the missionary was preaching as far south as Rickmansworth (*WMM* (1884), 799).

9   They were attached to the Luton, Ampthill, Biggleswade and Newport Pagnell circuits.

of 125 members to the circuit in twelve months. Quite simply more preachers meant that more places could be taken on to the circuit plan. In the past, even the places where a society existed had not always been able to enjoy regular preaching. Now it became possible to give time to places where there was as yet no society, like Barton, where a cottage was licensed for preaching in 1803, and Cranfield, where one was licensed in 1804.[10] The investment brought returns and the number of societies multiplied. In 1816 the Bedford circuit contained 11 societies only one of which, Bedford itself, had existed in 1806; and the Newport Pagnell circuit contained 11 societies only 5 of which had existed ten years earlier.[11]

Preachers cost money and although there was a virtuous spiral, by which additional preachers often won recruits whose contributions then met their stipends, it is evident that increasing collections were, in fact, a precursor of expansion, not simply a consequence. The economic boom of the war years put money into the pockets of many Methodists and they in turn put more into the collecting plates of their societies. The account book of the St Neots circuit, which records class and ticket money (members' basic subscriptions), shows an annual income in 1795 equivalent to 6s 4d per member; by 1810, the year that the Biggleswade circuit was formed, that had risen to 9s 8d; and by 1815 to 10s.[12] The accounts for class and ticket money in the Bedford circuit have not survived but the accounts for the annual collections in aid of the various connexional funds have. These show that in 1797 the members of the circuit contributed a total of £12 to the Kingswood School collection, the July collection and the Preachers' Fund, an average of 11d each. Seven years later they contributed £63 10s to those funds and a further £23 8s to the West India Mission, an average of 2s 1d each; by 1817 the average was over 2s 5d.[13] With more coming in to connexional funds from circuits across Britain, the connexion itself was able to do more to support promising local initiatives. In 1795/6 the Bedford circuit received a grant of £28 13s 6d to meet its deficit, about enough to pay all the costs associated with an unmarried preacher; twenty years later the circuits covering the same ground received grants worth £261 13s 6d, as well as having the costs of three preachers met directly from the missionary fund.[14]

Geographic expansion was not the only cause of the explosion in Wesleyan

---

[10] Welch, *Bedfordshire chapels*, 24 and 58.

[11] Bedford circuit stewards' accounts book 1817–37, BLARS, MB 12 and Newport Pagnell circuit book 1813–38 (CBS, NM 500/7/2). The eleven societies in 1816 were Aspley Guise and Salford in Bedfordshire; Bow Brickhill, Fenny Stratford, Hanslope, Little Brickhill, Moulsoe, Newport Pagnell, Stony Stratford, Water Eaton and Wavendon in Buckinghamshire. Hanslope and Stony Stratford appear to have been transferred from the Northampton circuit and Water Eaton from the Leighton Buzzard circuit.

[12] St Neots Wesleyan circuit stewards' account book 1793–1832, BLARS, MB 1346. See Plates 27 and 28 for examples of admission tickets.

[13] Bedfordshire Wesleyan circuit book and Bedford Wesleyan circuit stewards' accounts, BLARS, MB 1 and 12. Kingswood school collection, usually made in November, was to meet the costs of the boarding school for preachers' sons. The July Collection was an annual collection among the societies to provide the conference with funds to assist circuits in deficit. The Preachers' Fund provided support to 'worn-out' preachers and was supported by a private collection among 'a few of the more wealthy and liberal' (Crowther, *A portraiture of Methodism*, 301–7).

[14] The grants are detailed in the annual minutes of the Wesleyan conference.

membership, however. Once again, some existing societies experienced an extraordinary level of growth and this was at least as important as the creation of new societies. Three-quarters of the growth in the Leighton Buzzard circuit between 1812 and 1816 came from three well-established societies – Leighton Buzzard, Eaton Bray and Wing – that more than doubled their membership.[15] This growth also appears to have been related to the allocation of resources. A plan of Sunday preaching appointments in the circuit for November 1817 to May 1818 shows that at Leighton Buzzard itself at least two of the three services held each Sunday were led by one of the itinerant preachers and that at Eaton Bray and Wing, where two services were held each Sunday, they were led by an itinerant every other week. It also shows that at Stanbridge, Billington, Heath, Stoke Hammond, Great Brickhill and Soulbury, societies that experienced little or no growth, all the Sunday services were taken by the amateur local preachers.[16]

Contemporary observers appear to have been aware of the role that the professional preachers played as catalysts for growth. John Dredge, the junior itinerant at Bedford in 1816, was apparently a gifted preacher who 'studied to introduce a constant variety of matter, which was judiciously arranged, and impressively delivered.' His sermons, it was noted, 'attracted attention; and our congregations increased.'[17] Similar stories were told at Biggleswade and Luton. William Conquest, looking back in 1835 at the founding of the Biggleswade circuit, described how:

> John Ward was appointed to ... St Neots; and during his residence there, it was determined to make Biggleswade and the adjacent places into a separate Circuit, which took place in 1810. He then removed to Biggleswade, and God made him a special blessing to the people. During his ministry it became necessary to enlarge the chapel.[18]

Frederick Davis, likewise, tells how the Wesleyans in Luton were:

> ... but a very small congregation till the Rev. Maximilian Wilson, a noted preacher, was stationed here in the year 1808, (the first year that it became a circuit) who, being an intelligent and useful minister, introduced good order among the people; from that time they have increased in numbers and respectability.[19]

It was not only human resources that were invested in these societies. They were also the subject of an unprecedented level of capital investment. Arriving in the Bedford circuit in 1812, Isaac Bradnack immediately reached the conclusion that: 'We are losing ground for want of chapels. In many large towns and villages we have only small, inconvenient preaching-houses.'[20] He was clearly not alone in this judge-

[15] Leighton Buzzard Wesleyan circuit book 1812–27, BLARS, MB 1533.
[16] Preaching plan of the Leighton Buzzard Wesleyan circuit November 1817 to May 1818, BLARS, MB 224. The Leighton Buzzard society's membership increased from 71 in 1812 to 149 in 1816, Eaton Bray's from 47 to 91 and Wing's from 37 to 72. Billington's membership, by contrast, went from 8 to 10 and Stoke Hammond's from 22 to 21 (Leighton Buzzard Wesleyan circuit book 1812–27, BLARS, MB 1533).
[17] *WMM* (1822), 21
[18] *WMM* (1835), 213.
[19] Davis, *History of Luton*, 119–20.
[20] Rowland, *Memoirs of Isaac Bradnack*, 82.

ment for while in 1790 there had been only two purpose-built Wesleyan preaching-rooms in the whole county, by 1815 there were nineteen and some of them could now be described as chapels.[21] A preaching-room was essentially designed only for gatherings of the society, a chapel had a more ambitious function. The opening of such a building in Hull, in 1814, was described by Jabez Bunting as:

> a sort of new era in Methodism, and to have given it an impulse, a publicity, and a popularity such as it never had before. The very largeness of the chapel excited curiosity; and curiosity, there is reason to hope, will be so over-ruled in numerous instances, as to terminate in the production of genuine piety.[22]

The old preaching-house in Luton had been hidden down an alley and had offered a windowless façade to the would-be visitor. The new chapel, built in 1814, fronted on to a main street and was an elegant, self-confidently public building, designed to invite the attention of the passer-by and attract their attendance. It was a speculative venture and:

> It was said by many friends, as well as foes, 'to be too big by half, and that it would never be filled.' And I have heard the early trustees say that they almost feared at first to mention seat rents, as their main desire was to secure a congregation.[23]

The new chapel at Bedford, built in 1804, likewise, was of a very different order from the preaching-room that preceded it and was described as 'a neat and respectable brick-fronted building' with 'a certain air of snugness in its appearance and ... by no means destitute of modest and unassuming beauty.'[24]

With the opening of these chapels Methodism was able to recruit not only those who were willing to submit themselves to the rigorous discipline of the weekly class meeting, but those who simply wanted to hear a Sunday sermon. There had probably always been a few hearers round some of the Methodist societies but where Methodism was now offering regular public preaching, in a purpose-built chapel, led by a professional preacher, it seems that their numbers grew dramatically. The new chapel at Bedford was soon regularly filled and at Ampthill numbers increased so quickly that two years after a house was converted into the town's first Methodist chapel the society had to build a much larger meeting-place.[25] The impact of this new outer circle of non-members would have had a profound effect on those societies where they existed. It certainly provided a reservoir of potential recruits for the class meetings and may be one reason why these societies experienced such extraordinary growth in their membership.[26]

---

21 Eaton Bray (1795), Biggleswade (1795), Leighton Buzzard (1804), Bedford (1804), Lidlington (1805), Tempsford (1806), Riseley (1807), Radwell (1807), Great Barford (1808), Markyate (1808), Wootton (1811), Heath (1812), Ampthill (1813), Aspley Guise (1813), Luton (1814), Clophill (1814), Salford (1814), Dean (1815) and Marston Moretaine (1815).

22 Bunting, *Life of Jabez Bunting*, II, 80

23 Hawkes, *Rise of Wesleyan Sunday schools*, 10.

24 Quoted in Anderson, *Early Methodism in Bedford*, 24. See the 1814 chapel beside the later 1852 chapel in Plate 17.

25 Coles, *Youthful days*, 139.

26 William Cumberland apparently paid 'indefatigable attention to the outward hearers. He soon recognized such in the congregation; sought them out; apprized them of the advantages of christian communion; and encouraged them to give the right-hand of fellowship to the people of God' (Greeves, *Memorials of Wm Cumberland*, 31).

All of this investment in additional preachers and in bricks and mortar was dependent not only on an economic upturn but also on a quite profound change in outlook. Some Wesleyans had clearly ceased to pray 'keep us little and unknown' and were now importuning, 'Lord! Let this glorious work, be crowned with large success.'[27] It was a shift in mood and theology that was to transform religious communities of almost every tradition in the early nineteenth century, not only the Wesleyans, although they are often credited with its genesis. The truth, however, is that Methodists and Dissenters began to abandon the idea of their communities as 'a garden walled around' at about the same time and that, if anything, Dissent rather than Methodism took the lead.[28] The traditional view among Dissenters had been hostile to missionary activity, for if God had predestined men and women to heaven and hell then Christians who preached to anyone except the elect were not only practising a cruel deception on the damned but challenging God's sovereignty. From the late 1770s, a new outlook can be seen emerging.[29] The Northamptonshire Baptist Association, to which several Bedfordshire churches belonged, was a particular focus for the new thinking and Andrew Fuller, pastor of the church at Kettering, was its chief spokesman. Published in 1785, his book, *The Gospel of Christ Worthy of all Acceptation,* side-lined the bleaker aspects of predestination, with the argument that all men had a duty to believe, and opened the way for Dissenters to engage more positively with the world by advocating the responsibility of Christians to present all of mankind with the message of salvation.[30] It was in keeping with this new vision that, seven years later, the Northamptonshire Baptists formed the Baptist Missionary Society. The majority of Dissenting ministers in the county, if not always their congregations, seem to have come across to his position with extraordinary speed.[31] In 1797, Samuel Greathead, minister of Woburn Independent church, launched the Bedfordshire Union of Christians as an interdenominational society to support itinerant village preaching in the county. His original hope was that 'pious persons of the Established Church, of the late Mr. Wesley's Connexion; of the Unitas Fratrum, usually called Moravians; and of several Independent Churches, both Paedobaptists and Baptists' would all collaborate in the venture but the response was confined to Dissenters. The ministers of ten congregations in Bedfordshire and of six in neighbouring counties signed the original compact and drew up a plan to provide preaching in at least forty-six villages.[32]

The impact of Fullerism, and particularly of its practical expression in the Bedfordshire Union of Christians, on local Wesleyan communities was clearly

---

27 The words are from the hymn 'Come let our voices join' by William Budden, which appeared in the *Evangelical Magazine* in 1795 and was sung at the Sunday school anniversary in Leighton Buzzard in 1815 (Hymns to be sung at the Methodist chapel, Leighton Buzzard, BLARS, Z1115/1).

28 'We are a garden walled around, / Chosen and made peculiar ground; / A little spot enclosed by grace / Out of the world's wide wilderness' (Isaac Watts). See also Jones, *Congregationalism in England,* 105–45.

29 Lovegrove, *Established Church, sectarian people,* 18.

30 Watts, *Dissenters,* I, 456–61.

31 Fuller was the son-in-law of William Coles, minister of Maulden Baptist church; he took part in the ordination of Mr Perkins as minister of Luton Baptist church in 1802; and had baptised Joseph Patrick, a former Wesleyan preacher, who was appointed minister of the mixed communion church at Southill in 1804.

32 Brown and Prothero, *Bedfordshire Union of Christians,* 17–18 and 35–8.

considerable. At Dunstable the fledgling Wesleyan society received valuable support and encouragement from the Fullerite minister of Houghton Regis Baptist church but at Sheep Lane the Farey family, who had once been mainstays of the Bow Brick-hill Wesleyan society and on one occasion John Wesley's hosts, were won over from Methodism to Dissent.[33] Whether the Wesleyan circuit leadership were inspired by the new energy evident among Dissenters or felt threatened by it, there is no question that it provided the context in which they decided to embark on an expansionist programme of their own. Not everyone approved, fearing that such growth was, in Jabez Bunting's words, 'more swift than solid; more extensive than deep; more in the increase of numbers, than in the diffusion of that kind of piety, which shines as brightly & operates as visibly *at home* as in the prayer meeting and the crowded lovefeast.'[34] Thomas Edman, serving as an itinerant preacher on the Northampton circuit in 1801, was certainly unimpressed by the flood of new recruits, recording in his journal, 'I have reason to believe that there are four or five that have wakened under my preaching this last year.'[35] In fact, the majority of local Wesleyan societies continued to operate as essentially closed communities for some years.

Whatever the misgivings felt by some, the connexional structure of Wesleyanism was peculiarly well adapted to the new missionary spirit. Resources were funnelled to the centre, first of the local circuit and then of the body as a whole, giving the Wesleyan leadership far greater scope to direct operations than the voluntary associations of Dissent could ever achieve. After an initial burst of enthusiasm the Bedfordshire Union struggled both to attract subscriptions and to persuade local churches to release their ministers for village preaching. By 1818, over twenty years after its formation, the number of Dissenting congregations in the county had increased by perhaps as few as ten and many of the villages in which the Union had sponsored preaching had become hosts to Wesleyan societies.[36]

The Wesleyan presence in Bedfordshire, by contrast, had been utterly transformed. The three growth spurts – 1789 to 1793, 1799 to 1804 and 1808 to 1815 – had seen the number of Wesleyan societies multiply from half a dozen to forty-three.[37] Where

---

[33] Hews, *Spoils won in the day of battle*, 196–7; Welch, *Bedfordshire chapels*, 133; *Gentleman's Magazine* (1804), 182.

[34] Letter from Jabez Bunting to George Marsden 28 January 1813, Hempton, *Religion of the people*, 100.

[35] 'Extracts from the journal of Thomas Edman', 105.

[36] *Congregational Magazine* (1818), 48–51. The Dissenting congregations listed that year that had not existed in 1797 were at Clophill, Houghton Regis, Harrold, Hockliffe, Pavenham, Roxton, Shefford, Sandy, Toddington and Potton (the anti-Union congregation). Among the villages missioned by the Bedfordshire Union in its first years but in which the Wesleyans had subsequently established themselves were Eversholt, Little Brickhill, Heath, Billington, Elstow, Cople, Biddenham, Bromham, Clapham, Milton Ernest and Wilstead.

[37] For the societies of the Bedford and Newport Pagnell circuits in 1815 see above. A preaching plan for the Luton circuit covering October 1813 to April 1814 (BLARS, MB 497) shows fourteen preaching places where there had been 11 societies in 1806. Two societies, at How Green and Colney Heath, both in Hertfordshire had disappeared and 6 had been created, Hemel Hempstead, Hudnall, Kensworth, Mimms and Watford, all in Hertfordshire. The Leighton Buzzard Wesleyan circuit book 1812–27 (BLARS, MB 1533) has no entries for 1815 but shows 13 societies in 1816 where there had been 11 in 1806. Two societies, Swanbourne and Cublington, both in Buckinghamshire, had disappeared and 4 had been created, Billington and Woburn in Bedfordshire and Slapton and Soulbury in Buckinghamshire. The only record that survives for the short-lived Ampthill circuit is its baptism register but it is known from the Bedfordshire circuit book that 4 societies existing in 1806 lay within its territory, Greenfield, Houghton Conquest, Lidlington and Silsoe and, from the Bedford accounts book, that when the Ampthill

the largest society had previously mustered barely 40 members several now boasted four times that number; and the membership itself was now only the core of a wider community of both adults and children.

Peace and Decline 1815–1827
The remarkable expansion which Methodism enjoyed during the long years of the Napoleonic wars came swiftly to an end with the outbreak of peace. Between 1816 and 1821 the official membership of the five circuits that in 1793 had constituted the Bedford circuit fell from 1,764 to 1,586 and in the three circuits that had once been the St Ives circuit it fell from 891 to 713 (see Table 16). Given that preachers would have been reluctant to report losses, the decline was, if anything, probably even greater. At Leighton Buzzard in 1822 the circuit reported 610 members to conference but Jonathan Williams, the incoming superintendent, noted 'I found 568 members when I came and that was all.'[38] At Biggleswade they blamed their losses on the heterodox views of one of their preachers which, it was claimed, had unsettled the people. The truth, however, was that the decline was much more widespread than a single circuit or even a single county.[39] Across England the advance of Methodism was brought to a standstill, the annual increase of members sinking steadily between 1816 and 1820, when the conference was forced to announce a decrease of 5,000.[40] Bedfordshire suffered more than its share of the decline. In the area covered by the old Bedford and St Ives circuits nearly 14% of the membership was lost compared to 1% across the connexion as a whole. Worst hit was the Ampthill circuit which lost 70 of its 200 members and was forced to reunite with Bedford in 1819. Bedford suffered badly too, seeing nine of its village societies disappear altogether.[41]

The post-war economic depression played its part in this, just as the wartime boom had fed the preceding period of growth. As incomes tumbled so did collections. In the St Neots circuit, for which the best financial records survive, giving fell from 10s per member in 1815 to 6s 2d per member by 1819.[42] Even that may have been beyond some people and part of the decline in membership may have been that people simply could not afford to belong any longer. Grants too were progressively cut.[43] With less money coming in, a retrenchment in expenditure was unavoidable. The St Neots circuit resolved that:

circuit rejoined the Bedford circuit in 1819 there were societies at Ampthill, Clophill, Wilstead, Marston, Houghton Conquest, Lidlington and Eversholt. A licence was issued for a house in Greenfield in 1818, so that society may still have been in existence in 1815.
38 Michael Watts has suggested that the national drop in membership reported in 1820 was the result of superintendents pruning their membership lists to avoid a connexional levy but the local decline in membership began earlier and lasted longer than that and, as the Leighton Buzzard story shows, some people were still clearly overstating their membership (Watts, *Dissenters*, II, 407).
39 *WMM* (1835), 213.
40 Currie, Gilbert and Horsley, *Churches and churchgoers*, 140.
41 Clapham, Felmersham, Odell and Silsoe were gone by 1817; Biddenham, Bletsoe, Bromham, Cople and Elstow by 1825 (Bedford Wesleyan circuit stewards' account book 1817–37, BLARS, MB 12). Ampthill was not the only circuit to collapse. The Towcester circuit, formed in 1810, had to be re-united with Northampton in 1822 (see Appendix B for the sub-division of the Bedfordshire circuit).
42 St Neots Wesleyan circuit stewards' account book, BLARS, MB 1346. Accounts for the Newport Pagnell circuit tell a similar story with quarterly collections falling from £36 8s 6½d (3s 8d per member) at midsummer 1815 to £29 11s 6d (2s 10d per member) at midsummer 1820 (Newport Pagnell Wesleyan circuit stewards' account book 1814–34, CBS, NM 500/5/1).
43 By 1825 the grant for the circuits that had once formed the Bedford circuit was down to £121.

1st In consequence of the present embarrassed state of our circuit and also as the necessity does not now exist which formerly existed, for relieving the preachers 10s per qr. each as travelling expenses, that allowance be henceforth discontinued.

2nd That no stationary [sic], and the postage of no letters, be henceforth paid except such letters as relate to the official affairs of this circuit.[44]

Over the next two years the circuit's income fell still further and by 1821 the stewards were owed £42 13s 11d, the equivalent of eight months collections. The only way to resolve the crisis was to cut the number of paid preachers and at the conference that year the circuit went down from two men to one. Other circuits clearly faced similar problems: Bedford cut its staff from four to three in 1817 and then again from three to two in 1822; Luton and Biggleswade similarly downsized. In all, between 1815 and 1822 the number of Wesleyan itinerant preachers based in the county fell from thirteen to eight. With fewer preachers travelling the circuits some of the small outlying societies had to be abandoned, reducing membership and income still further. It was a dilemma that was recognised at the time, for when, in the late 1820s, the adjacent Aylesbury circuit was on the point of collapse the district meeting agreed that the solution was to send a second preacher so 'that the circuit may be raised and rendered better able to support itself'; the only problem was they did not have the £40 to pay for him.[45]

After 1821 membership of the Wesleyan connexion began to grow again and some of the local circuits appear to have shared, briefly, in that advance. The Leighton Buzzard circuit, in the south-west of the county, and the Biggleswade circuit, in the east, both recovered strongly and by the mid-1820s had substantially more members than they had had at the end of the war.[46] The key to this success appears, once again, to have been the geographic expansion of these circuits rather than any growth in the membership of the existing societies. There were 5 new societies created in the Leighton Buzzard circuit in the early 1820s, which accounted for more than two-thirds of its additional members, and probably 6 new societies in the Biggleswade circuit.[47] This upturn in membership brought with it an easing of financial pressures. In the Newport Pagnell circuit the quarterly contributions from the various societies rose from £29 11s 6d at midsummer 1820 to £38 6s 3½d at midsummer 1824, a rate of increase almost exactly in line with the rise in membership. The following year a third minister was appointed to mission the area around

[44] St Neots Wesleyan circuit stewards' account book, BLARS, MB 1346.

[45] Letter from the Aylesbury Wesleyan circuit stewards to the president of the Conference 10 July 1828, CBS, NM 100/5/1A.

[46] The Leighton Buzzard circuit had 535 members in 1816, which fell to a low of 484 in 1819 and reached 620 in 1824 before falling back again to 557 in 1827. The Biggleswade circuit fell from 235 members in 1816 to 156 in 1821 before recovering and reaching 354 in 1824 only to slip back again to 302 in 1827.

[47] The new societies on the Leighton Buzzard circuit were Sheep Lane and Eggington (both 1822), in Bedfordshire, and Mentmore (1822), Cheddington (1824) and Ivinghoe Aston (1825) in Buckinghamshire. Between 1819 and 1825 membership of the circuit grew by 74 members and these societies accounted for 53 of them (Leighton Buzzard Wesleyan circuit book, BLARS, MB 1533). Equivalent records for the Biggleswade circuit are lacking but new societies appear to have been formed at this stage at Stotfold and Arlesey in Bedfordshire, and at Newnham, Wymondley, Hinxworth and Therfield in Hertfordshire (Biggleswade Wesleyan circuit preaching plan 1825, Drew University, United Methodist archives, Marriott collection of British Wesleyan circuit plans).

Olney. In the St Neots circuit there was money to employ a second preacher again, in the Luton circuit too the number of preachers was increased and St Albans was launched as a separate circuit. There was even money for new chapels. Not a single Wesleyan chapel had been built in Bedfordshire between 1815 and 1821 but over the next three years the societies at Heath, Cardington, Toddington, Stotfold, Leagrave and Woburn all erected purpose-built meeting places.[48]

After 1824 the Bedford, Luton and Newport Pagnell circuits continued to experience modest numerical growth but Leighton Buzzard, Biggleswade, St Neots and Higham Ferrers either stood still or lost ground. Money was clearly tight. The accounts of the chapel trusts at Eaton Bray and Clophill both show pew rents falling.[49] Public collections in the Leighton Buzzard circuit fell from £48 6s in 1824 to £38 19s 11d in 1828.[50] Chapel-building ground to a halt once more, with no building work being reported in 1825, 1826 or 1827; the St Neots circuit had to cut its staff again and the Newport Pagnell circuit to abandon its Olney mission. In the Aylesbury circuit the furniture of the preacher's house was almost seized in lieu of unpaid rent, the circuit steward was owed £74 and the preacher himself £33. A letter to the conference explained:

> Such is the poverty of this agricultural district, 48 pay nothing to the cause being paupers, 48 only 6d. per quarter for class money and 12 others, who pay 1d. a week class money, pay no ticket money, making 108 who pay no quarterage. 76 others pay only 6d. per quarter ticket money making 184 out of 245 members who come short of 2/1 per quarter.[51]

The situation in Bedfordshire can hardly have been much better. By 1829, although membership of the local circuits had grown by about a third since 1816 (a rate of growth slightly in advance of the population as a whole and of the national connexion), they were employing about a third fewer preachers.[52]

With few chapels being built, the evolution of Wesleyanism from a network of closed societies into a denomination of public congregations seems to have come to a standstill as well.[53] As late as 1829, the overwhelming majority of local societies appear still to have been following the traditional, closed pattern of life. This was the year in which Church of England clergy were required by Parliament to make a return of the number of Dissenting meetings in their parish and to give an estimate of the number of people attending them. Unfortunately, many of the returns, including those for Bedfordshire, have not survived but the returns for the villages

---

[48]   London West (Wesleyan district) minutes of district meeting, MARC, MAB D157.5.

[49]   Pew rents at Eaton Bray fell from £14 2s 1d in 1820 to £11 11s 7d in 1824 and at Clophill from £7 1s 6d in 1823 to £3 18s 6d in 1826 (Eaton Bray and Clophill chapel account books, BLARS, MB 309 and 76).

[50]   From collections' totals published annually in the *WMM*.

[51]   Letter from the Aylesbury Wesleyan circuit stewards to the president of the Conference 10 July 1828, CBS, NM 100/5/1A.

[52]   Currie, Gilbert and Horsley, *Churches and churchgoers*, 140. The population of Bedfordshire is reckoned to have been 70,119 in 1811 and 95,483 in 1831 (VCH *Beds*, I, 113).

[53]   In 1825 a survey of Wesleyan property was carried out for the conference by Thomas Marriott, a London solicitor. Marriott fulfilled his brief by requiring the superintendents of every circuit to send him a copy of their circuit's preaching plan and to mark on it which of the places had a chapel. The collection of plans, bound together in a scrap book, is now in the United Methodist archives at Drew University, Madison, New Jersey. Marriott found forty-nine societies in Bedfordshire of which twenty-nine had some kind of chapel. There appear to have been still only nine Sunday schools.

Table 6. Wesleyan societies in the Leighton Buzzard and Newport Pagnell circuits noted in the Returns of the Buckinghamshire clergy, 1829

Place and date formed	Number of Members according to		Meeting place
	the clergy returns	*the circuit books*	*Private house or date preaching room or chapel established*
Bow Brickhill (by 1781)	60	19	House
Broughton (1817/8)	9 'prayer meeting in a private house'	19	House
Cheddington (1823/4)	10 'a private meeting'	8	House
Fenny Stratford (1806–13)	60	17	1813
Great Brickhill (1802)	10	8	1820
Hanslope (1806–14)	about 120	18	by 1825
Ivinghoe (1825)	'fluctuating'	23	House
Ledburn (1817)	–	8	House
Little Brickhill (1806–14)	30	12	1819
Mentmore (1820–22)	–	11	House
Moulsoe (1806–14)	40–50	15	House
Newport Pagnell (1806–14)	114	39	1815
Pitstone (1829)	10 'a private assembly'	?	House
Simpson (1823)	–	8	House
Slapton (1807–12)	34 or 35	38	1817
Soulbury (1813/4)	23 or 24	24	by 1825
Stewkley (by 1781)	80	78	by 1799
Stoke Goldington (1825)	–	4	House
Stoke Hammond (1803)	20	14	1816
Stony Stratford (1806–14)	30	30	by 1825
Water Eaton (1806)	–	4	House
Wavendon (1803)	20 or 30	54	by 1825
Wing (1802)	about 80	80	1813

Source: Returns of the clergy for Bucks 1829, Aylesbury, CBS, Q/W/G.

in Buckinghamshire that formed part of the Leighton Buzzard and Newport Pagnell circuits are available and provide a valuable glimpse into the balance of closed societies to open congregations (see Table 6). What is striking about the returns is just how close to the actual membership of the societies in question many of the estimates were, suggesting both that the local clergy were well informed and that the great majority of village societies still had no wider community of hearers and Sunday school scholars. Two returns actually describe the Wesleyan meeting in their parish as a private gathering. In all, of the twenty-three preaching places for which returns might have been made, 11 are described as having congregations no larger than their class membership and 5 appear to have been so private as to have avoided drawing any notice. The returns also show that the existence of a building set aside solely for preaching did not of itself necessarily mean that there was a body of hearers in that place beyond the society members. Most of the closed societies had either a purpose built preaching-room or at least one created by the conversion of some other building. Nor was this evolution simply a product of size, for the societies at Stewkley and Wing were quite large but both closed, while the society at Hanslope numbered 18 but drew a congregation of 120.[54]

Other kinds of Methodism

The growth of Wesleyan Methodism in this period contrasts strikingly with the fortunes of its eighteenth-century rivals. The Bedford Moravian congregation continued to pursue their self-limiting United Flocks policy, by which only the most determined applicants from outside the community were admitted to membership. There appears to have been only one attempt to extend their work beyond Bedford, the licensing of a house at Willington in 1811, and this was not sustained for long. The brethren's house and most of the business ventures which had been central to the life of the original settlement were given up by 1801 and the premises were put to use instead as a girl's boarding school. A new chapel was built in 1795 but it was almost a boast that numbers had not increased:

> Another point which merited and elicited the attention and thankful consideration of the congregation was this, that altho' it had not at any time been a numerous one yet it had never been subject to those fluctuations of sudden increase or decrease at certain periods in its history which has occurred in some other congregations.[55]

Even the Moravians, however, were not entirely immune to the surge of evangelical religious activity taking place around them and there was an unexpected accession of new congregations in the north of the county during the 1820s, thanks to John King Martyn, the curate of Pertenhall. A pupil of Charles Simeon, Martyn began his ministry as a conforming evangelical but, in a trajectory that mirrored that of an earlier generation of Methodists, gradually began to adopt practices that would bring him into conflict with the Church authorities. In 1809 he organised the serious element of his congregation into a society with rules on Methodist lines and, at about the same time, began to preach mid-week at farmhouses not only in his own parish but in those of other evangelical clergy, including Turvey. His society drew members from quite a wide area, including Long Stow and Kimbolton in Huntingdonshire where the incumbents were not evangelicals, and between 1817 and 1820 he bought properties in both villages which he fitted up as meeting-rooms. Attempting to stay within canon law, he did not preach in these rooms himself but arranged for sermons to be read. When he visited a dying society member in Kimbolton, however, and gave him communion, he exposed himself to prosecution and in 1823 resigned from the Church of England. Martyn had been in contact with the Bedford Moravian congregation since at least 1810, when his daughter had entered their school, and had preached for them as early as 1816. Following his resignation, he was received into the Moravian church together with his congregations at Kimbolton and Long Stow, the Pertenhall society remaining technically

---

[54] Returns of the clergy for Bucks 1829, CBS, Q/W/G.
[55] A brief account of the celebration of the centenary anniversary at Bedford January 17th 1845, BLARS, MO 672.

within the Church of England until the death of his father, the rector, in 1825.[56] A chapel, minister's house and burying ground were built at Pertenhall in 1827 and cottage preaching was sustained in a string of Bedfordshire villages including Tilbrook, Dean and Keysoe, as well as at Barham, Great Staughton, Swineshead, Covington and Old Weston in Huntingdonshire.[57]

John Berridge's death in 1793 scattered the Calvinistic Methodist societies of his circuit to a variety of winds. Some attempted to maintain the old path. At Potton the barn in which Berridge had preached continued to be open 'for occasional preaching to every good man, who made Christ Jesus, and him crucified, the alpha and omega of a sinner's salvation'; at Stotfold a group who were running a Sunday school were described as Calvinistic Methodists as late as 1833; and at Ely the society was absorbed into the Countess of Huntingdon's Connexion.[58] Some appear to have been courted and won by the newly formed St Ives Wesleyan circuit. At Tempsford,

> In the course of the year 1794, as Mr. Bennett was one day attending to some of the duties of his farm, he met with a stranger on horseback, with whom he entered into conversation. The interesting character of the surrounding scenery was mentioned, and an apparently casual reference to the great Author of nature soon led to more extended religious remark; and the parties, though strangers to each other, found that they could hold mutual converse on a subject which was dear to them both. The traveller told Mr. Bennett that his name was Thomas Linay; that he was a Methodist Preacher, then stationed at St. Ives; and that he was then on his way to Inksworth [Hinxworth], the residence of a truly pious lady, well known in that part of the country as Madam Harvey. He added, that as he had been riding through various villages on his way, he could not help greatly fearing that they were in a deplorable state of moral destitution; and that he earnestly desired to have an opportunity of preaching in some of them. [Mr Bennett's] heart responded to all this with joy; and he engaged Mr. Linay to hold divine service in his farm-house the next time he came that way … and thus was [Wesleyan] Methodism introduced into Tempsford.[59]

The following year Wesleyan preachers were invited into Biggleswade, Baldock and Norton by what appear to have been former followers of Berridge.[60] Many of his societies, of course, had already moved into Dissent and others now made the same journey. Independent churches were formed at Ashwell in 1793 and at Duxford in 1794; at other places the process was slower and it was not until 1801 that the congregation at Streatham constituted themselves as a Baptist church and 1812 before Haddenham took the same step.[61]

56 *Memoir of the Rev. J. K. Martyn*, 11–14, 22, 27, 30.
57 Welch, *Bedfordshire chapels*, 132 and 172; *Short sketches of the work carried out by … Protestant Episcopal Moravian Church in Lancashire*, 39.
58 Oxenham, *Fruits of the Bedfordshire Union*, 26
59 *WMM* (1841), 707–8.
60 The earliest account of the introduction of Wesleyan Methodism to Biggleswade dates from 1835. A Mr. Freeman is said to have invited the Wesleyan preachers to visit because he missed the 'ministry of an eminent and pious clergyman' that he had attended in another town. It seems quite likely, however, that this is a garbled memory of his previously having attended Berridge's preaching (*WMM* (1835), 212). At Baldock too, the Wesleyan narrative of Methodism's introduction to the town, cannot completely disguise the fact that there were already Methodists living there who were avid readers of Whitefield's sermons (*WMM* (1829), 290).
61 *Congregational Magazine* (1842), 36–7; (1819), 501; (1820), 57–8; and (1819), 631.

The Calvinistic Methodists who found their way into Dissent were by no means all enthusiastic supporters of Fullerism. Indeed, some of them proved to be among its most determined opponents. At Potton, some of Berridge's converts who had joined Gamlingay Baptist meeting seceded from that church when the minister, William Pain, began to preach Fullerite doctrines and to co-operate with the Bedfordshire Union of Christians.[62] However, perhaps the bitterest clash between Calvinistic Methodism and Fullerite Dissent occurred in the south of the county. Born at Aldbury in Hertfordshire, in 1768, Francis Hews was one of the first members of the Countess of Huntingdon's society at Berkhamsted and about 1786 began to preach in cottage meetings associated with that congregation and with the Whitefieldite-Baptist church at New Mill, near Tring. He was invited to preach for the Baptist church in Dunstable and by 1790 had become its minister. On Sunday evenings and weeknights he continued to preach in a number of villages including Markyate, Studham, Totternhoe and Westoning. Hews might have been expected to have been an enthusiastic supporter of the Bedfordshire Union of Christians but he was, in fact, a bitter opponent of Fullerism and a staunch supporter of William Huntington. Huntington was a Calvinistic Methodist preacher who had risen from poverty and obscurity to celebrity status as minister of Providence chapel in London and who maintained a traditional emphasis on the doctrine of election and man's utter dependence on the grace of God. Relations between the two camps were poisonous. The Baptist church at Houghton Regis, which had gone over to the Fullerite position, organised the formation of a second Baptist congregation in Dunstable in 1801. Hews, in turn, retaliated by forming rival congregations to the Baptist meetings in Luton and Toddington.[63] When Hews left Dunstable in 1810, he went to become minister of a Huntingtonian congregation in Northampton, the result of a secession from College Lane meeting-house, a Baptist church that had previously shown Calvinistic Methodist sympathies but was now enthusiastically Fullerite.[64] Half a century later Hews' congregations at Dunstable, Luton, Westoning and Northampton, and several of Berridge's former societies were all to be found among the Gospel Standard Baptists, a fellowship of hyper-Calvinistic, strict communion churches who were distinguished from other strict Baptists by their emphasis on 'experimental', that is heart-felt rather than head-led, religion. In this respect Bedfordshire's numerous Gospel Standard churches preserve to this day something of the tradition of eighteenth-century Calvinistic Methodism.

Some of Berridge's disciples, of course, remained within the Church of England and across the county there was a small but growing number of clergy who were still occasionally described by their contemporaries as Methodists but who would soon be thought of as Evangelicals. Robert Beachcroft, rector of Blunham from 1806 to 1830, held cottage lectures in the hamlets of his parish and was happy to be called a Methodist although he did not use the word of himself.[65] Legh Richmond, vicar of Turvey from 1805 to 1826, likewise held cottage meetings and published a hugely popular tract *The Dairyman's daughter*, based on the religious experience

62 Oxenham, *Fruits of the Bedfordshire Union*, 3–7; Evers, *Potton Baptists*, 11.
63 Hews, *Spoils won in the day of battle*, 189–90; Welch, *Bedfordshire chapels*, 108 and 173.
64 *Evangelical Magazine* (1810), 279.
65 Methuen, *Memoir of Robert Beachcroft*, 99.

of a young Wesleyan convert. All of these men, however, were canonically regular and followed Henry Venn and Charles Simeon in foreswearing itinerant preaching and accepting the discipline of a parish ministry.[66] Even Berridge's one-time curate and biographer, Richard Whittingham, the vicar of Potton, had given up itinerancy and the use of extempore public prayers by 1799.[67] The overlap between Methodism and the Church of England was fast disappearing.[68]

The villages of the Chiltern hills, which had been the scene of some of Francis Hews' first preaching engagements, were also home in the early 1800s to a small community of a movement whose place in the Methodist spectrum is often overlooked, the Southcottians. Joanna Southcott, the daughter of an unsuccessful Devon farmer, and sometime Methodist member, became a national celebrity between 1802 and 1814 as a result of her prophecies about the imminence of Christ's second coming. She drew heavily on the Methodist millenarian tradition and Methodists formed a large part of her following. George Turner, one of her most loyal adherents, even had a dream, which was much publicised, in which John Wesley returned from heaven and told him to 'Inform my Brethren that it is the Will of the Lord that they obey the Word of God which is made known.'[69] The movement was strong in London, Devon and in the industrial towns of the north. Preachers were appointed to districts and moved around at Joanna's direction, on a connexional system; chapels were built, the sacraments administered and large congregations gathered. A list of believers from about 1815 records the names of forty-one people in the neighbouring villages of Gaddesden, Little Gaddesden and Ashridge. The story of this Southcottian outpost appears to be entirely lost but it may not be coincidental that the Luton Wesleyan circuit gave up its preaching in Little Gaddesden in about 1813.[70]

Nationally, the war years also saw the emergence of a number of new Arminian Methodist groups, some of which grew to become national bodies rivalling the Wesleyans. Two themes recur in the emergence of many of these communities: tensions about the respective rights of the professional preachers and local officials (as, for instance, in the formation of the Methodist New Connexion) and disputes over the encouragement of uninhibited, emotional outburst in meetings (such as led to the founding of the Primitive Methodist Connexion). Bedfordshire was certainly not immune to these developments and in 1803 the Bedford Wesleyan circuit experienced its own local schism. In December 1802 William Johnson, a local preacher living at Eaton Bray, was censured for neglecting appointments and was asked, for the future, to 'submit to be plan'd by your superintendent, meet in Class regularly and attend to every other Branch of Methodist disapline.' Johnson attempted to dictate terms; he appears to have wanted to play a leading role in preaching at Eaton

[66] Berridge to the Countess of Huntingdon, 26 April 1777 and Berridge to John Thornton, 2 July 1785, Whittingham, *Works of Berridge*, 515–16 and 413–15.

[67] Oxenham, *Fruits of the Bedfordshire Union*, 37.

[68] There would continue to be exceptions. At North Marston in the Aylesbury circuit, William Pinnock, the perpetual curate, was a member of the Wesleyan class in 1822. Berridge's protégé, Rowland Hill minister of Surrey Chapel, remained technically a deacon of the Church of England until his death in 1833. The careers of Timothy Matthews and Robert Aitken will be touched on in the next chapter.

[69] Hopkins, *A woman to deliver her people*, 125.

[70] Hopkins, *A woman to deliver her people*, 221. The house of Robert Austin at Little Gaddesden was licensed by Wesleyan preachers in 1812 (Urwick, *Nonconformity in Herts*, 414). The village does not, however, appear on a Wesleyan circuit preaching plan for 1813 (BLARS, MB 497).

Bray chapel rather than being planned around the circuit, but there was clearly no question of this being acceptable and he withdrew taking about twenty members with him. The secessionists met in the home of James Gadsden at Northall, a hamlet in the adjacent parish of Edlesborough 'and crowds came ... till Numbers ware obliged to stand out of doors wishing and waiting admishion into the House of God.' It is interesting to note that from the beginning they 'administred the Ordinance of the Lord's Supper',[71] something still rare among Wesleyans and perhaps another factor in the schism.[72] During 1803 Johnson's people leased a building in Northall and fitted it up as a chapel but they also registered cottages at Billington, Slapton and Ivinghoe Aston. This little independent Methodist circuit had only a brief existence, however. In 1807 Johnson and eleven others announced that they had changed their views on baptism and were immersed by the minister of Leighton Buzzard Baptist church.[73] Ten other members withdrew in protest and the formation of Wesleyan societies at Billington, Slapton and Ivinghoe Aston suggests that they and others were reconciled to the old connexion.[74] As for Johnson and his remaining followers, they went on to be recognised as a Baptist church practising open communion.

Primitive Methodism had no significant presence in Bedfordshire until the 1830s but the connexion did mission Huntingdonshire in 1821 and, although the centre of gravity of this work had moved to Cambridge by 1823, Primitive Methodist preachers were certainly active on the county's eastern boundary.[75] It is also possible that another, related community, the United Revivalists, were present in Bedford itself. Formed by a disillusioned Primitive Methodist preacher, Robert Winfield, in Leicestershire in 1818, this relatively obscure body held their first conference in Northampton in 1821 and by 1823 had a total of 13 circuits, 25 travelling preachers (including a number of women), 71 local preachers, 20 chapels and perhaps as many as 5,000 members. A meteoric rise was followed by just as meteoric a fall and this little connexion was officially dissolved in about 1827.[76] Almost everything known about it is based on passing references in the records of other bodies and its geography has never been fully established. There is certainly evidence attesting to the presence of the Revivalists in northern Buckinghamshire and Northamptonshire. They were active in the Vale of Aylesbury around 1825/6 and eleven years later, in Aylesbury itself, Primitive Methodist missionaries still found themselves 'excluded from all local help' because

---

[71] Church book of Northall Baptist church (Northall Baptist Church).

[72] Johnson appears as Master Bitson in Buckmaster's *Village politician*, 64–5, where it is suggested that he was a strict Calvinist but there is no mention of this in the Northall church book.

[73] Tibbutt, *Baptists of Leighton Buzzard*, 28.

[74] James Leach and Thomas Newens, who signed an application to license a cottage at Billington with Johnson in 1803 (Welch, *Bedfordshire chapels*, 43), were Wesleyan members by 1812 as was Richard Turney who signed a license application for Slapton in 1804.

[75] Petty, *History of the Primitive Methodist Connexion*, 143–5 and 151; Tice, *History of Methodism in Cambridge*, 61. Primitive Methodist preachers were holding services at Eltisley in 1825 (Cambridge University Library, EDR, C1/6).

[76] Short, 'Robert Winfield and the Revivalists', 97. At least one Revivalist chapel is still standing, at Epwell in Oxfordshire (Stell, *Inventory of Nonconformist chapels and meeting-houses in central England*, 175). The United Revivalists were almost certainly the Ranter group with which John Clare, the Northamptonshire poet, was briefly involved.

there has been an imposter a few years ago, in this part, who has partly gone in the name of our people, styling himself a preacher of the P[rimitive] Methodist new community; he has preached at Aylesbury and the villages round; and has acted very immorally; and after some time got embarrassed in his circumstances, and made what the people call here, a light night of it, and off he went.[77]

In 1824 two Revivalist preachers were arrested at the instigation of the vicar of Newport Pagnell, and sentenced to hard labour by a clerical magistrate, after making a collection locally for a new chapel at Raunds, which was deemed vagrancy.[78] There was Revivalist activity around Buckingham.[79] At Northampton, as at Aylesbury, the Primitive Methodists would find that they had been there before them:

> The extinction of the Revivalists in this district notwithstanding their previous prosperity, rendered many of the inhabitants cautious respecting uniting with another new community; whilst the majority confounded the two denominations; imagining that as the Primitive Methodists sang many of the same hymns and tunes as the Revivalists had done, and resembled them in the open-air worship, and in some other respects, that they belonged to the same community, and were now making a second attempt to establish a cause, which, like the former, would prove ineffectual.[80]

Some local societies appear to have survived the dissolution of the connexion. In the 1829 Returns of the Clergy, the vicar of Emberton, in Buckinghamshire, refers to 'the Ranters' room at Olney' and when the Primitive Methodist preacher James Hurd was sent to Northampton in 1834 it was at the request of a group who may likewise have been a remnant of Revivalists.[81] There are no direct references to the Revivalists in Bedfordshire but the fact that a Primitive Methodist preacher was also sent to Bedford in 1834, and that the cause there was established so quickly, may suggest that his mission too was to absorb a surviving Revivalist group into the Primitive Methodist connexion.

Part 2 Methodist People

Maidens and Young Men
The two decades of war with revolutionary France saw not only an astonishing growth in Wesleyan numbers in Bedfordshire but also a dramatic transformation of the movement's social make-up. What had been an ageing community was suddenly awash with young people again. Between 1795 and 1804, the last year for which the Bedford circuit book gives comprehensive details of the marital status of members,

---

[77] *PMM* (1837), 307; see also Kussmaul, *Autobiography of Joseph Mayett*, 86.
[78] Davis, *Political change and continuity*, 64.
[79] *PMM* (1844), 485.
[80] Petty, *History of the Primitive Methodist Connexion*, 375–6.
[81] Ward, *Religious census of Northamptonshire*, 25. In 1827 something similar had also happened with the Revivalist circuit on the Norfolk/Suffolk border. George Wharton (of North Lopham) 'was for many years a member of the Wesleyan society. But for reasons known to himself he left that society, and joined the revivalists, so called. But when those people broke up, he came to Lynn with a preacher in 1827; and wished, with what were left, to be united with our Lynn circuit. So we took up Brandon as a branch' (*PMM* (1840), 254).

the proportion of members who were single more than doubled and the proportion who were widows and widowers halved.[82]

Table 7. Gender and marital status of Wesleyan members in Bedfordshire, 1804

	Single		Married		Widowed		Total
	no.	%	no.	%	no.	%	
Men	47	27%	120	69%	6	4%	173
Women	129	43%	134	45%	35	12%	298
All members	176	37%	254	54%	41	9%	471

Source: Bedfordshire Wesleyan circuit book, BLARS, MB 1.

Most of the recruits were women and during the boom years women came to form an increasing percentage of the membership, rising from slightly less than 60% of the membership in 1781 to 63% in 1806, and 66% by 1812. When Wesleyan membership declined after 1815, however, the percentage of women members seems to have fallen quite markedly and by 1819 may have been down to little more than 50%.[83] This disproportionate decline may owe something to the difficulty which those who were economically dependent on non-Methodist husbands and fathers had in affording the cost of membership during the economic downturn. It is certainly interesting that in southern Bedfordshire, where booming demand for straw plait was providing new opportunities for female employment, the proportion of women members remained steady. In the 1820s, when membership numbers picked up again, the gender ratio across the county gradually returned to the familiar 3:2.[84]

Backsliding
What is perhaps most notable about the new recruits, however, is just how short a time many of them remained in membership. Between midsummer 1804 and midsummer 1806 twenty-five men joined the societies in and around Leighton Buzzard, but by 1812 eighteen of them had disappeared from the membership roll.[85] If the retention rate had remained as it had been in the 1780s the number lost would have been only five.

The circuit books also suggest that the decline in membership was not caused by any significant diminution in the number of people joining Wesleyan societies. At Great Barford and Tempsford in the St Neots circuit, where the membership fell from seventy-one to sixty between 1815 and 1817, there were twenty-eight new recruits

---

82 Bedfordshire Wesleyan circuit book, BLARS, MB 1.
83 At Great Barford and Tempsford in the north-east of the county the proportion of women members fell from 61% in 1815 to 53% in 1819, and at Salford and Aspley Guise, in the south-west, women formed less than half the membership in 1816. In the Leighton Buzzard circuit, however, women accounted for around 64% of the members from 1814 to 1828.
84 At Great Barford and Tempsford the proportion of female members returned to 60% by 1824 and in the Newport Pagnell circuit it had reached 69% by 1830.
85 Bedfordshire Wesleyan and Leighton Buzzard Wesleyan circuit books, BLARS, MB 1 and 1533. The societies concerned were those at Billington, Eaton Bray, Heath, Leighton Buzzard, Stanbridge and Tilsworth.

during that period, one more than there had been between 1813 and 1815 when membership had risen from sixty-one to seventy.[86] The real cause of decline seems to have been that members were now remaining in membership for even shorter periods of time.[87] Faced with similar statistics E. P. Thompson was struck by 'the *impermanence* of the phenomenon of Methodist conversion.'[88] Whether such people abandoned Wesleyanism altogether, however, or simply gave up formal membership for a time as an austerity measure, the surviving records are too fragmentary to say.

The Butcher, the Baker, the Candlestick Maker

The Bedford circuit membership list for 1795 is the last that records members' occupations and it suggests that, at the beginning of this period, the men who belonged to the Wesleyan community were broadly representative of the social structure of the local population. Something over 50% were unskilled manual workers and about 20% were craftsmen. There were farmers, tradesmen and some clerical workers but no-one from the top tier of society. The women, however, tended to be disproportionately drawn from the lower economic strata: 85% were either married to unskilled workers or engaged in low paid work themselves.[89]

After 1795 the only glimpse of the economic status of Wesleyan Methodists available comes from baptism registers. Before 1815 the number of baptisms, and particularly of baptisms where the father's occupation is recorded, is simply too small to provide a reliable sample.[90] During the 1820s, however, although the number of Wesleyan members levelled off, the number of people turning to Wesleyan preachers for the baptism of their children continued to increase and provides a sample of credible size. What the registers show is a community that drew support from a wide spectrum of society, although still excluding the very wealthy. In the villages, the great majority of fathers, 69%, are recorded as labourers

---

[86] In the Bedfordshire societies of the Leighton Buzzard circuit (Leighton Buzzard, Heath, Eaton Bray, Stanbridge, Tilsworth, Billington and, after 1817, Woburn) there were 93 new recruits between 1812 and 1814 when their combined membership rose from 183 to 247 and 84 new recruits between 1817 and 1819, when membership sank from 302 to 295.

[87] Of the 27 recruits won at Great Barford and Tempsford between 1813 and 1815, 13 (48%) had gone by 1817. Of the 84 in the Bedfordshire societies of the Leighton Buzzard circuit between 1817 and 1819, 41 (49%) had gone by 1823.

[88] Thompson, *Making of the English working class*, 427.

[89] Taking the societies in Bedfordshire itself, of the 62 men in membership: 6 (10%) were farmers (including 2 yeoman); 5 (8%) were tradesmen (2 shopkeepers, a baker, a lacebuyer and a publican); 13 (21%) were artisans (4 shoemakers, 3 smiths, 2 curriers, 2 tailors, a saddler and a stonecutter) and 34 (55%) were labourers (inc 2 servants, 2 dairymen, 2 higglers, a sweep, a bricklayer, a brickmaker and a man described as poor). There were also now 5 men (8%) in what can very loosely be called clerical work (a schoolmaster, a clerk, a hospital keeper and a surgeon). Of the 119 women some occupational information is provided for all but 14. Four were farmers or married to farmers; 3 were shopkeepers and 3 mantuamakers; 3 were married to clerical workers and 3 to artisans.

[90] The names of 110 couples are recorded in the baptism registers of the Ampthill, Bedford, Biggleswade, Leighton Buzzard and Luton circuits before 1815 but the father's occupation is only given in 41 cases, two of whom were preachers. What the records show is that Methodist baptism was taken up first in the places where there was a chapel and by the better off. Six were farmers, eleven were tradesmen and twenty-one artisans. Only one was a labourer. This appears to contradict the view that better-off Methodists continued to use the Church of England to register births for fear of problems over inheritance (see Ward, *Early correspondence of Jabez Bunting*, 38).

and this seems to have been roughly in line with the general population.[91] It also accords with a description of the neighbouring Aylesbury circuit in 1828 where the members consisted 'principally of farm servants and their wives and children.'[92] In the towns for which there is information, Bedford and Biggleswade, the Wesleyan baptisms also broadly mirror the social structure of the general population with much higher proportions of artisans and tradesmen.[93]

Table 8. Wesleyan baptisms 1816–1829: occupation of father

Occupation	Villages		Bedford		Biggleswade		Total	
	no.	%	no.	%	no.	%	no.	%
Farmer	17	13%	0		7	21%	28	12%
Tradesman	10	7%	12	21.5%	4	12%	27	11%
Clerical worker	0		3	5%	2	6%	8	3%
Artisan	14	11%	29	52%	12	35%	58	24%
Labourer	91	69%	12	21.5%	9	26%	120	50%
Total	132	100%	56	100%	34	100%	241	100%

The figures represent all the baptisms that took place in the Ampthill, Bedford, Higham Ferrers and St Neots circuits.
Sources: Bedford Wesleyan baptism register 1810–37, BLARS, MB 2; Ampthill baptism register 1810–73; Higham Ferrers baptism register 1813–37; and St Neots baptism register 1797–1837, TNA, RG4/307, 1272 and 1370.

Networks of recruitment

If Wesleyan recruitment was not shaped by occupational status, it was channelled through a variety of social networks. The obituaries in the connexional magazines provide a rich seam of detail about individual stories, but with only a small proportion of recruits maintaining their membership as a lifelong commitment, the window they provide into these recruitment patterns is necessarily partial. They reflect the experiences of a small inner core of members and it is perhaps not surprising that many of these were now second-generation Methodists. Samuel Bennett junior followed his parents into membership of the Tempsford society in 1811:

> The Divine change ... was wrought in Samuel on the last Sunday in January, 1811, he being then about twenty years of age. Although very docile and amiable, and distinguished by affection for his parents and by good morals, yet, like many other young persons, he seems for years to have resisted the convictions of duty: but conscience still asserted her claim to be heard. ... During the earlier part of the day just mentioned, he had been reading, in the January Number of the Wesleyan-Methodist Magazine for the year, a memoir of the Rev. Robert Lomas; and in the evening he heard the late Rev. Frederick Calder preach a most impressive sermon on the words, 'Then Agrippa said unto Paul, Almost

[91]   In the 1831 census more than 60% of the men over the age of 20 in Bedfordshire (excluding Bedford itself) were employed as labourers (*Abstract of the population returns of Great Britain, 1831*, I, 9).
[92]   Letter from the Aylesbury Wesleyan circuit stewards to the president of the Conference 10 July 1828, CBS, NM 100/5/1A.
[93]   The 1831 census found that in the parishes of Bedford 54% of men were 'employed in retail trade or in handicraft as masters or workmen' and 25% were employed as labourers (*Abstract of the population returns of Great Britain 1831*, I, 9).

thou persuadest me to be a Christian.' (Acts xxvi. 28). On this occasion he was so completely filled with penitential sorrow, that, while he strove to unite with the congregation in singing after the close of the sermon, his voice faltered, and he fell back on his seat and wept. At the same time a younger brother was similarly affected. The family having arrived at home, the devout father proposed prayer; and, after engaging with great fervour himself, he asked Samuel to pray. Although it was with struggling hesitation, he made the effort, and for the first time his voice was heard, under the parental roof, making humble supplication to that Being who is 'plenteous in mercy to all them that call upon Him.'[94]

At Leighton Buzzard, the young Elizabeth Dumpleton joined when her mother died and the class-leader asked, 'Betsey, your mother is gone to glory: shall I have to take her name off the class-paper?'[95] At Little Brickhill Rebecca Pakes was taken to the class meeting by her mother from the age of nine and became a member in her own right at thirteen.[96]

If the act of becoming a Methodist was for some people an expression of independence, for the sons and daughters of Methodist families it was an act of dutiful submission. Pressure to conform may have been greater on girls than boys. Among the core membership it was certainly the case that girls tended to enter membership at a younger age. 54% of the women memorialised in obituaries had become members before they were 21 but only 33% of the men, for whom the peak age of recruitment was between 21 and 30 years of age.

Table 9. Age of Wesleyan recruits on entering membership, 1800–1829

	Under 21		21–30		31–40		Over 40		Total
	no.	%	no.	%	no.	%	no.	%	
Men	15	33	20	43	6	13	5	11	46
Women	28	54	14	26	5	10	5	20	52

Source: Obituaries of members of Bedfordshire circuits in the *Methodist Magazine* and its successors.

Servants, like children, may have felt some obligation to join the society. Mary Hardwick 'when young … was a servant in the family of Mr. Bennett, sen., who introduced Methodism into his house; and in the year 1798, while attending a lovefeast in her master's barn, she obtained peace with God through faith in the Lord Jesus Christ.'[97]

It is clear, however, that lateral as well as hierarchical relationships played a part in recruitment. Some were drawn into membership by brothers and sisters. When the young Thomas Coles became a member of the society at Stewkley in 1798 he was the first Methodist in his family but by 1806 he had won over his mother and four of his brothers.[98] When Elizabeth Ekins returned from boarding school:

94 *WMM* (1857), 194–5.
95 *WMM* (1837), 314.
96 *WMM* (1831), 208.
97 *WMM* (1854), 190.
98 Coles, *Youthful days,* 82–3.

she found her elder sister had joined the Methodist society. She saw that her sister was very much altered, had become plain in her dress, was very attentive to religious duties, and took delight in the means of grace. She found she could have no companion in her sister, unless she sought the Lord with her.[99]

Husbands and suitors too followed their wives and girlfriends into membership. Mary Dawson of Leighton Buzzard made her fiancé promise that he would not interfere in her attendance at class before she married him and his own name subsequently appears in the class lists.[100] Mary Howard of Bedford was one of those who were drawn in to Methodism by friends:

> When about 16 years of age, she was invited to spend an afternoon with a party of Christian friends. … The singing of hymns, the heavenly conversation, and the fervent prayers … produced a serious and lasting impression … her friends found no difficulty in prevailing upon her to attend the ministry of the Methodist Preachers.[101]

If parents, siblings, and friends all brought recruits into the Methodist fold, being absent from the support of such relationships could also provide the background to conversion. Several young people were recruited when they were away from home, either working, as apprentices or servants, or just visiting. John Darley, from Dunstable, became a Methodist while working in Nottingham; Mary Stevenson, from Hockliffe, while staying in Sheffield; and Thomas Row from Cople while an apprentice in Lincolnshire. George Coles was already a Methodist when he moved to Ampthill in 1806 to begin his apprenticeship but his account of those years gives an insight into the way in which Methodism provided a surrogate family for a lonely young man a long way from home: 'These dear old friends took me by the hand, and treated me with as much kindness as if I had been a brother, or a son.'[102]

One final thread that runs through many conversion narratives relating to this period is that recruits were often already hearers at Wesleyan public preaching. Mary Dawson occasionally attended both the Baptist and Methodist chapels in Leighton Buzzard in her teens until she was convinced 'that a closer union with people of God would … prove of considerable advantage to her' and applied to join a class.[103] Likewise Thomas Hine attended Radwell chapel at first occasionally and then more regularly and finally 'united himself in church-fellowship with the Wesleyan Methodists.'[104]

Part 3 Being a Methodist

Many of the features of eighteenth-century Methodist life continued unchanged into the early nineteenth century. Members continued to meet weekly in their classes and the itinerant preachers to travel their weekly circuits. New patterns of activity were also emerging, however, that would transform the very nature of some Methodist

---

99   *MM* (1816), 49.
100 *MM* (1814), 365; Leighton Buzzard Wesleyan circuit book 1812–27, BLARS, MB 1533.
101 *MM* (1814), 284.
102 Coles, *Youthful days*, 120.
103 *MM* (1814), 365.
104 *WMM* (1858), 770.

communities. One of the most significant changes was that an increasing number of men took on the role of lay or, as they were called, 'local' preachers. In 1796, the year that quarterly preachers' meetings were introduced across the connexion, the outgoing superintendent of the Bedford Wesleyan circuit wrote in the circuit book the names of seven men who supplemented the work of the professional 'itinerant' preachers in this way.[105] Three years later their numbers had almost doubled and by 1824 there were 59 local preachers, 5 exhorters and 18 prayer leaders active in the same area; which meant that approximately one in ten of the men in Wesleyan membership were involved in leading worship.[106]

George Coles' initiation into preaching was probably quite typical. It began with the superintendent of the Bedford circuit taking him aside one evening 'When I heard you speak in love-feast, a few Sabbaths since, I thought within myself, "The Lord has something for that young man to do: if he knows it, he ought to be encouraged; and if he does not, some one ought to tell him of it."' A few weeks later Coles was sent one Sunday morning to a village seven miles distant to 'explain a verse' to a society who met in a barn. The reports that reached the superintendent were clearly good for, 'without my knowledge or consent [he] put the initials of my name on the Local Preachers' Plan, and gave me plenty of appointments.' Within a year Coles had preached a formal trial sermon before the superintendent in the chapel at Bedford and his full name had been entered on the plan. He was twenty-two years old.[107]

Some of these amateur preachers were well-read. Samuel Copleston was a schoolmaster and John Curtiss of Wootton apparently had a good collection of second-hand books.[108] Occasionally attempts were made to improve their education: Thomas Hall, one of the junior itinerants on the Bedford circuit in 1813, 'formed the local preachers, exhorters and class leaders into an association, gave them their lessons and heard then recite.'[109] But the impression is left that stamina was in greater demand than learning. In the 1790s the local preachers seem to have preached for their own societies and perhaps one or two close by. So Robert Bull, who was living in Bierton in 1791, preached in his own village every Sunday evening and at Whitchurch on Sunday afternoons.[110] Mr Ewbank, who was living at Wendover in 1796, was 'at home two Sundays, and then out two Sundays. On one sabbath at *Bierton* at 2 o'clock, and at *Aston* at 6 o'clock; the next at *Whitchurch* 3 o'clock, and *Oving* 6 or 7 o'clock.'[111] Such preaching was clearly seen as a bonus and, when Mr Ewbank left Wendover, for a while the societies in Aylesbury Vale simply made do without Sunday preaching. By about 1800, however, local preachers were being deployed across the whole circuit at the superintendent's direction and could face

---

[105] The seven were: William Cumberland, Francis Downman, John Bowers, William Emmerton, Richard Partridge, Samuel Copleston and Henry Saunders.

[106] The total membership of the Bedford and Ampthill, Luton, St Albans, Newport Pagnell and Leighton Buzzard circuits in 1824 was 1,929, of whom no more than about 40% were probably men. There is no evidence of any women preachers in the Bedfordshire Wesleyan circuits.

[107] Coles, *Youthful days*, 146–7, and 150.

[108] Coles, *Youthful days*, 97–8 and 131–2.

[109] Coles, *Youthful days*, 141. A similar initiative appears to have been made in the Luton circuit in the 1830s (Balch, *Souvenir of a century of Wesleyan Methodism in Luton*, 14).

[110] *MM* (1816), 120.

[111] Durley, *Centenary annals*, 10.

having to travel a round trip of up to twenty miles on unmade roads, on foot and in all weathers, often returning late and in the dark.[112]

It became rare for them to preach for their own society. Richard Partridge, a local preacher from Leagrave, preached on two Sundays out of every three but only once in six months did that involve preaching in his own village.[113] This was exactly what William Johnson had protested against at Eaton Bray, and the willingness of the Wesleyan leadership to push matters to a schism rather than compromise on the arrangement suggests that it was seen as fulfilling an important function. It may be that it was intended to ensure that the local preachers remained auxiliaries to the itinerants and did not evolve into *de facto* ministers of their home congregations (as Johnson wished to do) thereby threatening the integrity of the circuit system.

Safely channelled through the discipline of the circuit preaching plan, the swelling number of volunteer preachers nevertheless brought about a transformation in the role of preaching in the communal life of Methodism. While the full-time itinerant preachers continued to carry out their circuits of mid-week preaching engagements, the local preachers made possible an explosion in regular Sunday preaching in the villages of Bedfordshire. The arrangements as to who would preach at each place on any particular Sunday were published every few months in a document called a preaching plan. The oldest surviving example from Bedfordshire covers the Luton Wesleyan circuit for the period October 1813 to April 1814 (Plate 24). Although, unlike some, it does not refer to the mid-week appointments of the three itinerant preachers, the basic six-week cycle of their circuits is still immediately evident.[114] Between them they managed to provide the main society in Luton with preaching on five Sundays out of six; 4 other societies on three Sundays out of six; another 3 on one Sunday in three, and 2 more with preaching on one Sunday in four. The local preachers not only filled the gaps to give all these societies preaching every Sunday but also provided regular preaching in 4 other places that the itinerants never visited on a Sunday. By 1824 there were 49 communities across Bedfordshire with regular Wesleyan Sunday preaching and in 20 of them the preaching was entirely provided by local preachers. In a further 19 they conducted the majority of the services, often all but one.[115]

The swelling number of preachers was such that in many places it was possible to offer not merely one Sunday sermon but several. George Coles, remembering the life of the Wesleyan society at Stewkley in 1805, recalled that: 'At half past ten, at two, and at six, we had public preaching either by the traveling or local preachers.'[116] The Luton plan for 1813/14 shows three Sunday services every week at Luton and St Albans, two services at 7 other societies and a single service at only 5 places. By

---

[112] Coles, *Youthful days*, 150–1. For the authority of the superintendent to make the plan, see Ward, *Early correspondence of Jabez Bunting*, 193–4.
[113] Luton Wesleyan circuit preaching plan 1813/14, BLARS, MB 497.
[114] Preachers 1 to 3 are the itinerants and their cycle can be seen to finish on successive Sundays at Luton (week 1), Harpenden (week 2), Tebworth and Dunstable (or St Albans) (week 3), Leagrave and Luton (week 4), St Albans (or Dagnall, Hudnall and Hemel Hempstead) (week 5), and finally Luton and Markyate (week 6).
[115] The Marriott collection of British circuit plans, Drew University, United Methodist archives.
[116] Coles, *Youthful days*, 82.

1825 there were 7 places across the county holding three services on a Sunday, 32 holding two, and only 10 holding one.

The most popular times for services were the afternoon and evening.[117] The often-made presumption that this was because Wesleyans were fitting their preaching around the morning service at their parish church ignores the fact that in country districts the most popular service in the parish church was usually the one held in the afternoon, leaving the morning for the unavoidable chores of agricultural life.[118] If the great majority of Wesleyan societies were happy to go head to head with the parish church in the afternoon, why did so many of them hold their second service in the evening rather than the morning? There were certainly some obvious disadvantages to holding a service at 6.00pm: the congregation had to travel after dark for half the year and there was an additional expense in providing candlelight, which may explain why neither church nor meeting-house held evening services. The success of the Wesleyans in recruiting women and young people in particular may, however, point to part of its attraction. When the day's work was done, while men might go to the alehouse, there was nothing for anyone else to do. John Buckmaster, recalling his boyhood, observed that, 'I occasionally went to [the Methodist] meetings to pass away the evening.'[119] Evening service was not a work of supererogation but a leisure activity, and the novelty of going out in the evening no doubt contributed both to its atmosphere and its success.

Wesleyan services not only became more frequent but also began to exhibit a more popular tone. There seems to have been gradually more hymn singing around the preaching, with a third hymn becoming standard, and in some places additional verses being sung at the beginning and end of the service.[120] Bands of musicians and choirs were formed both to lead the hymn singing and to provide anthems. One village society had a makeshift gallery for the singers as early as 1803 and at Ampthill the chapel, built in 1816, had 'a large choir of singers, with instruments of music, "to praise the Lord withal."'[121] With these greater musical resources came a new style of music. In 1811 George Coles heard the Bedford choir sing at the opening of Ampthill chapel:

> in the afternoon they sang one of Leach's tunes, called 'Tabernacle'. ... In the evening they sung an anthem, by the same author, called 'Canaan', – a most charming piece, and performed in a style superior to anything I had ever heard before. The contrast between this kind of singing, and nearly all other kinds with which I was acquainted, was great indeed.[122]

---

[117]   Of the fourteen preaching places on the Luton circuit in 1813, 5 held morning services, 10 afternoon services and 9 evening services. Of the twenty-six preaching places on the Leighton Buzzard and Higham Ferrers circuits in 1817, 7 held morning services, 21 afternoon services and 22 evening services. Of the forty-nine Wesleyan preaching places across Bedfordshire in 1825, 19 held morning services, 33 afternoon services and 42 evening services.

[118]   Knight, *Nineteenth-century church and English society*, 27. In 1851 the vicar of Willington observed that 'The afternoon services are always much better attended in country parishes than the morning services' (Bushby, 'Ecclesiastical census, Bedfordshire', 135).

[119]   Buckmaster, *Village politician*, 39. At Stewkley, in 1804, Methodist meetings of one kind or another got George Coles out of the house on as many as six nights some weeks (Coles, *Youthful days*, 82).

[120]   Service sheet for Bedford Wesleyan Sunday school anniversary 1825, MARC, MAW LHB 4.10.

[121]   Coles, *Youthful days*, 77 and 153. Slapton chapel, built in 1817, also had a musicians' gallery and a band composed of bass viols, fiddles, flutes and clarinets (Buckmaster, *Village politician*, 47).

[122]   Coles, *Youthful days*, 136–7.

James Leach's collection of tunes, published in 1797, was just one of a host of sources for a new fugal style of hymn settings that rapidly replaced the more restrained tunes which Methodists had sung in Wesley's day.[123] William Millard, who attended Lidlington chapel, even published his own collection of tunes, *The Branch, comprising Forty Psalm and Hymn Tunes,* in 1810. Many years later it would be remembered how in these days 'When the hymn was given out, the violinist struck the key note for the leader to pitch the tune. Then the precentor took the air, the viol poured in its bass, and the whole choir and congregation joined in the praise of God.'[124] The musical resources of some congregations was impressive. At Biggleswade the band consisted of first and second fiddles, flute, clarinet, trombone and two bass cellos.[125] At Northampton the accounts even suggest that the singers were paid but this can hardly have been a widespread practice in country areas.[126] Indeed, at Kempston the person leading the singing had only the support of a set of tuning forks and in many small societies they may not have had even that.[127]

Although this lively singing would eventually find its way into parish churches and Dissenting meetings, for a time at least it seems to have been the prerogative of the Wesleyans. At Ampthill, apparently, the singing in the parish church continued to be led by the clerk, just as Methodist singing had previously been by the preacher, but Coles found this 'so poor I could not endure it'; while the Baptist meeting, although having a group of singers, 'used no instruments' and sang 'only two parts of the harmony, the treble and bass.'[128] The importance of singing in the appeal of Methodism is attested in numerous obituaries from this period.[129] Coles too could 'well recollect hearing my brother say that it was the *singing* that brought him into the meeting, and eventually led him to join the society.'[130] Entering a Methodist preaching-house for the first time, a visitor would have seen:

> a company of plain-looking people, all on the same floor, the men on one side the room, and the women on the other; the minister … giving out a hymn, two lines at a time … I can easily suppose that 'the men sung with all their might' for they often used to do so … [and] that 'the women sung the repeats alone. '[131]

Such was the power of these hymns that their words became like a second scripture to Methodists so that when Susannah Owen of Whittlebury was dying, like many others, she repeated 'appropriate passages of Scripture, and verses of hymns' interchangeably.'[132]

---

[123] Lightwood, *Music of the Methodist hymn-book,* xviii; Coles, *Youthful days,* 126–7.
[124] Telford, *Two West-End chapels,* 132.
[125] Phillips, *Wesleyan Methodist church, Biggleswade circuit,* 8.
[126] Bowles, *One hundred and forty two years,* 21.
[127] Carnell, Booth and Tibbutt, *Eight thousand years: a Kempston history,* 85.
[128] Coles, *Youthful days,* 106.
[129] William Ekins' hymnbook was his constant companion; and John Marlow was deeply distressed when 'a complaint in his breast, and a cough … prevented him from joining with others in singing the praises of God which had been his delight' (*MM* (1816), 47 and *MM* (1810), 481). Susan Elger, if the *Methodist Magazine* is to be believed, looked forward to singing 'more sweet and loud' in heaven (*MM* (1809), 527). Letitia Norris too started attending Methodist meetings in 1795, because 'she was fond of singing' (*MM* (1816), 286).
[130] Coles, *Youthful days,* 69.
[131] Coles, *Youthful days,* 70.
[132] *MM* (1814), 793.

Changes in the music were not the only way in which Methodist worship was becoming more popular. A number of societies began to hold festivals of one kind or another which drew visitors from quite a distance. In 1807 members from the Bedford circuit had an outing to Quainton in the Oxford circuit to attend a day of fasting and prayer.[133] Love-feasts, in particular, were a great draw. These services, Moravian in their origin, were an opportunity not only for singing but also for anyone present to stand up and share their testimony, while biscuits and water were passed among the congregation. The earliest recorded Wesleyan love-feast in Bedfordshire was held at Tempsford in 1798 and there appears to have been an annual love-feast at Eaton Bray from soon after to which people came from as far away as Aylesbury.[134] The popularity of love-feasts was such that they quickly became an established part of the calendar of many societies.[135] Watch-night services, festivals of singing and prayer that continued until midnight (providing both a reason for young people to stay up late and a need for young women to be escorted home), also make their first appearance in local records at this period. The draw of a watch-night held in Bedford in 1827 was such that both Church people and Dissenters flocked to join the Methodists for the occasion.[136] Such occasions, however, were soon overshadowed as the high points in the year by the emergence of other events that had even greater popular appeal.

One of these was the chapel anniversary. The origins of this festival almost certainly lay in the celebrations that were held to mark the actual opening of new chapels. Partly motivated by a genuine sense of achievement but also by the very real need to secure financial contributions towards the cost of the project, trustees made every effort to put on a good show and draw a large crowd. Music played its part: the chapel at Slapton was 'opened with all the bass-viols, fiddles, flutes, and clarionets of the neighbourhood.'[137] Even more important, however, was a performance by a celebrity preacher. Joseph Benson, editor of the *Methodist Magazine*, was secured for the opening of Leighton Buzzard chapel in 1804 and Luton chapel in 1815. Samuel Bradburn, 'the Demosthenes of Methodism', was the preacher at the opening of Clophill chapel in 1814.[138] No expense was spared. The trustees of Northampton chapel spent £11 on preachers' travelling expenses for their opening in 1816; but it proved a good investment as the collections amounted to £114.[139] With ongoing expenses to meet, the annual anniversary of the chapel's opening was a good moment to revive the excitement of that day and to secure fresh donations. In fact, anniversaries were to become hugely important to the economy of Methodism. At Whitchurch, in the Aylesbury circuit, where the seat rents amounted to £11 in 1821, the anniversary collection yielded nearly £7.[140] These were festivals,

---

[133] Letter from John Goodson to Richard Gower, quoted in a manuscript history of Methodist circuits in Buckinghamshire by E. Ralph Bates now in the possession of the author.

[134] *WMM* (1854), 190; *WMM* (1848), 798; Coles, *Youthful days*, 76–9.

[135] In the Marriott collection of preaching plans for 1825, which provides a snapshot of only part of the year, 11 of the 49 Wesleyan societies in Bedfordshire are recorded as holding love-feasts (Drew University).

[136] Greeves, *Memorials of Wm Cumberland*, 40.

[137] Buckmaster, *Village politician*, 47.

[138] Coles, *Youthful days*, 158–9.

[139] Bowles, *One hundred and forty two years*, 3.

[140] Whitchurch Wesleyan chapel papers and accounts, CBS, NM 114/7/7.

moreover, not just for the Methodist faithful but quite deliberately marketed to the public as a whole with printed posters.[141]

The most successful anniversary preachers appear to have been those who eschewed the plainness and immediacy of the eighteenth-century sermon for a more dramatic and rhetorical style. It was said of Robert Newton, perhaps the foremost anniversary preacher among the Wesleyans, that 'he was pathetic in his strokes of tenderness and pictures of distress, – he was thrilling and powerful in his appeals.'[142] Indeed, a new, more emotional note seems to have been evident in Wesleyan preaching generally. Hugh Ransom, a junior preacher on the Ampthill circuit was 'zealous' in the pulpit and James Conquest, a Biggleswade local preacher, 'evinced an ardent desire to be useful to his hearers.'[143] William Cumberland 'seldom stood up ... but great feeling was soon manifested. Hearts were warmed, tears flowed apace, and all got a blessing'; while Maximilian Wilson's sermons were 'delivered with distinctness, earnestness, pathos and power.'[144]

While there may have been power in the performance of the preachers there is little to suggest that there was anything particularly striking in their message. In 1824 Susanna Row of Cardington noted in her diary the substance of a sermon that she had found 'very profitable'. It was preached by John Rowe, the superintendent of the Bedford circuit, and based on a text from the book of Genesis in which Abraham drives away the birds that are feeding on the carcases of a sacrifice he had made:

> He pointed out first the sacrifices that were required under the mosaic dispensation; stating that though they were no longer required under the gospel dispensation yet we in these days had also sacrifices to offer, mentioning particularly those of prayer and praise: he showed how these sacrifices were often marred, and rendered unacceptable to God, by being offered in a cold, heartless manner. ... He urged us to endeavour by watchfulness to drive away whatever we felt to be a hindrance. ... He concluded by encouraging us to *expect* the influences of the Holy Spirit, without which our own efforts would be vain.[145]

A similar focus on rather esoteric spiritual concerns seems to have dominated William Cumberland's sermons, for all his warmth and tears:

> *As new born babes, desire the sincere milk of the word, that ye may grow thereby.*
> How does the new-born babe desire the milk? Four ways:
> I.   It covets it, and nothing will do but the milk.
> II. It desires it through a sense of want.
> III. It desires it as nature has prepared it.
> IV. It hunts for it, and struggles for it.[146]

The richest source of material, the sermon notes of James Durley, a local preacher in the Aylesbury circuit, suggests that most of his sermons followed the theme of Man's sin, Christ's death, and the offer of forgiveness in return for faith but that he

---

[141] The earliest surviving local example relates to the Whitchurch anniversary of 1828 (CBS, NM 114/9/1/2).
[142] Rigg, *Sermons on special and ordinary occasions*, viii.
[143] Hall, *Memorials of Wesleyan Methodist Ministers*, 110; *MM* (1822), 67.
[144] Greeves, *Memorials of Wm Cumberland*, 37; *WMM* (1858), 966.
[145] Jones, *Memoir of the late Miss Susanna Row*, 23.
[146] Greeves, *Memorials of Wm Cumberland*, 39.

also preached quite a few expository sermons working through Biblical passages verse by verse offering advice to the faithful rather than a warning to sinners:

> Thus let us guard against the two fatal extremes never to grow weary and faint but to persevere hungering and thirsting and watching and praying with all prayer to the end of time expecting. On the other hand let us be careful not to trust in ourselves nor make a saviour of our works or exalt ourselves on account of our gifts or abilities or performances.[147]

One preacher, Richard Gower, superintendent of the Bedford circuit from 1818 to 1820, delivered sermons that were apparently 'remarkable for variety of matter'; but it should perhaps be deduced from that comment that the 'variety of matter' was sufficiently rare to be worthy of remark.[148]

Even if there was not much variation in what was said, the ever-changing succession of itinerants, who never spent more than three years on a circuit, brought with them a diverse range of exotic accents, from Yorkshire, Cornwall and Wales; and the ever-growing number of local preachers gave every Sunday a degree of novelty even in the villages.[149] Thirty years after he heard them, the voices of the preachers on the Ampthill circuit remained clear and distinct in George Coles' memory:

> Our local preachers were John Armstrong, a farmer by occupation, and a plain, pious, humble Christian, but not very gifted as a preacher; William Yates, a farmer also, equally plain, and equally pious, but much more gifted; and John Goss, a shoemaker, and by nature, I should think, as good a poet as Robert Bloomfield; John Curtiss also, a lace-dealer, one of the best local preachers with whom I was then acquainted. On one occasion he took for his text, Psalm lxvi, 16, and preached his own experience, which, to me, was very entertaining and profitable.[150]

It was not all heavy and tearful; many preachers used familiar language and were not above using humour. In one incident, the fame of which survived many years, John Leppington:

> In order forcibly to illustrate his subject, opened the pulpit door, and, placing himself on his back upon the short, steep handrail, he quickly slid to the bottom, and then vainly attempted to slide up again on his back, after which he walked up, re-entered the pulpit, and powerfully insisted on the danger of back-sliding – how easy to fall into sin, how difficult to obtain restoration.[151]

As Wesleyan preaching services became more numerous, more entertaining and more popular it is clear that they began to displace the class meeting as the focal moment of the local society's life. Looking back from his old age, George Coles could still name the preachers who visited Lidlington and Ampthill during the first two decades of the nineteenth century; he could even, in some instances, remember the texts on which they had preached; but he appears to have had no strong memory

---

[147] James Durley's sermon notes February 1811 to October 1812, CBS, DX 544/1.
[148] Hall, *Memorials of Wesleyan Methodist Ministers*, 232.
[149] Dunstable, for example saw 12 different preachers between October 1813 and April 1814 and Tebworth, 11.
[150] Coles, *Youthful days*, 131–2. Robert Bloomfield (1766–1823) was a peasant poet who enjoyed a certain vogue in the first decade of the nineteenth century. For the latter part of his life he lived at Shefford.
[151] Hawkes, *Rise of Wesleyan Sunday schools*, 6.

of his class leader or of the class meetings he attended. The rising importance of preaching within the Wesleyan community saw a concomitant raising of the status of preachers. The biographer of one local preacher was sure that his readers would not be surprised that he 'should have been called upon to exercise [his zeal and talents] in a more public manner than the mere office of leader admitted.'[152] Itinerant preachers began to be looked on as ministers and to be asked to baptise children and to preach funeral sermons, not only for society members but for villagers who attended the preaching services.[153] Some of them even began to take on the style of ministers. As early as 1813 Richard Eland

> walked to the house of God, dressed in a suit of rich black broadcloth, with breeches buttoned at the knee and fastened with a buckle, and black silk stockings and brightly-polished shoes, walking slowly and gracefully along in meditative mood, as if intent on holy things ... or that he had been brought up in London, or Cambridge, or Oxford, and that he wished to make Methodism appear respectable in the eyes of the world.[154]

The ambition to make Methodism respectable may also have played a part in the willingness shown by some Wesleyans to become involved in pan-evangelical committees. In 1797 the Wesleyans had held aloof from the Bedfordshire Union of Christians but, by 1812, the preachers of the Bedford circuit were enthusiastic supporters of the Bible Society and took their place on the platform with the Marquis of Tavistock at the inaugural meeting of a local branch.[155] The junior preacher's account of the proceedings for the *Methodist Magazine* veritably trembles with the excitement of such social acceptance:

> The noble President conducted himself with the greatest propriety; and in thus following in the steps of his father in this illustrious work of religion and charity, has set an excellent example to the young noblemen of the empire. ... [there was] the happiest spirit of zeal, benevolence and mutual regard.[156]

Six years later the same preacher, William Theobald, joined with Dissenting ministers from Bedfordshire and Huntingdonshire to launch an auxiliary of the Sunday School Union.[157]

A desire to see Methodism recognised as a fully-fledged Christian community alongside the Church and Dissent may also have lain behind the rapid and widespread introduction of communion, or sacrament, services in the first decade of the nineteenth century. There is no record of any of the Bedfordshire societies having sought permission from conference for such services before 1800 but by about

---

152 Greeves, *Memorials of Wm Cumberland*, 35.
153 The Luton preachers were baptising almost fifty children a year by 1824 (Luton Wesleyan circuit baptism register 1803–37, TNA RG8/1). Funeral sermons, on the evening of the burial, seem to have been fairly common by about 1815 (*MM* (1814), 366; *MM* (1816), 292 and 512). A manuscript funeral address from 1818 makes it clear that such sermons were not reserved for leading members. Elizabeth Shepherd, the subject of the address, was not well known to the preacher and had only shown signs of repentance during her last illness (CBS, NM 114/7/1).
154 Coles, *Youthful days*, 140–1.
155 *MM* (1812), 77. Intriguingly, the formation of the union was welcomed by the conference of the Methodist New Connexion, which had no presence in Bedfordshire (Crosland, 'The Bedford Association', 95).
156 *MM* (1812), 396.
157 *Evangelical Magazine* (1818), 442.

1815 almost half may have been holding sacrament services at least once a quarter.[158] The spread of these services has traditionally been presented as the result of popular demand but there is little evidence of their popularity. None of the surviving memoirs, obituaries or journals from this period mention participating in sacrament services and circuit preaching plans from the 1820s show a decline both in their frequency and in the number of places holding them.[159] This is not altogether surprising for while, from an ecclesiological perspective, the introduction of sacramental services may appear a natural step in the emergence of Wesleyan Methodism as a separate ecclesiastical community, in many ways it ran quite contrary to the tide which was carrying the movement out of its closed, sectarian backwater and into popular culture. With attendance restricted to members, and to those given special written permission by the superintendent, the sacrament service excluded the great majority of the people whom the new chapels, new preaching times and new music were attracting.[160]

In fact, the restrictive communion practice among Wesleyan Methodists is a reminder that the old patterns of Wesleyan thinking and practice continued to exist alongside the new throughout this period. In many, if not most, places congregations continued to consist primarily of members and regular attendance at the class meeting remained normative. Surviving class books from Bierton, North Marston and Whitchurch in the Aylesbury circuit, three 'closed' societies on the evidence of the 1829 clergy returns, show a very high rate of regularity in attendance as late as 1828.[161] Even in places like Bedford and Luton, with their new chapels, resident preachers and large congregations, some people continued to meet in class and even in bands; a few people continued the tradition of early morning meetings and others stayed after the evening preaching for a society meeting.[162]

The First Sunday Schools

Sunday preaching was not the only innovation that was eating away at the religious isolationism of traditional Wesleyan life. Several other new activities also began

---

[158]   St Albans and Stewkley, both in the Bedford circuit, sought permission in 1799 and 1802 respectively. Baldock, in the St Neots circuit, sought permission in 1800. Preaching plans for the Luton, Leighton Buzzard and Higham Ferrers circuits show that by about 1815, nine of the fifteen Bedfordshire societies in those circuits were holding sacramental services.

[159]   Thanks to the Marriott collection, preaching plans survive for all the local circuits in 1825 and they show only 17 of the 49 Wesleyan societies in Bedfordshire holding sacramental services. Two societies, Heath and Woburn, appear to have given them up and at Leighton Buzzard, Eaton Bray, Markyate and Tebworth their frequency appears to have been reduced.

[160]   Participation in the sacrament was restricted to members and to those given special tickets of admission. An example of such a ticket survives, uncatalogued, in the archive of the Aylesbury Wesleyan circuit, CBS.

[161]   At Whitchurch, in 1828, there were 13 members in Ann Durley's class: 2 had a very poor attendance but the remaining 11 had an 83% attendance rate even in July and August, the harvest months (Whitchurch Wesleyan class books 1821–81, CBS, NM 114/5/1).

[162]   Elizabeth Ekins 'began to meet in band' at Raunds with her sister and another young woman about 1816 (*MM* (1816), 50). There were 7.00am prayer meetings on a Sunday at Stewkley, Riseley and Raunds during this period, though poorly attended (Coles, *Youthful days*, 82; Harris, *To serve the present age*, 2; *MM* (1816), 25). Isaac Bradnack's diary for 1808 records: 'After preaching, in meeting the society I read our Rules, which appeared to give universal satisfaction' (Rowland, *Memoirs of Isaac Bradnack*, 66). Mary Howard's conversion took place in Bedford chapel 'during the meeting of the society after preaching' on a Monday evening in 1804 (*MM* (1814), 285).

both to make their mark on the rhythm of the Methodist calendar and to change Methodism's relationship with the wider community. Perhaps the most important was the Sunday school. The local impetus for these schools seems to have come from the same people and the same thinking that were transforming Wesleyan preaching services into public worship. John Leppington, the superintendent who oversaw the building of large chapels at Bedford and Leighton Buzzard, was also responsible for initiating the first Wesleyan Sunday school in Bedfordshire at Luton in 1803.[163] At Ampthill too, the launch of a Sunday school seems to have followed on naturally from the opening of the Methodist society's first chapel.[164]

Thomas Laqueur's study of the British Sunday school movement, which drew heavily on evidence from the industrial mill towns, concluded that laymen took the dominant role in the launching of Sunday schools but it is striking that the Wesleyan schools in Bedfordshire were principally found, like the large congregations of hearers, in the places where the itinerant preachers concentrated their Sunday labours and presumably had greatest influence.[165] Of the nine Wesleyan Sunday schools in Bedfordshire in 1825, six were in places where the itinerants were actually resident.[166]

The schools, like the new chapels, were hugely popular. At Markyate, there were 119 children enrolled by 1818, at Luton there may have been as many as 150, and even in the hamlet of Leagrave the school attracted 84 scholars.[167] Nevertheless, the majority of Wesleyan societies were slow to emulate these ventures and it was not until the 1830s that Sunday schools became commonplace. Cost may have been a factor, for even though they were staffed by volunteers the schools were not cheap to run. The outgoings of the Sunday school at Whitchurch, in the Aylesbury circuit, were £10 8s 10d in 1825, a hefty additional commitment for a society whose annual contribution to circuit expenses was only about £16.[168] There may also, however, have been objections on principle. There was certainly fierce debate, in 1822, when a Sunday school was proposed in connection with the Baptist church at Quainton, in Buckinghamshire, a congregation that had begun life as a Wesleyan society. Those in favour of the proposal felt that 'a Sunday School ... would be the means to increase the Congregation for they said if they taught peoples Children the parents of the Children would attend the chapel.' Others, however, including one who had

---

163 'Mr Leppington promised the Luton friends that if they would raise a Sunday School, and furnish a room, he would provide all the necessary books free of cost for one year' Hawkes, *Rise of Wesleyan Sunday schools*, 6.

164 George Coles recalled that 'Regular preaching having now been established among us, it was thought that we must open a Sabbath school' (Coles, *Youthful days*, 137–8).

165 Laqueur, *Religion and respectability*, 33.

166 Hawkes, *Rise of Wesleyan Sunday schools*, 5–7; Coles, *Youthful days*, 138. Biggleswade Sunday school seems to date from 1810 (Phillips, *Wesleyan Methodist church, Biggleswade Circuit*, 9). The accounts of the Leighton Buzzard Wesleyan Sunday school begin in 1814 (BLARS, MB 251) and Bedford appears to have started the same year (Powers, *Brief memoir of Sarah Fisher*, 3). Leagrave Sunday school was active by 1819 (Franklin, *Century and a half and more*, 4). Markyate and Tempsford are both mentioned in the 'Digest of returns to a circular letter from the select committee on education of the poor &c. 1818' (reprinted in Bushby, *Bedfordshire schoolchild*, 40 and 51). Tebworth existed by the early 1820s (*WMM* (1824), 501).

167 Bushby, *Bedfordshire schoolchild*, 40; Hawkes, *Rise of Wesleyan Sunday schools*, 17; Franklin, *Century and a half and more*, 4.

168 Whitchurch Sunday School accounts 1824–8, CBS, NM 114/6/1.

been brought up a Wesleyan, opposed the idea, arguing that 'a thorough reformation in our own Conduct was the most likly means to increase the Congregation.'[169] Many Methodists it would seem agreed; the purpose of their societies was to discipline their own sinful hearts, not to teach their neighbours' children how to read.

The limited interest among the Wesleyans is all the more striking when contrasted with the Church of England's enthusiasm for Sunday schools. By 1818 sixty-four Bedfordshire parishes, about half the total, supported a Sunday school, and over 4,000 children were enrolled. The parish church at Podington was typical of many, having 'A Sunday school for the education of twenty-eight boys and twenty-one girls, supported partly by voluntary subscriptions and partly by a parish rate.' It taught reading (but not writing), and instructed the children 'in the first principles of religion according to the Established Church.'[170] If the purpose of Church Sunday schools was to shore up support for the Established church, and to provide a bulwark against the suddenly rising tide of Methodism and Dissent, they may well have been a serious miscalculation. It has often been argued that Sunday schools were an important engine of Methodist growth and there is evidence that Methodist recruitment did rely in large measure on a religious upbringing. In Bedfordshire, however, it appears that it was the Church of England, rather than the Methodists themselves, who inadvertently trained up this pool of potential recruits.

Where Wesleyan Sunday schools were founded it is evident that their primary objective was, from the beginning, religious rather than educational. The public announcement of the opening of a school at Whitchurch, in 1823, made clear that its object was to make the children 'followers of him who said "learn of me"'.[171] Like the Baptists at Quainton, Wesleyans saw a Sunday school as a doorway into homes that might otherwise be shut to them. Teachers calling on their pupils might leave a tract for the other members of the household to read or the children themselves might bring home some spark of religious truth which would lighten their parents' darkness. The story of John Swanell of St Neots, told in the obituary column of the *Wesleyan Methodist Magazine*, expresses the ideal outcome of the Sunday school's influence. John was a drunken sabbath-breaker but

> His daughter, then comparatively a child, attended the Methodist Sunday-School, and had little books given her as rewards: these she read to her father; and by this means he was induced to hear the Methodist Ministers. ... He was enabled to believe with his heart unto righteousness.[172]

Sarah Fisher of Bedford, whose short life was memorialised in a locally produced tract, likewise often went home and told her parents what she had learnt in the Sunday school, the preacher's text and the substance of sermons.[173]

It was not merely into the homes of sinners, however, that Wesleyans appear to have hoped that their schools would give them a new entrée. The printed announcement of the launch of the Whitchurch school was made to the 'Benevolent Public'

169   Kussmaul, *Autobiography of Joseph Mayett*, 75.
170   Bushby, *Bedfordshire schoolchild*, 37–59.
171   Whitchurch Wesleyan Sunday school rules and regulations 1821 (Whitchurch Methodist church vestry).
172   *WMM* (1826), 574–5.
173   Powers, *Memoir of Sarah Fisher*, 4.

and it is fair to conclude that it was aimed at people who were literate, affluent and beyond the narrow boundaries of the Methodist community. In Bedford, much was made of the young Sarah Fisher's faithful acceptance of her terminal illness and members of the wider community, including apparently two Jewish women, were encouraged to visit the dying child and see for themselves the miraculous effects of a Wesleyan Sunday school education: 'Numbers hearing of the happy state of her mind, daily flocked to witness the truth of what was rumoured abroad respecting this amiable child'.[174] Sunday schools, it seems, were viewed as a vehicle to enhance Methodism's reputation among its better-off neighbours, at a time when it was under suspicion, and perhaps even secure their financial support, at a time when it was chronically short of funds. All these motives – proselytization, respectability and money – are evident in the emergence of what would become one of the great festivals of the Methodist year, the Sunday school anniversary. As early as 1815 the anniversary service at Leighton Buzzard was a sufficiently major affair to justify the printing of special hymn-sheets and by 1818 even the Leagrave anniversary justified the expense of a guest preacher.[175] A collection in aid of the school was, of course, central to the occasion, but to draw a crowd and loosen purse-strings there were musical performances by the children and the latest hymns. This was the very acme of the new Methodism, religion as a form of popular entertainment.

The weekly cycle of Sunday school life was more mundane. At Leighton Buzzard, school began at eight o'clock in the summer and nine in the winter and continued until half-past ten when the children took their places in the chapel for the morning service. In the afternoon there were two sessions, one from one o'clock until about half-past two, which appears to have been for the younger children, and another from about half-past two until half-past four for the older children who had been to the afternoon service while the earlier session was in progress.[176] At Ampthill even the school sessions were given over in part to devotional exercises, with a hymn, a prayer, a chapter of the Bible and an address preceding the actual lessons.[177] At first the only books available were Wesley's hymns and the Bible but some educational material was gradually introduced. At Luton, the lessons were 'pasted on thin boards, about six inches long and three wide, square at the top and rounded off where they were held in the hand, with the alphabet on one side and short words on the other.'[178] The regulations of the Leighton Buzzard Sunday school left open the possibility of teaching writing as well as reading but strictly forbade 'the teaching of Accompts'.[179] Whether writing was ever taught is not clear but it would have been against official Wesleyan policy which viewed writing on a Sunday to be a breach of the fourth commandment.

---

174 Powers, *Memoir of Sarah Fisher*, 6.
175 Hymns to be sung at the Methodist chapel, Leighton Buzzard, BLARS, Z1115/1; Franklin, *Century and a half and more*, 4. See also Service sheet for Bedford Wesleyan Sunday school anniversary 1825, MARC, MAW LHB 4.10. In 1818 the Northampton Sunday school spent £3 on the guest preacher's travelling expenses, £1 17s 6d on 700 hymn-sheets and 5s on paying someone to teach the children to sing, but the collection on the day exceeded £20 (Bowles, *One hundred and forty two years*, 9).
176 Brigg, *Methodism in the Leighton Buzzard circuit*.
177 Coles, *Youthful days*, 138.
178 Hawkes, *Rise of Wesleyan Sunday schools*, 20.
179 Brigg, *Methodism in the Leighton Buzzard circuit*.

Securing regular attendance and good behaviour were not always easy. At Leighton Buzzard each child was required to pay the treasurer 1d each week as a kind of bond, with the money being returned at the end of the year if the child had not been expelled or ceased to attend.[180] At Northampton more drastic steps were required and it was resolved that 'a scaffold be erected at the end of the school room to reform those boys that are not so good as they should be.'[181]

The Missionary Society

Collections for the West India Mission are first mentioned in the Bedford circuit book in 1802. In that year John Leppington sent £11 13s 5d to Dr Coke and by 1806, when Coke himself visited the area, the annual total had risen to £24 10s 6d, an amount equivalent to the circuit's contribution to Kingswood school and three times the size of the amount collected for the worn-out preachers' fund.[182] That same year Elizabeth Harvey, Wesley's hostess on many occasions during the 1780s though never a Wesleyan member herself, left £2,400 to Methodist missions under the terms of her will.[183] It was an early indication that, perhaps to an even greater degree than their Sunday schools, Methodist overseas missionary work might win for the movement the approval of the social élite and even their financial support.[184]

The missionary cause soon became much more than simply the beneficiary of an annual collection among the societies. In April 1817 a Bedfordshire branch missionary society was formed to recruit collectors, mainly young women, and gather weekly subscriptions.[185] By 1825 most circuits, and even some individual congregations, had organised their own missionary societies.[186] The initiative seems, once again, to have come largely from the professional preachers: the secretary of the provisional committee at Bedford was the superintendent, John Smith, while at Aylesbury the junior minister was the first secretary of the society and the superintendent, the treasurer.[187] In some places monthly missionary prayer meetings were introduced at which articles from *Missionary Notices* were read out, rather in the manner of the old Moravian letter days, but these appear to have had a rather chequered existence.[188] The real impact of the missionary societies on the calendar of Methodist life was undoubtedly their annual meetings which immediately became

---

[180] Brigg, *Methodism in the Leighton Buzzard circuit.*

[181] Bowles, *One hundred and forty two years*, 9.

[182] Bedfordshire Wesleyan circuit book 1781–1806, BLARS, MB 1. Coke spent two weeks at Bedford and Biddenham in 1806 (Vickers, *Thomas Coke*, 420–3).

[183] Will of Elizabeth Harvey, TNA, PROB11/1459/128.

[184] Early subscribers included William Wilberforce, Thomas Haweis and the Earl of Belvidere (Vickers, *Thomas Coke*, 266).

[185] Poster for the inaugural meeting of Bedfordshire Wesleyan missionary society 1817, BLARS, X 37/42/3. Sophia Potts of Toddington was one of the first collectors (*MM* (1821), 536).

[186] Luton Wesleyan circuit missionary society accounts 1825–98 and Biggleswade Wesleyan circuit missionary society accounts 1823–47, BLARS, MB 394 and 862; Poster for first anniversary of Aylesbury Wesleyan circuit missionary society 1825 and poster for Whitchurch Wesleyan missionary society 1826, CBS, NM 100/9/1/1 and 114/9/1/1.

[187] Invitation to inaugural meeting of Bedfordshire Wesleyan missionary society, BLARS, X 37/42/3; Subscription registers for Whitchurch Wesleyan missionary society, CBS, NM 114/4/2.

[188] At Aylesbury the monthly missionary prayer meetings were introduced in 1826 but abandoned by 1829, reintroduced briefly in 1837 and then again in 1840 (Aylesbury Wesleyan circuit preaching plans 1813–80, CBS, NM 100/8/1). Missionary prayer meetings were also held for a while at Whitchurch (Whitchurch Wesleyan missionary society reports, CBS, NM 114/4/2).

one of the festivals of the Methodist year. A poster for the inaugural meeting of the Bedfordshire branch shows events over two days, including three sermons by leading London ministers as well as the main missionary meeting. Considerable space was given to listing the exotic places in which Wesleyan missionaries were at work – Jaffnapatam, Sierra Leone, Tortola and the Virgin Islands – and such were the numbers anticipated that, in a piece of interdenominational co-operation, the final service was moved from the Wesleyan chapel in Bedford to the town's Old Meeting.

At the outset these missionary meetings seem to have been deliberately staged as major public events rather than as a simply Methodist festival. The arrangements for the first anniversary of the Aylesbury auxiliary society, in 1825, certainly suggest that the aim was not merely to deliver a good turn-out of Wesleyans but to attract support from respectable and affluent members of the wider community, perhaps even the kind of evangelical gentry that Wesley had been able to count on for hospitality and patronage. So the meeting was announced by public posters and scheduled for a workday morning rather than a Sunday. It was held in the County Hall, by permission of the High-Sheriff, rather than in the chapel. It was chaired by a gentleman, Lancelot Hanslope JP, and structured around a series of formal resolutions. The flyers were addressed Sirs rather than Brethren or Friends, and the front seats in the hall were reserved for the Ladies.[189] Perhaps the most telling detail of all is that the lunch served in the White Hart Inn after the meeting cost 2s 6d a head, and this in a circuit where 184 out of 245 members could not afford 1d a week and 1s a quarter in class and ticket money.[190]

Preserved in the archives of the Aylesbury circuit are manuscripts of five addresses given at missionary meetings, four speeches from Whitchurch and one from Aylesbury. These also suggest that the expected audience at these events was both denominationally mixed and rather better educated than the mass of Methodist members. The sophistication of the arguments employed contrasts strikingly with the unvarying predictability of the sermons considered earlier. Methodist missionaries were effecting the moral reformation of a dark world where widow-burning and child-sacrifice were common place. They were engaged in a struggle for the soul of Britain's empire with modern 'infidels' who were interested only in financial gain and would cause God to withdraw his blessing from the nation if unchecked. They were champions of moderate, sensible Christianity exposing the errors of the pre-millenarian enthusiasts who wanted to leave the conversion of the world to Jesus on his return. They were unsectarian Christians working in a common cause with evangelical Christians of every hue: 'the Methodist stream, the Moravian stream, the Church of England stream, the Baptist stream, the Congregationalist stream, and other streams' all slaking 'the thirst of a famishing world.'[191] It was clearly a message not just designed to inspire Methodists to give but carefully crafted to play well with wealthy evangelicals from both the church and meeting-house.

---

[189] Poster for first anniversary Aylesbury Wesleyan circuit missionary society, CBS, NM 114/4/2.

[190] Letter from the Aylesbury Wesleyan circuit stewards to the president of the Conference 10 July 1828, CBS, NM 100/5/1A.

[191] Four speeches survive from the Whitchurch Wesleyan missionary meeting in 1833 and one from the Aylesbury Wesleyan circuit missionary meeting of 1834, CBS, NM 114/4/23–25, 27 and 28.

These ambitions may have achieved some initial success. Three Church of England clergymen joined the platform at a missionary meeting in Luton and a leading Dissenter took the chair at the Bedford meeting in 1822.[192] The financial accounts for Whitchurch, in the Aylesbury circuit, show that some two-thirds of the people subscribing to the missionary society in 1827 were neither members nor pew-holders.[193] It was not to be sustained, however, and by the 1830s missionary meetings had evolved into a more obviously denominational event. At Aylesbury the dinner at the White Hart was never repeated and although the meeting in the County Hall continued to be held until the 1840s it was moved to the early evening when it was easier for working people to attend. The public meeting was, in any case, becoming a less important part of the anniversary. In 1825 a preparatory sermon had been preached on the evening before the anniversary but by 1834 the sermon had been moved to a Sunday and was being given top billing on the posters.[194]

One of the key purposes of both the missionary meeting and the missionary sermon was, of course, to provide an opportunity to take a collection in aid of missionary society funds. Whatever disappointment the missionary anniversary may have been in attracting a different class of support for Methodism, as a means of generating funds it was clearly successful. In 1806 the collections for missions held in the Bedford circuit had represented the equivalent of 6d per member, but by 1827 they represented 4s per member.[195] This level of generosity is all the more striking when set in the context of the parlous financial state of the local circuits. The accounts of the Whitchurch society provide a stark example. A chapel had been built in the village in 1808 and enlarged in 1815 at a total cost of £464 4s 3d, three-quarters of which was raised on loans. In 1821 the annual interest payment owed on that debt was £18 3s and the annual income of the trustees from seat rents and the anniversary collection was £17 18s 6d. By 1830 the trustees' total income had fallen to £8 14s and the debt on the property had risen to twice its value but the contribution to missions stood at £8 3s 4½d.[196] The first annual report of the Whitchurch missionary association in 1827 had acknowledged that:

> As the inhabitants of this place subscribe both to the Sunday school and the tract society, it was feared by some that the application for subscriptions for the missionary purpose would be detrimental to these institutions.

It insisted, however, that

> Experience, however, proves that the excitement of liberality, and the awakening of compassionate exertions on behalf of the destitute Heathen, will rather deepen the sensibilities of the heart and expand into a broader stream the charities which it sends forth for the benefit of kindred objects.[197]

It is hard to avoid the observation that the amount raised for missions almost exactly matches the decline in the chapel trustees' income or that in the local circuit

[192]   *MM* (1822), 478.
[193]   Whitchurch Wesleyan missionary society collection books, CBS, NM 114/4/2/18.
[194]   Poster for first anniversary of Aylesbury Wesleyan circuit missionary society 1825, and Poster for annual missionary sermons 1834, CBS, NM 100/9/1/1 and 114/9/1.
[195]   Bedfordshire Wesleyan circuit book 1781–1806, BLARS, MB 1.
[196]   Whitchurch Wesleyan chapel papers and accounts 1821–79, CBS, NM 114/7/7.
[197]   Whitchurch Wesleyan missionary society report 1827, CBS, NM 114/3/6/26.

as a whole the total amount sent to support foreign missions was almost identical to the deficit that necessitated a cut in the number of paid preachers and an inevitable limiting of the circuit's capacity to expand.[198]

There was more to the missionary cause than money and respectability; there was a certain romance that transformed Methodism from being an intensely local phenomenon into an imperial, if not cosmic, cause. Stirred by that vision, or by the opportunity to see foreign lands, a string of local young men, beginning in 1806 with John Constable from St Albans, applied to be missionaries. William Peet, a 25-year-old weaver from Bedford, offered to go to 'any part of the world', as did Edward Handscombe from Biggleswade, though he subsequently changed his mind.[199] Henry Fleet, from Bierton in the Aylesbury circuit, offered himself for missionary work 'in any part of the world the conference may think proper to appoint him, except Sierra Leone.' Perhaps inevitably it was to Sierra Leone that he was sent, with his new wife, Hannah Tearle from Stanbridge. She died before reaching their destination and he survived only a few months. They were both 22 years old.[200] Others were more fortunate. John Manton, from Biggleswade, was sent to Van Diemen's Land, where he became a prominent public figure.

The Upright Walk

It was not only in Methodism's communal life that change was evident during these years. The personal discipline of Wesleyans also appears to have evolved. High moral standards had always been part of the expectations of Wesleyan membership but when the community began to grow at an unprecedented rate the outward behaviour of members seems to have acquired even greater importance. In the eighteenth century the obituaries published in the *Arminian Magazine* had focussed primarily on the spiritual experience of their subjects, their struggle to feel forgiven and the ebb and flow of their joy and despair. Only one of the hagiographies relating to members of the Bedfordshire circuit written before 1800 makes any reference to the outward behaviour of its subject: William Parker was apparently 'a great example of good works.'[201] After 1800 such comments become commonplace. The outward conduct of Sophia Potts of Toddington was 'blameless'; Virtue Kingham of Luton was 'irreproachable'; John Ranshall of Bedford displayed the 'strictest integrity'; in fact, forty-two of the fifty-three obituaries published between 1800 and 1830 specifically praised the exemplary behaviour of the departed.[202]

One possible explanation for this shift in emphasis is that it reflects a change in the way in which ordinary Methodists saw themselves and practised their faith. They were no longer overwhelmed by their unworthiness, but rather more willing to believe that they had been transformed into better people and genuinely placed greater emphasis on the outward signs of that transformation. John Marlow's obit-

---

[198] Between 1826 and 1828 the Aylesbury circuit steward had to advance the circuit £74 to cover its deficit and an arrangement for sharing a second preacher with a neighbouring circuit had to be abandoned. In the same period the circuit sent £82 to the missionary fund (Letter from the Aylesbury Wesleyan circuit stewards to the president of the Conference, 10 July 1828, CBS, NM 100/5/1A).
[199] London west Wesleyan district minutes 1824 and 1827, MARC.
[200] *WMM* (1839), 85–6, 851–2; (1840), 328–9.
[201] *AM* (1785), 624.
[202] *MM* (1821), 535; *WMM* (1828), 215; *MM* (1825), 142.

uary in 1810 claims that after his conversion 'the change soon became visible to all around him' and Mary Gilbert's in 1816 that it was 'evident to all around her that she was the subject of real change.'[203] This self-confident superiority, or 'spiritual snobbishness' as Stuart Andrews has called it, may have been a contributory factor in Methodism's growth, attracting those who aspired to be a little better, a little more respectable, than their neighbours.[204]

Another explanation is that the increasing emphasis on moral standards in the model lives enshrined in the *Methodist Magazine*, as the *Arminian Magazine* was renamed in 1798, is not a reflection of what was happening in the towns and villages of Bedfordshire but of what was going on in the heads of the preachers who wrote those obituaries and, even more importantly, of the editors who selected them for publication. The emphasis on high moral standards in fact reflects a concern that these could no longer be taken for granted. Was there some edge to the comment in Mary Wale's obituary that she had 'proved the sincerity of her profession by an upright walk'?[205] Or in Mr Blunt's, that he had 'walked worthy of his high vocation'?[206] It is certainly interesting that steadiness and consistency are perhaps the most frequently celebrated virtues in the obituaries of this period and yet it is known that the turnover of members had increased dramatically. Indeed, it is quite possible that the virtues most celebrated were those that were least evident, and that what the obituaries reveal is that early nineteenth-century Methodists were often irregular in their attendance, neglectful of private devotions, showy in their dress, unsupportive of the preachers and reluctant to part with their cash. The truth may well be that these explanations are not mutually exclusive.

Aspiration and Respectability

Among the records of the Wesleyan chapels at Whitchurch and Bierton in Buckinghamshire are plans of the interior layouts of the two chapels from the 1820s. Both show a departure from the old custom of backless forms and segregated sexes, and the introduction of clear social distinctions in the seating arrangements for Methodist worship. At the front of both chapels, either side of the pulpit, there were now pews allocated to the families of the chapels' principal supporters. At Whitchurch, the central body of the chapel was then given over to pews reserved for the other members of the congregation able to pay for their seats. At Bierton, it appears the rentable pews occupied the first rows of seating either side of a central aisle. In both cases the poor were consigned to the extremities and at Whitchurch they seem to have been allocated moveable benches.[207] This was the kind of Methodist congregation that William Cobbett stumbled across, riding through Kent in 1823:

> Coming through the village of Benenden, I heard a man, at my right, talking very loud about *houses! houses! houses!* It was a Methodist parson ... 'Do you KNOW,' said he, laying great stress on the word KNOW: 'do you KNOW, that you have ready for you houses, houses I say; I say do you KNOW; do you

[203] *MM* (1810), 482; *MM* (1816), 213.
[204] Andrews, *Methodism and society*, 70.
[205] *WMM* (1828), 645.
[206] *WMM* (1827), 431.
[207] Bierton Wesleyan chapel steward's book, 1827–60 and Whitchurch Wesleyan chapel steward's accounts 1808–87, CBS, NM 102/3/1 and NM 114/3/6.

KNOW that you have houses in the heavens not made with hands? Do you KNOW this from *experience?*' ... Some girls whom I saw in the room, plump and rosy as could be, did not seem at all daunted by these menaces; and indeed, they appeared to me to be thinking much more about getting houses for themselves *in this world first:* just to *see a little* before they entered, or endeavoured to enter, or even thought much about, those *'houses'* of which the parson was speaking.[208]

Indeed, the obituaries of local Methodists from this period regularly assert the material blessings which attended religious faithfulness. Sarah Thorpe of Buckingham, for example, was a widow with a large family to support 'but from the time she sought the Lord, an evident blessing attended the work of her hands, so that she and her family had all things needful.'[209] Nor was this entirely wishful thinking, for as Methodism grew the network of Methodists became a significant economic interest. When Daniel Pressland of Higham Ferrers set up his own business about 1800:

Money was offered to him on loan to any extent he might require; and by one generous friend a considerable sum of money was put into his hands. ... God was with him, and he prospered in all that he undertook; so that he was soon enabled to repay the loans with which he had been kindly assisted, and to enlarge his own business by his increasing capital. A number of persons from the adjacent villages ... flocked to [his shop] as purchasers; and some of them, many years after, exhibited the articles which they had first purchased, having kept them as relics of the occasion.[210]

Little wonder that, in 1813, an anonymous pamphleteer wrote of Methodism that 'The immediate temporal advantages which people of the lower classes feel as soon as they enter the society must be numbered among the most efficient causes of its rapid and continual increase.'[211] Whether there was real material benefit for the majority of those who joined must be questionable but the prospect of it certainly seems to have been part of Methodism's appeal and to have been actively marketed as such by the Wesleyans themselves.

Even when there was no material benefit, Methodism may still have provided much that appealed to the ambitious and aspiring. When Samuel Bennett moved to Tempsford from Leicestershire he was labelled the 'new farmer' by his neighbours and clearly struggled to establish his place in the local social hierarchy. Founding a Methodist society created a new social space within which he immediately became a senior and respected figure.[212] William Hale White pointed to a similar function of the Wesleyan chapel in 'Cowfold', his fictionalised version of Bedford. Its principal supporter was a businessman who thought himself a cut above the shopkeepers at the meeting-house but knew he would be overshadowed at the parish church.[213]

More generally, attending the smart new chapel of the successful new religious community may have worked for women and men of the early nineteenth century

---

208 Cobbett, *Rural rides*, 181–2.
209 *MM* (1810), 243
210 *WMM* (1845), 839–40.
211 Quoted in Warner, *Wesleyan movement in the industrial revolution*, 191.
212 *WMM* (1841), 707–9.
213 Rutherford, *Tanner's Lane*, 196.

as designer labels do for their twenty-first-century descendants, providing status by association.

Part 4 Methodists and Politics

The Politics of Self-defence

A movement that enjoyed such a degree of popular support clearly had the potential to become a political force and there were moments when it showed signs of becoming one. Francis Hews had no qualms about using his pulpit in Dunstable to wade into deep political waters and in about 1799 preached

> against the covetousness of farmers, who were getting up corn so high, as to distress many families; and glorying in their wickedness, in so doing. I said, I thought there had been many a man hanged at Tyburn, that, in point of roguishness, no more deserved it, than some farmers; and so I think still.[214]

Seventeen years later a Methodist printer would be imprisoned in Northampton gaol for political libel.[215]

The full potential of Methodist political muscle was laid bare in 1811 when concern about the movement's growth prompted Lord Sidmouth to bring a bill before parliament that would have effectively outlawed the Methodist circuit system.[216] Preachers would have been licensed only to an individual congregation and the license would have required the support of several local residents of substance.

George Coles later recalled the speed with which Bedfordshire Wesleyans responded:

> When Lord Sidmouth's bill, for the suppression of what the Church considered unordained and unauthorized preachers, was brought into parliament, Mr Curtiss [a local preacher] took a very active part in obtaining signatures to petitions against the bill. These petitions were drawn up in legal form on sheets of parchment about three feet wide and four feet long, beautifully engrossed, and addressed 'To the lords spiritual and temporal' of the British realm. ... This was the only instance that ever occurred in which I felt it to be my duty and privilege to sign a petition to the British legislature, ... But I was indebted to the vigilance and activity of Mr Curtiss for the opportunity. He mounted his horse and rode through the country like an 'express,' and wherever he found a Methodist, or a Protestant dissenter, whose signature he was likely to obtain, he presented the petition.[217]

The petition from the Wesleyan society at Wing, in the Leighton Buzzard circuit, is one of the few that have survived but it amply demonstrates the unity of purpose which the bill provoked.[218] The society managed to collect twenty-six signatures even though a year later it would still have only thirteen men amongst its members. Another petition, from Aylesbury, clearly shows Wesleyans and evan-

214 Hews, *Spoils won in the day of battle*, 185.
215 Hobsbawm, 'Methodism and the threat of revolution in Britain', 23–33.
216 Davis, *Political change and continuity*, 66.
217 Coles, *Youthful days*, 132–3.
218 Petition to the House of Lords from the Protestant Dissenters of Wing, CBS, DX 603/8.

gelical Dissenters making common cause. So strong was the reaction to the bill, from across the country, that it was lost in the House of Lords on its second reading without a division.

Having seen off the threat to their circuit preaching, the Wesleyans appear to have stepped immediately back into the political shadows. There is no record of local circuits petitioning parliament again until the 1840s nor of them taking an official stance on any political issue until the election of 1830.[219]

In fact, there is clear evidence that local Wesleyans were actively encouraged to abstain from politics. In one election-tide sermon, at Luton, they were apparently warned that 'Although they were to give their votes they … were to take no prominent part as partisans and canvassers of either side … [for] political excitement was incompatible with a healthy spiritual state and … mixing in party-strife would be destructive to religious peace of mind.'[220] When the few members who were voters went to the poll, the others were called to a prayer meeting to ask God 'that the followers of John Wesley might not be embroiled in the conflict then raging around them.' At Bedford too, William Cumberland, the aged patriarch of the society, expressed himself 'more than ordinarily happy and more detached from the world … during the late contested election; which agitated so many minds. – "Now", said he, "is the time to pray to be kept from all evil"'.[221] This was certainly connexional policy and the official obituaries of itinerant preachers from this period are careful to underscore their commitment to the old Church of England doctrine of Passive Obedience. Joseph Hallam for one 'prayed with great fervour and affection for the king and the great men of the land'; John Crickett was likewise 'a steady loyalist, even when the French Revolution had unhappily excited in this country a spirit of disaffection'; and Isaac Bradnack 'avoided all intermeddling with these matters.'[222]

Although there may be doubts about how rank-and-file Wesleyans responded to this teaching in the industrial districts of northern England, in Bedfordshire at least the poll-books suggest that most members accepted it. If they cast their votes as a civic duty that was a matter quite separate from the business of being a Methodist. In the 1790 borough election there were eight electors who were Wesleyan members. Four of them did not vote and those who did all gave their support to William Colhoun, a candidate backed by the Duke of Bedford but who, as a Jamaican slave-owner, might have been thought objectionable to Methodists. In 1807, only 17 Wesleyan members can be identified among the voters in a poll of the shire, 9 of whom plumped for John Osborn, the candidate of the Tory gentry, as against 5 who voted for Francis Pym and Richard Fitzpatrick, the duke's candidates, and 2 who split their votes between the two camps. The shire polls of 1820 and 1826 paint a very similar picture, with only a handful of Wesleyans qualified to vote and those

219 The *Methodist Magazine* carries a long and detailed account of a county meeting in Bedford in 1823 which submitted a petition to parliament on the practice of widow-burning in India, a popular evangelical cause since before 1813, but there is no indication that any Wesleyans took part in the proceedings (*MM* (1823), 442–8).
220 *Luton Reporter* 20 July 1895.
221 Greeves, *Memorials of Wm Cumberland*, 52.
222 Hall, *Memorials of Wesleyan Methodist Ministers*, 40 and 42; Rowland, *Memoirs of Isaac Bradnack*, 122.

who used their vote almost evenly divided in their support for the different candidates. Most tellingly perhaps, having been disproportionately represented on the Bedford corporation in the eighteenth century, no Wesleyan appears to have sat on that body in the first three decades of the nineteenth century.

The 'no politics' rule of the Wesleyan connexion has often been represented as something imposed upon the movement by a national leadership who were either frightened by Sidmouth's bill or working to a politically conservative agenda. In Bedfordshire it seems to have been a genuine expression of the community's active disinterest in politics and to re-enforce the impression that the growth of Methodism locally in the early nineteenth century owed much more to a rising tide of aspiration than to an upsurge of feeling against the establishment.

Part 5 Contemporary Responses to Methodism

The rapid growth of Methodism and evangelical Dissent did not go unnoticed. Robert Woodward, vicar of Harrold, raised an alarm about the 'additional number of dissenting teachers dispersed among us, and an increase of meetings and conventicles' as early as 1799.[223] A second, enlarged edition of his book appeared in 1802 and reported on a worsening situation in which 'separation from the church has for the last few years increased beyond all credibility, and an inconceivable number of new meeting houses have been built.'[224] Woodward evidently wrote from close observation of what was happening in his own and neighbouring parishes. His description of the way in which new congregations were established closely mirrors the accounts given in Methodist sources:

> Their method in causing and increasing divisions, is as follows. In a parish where there were no dissenters, nor dissenting meetings; application is made to some inhabitant with whom there is a probability of succeeding, to use his house or barn as a place of meeting, to pray, and to preach the Gospel. If unsuccessful, then a dissenter is contrived to be settled in that parish: a meeting is soon afterwards announced; the novelty induces the neighbours to assemble: When the different mode of religious service, together with new and uncouth expressions, are disgusting to some; others mock and laugh. ... Some few are gained over to believe their erroneous doctrines of a new, easier, and better road to Salvation, than through the Church of God. These meetings once commenced, continue, and become established.[225]

Although he uses the term Dissent throughout the book, it is clear from the local examples which he quotes that Woodward was writing as much about Methodists as Baptists and Independents.[226] It seems highly unlikely that he was unaware of the distinctions between the two; only a few years before, in the episcopal visitation of 1788, the Bedfordshire clergy had been asked to report separately on Method-

---

[223] Woodward, *Candid Consideration of the Causes and Pretences for Separation from the Ancient Established Church*, iii.
[224] Woodward, *Causes and pretences*, 124.
[225] Woodward, *Causes and pretences*, 47–8.
[226] Woodward, *Causes and pretences*, 123. His list of 'Dissenting' congregations includes Milton Ernest and Tebworth, both Wesleyan congregations.

ists and Dissenters in their parishes and the returns suggest that they generally had no real difficulty in doing so. Rather, his lumping the new congregations together as belonging to one movement underlines the fact that Methodists and Dissenters were now operating in a very similar way and his use of the word Dissent rather than Methodist to describe them suggests that it was not what he associated with traditional Methodism. For Woodward, as a parish clergyman, the real issue with the multiplication of cottage meetings was that they undermined the status of the clergy, by allowing 'crafty tradesmen, low mechanics, and illiterate labourers' to assume the role of rival sources of religious and moral guidance, spiritual comfort and rites of passage. The results of this, he clearly felt, were already tangible: 'These audacious assertions and insinuations, place the clergy in a very unfavourable light ... disliked by many of the parishioners, perhaps by most of them.'[227]

Others viewed the proliferation of preachers and meetings with even greater apprehension, fearing that it endangered not only the status of the village parson but also the *status quo* of society as a whole. Samuel Horsley, who had been archdeacon of St Albans in the 1780s, was one of those who saw a dark conspiracy at work:

> In many parts of the kingdom new conventicles have been opened in great number, and congregations formed of one knows not what denomination. The pastor is often, in appearance at least, an illiterate peasant, or mechanic. The congregation is visited occasionally by preachers from a distance. Sunday-schools are opened in connection, with these conventicles. There is much reason to suspect, that the expences of these schools and conventicles are defrayed by associations formed in different places. ... It is very remarkable, that these new congregations of non-descripts have been mostly formed, since the Jacobins have been laid under the restraint of those two most salutary statutes, commonly known by the names of the Sedition and the Treason Bill. ... The Jacobins of this country, I very much fear, are at this moment, making a tool of Methodism ...[228]

The archdeacon of Buckingham, likewise feared that the Bedfordshire Union of Christians would 'produce discord and division among the people, and destroy religious communion, which is the bond of society.' He too drew parallels with revolutionary France and warned that 'Innovators and reformers should keep these things in remembrance.'[229]

Nor was it just the clergy who were nervous. Lewis Harrison, Baroness Lucas's steward, carefully monitored the progress of Methodism in the villages on her estate, applying pressure on people who played any leading part and buying property to prevent it being acquired for a chapel.[230] There is strong evidence, from across southern England, that the attitude towards Methodism among magistrates noticeably hardened.[231] At Green's Norton, in Northamptonshire, Methodists were fined heavily for holding a service in a street:

---

227 Woodward, *Causes and pretences*, 176.
228 Horsley, *The charge of Samuel, Bishop of Rochester, to the clergy 1800*, 19–20.
229 Heslop, *Two sermons and a charge*, 54 and 58.
230 BLARS, L 30/11/132/108, 122, 124 and 141.
231 The three incidents used by John S. Simon to illustrate his article on the subject took place at Great Barfield in Essex, at Pershore in Worcestershire, and in Berkshire (Simon, 'Repeal of the Conventicle Act', 103–8).

> Last Sunday was distributed to the Poor of Greens-Norton … £6 19s 8d being
> the third Parts of several Penalties levied on a Number of People called Method-
> ists, under the Statute of the 22d of Charles the Second, for unlawfully assem-
> bling in the Streets of the said Parish. – By these Convictions, it is now clearly
> ascertained, that all Assemblies and Conventicles held in the Streets, or any
> Place not properly licensed, are unlawful; and the Parties present, if amounting
> to the Number of five (as well the Hearers as the Preachers) are liable to the
> several Penalties imposed by the said Act …[232]

In Buckinghamshire magistrates pre-empted Lord Sidmouth's bill by simply
refusing to grant licences to itinerant preachers from early in 1809, and in 1811 even
refused one to the pastor of a settled congregation.[233] In Bedfordshire the political
strength of the older Dissenting congregations may have offered some protection but
even a supposed friend of Dissent, like the Duke of Bedford, could not be entirely
relied upon, and threatened at least one tenant who licensed his home for preaching.[234] Local Wesleyans certainly seem to have felt vulnerable to legal penalties and
this is reflected in the increasing care which they took, from the 1790s onwards, to
ensure that their meetings were licensed.[235]

A more common problem than official harassment appears to have been the
disruption of meetings by local youths. Francis Hews records that at Ivinghoe Aston
a group of farm servants came to the door of the barn where he was preaching:

> Some of them soon pulled off their hats, when they bid the others do so likewise,
> but they refused: 'Then', said they, 'we will knock them off, and your heads
> with them; ' and immediately drew off, and went to fighting. …When worship
> was over, the people all went out of the barn, and these men, standing in two
> rows, through which they passed, waited for me. … 'Take hold of him,' said
> several, 'Damn you,' said the rest, 'do it yourself.' With this, they fell to fighting
> again, and were so engaged, until I got quite away.[236]

At Aylesbury, the Wesleyans sought legal advice about how best to protect meetings from being disrupted, at Buckingham they put up posters warning of the penalties for disturbing religious meetings.[237] At Beeston they actually carried through a
prosecution. The magistrate's notes for the case survive:

> THURSDAY, NOVR. 28, 1811
> Richard Bird of Beeston to complain of Samuel Skilleter, Jeremiah Skilleter
> and William Hilsley for disturbing the congregation of a Methodist Meeting in
> Beeston Green on Sunday evening, Novr. 10. Granted a warrant. …
> FRIDAY, NOVR. 29, 1811 …
> Samuel and Jeremiah Skilliter and William Hilsley brought by warrant for
> wilfully interupting divine service in the meeting at Beeston on Sunday Novr 10.
> Richard Bird sworn; J. Skilleter & William [Hilsley] came into the chapel and
> sat down at morning service, began to talk, whistle and cough; were reproved

---

[232] *Northampton Mercury,* 12 January 1788, p. 3, col. 4.

[233] Davis, *Political change and continuity,* 66; Davis, *Dissent in politics,* 161.

[234] John Farey, who had been Wesley's host in 1788, obtained a licence for his house for Baptist meetings in 1792 and was given notice to quit his farm by the duke (Welch, *Bedfordshire chapels,* 133; John
Farey to Mr Gotobed, 2 July 1793, BLARS, R3/1763).

[235] 'Extracts from the journal of Thomas Edman', 104.

[236] Hews, *Spoils won in the day of battle,* 122–3.

[237] Durley, *Centenary annals,* 13; Poster 'Caution. Penalty on disturbing religious assemblies' c.1812,
Buckingham, Brackley and Bicester Methodist circuit records, Northants RO, BBMC/199; Cirket,
Samuel Whitbread's notebooks, 71–4.

by James Jeeves, one of the congregation; took no notice. Ann the wife of the witness then reproved them, after which they behaved better. After service witness spoke to them and they jeered him. Samuel Skilliter came to the chapel in the evening and disturbed the congregation very much ...
SUNDAY, DECR 1, 1811
The boys from Beeston again about the disturbance in the chapel. ... Ordered the boys to be flogged; lesser ones 6, bigger 10 stripes. Parent paid the constable's expenses.[238]

The impression is given that many of the incidents of disruption were of a similar nature. It was not that Methodism provoked organised or deliberate opposition from local communities, it was simply that, in gathering crowds of young people for an evening's entertainment and diversion, the Methodists sometimes found their audiences hard to manage.

There were, of course, still men who objected to their wives disappearing to religious meetings, like the man at Milton Ernest who disrupted a service and drove his wife home 'on a dark winter's evening, with blows and oaths.'[239] There were parish clergy who continued to resent the criticism of their labours implicit in the success of the Methodist preachers.[240] There were even those who continued to object to the Arminian theology of the Wesleyans. It is reported that three young men from Potton were forbidden from attending the Biggleswade chapel in 1796 when their parents discovered the doctrine of freewill expressed in the hymn-book they brought home:

> But all, before they hence remove,
> May mansions for themselves prepare
> In that eternal house above;
> And, O my God, shall I be there?[241]

There must be some doubt, however, as to how widely such concerns were shared. Even among the clergy there were men who took a more relaxed view. At Stewkley the minister held George Coles's brother in such esteem that he allowed him to introduce hymn singing at the graveside of 'those who died in the Lord.'[242] Daniel Basley, the curate at Luton, was similarly happy to accommodate the practice, as long as the mourners allowed him to absent himself before the singing began.[243] The invitation to participate in the Bedfordshire Union, the involvement of Wesleyans in the local auxiliary of the Bible Society, public support for Methodist

---

238   Cirket, *Samuel Whitbread's notebooks*, 71–4.
239   *WMM* (1864), 426.
240   See John Crowe, *Some remarks on the address of the Rev. R. Exton*; and John Ward, *A brief vindication of the Wesleyan Methodists*, for the Methodist side of a pamphlet war initiated by the curate of Green's Norton in Northamptonshire. Unfortunately, neither of Exton's pamphlets, nor an anonymous one in support of him, appear to have survived. See also Richard Shepherd, *No false alarm*.
241   Williams, *The veteran school-superintendent*, 13. The Wesleyans were also a target of Francis Hews's *Spoils won in the day of battle* (see pages 196 and 200). An anonymous Wesleyan replied in verse with *The spoiler spoiled* and Hews may have gone into print again with *The little child well flogged for lying* but no copy has been traced. See also Edward Griffin, *Strictures upon a publication entitled 'A brand plucked out of the fire'* and the response of the Wesleyan preacher W. P. Davies, *A refutation of the charges alleged against the writer of Kendall's narrative*.
242   Coles, *Youthful days*, 72.
243   'Bedford Methodism', *The Bedford Methodist Monthly Magazine* (1894), BLARS, X 302/7/1.

missionary societies, and, above all, the popularity of Wesleyan preaching services all suggest that Methodism was seen in a generally positive light by a wide section of the population. Indeed, Methodism had become an everyday feature of Bedfordshire life and even for a non-Methodist like John Pedley, a farmer and diarist from Great Barford, attending a Methodist meeting was really a quite normal event: 'In the evening I rode into the town. Was to hear a preacher as belongs to the chapel in White Horse Street in Bedford at William Gross's.'[244]

Part 6 Methodism on the eve of the Swing Riots

The landscape of Methodism in Bedfordshire in 1829 was almost unrecognisable from forty years earlier. Calvinistic Methodism had largely disappeared, either into Dissent or into the Evangelical party of the Church of England; the distinctive communal life of the Moravians had largely been abandoned; and the Wesleyans, by whom the name Methodist was now almost exclusively appropriated, had been transformed. What had once been a small circle of little societies was now a substantial community. Many of the individual societies were still small but in the towns of Bedfordshire, and a few other places, the Wesleyans were operating on a very different scale. The small, back street preaching rooms had been replaced with prominent, main street chapels. The class meeting, with its strict discipline, had yielded precedence in the weekly round to a Sunday preaching service that was popular and entertaining. The old emphasis on the cultivation of an inner, emotional security had given way to a new focus on outward behaviour. There was more to do now, local preaching, acting as a trustee, chapel steward or chapel keeper, teaching in the Sunday school, collecting for the missionary society; but there was also the option of doing less, of simply turning up for the preaching and singing, perhaps even just for the new festivals that punctuated the annual cycle – the chapel, Sunday school and missionary anniversaries. Most societies still had no chapel, no Sunday school and few adherents but even in these smaller societies, a high turnover of membership meant the Wesleyan class meeting was no longer such a closed world.

Methodism had become a vehicle for expressing popular religious feeling but its older traditions were not entirely forgotten and they could sometimes jar with the new spirit. John Leppington's credentials as a modernising superintendent, building chapels, enlivening worship and founding Sunday schools, have already been established, but there were limits to how far even he was prepared to accommodate popular sentiment.

> On one occasion in connection with the Christmas Festival some of the friends desired to decorate the Methodist chapel. With loving hands the decorations of holly and evergreen were completed. This however seems to have greatly perturbed the good Methodist Preacher, for he discerned in it a movement towards something not Methodistic. Early on the Christmas morning he arose from his bed and tried to enter the chapel, but found the chapel door locked. Not to be daunted however, he surveyed the building and discovering one of the windows open he crawled through, and with iconoclastic zeal swept away the

---

[244] Emmison, 'John Pedley of Great Barford, 1773–95', 108.

decorations, so that when the congregation gathered the chapel stood out in all its austere and simple unadornment, much to the surprise and grief of the ladies who had so zealously engaged in this work of decoration.[245]

In the decade after 1830 such tensions would multiply.

---

[245] Pages from *Bedford Methodist Monthly Magazine* 1894, BLARS, X 302/7/1. It was also said that Leppington reproved a member at Luton from the pulpit for looking at the clock during his sermon: 'Give Brother Hawkes his hat, he is worried that his pudding will spoil' (Hawkes, *Rise of Wesleyan Sunday schools*, 8). The incidents may explain why Coles wrote of him, 'a strict disciplinarian, rather arbitrary in his government, and on that account not a favourite with the people' (Coles, *Youthful days*, 75).

Chapter Three

Popular Protests: the third rise of Methodism 1830–1851

Part 1 Narrative

The Religion of the People

After more than a decade of decline and stagnation, at the end of the 1820s Wesleyan membership, in the south of the county at least, began once again to expand rapidly (see Table 16). Between June 1827 and June 1830 the Bedford, Luton and Leighton Buzzard circuits saw their combined membership rise from 1,491 to 2,160, an increase of nearly 45% in three years, more than eleven times the rate of growth reported by the denomination nationally.[1] For the next two years numbers levelled out, but in 1832 the rapid growth resumed and this time the Biggleswade, St Neots and Higham Ferrers circuits also reported large numbers of new members.[2] Between 1832 and 1835 membership of the six circuits increased by over 50%, almost four times the rate of growth reported by the connexion across England as a whole.[3] The cumulative effect of these two bursts of growth was to bring Wesleyan membership in the county close to three thousand, or about 5% of the adult population. Across England as a whole the figure was only 2%. Bedfordshire had become a Wesleyan stronghold.

As in the war years, geographic expansion was one of the drivers of numerical growth. Between 1828 and 1836, 10 societies were added to the Bedford circuit, 12 to the Biggleswade circuit and 10 to the Luton circuit.[4] By 1835 there were approximately 65 Wesleyan societies in Bedfordshire itself, covering more than half the parishes. The process of expansion, however, appears to have followed a significantly different course. In the past new societies had first been added to the weekly rounds of the professional itinerant preachers and then added to the Sunday preaching-plan to be supplied by local preachers. Now, it appears, the process was reversed and the initiative was in the hands of the amateurs. In the Biggleswade circuit, it was reported that:

---

[1] Across England Wesleyan membership rose by 3.9%, from 223,449 to 232,074.
[2] The only circuit with societies in Bedfordshire not to experience dramatic growth was Newport Pagnell, the membership of which was 286 in 1827 and 335 in 1835, an increase of 20% in 8 years.
[3] Between the conference of 1832 and that of 1835 the combined membership of the Bedford, Leighton Buzzard, Biggleswade, Luton, St Neots, and Higham Ferrers circuits rose from 3,127 to 4,696. Across England Wesleyan membership rose by about 13%, from 239,478 to 271,416.
[4] The St Albans circuit added seven places to its preaching plan in a single year (*The Watchman* 8 July 1835).

About thirty years ago, Ashwell was statedly visited by the Itinerant Preachers; but they afterwards desisted from their labours; ... [but more recently] the divine blessing having accompanied the word of life, as occasionally administered by our Local Preachers, a society was formed, and the place taken on the Circuit plan.[5]

In the Luton circuit

Methodism was introduced into Barton by one of our zealous local preachers, who first opened his commission in the public street, and whose labours, in conjunction with his brethren, have not been in vain. A small barn was fitted up. ... A hopeful society of about thirty has been formed.[6]

In fact, preaching plans from both the Luton and Bedford circuits show numerous new societies receiving Sunday visits from local preachers that were not part of the itinerants' mid-week circuits.[7] There was certainly no significant increase in the staffing of the local circuits during this period. A third itinerant was added to the Biggleswade circuit in 1833, to reside at Hitchin, and a third to the Luton circuit in 1834, to reside at Dunstable, but that still only took the total number of professional Wesleyan preachers in Bedfordshire to sixteen.[8]

Not all the growth, however, came from new societies. The Leighton Buzzard circuit added only one village to its bounds but it increased its membership by almost five hundred; and in the Luton circuit two-thirds of the growth came from existing societies. Unlike the situation twenty years earlier, when dramatic growth had been largely confined to the places where the itinerants concentrated their labours, this time the growth was, if anything, stronger in the smaller village societies served by the local preachers.[9] The increase in membership was, in any case, only the tip of the iceberg. Village, as well as town, societies now attracted large congregations of hearers. A report on the Biggleswade circuit in 1835 found almost all the preaching places struggling to cope with the number of people attending. At Biggleswade itself, 'although the new chapel contains more than twice as many pews as did the old one, yet they are nearly all let; and every succeeding Sabbath, since the opening, in the afternoon and evening, the chapel has been entirely filled with devout and attentive hearers.' At Beeston, a hamlet a few miles to the north, a chapel opened in December 1832 had already had to be extended by the spring of 1834. At Hinxworth, the new chapel was filled with worshippers. At Shefford, a village where a room capable of holding about 100 people had been rented even though there was no society, the preaching had proved so popular that a chapel had been built and 'the congregations have so much increased that they could not

---

5   *WMM* (1834), 216.
6   *The Watchman* 22 July 1835.
7   Luton Wesleyan circuit preaching plan July–October 1843, BLARS, MB 1824/1; Bedford Wesleyan circuit preaching plan May–August 1839, BLARS, MB 124.
8   When the additional preacher was allocated to the Biggleswade circuit in 1833, to be stationed at Hitchin, it was directed that his labours should be shared with Luton. The following year it was agreed that the Hitchin preacher should work exclusively for the Biggleswade circuit and that an additional preacher should be secured for Luton. The societies at Barton, Gravenhurst, Shillington, Lilley, Hexton and Offley all seem to date from this period (Bedford Wesleyan District, minutes of district meetings 1833 and 1834, MARC).
9   The Leighton Buzzard circuit book shows the membership of the main societies growing by an average of 71% while the smaller societies, served by the local preachers, grew by 103%.

have been admitted into the place previously occupied [and] an increasing society has also been formed.' At Hitchin, a chapel that was only four years old had to be replaced with a larger one and, in the village of Newnham, a chapel had been built 'capable of holding all the inhabitants of the village.'[10]

It is clear from the minutes of the district meetings that other circuits were experiencing the same transformation. Between 1828 and 1835 permission was given for 8 new chapels to be built in Bedfordshire, another 8 to be enlarged and 3 more to be replaced completely. Three other chapels, built without prior permission, received retrospective sanction and a further 13 appear to have been built not only without prior permission but without even the pretence of official approval.[11] The situation on the ground was changing so rapidly that the connexional structures were overwhelmed. In fact, congregations appear to have been growing at an even faster rate than membership. Applications for permission to build a chapel in the early 1830s reported an average ratio of members to hearers of about 1:2 but by 1834 it was 1:3 and by 1840 nearly 1:4.[12] Wesleyan Sunday schools also multiplied, so that by 1833 there were nearly thirty in Bedfordshire, with about 2,800 children on their rolls. If not only members but hearers and Sunday school children as well are taken into account, by 1835 the entire Wesleyan community in Bedfordshire, was in the region of eighteen thousand, or 18% of the total population. It was not, of course, evenly spread and in some areas Wesleyans may even have been in the majority. At Slapton, in the Leighton Buzzard circuit, according to one source three-quarters of the village were Methodists.[13]

Writing of this sudden influx of new faces, the Revd William Piggott would later recall that:

> About that time the cholera visited this locality, and many fell victims to this awful disease, and especially in those towns where wickedness most prevailed. In Bicester the mortality was great, whilst in Leighton we had but one death. The people saw and acknowledged the hand of God, flocked to the different places of worship, and humbled themselves under the mighty hand of God.

About five hundred people were admitted on trial in the course of three months in 1834 and there were emotional scenes at some services:

> One week evening the Chapel was crowded to excess, and some who came to ridicule soon became bathed in tears of penitence; about eleven or twelve o'clock we tried in vain to dismiss the congregation, for as soon as the doxology

---

[10] *WMM* (1833), 218 and (1835), 213–14.

[11] Permission was given to enlarge Leighton Buzzard (1828), Eaton Bray (1829), Dunstable, Toddington and Leagrave (1832), Luton and Beeston (1834) and Heath (1835). Permission to enlarge Bedford chapel (1831) was superseded by the decision to replace it (1832). Approval for the replacement of existing chapels was also given to Great Barford (1832) and Biggleswade (1834); and for new chapels at Dunstable (1829), Beeston and Hockliffe (1833), Ridgmont (1834) and Barton (1835). Retrospective permission was given for Turvey (1829) and for Harlington and Shefford (1835) (London (West) Wesleyan District minutes 1822–31 and Bedford Wesleyan district minutes 1832–6, MARC). Chapels at Aley Green, Arlesey, Billington, Chalk Hill, Chalton, Hogsty End, Houghton Conquest, Langford, Milton Ernest, Pavenham, Stanbridge, Tilsworth, Wilstead and Wingfield appear to have been built without any kind of permission.

[12] The five societies applying between 1831 and 1833 had 455 members and 1220 regular hearers; the five societies in 1834 had 311 members and 1270 hearers; while the ten societies in 1839–40 had 432 members and 1,910 hearers.

[13] Buckmaster, *Village politician*, 61.

was sung and the benediction was pronounced, those who were leaving returned. As I felt exhausted, I went to the door to breathe a little fresh air, and, to my great surprise, the labourers were going to their work, it being about five o'clock in the morning. There were several on their knees in the Chapel, whom with difficulty we persuaded to leave and come another night.[14]

An account of events in a neighbouring circuit paints a very similar picture of the impact which the cholera epidemic had on local religious life:

The Revs George Warren and John Killick were then the ministers in the Aylesbury Circuit; and they, hearing in this visitation a call to the people to repent, held special services in various places. ... when we reached the chapel [at Buckland], we found it filled with people in a very excited state. ... I went again the next night, and preached from Amos iv, 12: 'Prepare to meet thy God.' A prayer-meeting was held after each service, when in every part of the chapel there were strong cryings, tears and prayers to Him Who was able to save.[15]

Revivals of this kind, episodes of communal religious excitement, often initially sparked by danger or disaster but quickly taking on a dynamic of their own, are a well-documented feature of evangelical Protestant culture.[16] It does not, however, by itself explain a pattern of growth that had already been under way for a number of years. A revival may well have provided the culmination of that process, drawing back into the fold lapsed recruits from previous years, but it was not the starting point.

Another account of Wesleyan Methodism in the early 1830s can be found in the autobiography of John Buckmaster. Growing up in Slapton, Buckmaster had attended Methodist meetings and had known many of the local Methodist leaders but he was not a Methodist himself. In his memory Methodism had been an expression of popular protest born out of the sharp social tensions which marked those years. It is certainly interesting that, whereas from 1790 to 1828 Methodist fortunes had broadly tracked those of the local economy, boom being matched by growth and bust by decline, the surge in membership between 1828 and 1836 took place against the backdrop of a deepening agricultural depression, mounting population pressures and widespread distress as the existing Poor Law structures buckled under the strain of the demand. In 1830 the Duke of Bedford's steward calculated that an agricultural labourer needed to earn 10s per week but that local farmers were only paying 8s or 9s and that the men employed by the overseers received as little as 3s. Many families may have been on the point of starvation.[17] The unremitting wretchedness of the conditions in many villages created a tense and acrimonious atmosphere. At Blunham, the rector described how the labourers

being generally disaffected to their employers, [worked] unwillingly and wastefully. The disaffection is in great measure to be attributed to continual disputes respecting the Parish Relief, and it has doubtless been aggravated by agitators. ... In this neighbourhood the object has been, by keeping the Farmers in awe,

---

14 Brigg, *Methodism in the Leighton Buzzard circuit*. Piggott was the junior preacher on the Leighton Buzzard circuit from 1831 to 1834.

15 Rowe, *Mary Calvert*, 8–9.

16 There may have been another revival in western Bedfordshire in 1859–60 (Orr, *The second evangelical awakening*, 124).

17 Godber, *History of Bedfordshire*, 416–17.

to extort higher wages, and a greater parochial allowance: when this is refused, policy and revenge produce incendiarism. It has been threatened in Vestry where relief has been refused, and the relief has, in consequence, been granted.[18]

In many places threats were acted upon and, between 1828 and 1836, there was rioting, vandalism, arson and animal maiming, across the county.[19]

Attending Wesleyan meetings was also a form of protest, for the Church of England, which was so inextricably involved in landownership, was often the most visible expression of the established order in a village and therefore the most identifiable target of resentment.[20] The vicar of Kempston, for one, came to think himself fortunate if he managed to pass labourers on the road without being insulted by them and the vicar of Westoning found that the farmers of his parish were encouraging them in this hostility:

> In this parish some of the farmers accompanied the labourers, when they surrounded me in the village, and demanded higher pay: on their making this demand, the farmers exclaimed against the pressure of rent and *tithe*. Neither the landlords nor the lay rector resided in the parish; therefore the labouring poor surrounded me, instigated (as I am credibly informed) *by the farmers.*[21]

With so many of the clergy prominently involved in the magistracy, any attempt to impose order after some outbreak of discontent only served to damage relations further. At Stotfold, the curate, the Revd John Lafont, was at the forefront in the suppression of a riot by agricultural labourers in 1830. On the Sunday following the trial of the rioters the service in the parish church was disrupted and Lafont never conducted a baptism or burial in the village again.[22] At Slapton, John Buckmaster makes a direct link between such antagonism and the growth of Methodism, remembering that Methodist preachers were invited to the village 'out of pure ill-nature' against the curate as a result of a dispute about the use of the church rates, and that very soon:

> No one but the parish clerk stood by the curate, and all sorts of disagreeable things were circulated about him: he didn't preach the gospel; the church was no good to any one, it only robbed them of the charities; the curate was a whited sepulchre; he had never experienced the influence of converting grace; he was the blind leading the blind. The result was that no one went to church, and for weeks the door was never unlocked.[23]

The Turn of the Tide

The rapid membership growth of the early 1830s reached its peak about 1835 and was followed by a period of decline, as many of those who had begun to attend classes lost interest and fell by the wayside. Between 1835 and 1838 the Bedfordshire circuits lost four hundred members, about 8% of their total membership (see

---

[18] Agar, *Bedfordshire farm worker*, 72–9, reprinted from the *Report from His Majesty's commissioners for inquiring into the administration and practical operation of the Poor Laws*, 1834.
[19] Godber, *History of Bedfordshire*, 417–19 and Cirket, 'The 1830 Riots in Bedfordshire', 75–112.
[20] Obelkevich has made a similar observation in relation to Primitive Methodism in Lincolnshire a generation later (Obelkevich, *Religion and rural society*, 257).
[21] Agar, *Bedfordshire farm worker*, 74 and 78–9.
[22] Cirket, 'The 1830 riots in Bedfordshire', 96–100.
[23] Buckmaster, *Village politician*, 37–8.

Table 16).[24] There were great celebrations in 1839 to mark what Wesleyans regarded as the centenary of Methodism and almost all the local circuits contributed by dutifully recording healthy increases in their statistics. The centenary over, however, reports of increased membership became patchier. Over the next decade Wesleyan membership across the county grew by an average of less than 1% a year, significantly below the growth in the population as a whole, and even this may overstate the true situation (see Table 15).[25]

In most of the towns membership is recorded as having grown strongly. Between 1841 and 1851, the Bedford society grew from 297 members to 429, the Biggleswade society from 93 to 120 and the Luton society from 331 to 406. At Bedford and Biggleswade, though not at Luton, this was sufficient to outpace the growing population.[26] The figures, however, are quite misleading. Nationally there was a move during the 1840s towards allowing regular hearers who contributed financially to be re-classified as full members without requiring them to attend a class meeting; and locally it is evident that the ratio of members to hearers changed dramatically.[27] In reality, the congregations in all three towns declined significantly. At Biggleswade, the 742-seater chapel, which had been 'entirely filled with devout and attentive hearers' every Sabbath evening in 1835, was less than half-full in 1851. At Luton, where as recently as 1845 the Victoria Rooms had had to be hired for an overflow service, and at Bedford, where they had similarly hired a chapel in Russell Street in 1838, a third of the pews were empty.[28]

In many of the villages even the membership levels fell but this was disguised to some extent by the continuing multiplication of societies. The north of the county, where the Wesleyans were relatively weakly represented, faired best. In 1841 there had been fourteen village societies north of the river Ouse, with a combined membership of 238. By 1851 five had lost members and two had failed completely but the formation of four new societies lifted the membership total to 305.[29] Congregations

---

24   The six Wesleyan circuits with societies in Bedfordshire fell from a combined total of 5,031 members to 4,631.

25   In 1841 the membership of the six circuits with societies in Bedfordshire was 5,564. By 1851 the six circuits had become eight (Hitchin had been created from Biggleswade in 1842 and Dunstable from Luton in 1843) and the membership had risen to 6,071; an increase of 9% in ten years. In the same period the population of the county had increased by more than 15%.

26   The population of Bedford increased by 31% between 1841 and 1851, and membership of the Bedford Wesleyan society by 44%. The population of Luton grew by 82% and Wesleyan membership by only 23%.

27   Gregory, *Side lights on the conflicts of Methodism*, 426–8. At St Albans in 1848, Thomas Collins referred to 'The modern system of being members without being in class' (Coley, *Life of Thomas Collins*, 279). By 1851 members outnumbered non-members in the congregations at Bedford and Luton and at Biggleswade the ratio had fallen to 1:2.

28   Hawkes, *Rise of Wesleyan Sunday schools*, 14–15; *Luton Reporter* 3 September 1892. In 1846 it was recorded that 'more than 100 applications have been made for sittings at the Wesleyan Chapel, but in vain' (*Ceylon Baptist Church: centenary brochure*, 14; Bedford Wesleyan circuit, minutes of local preachers' meeting 31 December 1838, BLARS, MB 9). This appears to be the chapel used by the Primitive Methodists prior to the opening of their Hassett Street chapel. Membership of the Dunstable society is not recorded after 1842 but, based on the class-money contributed, it rose from 165 in 1841 to about 400 in 1851; a rate of increase well in advance of population growth. The ratio of members to hearers, however, seems to have fallen, as at Bedford and Luton, with 650 adults present at the best attended service.

29   The societies that failed were at Harrold and Odell. The new societies were at Tilbrook and Knotting in the Higham Ferrers circuit and at Everton and Honeydon in the St Neots circuit.

here also appear to have held up well. The religious census figures show that hearers outnumbered members by a ratio of 6:1 and that the chapels were generally well-filled.[30] In the south too, falling membership in the villages of the Luton circuit was off-set by the creation of new societies. Here the expansion seems to have been quite consciously planned. In the autumn of 1840 four laymen undertook to guarantee the salary of a hired local preacher to work the outlying parts of the circuit. The results of this experiment were sufficiently encouraging for a committee to be appointed the following spring to raise the funds to support an itinerant preacher and his family.[31] The fourth minister in turn paved the way for the division of the circuit in 1843. The result was that between 1841 and 1851 the number of village societies in the Luton circuit increased from twenty-nine to thirty-seven. Even this achievement, only maintained the membership at its 1841 level and took no account of population growth. Moreover, in many villages the decline in attendance at services seems, if anything, to have been more severe than the falling away of membership. When the chapel at Harpenden had been built in 1839 the society had numbered 117 and the congregation four hundred, by 1851 the membership had slipped to seventy-two but the congregation had dropped to 212. Across the Luton circuit the ratio of hearers to members in 1851 was barely 3:1 and it would have been even lower if there had not been a string of new Sunday schools. The number of Wesleyan Sunday schools in the county almost doubled, from twenty-nine in 1833 to fifty-nine in 1851, increasing the number of children involved from about 2,800 to 5,380. Half of the new schools were in the Luton and Dunstable circuits and their scholars, for whom attendance at services was compulsory, accounted for a third of the people present at worship in 1851, twice the proportion found in the north of the county.

The area in which Wesleyan support seems to have fallen away most dramatically during the 1840s was in its former heartland, south-west of Bedford towards Leighton Buzzard. Here Methodism was already established in almost every village and there were few opportunities to offset the decline in existing societies by creating new ones in neighbouring communities. At Ampthill the society's membership fell from a peak of 164 members in 1840 to 60 in 1851, at Wootton from 68 in 1839 to 33, and at Marston Moretaine from 120 to 89. At Cranfield, Salford and Aspley Guise the combined membership fell from 118 in 1841 to 45 by 1851, while three other societies, at Flitwick, Maulden and Pulloxhill, disappeared altogether.[32] Attendance at worship appears to have followed a similar trajectory. At Cranfield, where there had been a congregation of 150 in 1839, there were only 60 people at

---

[30] The eleven societies for which there are census returns had a combined membership of 262 and the total attendance at their best attended services was 1,602. The chapels and meeting-places had an average occupancy of over 90%.

[31] A printed address was distributed to class-leaders throughout the circuit and they were exhorted to 'make a personal application to each of their members requesting them to contribute their quota weekly, and to increase it, where they think there is the ability'; a special society meeting was held in every place in the circuit 'in order to impress upon our Members the necessity of acting Methodistically in reference to the Class monies and Quarterage'; and it was arranged that 'in order to meet the additional expenditure of the circuit' the quarterly collection would in future be taken at every service on the appointed day, not just at the main one, and would be made 'in the pews and not at the doors' (Luton Wesleyan circuit minutes of quarterly meetings 1 October 1840, 25 March 1841, 24 June 1841, 30 December 1841 and 31 March 1842, BLARS, MB 498).

[32] Newport Pagnell Wesleyan circuit, schedule book 1837–47 and 1847–60, CBS, NM 500/7/3 and 4.

the best-attended service in 1851 and at Water Eaton, in the Newport Pagnell circuit, where there had been 300 in 1841 there were only 96. In three chapels more than half the seats were always empty and across the district the average occupancy even at the most popular services was less than 75%.

Overall, between 1841 and 1851 the number of adults attending Wesleyan worship in Bedfordshire may have fallen by as much as a third.[33] Arriving in the St Albans circuit, Thomas Collins found:

> Things are low. The circuit debt is £60. Several chapel cases are deplorable. The Societies are faint. On my first Sabbath at Rickmansworth I rose and went to the early prayer-meeting: there were present but two young women and two children.[34]

'Low' was also the word used to describe the situation at Wellingborough and Thrapston, while at Kettering Benjamin Gregory found attendance 'very disheartening.'[35] In 1847, the Bedford and Northampton district meeting received a request from the Kettering circuit for permission to sell a chapel at Broughton, in Northamptonshire, the congregation having 'entirely dwindled away.'[36] It was the first time that a chapel in the district, as opposed to a preaching place, had failed. Seven years later the first closure occurred in Bedfordshire itself, when the quarterly meeting of the Bedford circuit resolved 'that the preaching at Moggerhanger be given up, and the trustees recommended by this meeting to apply to conference for power to sell the chapel or to convert it to cottages.'[37] Chapel closures would remain unusual, although not unknown, occurrences for several decades to come but they provide the starkest evidence of all that a tide which had been rising for half a century was beginning to ebb.

One of the reasons for this reversal in fortunes was that the Wesleyans were financially overstretched. They had responded to the surge in membership in the 1830s with an ambitious building programme and it had come with a price tag. The new chapel at Bedford, built in 1832, cost £1,676, but that was dwarfed by the bill for the new chapel at Biggleswade in 1843 which was £2,500.[38] Even a modest village chapel like that at Turvey, built in 1829, cost £180.[39] The overall expenditure on building projects within the county was probably in excess of £10,000 and although some of this was paid for in cash there was a heavy burden of debt. By 1838, in the Bedford circuit alone, the chapel trusts owed £4,600. Servicing the debt became a major pre-occupation and the constant calls for money were a deterrent to attendance by the poor. Samuel Wagstaff, an agricultural labourer at Caldecote near Biggleswade, joined the Wesleyans for a time 'but their continual calls for money made him feel that money was all they preached for' and he decided to attend

---

[33] In the north and east of the county, where membership had held steady as a proportion of the population since 1841, members constituted 16% of adult attendants, by Watts' calculation. If that ratio had been true across the county in 1841 the number of adult attendants would have been 21,650 but in 1851 the number of adult attendants was only 16,786.

[34] Coley, *Life of Thomas Collins*, 246.

[35] *WMM* (1893), 934 and 939; *The Watchman* 29 January 1845.

[36] Bedford and Northampton Wesleyan district, minutes of district meeting 1847, MARC.

[37] Bedford Wesleyan circuit, minutes of quarterly meeting 29 March 1854, BLARS, MB 6.

[38] Anderson, *Early Methodism in Bedford*, 22; *WMM* (1835), 214.

[39] *WMM* (1829), 475.

a Baptist meeting instead.[40] High levels of indebtedness may also have stymied Wesleyan attempts to respond to the growth of Luton. A satellite cause was begun in the town, in the new district of Wellington Street, but, whether through lack of cash or concern for the effect on the finances of the existing chapel, was not seen through. The way was left open for the Baptists who were swift to act. A Union church of Baptists and Independents had been formed by a secession from the Luton Baptist meeting in 1836, but the two congregations then co-operated to take advantage of the Wesleyans' failure and jointly founded a third Baptist church, Ceylon, in Wellington Street in 1845.[41] The result was that, while Wesleyan attendance in Luton declined, between 1835 and 1851 attendance at Baptist worship tripled.

The chapel building programme had been financed and carried forward, not by the surge of new members, but by an existing core of better-off Wesleyans. At Hitchin, and in many of the neighbouring villages, much of the building work was financed by one man, Thomas Ward, who contributed something in the region of £2,000. Elsewhere the money seems to have come from people who were comfortable rather than wealthy. At Bedford, the largest contributor to the chapel was Mrs Pheasant, a widow who is described as having done 'much good with an income comparatively limited'; she gave £150. Miss Dennis gave £100, and then 'four others gave £50, five gave £20, eight gave £10 and twenty-three people gave £5', accounting for £745 out of a total subscription of £863.[42] At Biggleswade the sums were similar, 'three of the trustees subscribed £50 each; others £30, £20, &c., &c.; so that the subscriptions soon amounted to £400.'[43] A list of these trustees, and their occupations, survives: a gentleman, two farmers, a yeoman, a draper, an ironmonger, a mealman, a schoolmaster and a plumber.[44] Widows and shopkeepers seem unlikely paymasters for an agrarian protest movement and there is no reason to assume that it was their intention to be so. William Conquest, himself a trustee of seven chapels, explained their motivation in his account of the building programme in the Biggleswade circuit:

> For many years this circuit did nothing, comparatively, for God or for the souls of men: satisfied themselves with the enjoyment of Gospel blessings, the wants of those places by which the societies were surrounded called forth no adequate exertions. The Lord now evidently calls upon us to spread his truth, and to shake off the supineness of bygone days. ... that even those who profess religion, but are too careful of what a kind Providence has committed to their trust, to expend it even in attempting to rescue from perdition the fallen race of man, should condemn us for such undertakings, is no cause of grief. God loves a cheerful giver. The liberality of our friends in this Circuit has furnished a theme of wonder to all parties in the neighbourhood; and let it still do so. ... not one of them repents, or has any cause to repent, of what he has done for God. They have acted from a spirit of gratitude.[45]

In other words, the building programme represented a final victory over the traditional, closed Methodism of the eighteenth century, whose followers 'satisfied

---

[40]   Bartholomew, '19th Century missiology of the LDS Bedfordshire Conference', 126.
[41]   *Ceylon Baptist Church: centenary brochure*, 14.
[42]   List of subscriptions to Bedford Wesleyan chapel, 1832, BLARS, MB 25; *WMM* (1834), 557.
[43]   *WMM* (1835), 214.
[44]   Biggleswade Wesleyan circuit schedule book 1838–52, BLARS, MB 834.
[45]   *WMM* (1835), 214–15.

Plate 1. Francis Okley, 1719–1794
Okeley was only 17 when he formed his religious society in Bedford in 1736. In later life he was minister of the Moravian congregation at Northampton.
Source: BLARS Z50/141/1.

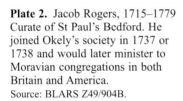

Plate 2. Jacob Rogers, 1715–1779
Curate of St Paul's Bedford. He joined Okely's society in 1737 or 1738 and would later minister to Moravian congregations in both Britain and America.
Source: BLARS Z49/904B.

Plate 3. Benjamin Ingham, 1712–1772
The first Methodist preacher to visit Bedfordshire in December 1738. He went on to join the Moravians but later founded his own connexion.

Plate 4. John Berridge, 1716–1793, vicar of Everton, Bedfordshire
A leading figure in the eighteenth-century Methodist movement and one of the principal preachers at the London Tabernacle after Whitefield's death.

Plate 5. John Wesley, 1703–1791
Organiser of what would eventually become the largest of the Methodist connexions and a regular visitor to Bedfordshire for almost 40 years.

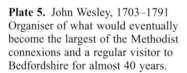

Plate 6. John Murlin, 1722–1799
Known as 'The Weeping Prophet'. He spent time in Bedford in 1760 and again in 1762 when the local Wesleyan society was an outpost of the London circuit.

Plate 7. Francis Asbury, 1745–1816
Junior preacher on the Bedfordshire
circuit in 1767/8 and again in 1769/70.
He went on to become the guiding
force of American Methodism.

Plate 8. William Cumberland, c.1759–1833
A class leader and local preacher at Bedford
for more than 40 years.
Source: Frontispiece of Greeves, *Memorials of
William Cumberland*, 1874.

Plate 9. Maximilian Wilson, 1777–1857
Superintendent of the Luton Wesleyan
circuit (1808–10 and 1832–35), Bedford
circuit (1827–30 and 1838–41), Leighton
Buzzard circuit (1844–6) and Chairman
of the Bedford district (1832–35) and
the Bedford and Northampton district
(1838–41 and 1844–46).

Plate 10. George Coles, 1791–1858, author of *My youthful days*
Born at Stewkley and apprenticed to a shopkeeper at Ampthill, his autobiography is a major source for Bedfordshire Methodist history.
Credit: Stephanie McCurdy

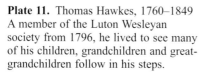

Plate 11. Thomas Hawkes, 1760–1849
A member of the Luton Wesleyan society from 1796, he lived to see many of his children, grandchildren and great-grandchildren follow in his steps.

Plate 12. Susanna Row, 1792–1866
Class leader at Cardington and part of the affluent cousinhood that dominated the Wesleyan societies of Bedfordshire in the mid-nineteenth century.
Source: Frontispiece of Jones, *Memoir of the late Miss Susanna Row, of Cardington, Bedfordshire*, 1876.

Plate 13. Timothy Matthews, 1795–1845
Chaplain to Bedford's House of Industry,
Matthews was an evangelical Churchman
strongly influenced by the Wesleyan
Methodism of his wife's family.
Source: frontispiece of Thomas Wright, *The Life
of the Rev. Timothy Richard Matthews*, 1910.

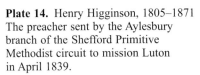

Plate 14. Henry Higginson, 1805–1871
The preacher sent by the Aylesbury
branch of the Shefford Primitive
Methodist circuit to mission Luton
in April 1839.

Plate 15. John Guy, 1811–1887
The first Primitive Methodist preacher
to visit Biggleswade. On a prior visit to
Hitchin he is said to have been beaten
with a dead cat.

Plate 16. Remains of Leighton Buzzard Wesleyan chapel, 1804
Built just three years after the formation of the society and extended several times, it was eventually replaced in 1865.

Plate 17. Bedford Methodist chapel, 1804
'A neat and respectable' building erected during the superintendency of John Leppington to replace an eighteenth-century preaching-house on the same site.
Source: BLARS, Z153/39.

Plate 18. Bedford Wesleyan chapel, 1832
Built on the site of its two predecessors (now the Central Library), it cost £1,676 and
seated 1,120 people.

Plate 19. Biggleswade Wesleyan chapel, 1834
Designed by William Jenkins, it cost £2,500 and seated 800 people.

Plate 20. Tebworth Wesleyan chapel, 1842
The first venture into gothic by local Methodists.

Plate 21. Bedford Primitive Methodist Chapel, 1849
Built on the footings of the previous chapel (erected in 1838), it cost £538 and sat 500 people.
Source: BLARS, X302/23/2, photograph 1938.

Plate 22. New Wesleyan Chapel, Luton, 1852
Designed by W. W. Pocock, it cost £3,650, and sat 1,800. To the left is the previous chapel, built in 1814.
Source: Lithograph by John Sunman Austin.

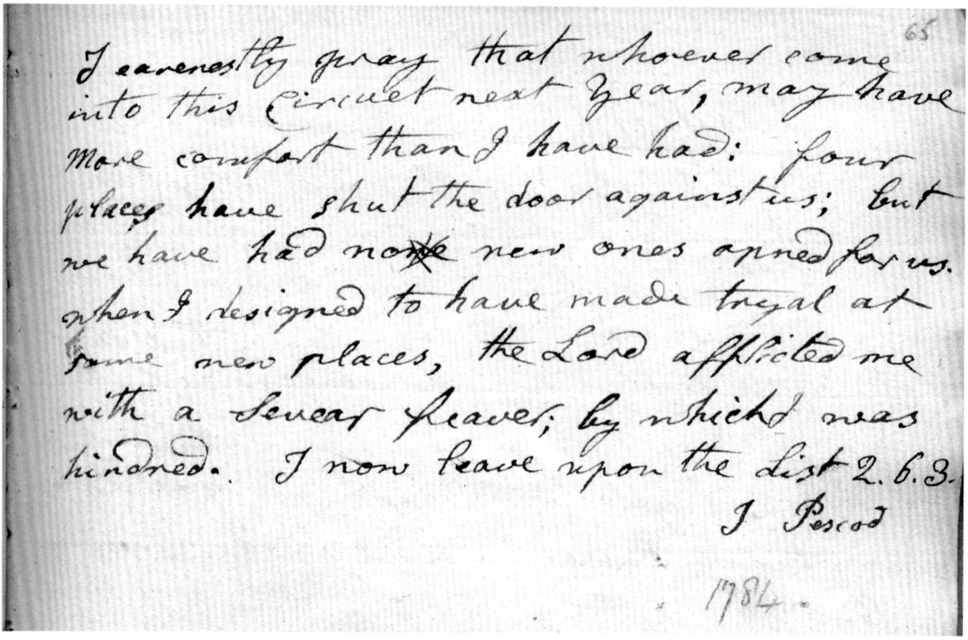

I earnestly pray that whoever come
into this circuet next Year, may have
More comfort than I have had: four
places have shut the door against us; but
we have had none new ones opned for us.
when I designed to have made tryal at
same new places, the Lord afflicted me
with a Sevear feaver; by which was
hindred. I now leave upon the list 2. 6. 3.

J Pescod

1784.

Plate 23. Bedfordshire Wesleyan circuit book, 'I earnestly pray …'
A message left by the outgoing Assistant, Joseph Pescod, for his successor in the summer
of 1784.
Source: BLARS, MB 1 p. 65.

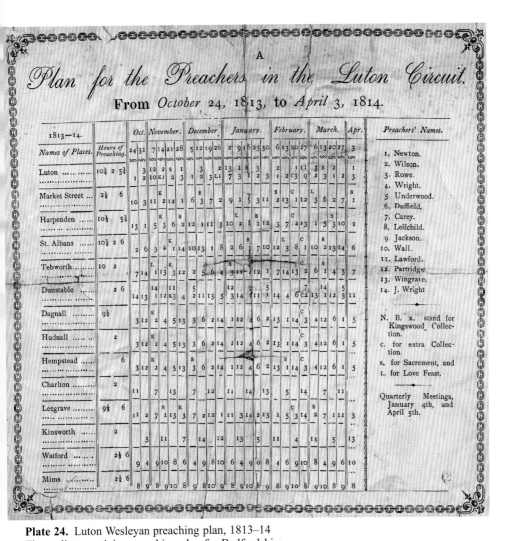

Plate 24. Luton Wesleyan preaching plan, 1813–14
The earliest surviving preaching plan for Bedfordshire.
(Source: BLARS, Luton Wesleyan preaching plan 1813–14, MB 497)

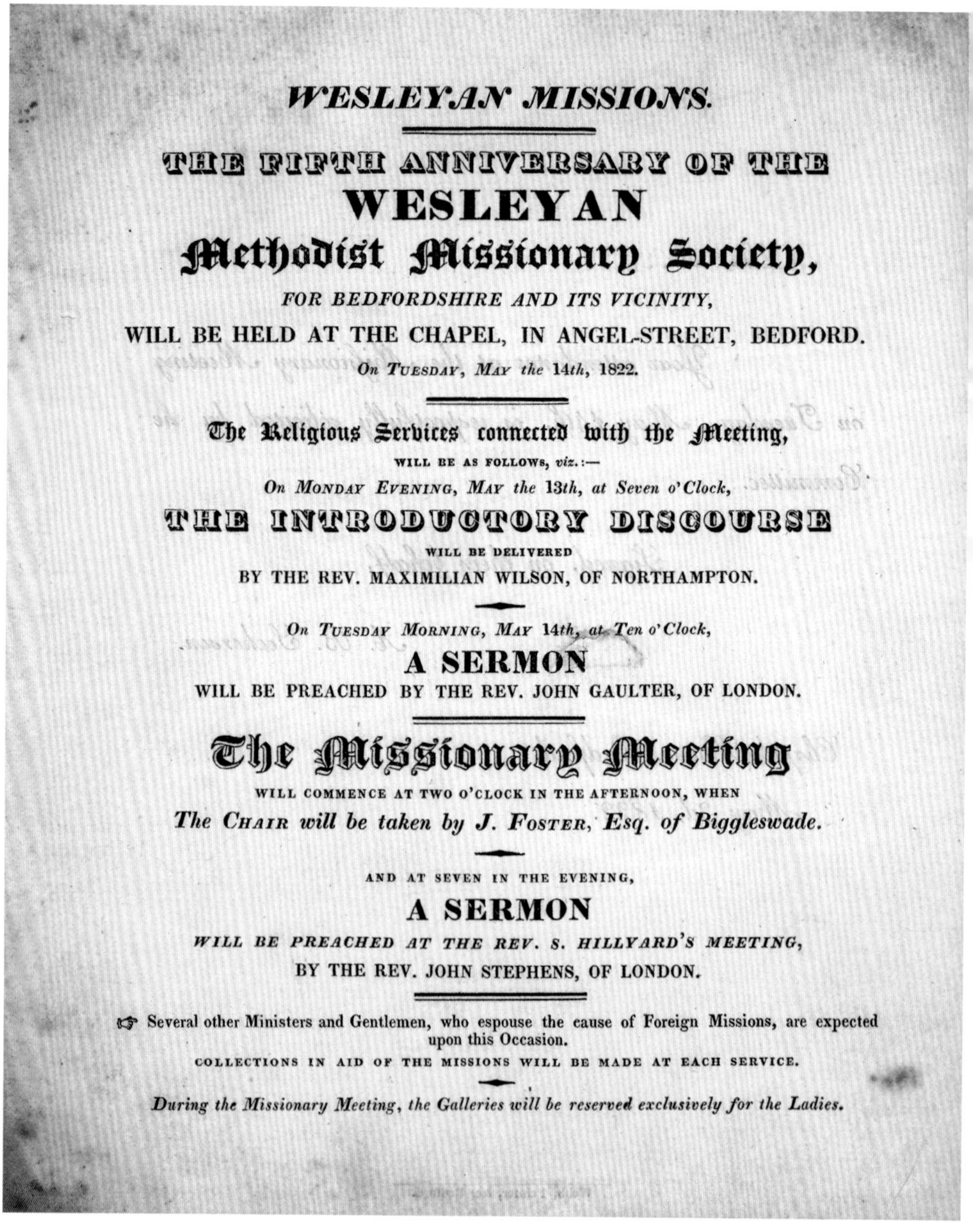

WESLEYAN MISSIONS.

THE FIFTH ANNIVERSARY OF THE

WESLEYAN
Methodist Missionary Society,

FOR BEDFORDSHIRE AND ITS VICINITY,

WILL BE HELD AT THE CHAPEL, IN ANGEL-STREET, BEDFORD.

On TUESDAY, MAY the 14th, 1822.

The Religious Services connected with the Meeting,

WILL BE AS FOLLOWS, viz.:—

On MONDAY EVENING, MAY the 13th, at Seven o'Clock,

THE INTRODUCTORY DISCOURSE

WILL BE DELIVERED

BY THE REV. MAXIMILIAN WILSON, OF NORTHAMPTON.

On TUESDAY MORNING, MAY 14th, at Ten o'Clock,

A SERMON

WILL BE PREACHED BY THE REV. JOHN GAULTER, OF LONDON.

The Missionary Meeting

WILL COMMENCE AT TWO O'CLOCK IN THE AFTERNOON, WHEN

The CHAIR will be taken by J. FOSTER, Esq. of Biggleswade.

AND AT SEVEN IN THE EVENING,

A SERMON

WILL BE PREACHED AT THE REV. S. HILLYARD'S MEETING,

BY THE REV. JOHN STEPHENS, OF LONDON.

☞ Several other Ministers and Gentlemen, who espouse the cause of Foreign Missions, are expected
upon this Occasion.
COLLECTIONS IN AID OF THE MISSIONS WILL BE MADE AT EACH SERVICE.

During the Missionary Meeting, the Galleries will be reserved exclusively for the Ladies.

Plate 25. Poster for Bedford Wesleyan missionary anniversary, 1822
Missionary, Chapel and Sunday school anniversaries were not only festivals of the
Methodist community but public entertainments.
Source: BLARS, X37/42/5.

Fourth QUARTERLY SCHEDULE FOR THE YEAR 18 38-9

Showing the State of the METHODIST SOCIETIES in the *Biggleswade & Hitchin* — Circuit, at the VISITATION of the CLASSES, for the Quarter ending *June 1839*

N. B. Every Superintendent is to provide for himself, and for each of his Colleagues, every Quarter, one or more Copies of this Schedule, the *Blanks* in which they are to fill up, in reference to *every distinct Class* to which they give Tickets; arranging the Classes under the Head of the Society to which they severally belong. The Schedules, thus filled up, are to be collected at the close of each Visitation, by the Superintendent; who, from these Documents, is to compile, every Quarter, one General Schedule, containing a View, *not of the Classes in detail,* but only of the SOCIETIES in his Circuit, taken collectively; for which purpose, also, he may conveniently use one of these printed Forms. These General Circuit-Schedules are to be produced when required, at the District-Meeting, and at the Conference. *See Minutes of 1820; Answer to Q. 26; Art. 28; Page 74.*

Names of Leaders or of Societies.	Now admitted on Trial.	New Members now fully received.	Members received from other Circuits.	Removals to other Circuits.	Members received from other Classes.	Members removed to other Classes.	Deaths.	Back-sliders.	Conver-sions.	Number of Believers.	Number in Bands.	Number now in Society; those on Trial not included.	Net Increase of Members this Quarter.	Net Decrease of Members this Quarter.	Quarterage. £ s. d.	Yearly Collection. £ s. d.
Ashwell Kitchener Mr.	4	7						3				25	3			
Garrard Mr.		2										12				
Newnham Hine Mr.												10				
Hinxworth Squires Mr.								1				18		1		
Norton Maxwell Mr.												25				
Pirton Preachers G.		2										12	2			
Shefford Inskip Mr.												10				
Marshall Mr.		4										10	4			
Walkern Aldridge Mr.	1	1										13	1			
Wright Mr.	2	1										9	1			
Ickleford Raban Mr.												10				
Royston Andrew Mr.				1								6		1		
Graveley Mackiness Mr.												5				
Codicote												5	5			
Clifton Usher Mr.	2							1				6	6			
Brought forward	35	31		1	2	3	2	7				465	40	14		
	44	48		2	2	3	2	12				641	62	16	46 Increase	

Plate 26. Biggleswade Wesleyan circuit schedule book, June 1839
From 1836 changes in the membership of each class were recorded every quarter, noting admissions, transfers, deaths and backsliders.
Source: BLARS, MB 834 p. 9.

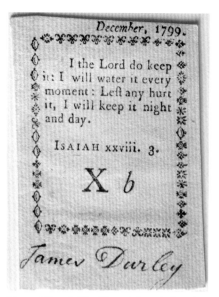
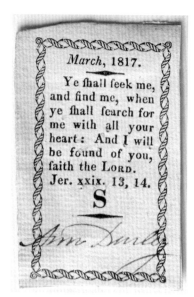

Plates 27 and 28. Class tickets belonging to James and Ann Durley of Bierton, 1799 and 1817
Issued quarterly, such tickets confirmed that recipients continued to meet the moral, spiritual and financial commitments of membership.

Plate 29. Wesleyan and Primitive Methodist tea services

Plate 30. Ridgmont Wesleyan Chapel decorated saucer
From the 1840s tea meetings were an important source of income, as well as being popular social occasions. Many local chapels invested in their own crockery.

Plate 31. London Wesleyan Missionary Bazaar, 1842
The tasteful arrangement of stalls at a bazaar in aid of St Neots Wesleyan chapel in 1850
won warm approbation from visitors, and raised £107.
Source: *London Illustrated News.*

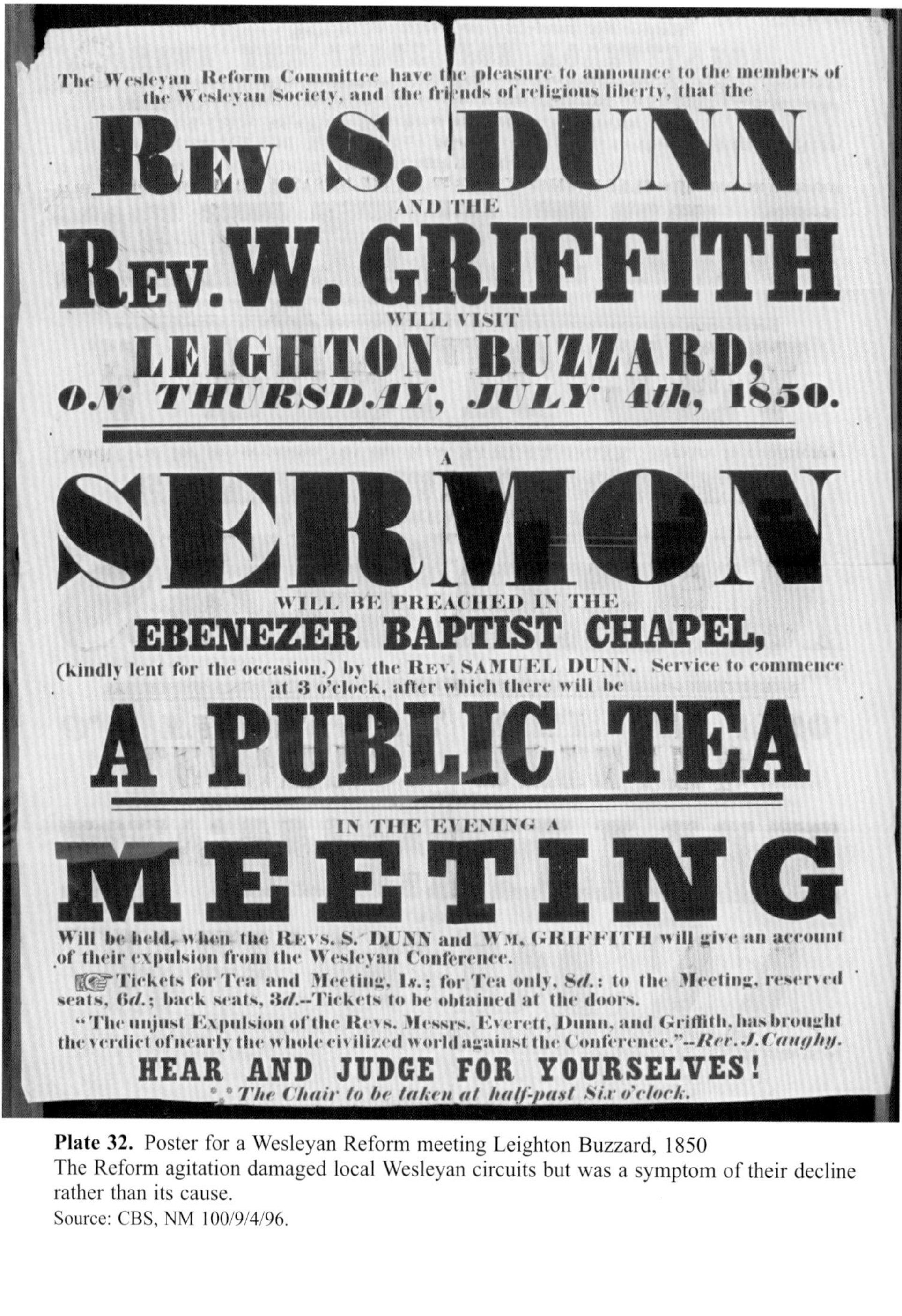

Plate 32. Poster for a Wesleyan Reform meeting Leighton Buzzard, 1850
The Reform agitation damaged local Wesleyan circuits but was a symptom of their decline
rather than its cause.
Source: CBS, NM 100/9/4/96.

themselves with the enjoyment of God's blessing', by those who had bought in to the more optimistic, expansionist theology of the 1790s and wanted 'to rescue from perdition the fallen race of man.'[46]

There were, however, clearly tensions between long-standing Wesleyans and the new recruits. John Buckmaster's account of chapel life at Slapton, recalls how a radical shoemaker, who took his rejection of the established order beyond simply attending the Methodist chapel and spoke out publicly against the imposition of the tithe, quickly found himself at odds with the chapel elders:

> Some began to say that ... he ought to have kept his tongue quiet ... and one or two of his staunchest supporters turned against him, and others spoke disparagingly of him. What they most wanted was their prayer-meetings, and the Methodists were divided on the conduct of the shoemaker. The younger Methodists supported him, the elder Methodists were against him.[47]

Although the crowds who filled the pews of the new chapels may have come to make a social protest, what they had joined was not a protest movement but a campaign to save mankind from sin and through the late 1830s and the 1840s the Wesleyan élite were content to sacrifice the movement's popularity to ensure that that remained the case. Great Brickhill, in the Leighton Buzzard circuit, was one of the societies that experienced a flood of newcomers but

> This was too much for the faith of the older members, to believe that God could save so many, and amongst them some of the worst people in the village, was beyond the strength of their faith, consequently they treated these new converts with coolness and neglect ... the result was that most of them got discouraged and gave up.[48]

A young minister working in the district in the early 1840s was similarly dismissive:

> I tried to gather a Bible-class of young men; but our leading families comprised no sons of a suitable age, and the young working-men were far more disposed to give instruction than receive it. At our first meeting, they told me through their spokesman that they could take no interest in systematic or continuous instruction of any kind, that the only sort of class they cared for was one in which *they* should choose the subjects and lay down their own laws of discussion ... Seeing that I could find a better investment of my time ... I recommended them to find some other place of meeting.[49]

The Wesleyans had never been a community that fostered or organised protest; it had simply been that some of their meetings lent themselves to appropriation for that purpose. As itinerant preachers and trustees responded to the upsurge in membership by endeavouring to impose greater decorum, respectability and control, Wesleyan societies ceased to provide the opportunity for popular expression and lost the appeal which they had briefly enjoyed among the rural poor. It could be argued that with the economic situation beginning to improve in the late 1830s and

---

[46] It is interesting to note that Jabez Bunting disapproved of the wave of chapel building in the 1830s, not just in Bedfordshire but across the country. He is reported to have said in 1839: 'fewer chapels and more horses would save more souls' (Gregory, *Side lights on the conflicts of Methodism*, 315).

[47] Buckmaster, *Village politician*, 45.

[48] Brigg, *Methodism in Leighton Buzzard circuit*.

[49] *WMM* (1893), 935.

social tensions easing, it was perhaps inevitable that attendance at Methodist meetings should decline as well. The fact, that other, more unambiguously-plebeian, Methodist groups were able to establish themselves in the county at exactly this moment suggests that the decline of Wesleyan Methodism reflected, at least in part, a specific disillusionment with its ability, or willingness, to represent the labourer and his family.

A further factor in the decline of Wesleyan Methodism may have been increasing competition from a resurgent Church of England. From the 1830s through to 1851 and beyond, the parish clergy took energetic steps to build on the Church's pre-eminence in Sunday schools by opening parochially-controlled day schools. Between 1833 and 1851 the number of parishes in the county boasting such facilities rose from seventeen to sixty-seven.[50] Evidence that these schools were used as bulwarks against Dissent is considerable, and it was standard practice to require children attending them to attend the parish church on Sundays.[51] Indeed, after 1830 it is not uncommon to find examples of various kinds of overt pressure being brought to bear in support of attendance at the parish church. At Oakley, the Primitive Methodists found that:

> Pastoral-aid societies and sundry gratuities and privileges, which are at the disposal of the parliamentary church agents, become a great snare to the poor in these parts; and already a strong opposition is put forth against our young and promising sabbath-school. … Several children have been discharged from the national day-school, and deprived of the church's 'benefit club' because they have entered our school.[52]

Perhaps even more ominously for the Wesleyans, by the middle of the nineteenth century the clergy had begun to learn from Methodist successes. In particular, parish churches were beginning to offer evening services, until now almost a Methodist preserve. By 1851 this was the best attended service of the day for the Church of England in Luton, Dunstable, Leighton Buzzard and even a few villages. At Bedford, where an evening service was introduced at St Paul's in 1834, it was enthusiastically noted that the congregation at the Old Meeting was immediately 'very much thinned' and it is hard to avoid the conclusion that some of the people at evening service in Luton parish church in March 1851 would have been occupying the now empty seats in the Wesleyan chapel before such services were commenced six months earlier.[53]

Primitive Methodism

The Church of England was not the only competitor to which the Wesleyan fold was beginning to lose lambs. The 1830s also saw a significant attempt by the Primitive Methodists, or Ranters as they were often known, to establish themselves in Bedfordshire. A largely working-class movement that originated in north Stafford-

[50] Bushby, *Bedfordshire schoolchild*, 61–84 and 123.
[51] Knight, *Nineteenth-Century Church and English society*, 191.
[52] *PMM* (1850), 121.
[53] Letter from Henry Tattam to Bishop of Lincoln, 24 February 1834, Varley, 'A Bedfordshire clergyman of the reform era and his bishop', 139; Bushby, 'Ecclesiastical census, Bedfordshire', 182–3.

shire during the Napoleonic wars, Primitive Methodism saw itself as a return to the spirit of the early Methodists but was actually influenced by accounts of a new style of revivalism that had developed in America. The movement was more than twenty years old, when the quarterly meeting of the Nottingham Primitive Methodist circuit decided, in March 1834, to send a young man called Thomas Clements to Bedford.[54] As has already been suggested, Clements' task may well have been to absorb an existing group of former Revivalists into the Primitive Methodist connexion. It is even possible that he was a former Revivalist preacher himself as he is not previously listed as a Primitive Methodist preacher. He certainly established himself in Bedford with great speed. On 30 June 1834 he obtained a licence for the house of Mrs Blackwell and within a few months had sufficient support that, when the General Missionary committee overruled his appointment by the Nottingham circuit, he was able to sustain himself and his work unaided.[55] Calling himself an Independent Primitive Methodist, Clements went on to open a rented chapel in Russell Street in June 1835 and in September 1838 to lay the foundation stone for a new chapel in Hassett Street capable of seating 180 people, with a preacher's house attached, at a cost of £538 4s 4½d.[56] At the Primitive Methodists' conference of 1839, he and his society of 40 members were accepted back into the Primitive Methodist connexion as a mission of the Hull circuit and a second preacher, Henry Alderslade, was sent to assist him in the work.

Within six months Clements and Alderslade had created four new societies and doubled the membership of the mission but at the following conference both were stationed to new appointments.[57] Clements was not gone for long, however. Stung by accusations that he had embezzled funds and stolen furniture from the minister's house, he called a public meeting in Bedford in May 1841 to set out his defence.[58] Within days the mission was riven with dissension: an official meeting on 10 June

---

[54] Petty, *History of the Primitive Methodist Connexion*, 416; Kendall, *Origin and history of the Primitive Methodist Church*, II, 419. Census returns suggest that he was born in 1803 so that he would have been thirty-one when he first came to Bedford.

[55] Welch, *Bedfordshire chapels*, 30.

[56] *Cambridge Independent Press* 6 June 1835 and 2 December 1837; *Bedford Mercury* 10 and 24 February 1838, 3 March 1838 and 8 September 1838; Hull Primitive Methodist district chapel schedule 1849, Hull History Centre. Petty's assertion that Clements had little success seems ill-founded (Petty, *History of the Primitive Methodist Connexion*, 416). Nor do relations with the Primitive Methodist connexion appear to have been as distant during these years as he implies, for in July 1837 John Flesher, superintendent of the Primitive Methodist's London circuit, preached two sermons in Bedford in aid of 'the Primitive Methodist chapel' (*Bedford Mercury* 15 July 1837, p. 4, col. 3).

[57] Petty claims that the two men 'could not agree, and the societies were divided' (Petty, *History of the Primitive Methodist Connexion*, 416–17). The Hull quarterly meeting was sufficiently concerned about how they would take this news to pass two minutes on the subject in the course of a single meeting: '24. That both preachers at Bedford be affectionately requested to make no stir about their removal from Bedford ... 26. That Bro. Harland request the Bedford preachers to be careful not to unsettle the people, in consequence of their removal and if they (the people) manifest dissatisfaction the preachers are hereby requested to use their utmost influence to promote tranquillity.' In the event both men appear to have departed in peace (Hull Primitive Methodist circuit minutes of quarterly meeting June 1840, BLARS, MB 182).

[58] 'The meeting was a most stormy one ... but on a show of hands being called for, Mr Clements was declared to have vindicated himself by a large majority.' The *Bedford Mercury* picked up the story on 22 May 1841 and the following week Clements' successor, Jeremiah Dodsworth, felt compelled to go into print with his own account of the affair (*Bedford Mercury* 22 May 1841, p. 4, col. 2 and 29 May 1841, p. 1, col. 5).

noted that, 'T. Waldocks name be taken off the preachers' plan he having left the society and joined Mr Clements'; and another in March 1842 that sixty-six names 'have been taken from our Class Books during the last twelve months' including '30 fallen and 22 divisionists'.[59] Given that the membership of the mission in 1841 had only been 120, it was a serious blow. Work progressed, however, and by 1849 the Bedford chapel was said to be full at the principal Sunday services and to have a congregation of fifty for the weeknight preaching. Later that year it was almost entirely re-built to seat around 500. In 1850 it was said that attendance at Sunday services had risen to 300; and on the evening of the 1851 census of religious worship the congregation numbered 460. Village societies also multiplied: there were eleven on the circuit in 1847. Some of these met in makeshift chapels. At Lidlington an old bakehouse was leased and fitted out, at Pavenham a barn; most met in a member's cottage. Not until 1849 was the first village chapel built, at Oakley.

In the meantime, Primitive Methodist missionaries had begun to descend on other parts of the county from almost every direction. From the west, preachers of the Shefford circuit, in Berkshire, had reached Aylesbury in 1836 and by April 1837 were publishing a preaching plan for a Leighton Buzzard mission.[60] It was re-absorbed into the Aylesbury circuit within a few months but the work continued and Primitive Methodist preachers reached Toddington later that year.[61] Two years after that, in 1839, the Aylesbury branch sent Henry Higginson to begin the work at Luton. Higginson met with immediate success. Within seven months a chapel had been built and within four years Luton was the head of an independent circuit containing 190 members in thirteen societies.[62] From the south, preachers of the Hertford mission of the Reading circuit began visiting Stotfold in January 1845 and were using Baldock as a base from which to mission Biggleswade by 1847.[63] Meanwhile from the east, missionaries from the Buckden branch of the Wisbech circuit formed their first society in Bedfordshire at Wyboston in 1849.[64] By 1851 there were at least 38 societies, 7 purpose-built chapels, 5 travelling preachers and some six hundred members in the county.[65] In seventeen years the Primitive Meth-

[59] Bedford Primitive Methodist mission minutes of preparatory quarterly meeting 22 March 1842, BLARS, MB 182. The 'divisionists' went on to build Bedford Tabernacle, which opened in October 1842. The following year Clements was ordained as their minister by the Baptist ministers of Carlton, Cranfield and Riseley (*Baptist Magazine* (1843), 667–8). The church does not appear to have survived long, however, for by 1851 Clements was pastor of Desborough Baptist church in Northamptonshire and the Tabernacle had disappeared without trace (Ward, *Religious census of Northamptonshire*, 159–60).
[60] It provided for Sunday preaching at Leighton Buzzard and Heath and weeknight preaching at Stanbridge.
[61] Shefford Primitive Methodist circuit preaching plans 1836–7, Berkshire Record Office, D/MC2/5A/1; *PMM* (1849), 188 and (1860), 757.
[62] Petty, *History of the Primitive Methodist Connexion*, 358.
[63] *PMM* (1847), 701 and 740.
[64] Buckden Primitive Methodist mission quarterly accounts 1845–71, BLARS, MB 1045.
[65] There were two preachers on the Bedford mission and two on the Luton circuit; and it looks as if one of the preachers on the Baldock mission, John Guy, was living in Biggleswade from 1848 (Welch, *Bedfordshire chapels*, 41). Membership of the Bedford mission, all of the societies of which were in Bedfordshire, was 190 in 1851; there were 48 members in Bedfordshire societies of the Aylesbury circuit and 35 in the Buckden mission. The Luton circuit (280 members), Newport Pagnell mission (190 members) and Baldock mission (183 members) straddled county boundaries and it is difficult to be certain how many of their members were in Bedfordshire. The chapels were at Bedford (1838, rebuilt 1849, see Plate 21), Luton (1839), Stanbridge (1842), Stotfold (1847), Toddington (1848), Oakley (1849) and Woburn Sands (1849).

odists had achieved what had taken the Wesleyans half a century. Moreover, they had done it at a time when the Wesleyans themselves were experiencing widespread stagnation and decline.

Paradoxically, for a community famed for being unlettered and impoverished, the Primitive Methodists seem to have owed much of their success to bold strategic planning and shrewd financial investment. Henry Higginson's mission to Luton, to take one example, was anything but accidental; it was the outcome of a deliberate decision made by the officeholders of the societies in the Aylesbury branch:

> This mission station decided at the March Quarterly Meeting of 1839, to send missionaries to Dunstable, Luton, and other places in the vicinity. ... On April 21st, 1839, the Revs. Henry Higginson and Samuel Turner opened their Mission at Houghton Regis by singing in the streets. In the afternoon, Mr Higginson preached in the open-air at Dunstable, and Mr Turner delivered an address. They then proceeded to Luton, and Mr Turner preached on the Market Hill, and Mr Higginson gave an address. During the week they visited Markyate Street, Kensworth, Caddington, and Chorlton, preaching at each place. On the following Sabbath evening Mr Higginson preached to a large assembly on the Market Hill. ... He had not been in Luton more than two months, when he caught a fever through visiting some sick people. ... On his recovery he removed in July to Marlborough.[66]

None of the societies which undertook to support this mission had been in existence for more than three years and none had yet managed to provide themselves with a permanent home, but the meeting took the extraordinarily far-sighted decision to invest a significant part of their meagre income paying one of their travelling preachers to spend several months preaching in the towns and villages of south Bedfordshire rather than for their own congregations.

Striking though this decision is, it was far from unique. Indeed, strategic mission planning, albeit on a smaller scale, seems to have been a routine matter at quarterly meetings during the 1840s. The minutes of the Bedford mission are typical:

> December 16th 1839 ... Kempston and Oakley to be missioned ...
> March 11th 1841 ... That we endeavour to mission Millbrook, Turvey, Olney, Woburn and Elstow ...
> June 10th 1841 ... That we endeavour to mission Olney next quarter, it being a market town, and their being no Methodist interest there ...
> June 21st 1842 ... That the word 'Mission' be put on the plan for Maulden and that it be supplied as judiciously as possible in connection with Ampthill ...
> March 21st 1843 ... That Goldington be missioned by the travelling preachers the first time that either of them are at liberty on a Friday evening ...[67]

Planning was only part of the story; it was frequently matched by an equally extraordinary opportunism. Oakley, north of Bedford, was to prove to be one of the strongest village societies in the county but it grew out of an attempt to mission the neighbouring village of Clapham in 1839. Ann Cocking walked across to Clapham to hear Henry Alderslade preach out of curiosity and at the end of the service told him: 'I live at Oakley, the next village, and if you will come you shall preach in

---

[66] *Introduction of Primitive Methodism into Luton, 1839*, 5–6.
[67] Bedford Primitive Methodist mission, minutes of preparatory quarterly meetings 1840–3, BLARS, MB 182.

my house.'[68] A preacher was sent and the work began. In 1846 the Hertford mission had made a second attempt to establish a foothold in the town of Hitchin but an invitation to preach in Biggleswade led to a radical shift in resources. John Guy preached the first sermons in the open air on 1 August 1847 and found a good response. Weekly open-air services were immediately begun and quickly established a Sunday afternoon congregation of four to five hundred and a Sunday evening congregation of six to seven hundred. Preaching in Hitchin was abandoned and instead the mission committed itself to sending one of its two travelling preachers to Biggleswade each Sunday and on at least one weekday.[69] In fact, the minutes of all the missions and circuits record a constant process of re-assessing priorities in the light of developments. During 1844 alone, the quarterly board of the Luton circuit added 2 preaching places to their plan, dropped 5 and altered the timing or number of services at 3.[70]

Above all, the missionary work of the Primitive Methodists was marked by relentless hard work. George Price's journal of his work on the Aylesbury mission in March 1836 gives a vivid insight into the physical labour involved:

> Monday, April 4. Walked seven miles to North Marston; informed a few of the inhabitants that I should preach there on Wednesday evening.
> Walked five miles to Ashton Abbots, called from house to house, and informed the people I should preach in the open air. A great number came, I had power in delivering the word; and many paid good attention. We have now one in the society, who professes to have obtained his first good under that sermon. Praise the Lord.
> Tuesday, 5. Walked to Wingrave. Told a few of the inhabitants I should preach there in the open air at ten o'clock next Sunday morning. Walked to Wing, called from house to house telling the people I intended to preach in the open air in the evening. But the rain coming on very heavy, I had the grant to preach in a house.
> Wednesday, 6. On my way to N. Marston, I called at Cublington, told a few persons they might expect preaching there in the open air on the next Wednesday evening. I went on through the heavy rain to N. Marston. I began to fear I should not preach. But a little before six the rain abated, and I preached with good liberty to a large and attentive congregation. To get a bed I was obliged to walk seven miles to Aylesbury.
> Thursday, 7. Preached with enlargement of heart, in the open air in Bishopstone Lane, to a large and attentive congregation. Good was done.
> Sunday, April 10. Preached at Wingrave at ten in the morning in the open air. … Preached at Weedon at half-past one in the open air. A large congregation. … Preached at Whitchurch at half-past four; and though it was not properly known, I judge there were between two or three hundred who paid good attention. At half-past six preached at Hardwick.'[71]

By 1851 at least sixty-eight towns and villages in Bedfordshire had been visited by Primitive Methodist preachers. It was a strategy of growth through geographic

---

[68] *PMM* (1861), 247.
[69] The first attempt to mission Hitchin was made in 1839, the second in 1845 (*PMM* (1846), 26). The town was still listed as a Primitive Methodist preaching place in Upton's survey of 1847 but is not mentioned in a review of work on the mission in 1849 (Burg, *Religion in Hertfordshire*, 41; *PMM* (1849), 368). For the progress of the work in Biggleswade see *PMM* (1847), 739–41 and (1848), 308–9.
[70] Luton Primitive Methodist circuit quarterly meeting minutes 1843–57, BLARS, MB 250.
[71] *PMM* (1837), 308.

expansion and, in that sense, harkened back to the approach of Wesleyan Methodism half a century earlier. However, the way in which it was pursued – relentlessly knocking on as many doors as possible to find which ones might open – was something quite new.

After only seventeen years' work in the county, the Primitive Methodists had more adults attending their services than the Independents, and almost a third as many as the Wesleyans.[72] It was an astonishing achievement but it is probably a mark of the transience and instability of many Primitive societies that the enumerators of the 1851 religious census found barely half of them.

Moravians, Matthewsites and Mormons

By the 1830s the Calvinistic Methodism tradition had all but disappeared from Bedfordshire. The final footnote of its history was perhaps written with the death, in 1845, of Richard Whittingham, John Berridge's former curate and for thirty-nine years vicar of Potton. It was the signal for 'many of the most influential and spiritually-minded of Mr. Whittingham's congregation' to withdraw from the parish church and form themselves into an Independent church.[73]

The Moravians, however, continued to flourish. In 1836 the chapel at Kimbolton, where John King Martyn based himself, was extended to seat six hundred, and in the 1840s was apparently regularly full, making it the second largest Moravian congregation in the country.[74] A building was fitted out as a chapel at Tilbrook in 1839 and this was replaced by a purpose-built structure in 1853.[75] By 1851 the various offshoots of the original Bedford settlement, which spread over Bedfordshire, Huntingdonshire and Northamptonshire, accounted for about a third of all the Moravian congregations in England and Wales.[76]

Bishop Martyn was not the only Bedfordshire curate to leave the Church of England after having come under Methodist influence. The story of the Revd Timothy Matthews has attracted considerable interest over the years but no coherent account of his career and its place in the wider history of early Victorian evangelicalism has ever been published.[77] Like Martyn, he was a disciple of the Cambridge evangelical Charles Simeon. He was appointed to Bolnhurst and Colmworth in

---

[72] With adjustment for congregations that were overlooked, the total number of adults attending Primitive Methodist worship, by Watts' calculation, was 5,330; the Wesleyan figure was 16,786; the Independents 4,400; the Baptists 13,965; and the Union congregations 3,289.

[73] Gilman, *Hundred years at the Congregational Church in Potton*, 7. The same had happened at Turvey on the death of Legh Richmond in 1827. In Hertfordshire, by contrast, Calvinistic Methodism was visibly sustained both by the presence of the Countess of Huntingdon's college at Cheshunt, with its mission stations, and by the work of Bernard Gilpin, rector of St Andrew's, Hertford, a convert to Huntingtonianism who resigned his living in 1835 and founded congregations in Hertford and Hitchin.

[74] For Martyn's earlier career, see pp. 91–2. In 1836 he moved to Ockbrook in Derbyshire to become bishop of the Moravian churches in Britain.

[75] *Short sketches of the work carried out by the ... Moravian Church in Lancashire*, 39.

[76] The 1851 census of religious worship found thirty-two Moravian places of worship in England and Wales, but missed the preaching at Tilbrook, Dean and Keysoe. The congregation at Woodford Halse in Northamptonshire had been a society of the Bedford settlement in the eighteenth century, as had its preaching stations at Culworth and Eydon. The Woodford congregation was in turn responsible for Moravian work in Warwickshire at Priors Marston, Stratford-upon-Avon and Grafton.

[77] There were several obituaries at the time of his death and a biography by Thomas Wright was published in 1934 but all these accounts simplify and distort Matthews' career to make it conform to evangelical ideals.

1818 and in June 1821 he married Ann Fielding, the daughter of a Wesleyan local preacher. Through her family he became increasingly influenced by Wesleyan teaching and practice. By 1828 he had introduced prayer-meetings and class meetings to the parish, and two years later wrote of 'the debt I owe, as a Minister of the Church of England, as well as many of my people, to the doctrine and discipline of Methodism.'[78] His powerful, eschatological preaching, often based on texts from the book of Revelation, won him appointment in 1825 to the post of chaplain at the House of Industry in Bedford; the chapel of which, as well as serving the needs of the impecunious inmates, had already become a fashionable centre of evangelical preaching, drawing a large, well-heeled congregation that included not only Church people but Dissenters, Moravians and Methodists.[79] Here he formed a society, issued membership tickets, held love-feasts and used the Wesleyan catechism. Such were the crowds that came to the services that a gallery had to be added to the chapel to increase the capacity to five hundred and there was even talk of building a new chapel capable of accommodating as many as one thousand hearers.[80] Then events took a different course.

George West was an Irishman of 'Herculean stature' who by all accounts had kissed the Blarney stone. He was originally a Wesleyan local preacher in Londonderry but in 1816 was recruited as a paid itinerant by the Primitive Wesleyan connexion, a newly-formed group of Irish Methodists opposed to separation from the established church.[81] Without permission from the connexion he sailed for Quebec in 1820 where he formed a society on Primitive Wesleyan principles before moving on to New Brunswick where he did the same. By 1826, however, he was back in Ireland and, having failed to gain re-admission to the connexion, he headed for Hull, where he became involved with a short-lived community known as the Church Methodists. Crossing the Atlantic again, he went to the United States where he was ordained by the Episcopalian Bishop of Ohio. Impressed by West's extraordinary skills as an orator, the bishop sent him back to Britain in 1827 on a fundraising trip. When West returned to Ohio the bishop discovered, as others had done before, that he was highly unreliable with money and there was an acrimonious parting of the ways. Nothing daunted, West sailed once more for Liverpool where he presented himself to old acquaintances as a properly consecrated bishop of the previously unknown Primitive Episcopal Church. In February 1831 he was invited to become co-pastor of All Saints, a 2,500-seater unlicensed proprietary chapel in the city, and from this base he began to build up his new denomination.[82] In October 1831 he issued a circular letter to the clergy of the Church of England, introducing the Primitive Episcopal Church as a church based on the Old and New Testaments and loyal to the King, with an elected episcopacy and a large measure of congregational independ-

---

[78] WMM (1830), 512.

[79] Matthews assumed the chaplaincy in 1825 when he lost the curacy of Bolnhurst and moved to Bedford in 1830 when he lost the Colmworth curacy. He lived in Old Priory and supplemented his small stipend by tutoring. Legh Richmond, rector of Turvey, and John King Martyn had both been regular preachers in the chapel (Varley, 'A Bedfordshire clergyman of the reform era and his bishop', 116; Wright, Life of Matthews, 12–22).

[80] Varley, 'A Bedfordshire clergyman of the reform era and his bishop', 117, 118–21.

[81] West has yet to find a biographer but a brief summary of his life is in Roddie, 'Keeping the faith', 232–3.

[82] Thom, 'Liverpool churches and chapels' 169–78.

ence. A summary of the circular appeared in the *Bedford Chronicle* on 5 January 1832 and that may well have been how Matthews heard of it.[83]

Frustrated by the Bishop of Lincoln's reluctance to support his proposal to build a new chapel of ease for his growing congregation, Matthews was instantly drawn to West's project. After the ecclesiastical equivalent of a whirlwind romance, he was consecrated as a bishop of the Primitive Episcopal Church on 8 February 1832 in the chapel of the Bedford House of Industry. A week later, in Liverpool, he shared with West in the consecration of All Saints and the ordination of six deacons.[84]

Returning to Bedford, Matthews found that some of the directors of the House of Industry had taken grave exception to his actions and, by a majority of one, had dismissed him from his post and shut the chapel.[85]

Nothing daunted, Matthews and his supporters immediately announced plans to build their own church and, in the meantime, hired an old meeting house. Nineteen weeks later the 500-seater Christ Church was opened in Conduit Street (later Bromham Road), Bedford at a cost of £2,000.[86] Here Matthews conducted services according to West's revised version of the Book of Common Prayer, dressed in a surplice, and assisted by a clerk and choir.[87] But by then the Primitive Episcopal Church was already disintegrating. Henry Turner, the original pastor of All Saints in Liverpool, having become increasingly uneasy about West's credentials, took the dramatic step at the end of March of excluding him from the pulpit which led to a full-blown riot. Within days West had consecrated another church, St Clements, and within weeks was laying the foundation stones for a new building, claiming to have subscriptions amounting to £3,000, but the party was over. The third, and last, issue of the *Primitive Episcopal Church Magazine* appeared in June 1832 and by February 1833 West had left the city.[88] All that remained of the new denomination was Matthews's Bedford congregation and a second, in Preston, presided over by his brother-in-law, a former Wesleyan preacher, James Fielding.

There were apparently nine hundred members in Bedford and the surrounding villages (more than in the Bedford Wesleyan circuit) but the mortgage on Christ

---

[83] Varley, 'A Bedfordshire clergyman of the reform era and his bishop', 123.

[84] Two days later West also consecrated a second building in the city, used by a congregation of Jewish converts who had placed themselves under his jurisdiction (Thom, 'Liverpool churches and chapels' 174–5).

[85] Varley, 'A Bedfordshire clergyman of the reform era and his bishop', 124–7.

[86] 'A new church is to be built in this town, to be entitled the "New Primitive Episcopal Church", the members of which profess the same religious principles as those of the Church of England. A new Prayer Book is just published, under the direction of Bishop West, of Liverpool, being a revision of the Book of Common Prayer' (*Bucks Herald* 24 March 1832, p. 3, col. 3). Henry Tattam, rector of St Cuthbert's, Bedford to Bishop Kaye 22 March 1832, Varley, 'A Bedfordshire clergyman of the reform era and his bishop', 124.

[87] Wright, *Life of Matthews*, 21–3; Matthews to Bishop Kaye 2 May 1835, Varley, 'A Bedfordshire clergyman of the reform era and his bishop', 130–1.

[88] Thom, 'Liverpool churches and chapels' 175–7. West appears to have headed back to America. He was defrocked by the Episcopalians in 1836 but was subsequently recognised as a Presbyterian minister by the Presbytery of Brooklyn before being struck off by them in 1843 for drunkenness. From 1846 to 1847 he was incumbent of the Scottish Episcopal parish of Old St Paul's, Edinburgh but by 1849 was lecturing in Richmond, Virginia. He was in Albany, New York in 1850 but then his trail goes cold. He was described by one contemporary as 'a great rogue.'

Church was crippling.[89] In April 1835, while simultaneously negotiating with the nascent Catholic Apostolic Church (a millenarian, proto-pentecostalist movement), Matthews wrote to the Bishop of Lincoln 'to inform your Lordship that we are convinced of our error in having stood so long by ourselves' and to 'earnestly solicit your Lordship to admit myself, congregation and Buildings into connexion with the Establishment.'[90] James Fielding, in Preston, was not amused, and wrote to other family members: 'I assure you it has been a heavy trial to me. I am now left alone – not a single brother minister to communicate with. It seems strange that I should have been almost forced into the work and then deserted.'[91] Negotiations with the bishop came to nothing and in August 1836 Matthews was in Preston preaching once again as bishop of the Primitive Episcopalians.[92]

Back in Bedfordshire, Matthews resumed his efforts at building up a circuit of village preaching places. A licence was obtained for a chapel at North Crawley in 1838 and there are references to preaching at Moulsoe, Newport Pagnell and Northampton.[93] At the same time he entered into a new partnership with another freelance Church of England clergyman and believer in the imminence of the second coming, the Revd Robert Aitken. Like Matthews, Aitken had been greatly drawn to Methodism and had even sought admission to the Wesleyan connexion.[94] Rebuffed, he had entered into negotiations with the Wesleyan Methodist Association with a view to becoming minister of their congregation in Liverpool but in the event formed his own Christian Society there in December 1835. In less than twelve months he had 1,500 members, within two years he had congregations across Lancashire, Yorkshire and Staffordshire, and within three he had opened at least two chapels in London. Pressed to cope with this rapid growth he entered into fresh negotiations with the Wesleyan Methodist Association but found a more willing helper in Timothy Matthews.[95] For most of 1839 Matthews was away from Bedford preaching

[89]   Ann Matthews to Joseph Fielding 18 March 1833, quoted in Jensen and Thorp, *Mormons in early Victorian Britain*, 53–4. Mention is made in that letter of members at Barford; a membership ticket, dated November 1833, survives for Mary Dickens of Riseley; and in June 1834 an 'Episcopal church' was licensed in Ravensden, probably a converted barn (Harris, *To serve the present age*, 5; Welch, *Bedfordshire chapels*, 138).

[90]   Matthews to Bishop Kaye 16 April 1835 and Tattam to Bishop Kaye 11 May 1835, Varley, 'A Bedfordshire clergyman of the reform era and his bishop', 127–8 and 136–7. The Catholic Apostolic Church went on to establish a congregation of its own in Bedford but its relationship to Matthews' work is unclear (*Bedford Mercury*, 18 November 1837; Carter, *Anglican evangelicals*; Bushby, 'Ecclesiastical census, Bedfordshire', 132).

[91]   James Fielding to Joseph Fielding, 23 October 1835, quoted in Jensen and Thorp, *Mormons in early Victorian Britain*, 55.

[92]   Matthews to Bishop Kaye, 10 August 1876, Varley, 'A Bedfordshire clergyman of the reform era and his bishop', 138.

[93]   Certificate of registration for North Crawley, CBS, NM 514/7/1; Wright, *Life of Matthews*, 37; Adams, *A few plain facts, shewing the folly, wickedness and imposition of the Rev. Timothy R. Matthews* (1841).

[94]   For an account of Aitkin's career see Thorp, 'Popular preaching and millennial expectations', 103–17 and Chapman, *Rev. Robert Aitken*, (1982). Aitken preached in Dunstable Wesleyan chapel on 8 January 1835 when he was seeking admission to the Wesleyan connexion but was refused use of the same chapel three years later and had to borrow a Baptist chapel instead (Ward, *Early Victorian Methodism*, 119; *Bedford Mercury* 6 October 1838).

[95]   Gowland, *Methodist secessions*, 106–7.

for Aitkin, but it was to be a short-lived partnership.[96] In 1840 Aitken dissolved the Christian Society and returned to the Church of England, leaving Matthews to make his way back to Bedford again and to his circuit of village preaching. This appears now to have been extended to include Burton Latimer, in Northamptonshire, and a congregation in Leicester.

It is clear that Matthews' following ebbed and flowed. In 1838 the rector of St Cuthbert's, Bedford reported to the Bishop of Lincoln that:

> Mr Matthews is going on much as usual, changing with almost every changing month. His congregation had nearly all forsaken him, he therefore found it necessary to adopt some new thing; and has had recourse accordingly to immersion, as the only right mode of administering the ordinance of Baptism. By this, and a miracle it is pretended he performed, and by his extravagant noisy meetings, he has for a time increased the numbers of his followers.[97]

In 1844, he gave communion to two hundred people at Bedford one Sunday, which suggests a congregation very much larger, and ordered four hundred quarterly tickets from the printer (less than half the requirement of the Bedford Wesleyan circuit but more than twice that of the Bedford Primitive Methodist mission).[98] The full extent of his activities in the surrounding villages is impossible to reconstruct but he had the help of several lay preachers and it was claimed, shortly after his death, that 'in a vast number of villages the well-known sound of his bugle would, at any hour, gather round him a congregation'.[99] Even after Matthews's death in 1845, Christ Church and the village societies attached to it had sufficient strength to survive as a body and to employ a series of ministers. According to one account the work at Christ Church was carried on by John FitzGerald (the brother of Edward FitzGerald) and then by two missionaries called Garth and Morton, who also served the village congregations Matthews had founded.[100] By 1851, however, Matthews's circuit had almost completely disintegrated. The congregation in Bedford was reduced to a tiny remnant and the only other survivor was a barn-chapel at Ravensden, the congregation of which described themselves as Matthuite Baptists.[101]

In local histories Matthews has usually been treated as a curiosity, an eccentric character from the fringe of religious life, but in fact his millenarian theology was both within a strong Methodist tradition and very much of his time.[102] The 1830s witnessed a general upsurge in millenarian expectation and prophets of the apoca-

---

[96]   His sermon register records eighty-six preaching engagements in Liverpool that year (Wright, *Life of Matthews*, 44–5).
[97]   Tattam to Bishop Kaye, 15 June 1838, Varley, 'A Bedfordshire clergyman of the reform era and his bishop', 139.
[98]   Wright, *Life of Matthews*, 98 and 100.
[99]   Chalmers, 'Biographical sketch of the Rev. T. R. Matthews', 259. For Matthews' use of exhorters and pastoral letters see Wright, *Life of Matthews*, 54–6 and 82–4.
[100]   Wright, *Life of Matthews*, 174.
[101]   There were only seventy people in the 700 seats of Christ Church even at the best attended service, but sixty people in the 75 seats at Ravensden (Bushby, 'Ecclesiastical census, Bedfordshire', 132 and 137). Two congregations in Northamptonshire recorded in the census may also have had origins in Matthews work, a Millenarian Baptist chapel in Grafton Street, Northampton and a Christian Brethren chapel at Moulton. The congregation at North Crawley appears to have become Mormons.
[102]   See, for example, Sharp, 'An eccentric Bedford evangelist', 65–7. Gowland makes a similar case for the essential similarities between Aitkins' appeal and a, by now, old-fashioned kind of Methodism (Gowland, *Methodist secessions*, 46).

lypse, like the man calling himself the angel Gabriel who appeared in the west of the county in 1838, were commonplace.[103] Matthews' community had connections with a network of similar groups across the country, including not only the Catholic Apostolics and the Christian Society but the Arminian Methodists of Derby, the Peculiar People (another millenarian Methodist offshoot based in London and Essex) and through John Bowes, a former Aitkenite, with the Brethren movement.[104] Nor did such views alienate Matthews from mainstream Wesleyanism. He received invitations from all round the country to preach at the opening of Wesleyan chapels and one of his last sermons, on 'the destruction of the kingdoms under the symbol of the image of Daniel', was for a Wesleyan congregation in London.[105] Locally, at least one Wesleyan local preacher helped on his circuit and there seems to have been a two-way traffic of members between the communities.[106]

Millenarianism had always formed an important thread in Methodist spirituality. John Wesley's sermon before the Bedford assizes in 1758 had had an apocalyptic theme:

> there are abundant magazines of fire ready prepared, and treasured up against the day of the Lord. How soon may a comet, commissioned by him, travel down from the most distant parts of the universe? And were it to fix upon the earth in its return from the sun, when it is some thousand times hotter than a red-hot cannon-ball, who does not see what must be the immediate consequence?[107]

Thirty years later he quoted approvingly, to a congregation in Bradford, the opinion of Johann Bengel, a German Pietist, that the millennial reign of Christ would begin in 1836; and his hymn-book catechized Methodist congregations in an expectation of the second advent:

> Nature's end we wait to see,
> And hear her final groan.
> Let this earth dissolve, and blend
> In death the wicked and the just;
> Let those pond'rous orbs descend,
> And grind us into dust.[108]

Many of the early Methodist leaders shared the same sense of anticipation. John Fletcher's first letter to Wesley, in 1755, predicted that 'we are come to the last

---

103   *Bedford Mercury* 10 November 1838, p. 4, col. 4.

104   Matthews to Bishop Kaye, 2 May 1835, Varley, 'A Bedfordshire clergyman of the reform era and his bishop', 130–1; Sorrell, *Peculiar People*, 13–29; Bowes, *Autobiography*, 271; Bowes, *Truth Promoter*, vol. 1, 216. In the 1851 religious census Christ Church was described as a congregation of 'Christian Brethren' (Bushby, 'Ecclesiastical census, Bedfordshire', 132).

105   Wright, *Life of Matthews*, 122.

106   John Prior, a Wesleyan local preacher, was censored for preaching for Matthews (Bedford Wesleyan circuit minutes of local preachers' meeting 27 September 1841, BLARS, MB 9). The Wesleyans gave up preaching in Ravensden two years after Matthews obtained a license for his chapel there (Bedford Wesleyan circuit minutes of local preachers' meeting 4 October 1836, BLARS, MB 9). At Riseley Mary Bass was converted by Matthews but attended the Wesleyan chapel as it was more convenient (Harris, *To serve the present age*, 4). Both the chapel at North Crawley and Christ Church eventually passed into Wesleyan hands.

107   *Works of Wesley*, I, 369. The sermon also referred to earthquakes as presaging the Second Coming, a view that Matthews shared (*Ibid.*, 357; Wright, *Life of Matthews*, 203).

108   *Works of Wesley*, VII, 155.

times, the grand catastrophe of God's drama draws near apace.'[109] David Simpson, the Methodist curate of Buckingham; Thomas Hartley, the friend of the Countess of Huntingdon and vicar of Winwick in Northamptonshire; and Thomas Taylor, a Wesleyan who preached at Luton in 1781, all published millenarian works.[110] By the latter part of the nineteenth century such views had fallen out of fashion and were generally excised from accounts of early Methodism.[111] In fact, not only was millenarian sentiment widespread in eighteenth-century Methodism but it continued to exercise a powerful appeal well into the second quarter of the nineteenth century. Thomas Coke, who was responsible for the home missionaries that transformed Wesleyan Methodism in Bedfordshire during the Napoleonic wars, interpreted those wars as the 'awful commotions which should precede that reign of righteousness which Christ shall establish on the earth' and predicted that 'the final overthrow of the Mahometan, Papal and Infidel powers, will probably take place about the year 1866.'[112] In the 1820s, John King Martyn wrote that 'the time is soon coming, when ... the Lord himself will direct all things in his millennial church.'[113] In the 1830s, Maximilian Wilson told the Wesleyans of Luton that the controversy over their connexion's Theological Institution was a sign that the new dispensation was approaching, when 'Messiah shall take to himself the mighty power and reign.'[114] Even as late as the early 1840s the platform at a local Wesleyan missionary meeting still 'united Millenarian views with missionary ardour.'[115]

If Matthews' career is an important reminder of this millenarian dimension in late Georgian Methodism, the history of another millenarian group which he helped to introduce to the county seems rather to underscore the point. It began in 1837 when two Americans arrived in Bedford with letters of introduction to Timothy Matthews from one of his brothers-in-law, Joseph Fielding, who had emigrated to Canada in 1832 where he had, at first, continued to be an active Methodist but in 1836 had converted to Mormonism.[116] In June 1837 he was among the small group of Mormon missionaries sent to begin work in England and it was in the Primitive Episcopal chapel in Preston of which his brother, James Fielding, was minister that the first Mormon sermon in Britain was preached on 23 July 1837.[117] Ten days later Elders Goodson and Richards arrived on Matthews' doorstep. According to an account published three years later, Matthews at first welcomed the missionaries and

---

[109] *Works of Wesley*, XXVI, 614.

[110] Simpson, *Key to the prophecies*; Hartley, *Paradise restored*; Taylor, *Ten sermons on the millennium*.

[111] Luke Tyerman even commented on the silence that had fallen over Wesley's millenarian views (Tyerman, *Life of Wesley*, II, 523–4).

[112] Quoted in Vickers, *Thomas Coke*, 330.

[113] *Memoir of the Rev. J. K. Martyn*, 25.

[114] *Two sermons delivered at the Methodist chapel Luton*, 15.

[115] *WMM* (1893), 936. Intriguingly, Benjamin Gregory remembered that one local minister insisted on wearing 'a blue suit of rustic texture and of rustic make – for, like Adam Clarke and Daniel Isaac, he discarded black', a practice that strangely echoes a Southcottian custom, 'The believers were not to wear black, which signifies mourning and the powers of darkness, but blue, which is an emblem of faith' (Harrison, *The second coming*, 121).

[116] Two of Joseph's sisters had emigrated to Canada with him and similarly converted. Mary married Hyrum Smith, older brother of the Mormon prophet Joseph Smith, in 1836 and in 1837 Mercy married another leading Mormon, Robert Thompson (Jensen and Thorp, *Mormons in early Victorian Britain*, 51).

[117] Jensen and Thorp, *Mormons in early Victorian Britain*, 56–9. For James Fielding's church see Atticus, *Our churches and chapels*, 104.

allowed them to use the vestry of Christ Church for a series of evening lectures.[118] This might seem surprising but much of the Mormons' message – the imminence of the Latter Days, the need for the faithful to gather, miraculous revelations and even the idea that America had been home to the lost tribes of ancient Israel – were common currency at the time.[119] By 14 August 1837, news arrived from Preston that the visitors had persuaded a significant part of James Fielding's congregation to forsake the Primitive Episcopal Church and be baptised into the church of the Latter Day Saints. Matthews' mood changed and a few days later Mrs Matthews was writing to her brother Joseph that both she and her husband looked on Mormonism as a cunning fable and the Book of Mormon as a fraud.[120] It was too late. In both Bedford and Northampton members of Matthews' own congregations were already being baptised into the new community.

The links between early Mormonism and Methodism have not, as yet, attracted a great deal of notice from writers on Methodist history but they have been well documented from a Mormon perspective. The *Bucks Herald* described the 'Mormonites' as a 'split off that queerest of all queer sects, the Ranters' and it is clear that there was quite widespread confusion between the two predominantly working class, teetotal sects.[121] At Dover, in 1851, the registrar compiling the census of religious worship discovered that what he had been told was a Primitive Methodist congregation was 'nothing but an out-door gathering of Mormons.'[122] Sometimes the confusion was understandable. At Holbeach, in Lincolnshire, in 1848, the Mormons preached from the same wagon in the same field that the Primitive Methodists had used earlier the same day.[123] Mormon ecclesiology, by which local branches were organised into conferences, serviced by paid itinerants who spent their weeks travelling from branch to branch, and Sunday services were mostly led by unpaid local preachers, clearly owed a debt to Methodism. So too did Mormon expectations of the apocalypse, as was made clear in an article on 'John Wesley – Latter Day Saint' that appeared in one of the earliest issues of the *Millennial Star*.[124] The most telling evidence of the relationship between the two movements, however, is the high proportion of Mormon recruits that were drawn from Methodist ranks. Nationally about 40% of Latter Day Saints were converts from Methodism and locally all of the branches were formed in places where Methodist societies already existed.[125] The threat which Mormonism posed to mainstream Methodism is perhaps best attested by the prominence which Wesleyan leaders took in attacking the movement. At Eaton Bray the Wesleyan minister organised a public meeting, at Dunstable

---

[118] *Millennial Star,* vol. 1, no. 12 (April 1841), 292–4.
[119] I am grateful to Dr Richard Cogley, at Southern Methodist University, for a crash course in the history of American Puritan eschatology.
[120] Ann Matthews to Joseph Fielding 20 August 1837, quoted in Jensen and Thorp, *Mormons in early Victorian Britain,* 61.
[121] *Bucks Herald* 20 July 1844, p. 6, col. 2.
[122] Roake, *Religious worship in Kent,* 352.
[123] *Spalding Free Press* 6 June 1848.
[124] *Millennial Star,* vol. 2, no. 2 (June 1841), 23.
[125] Thorp, 'The religious background of Mormon converts in Britain', 60.

a local preacher published two anti-Mormon pamphlets, and at St Ives Methodists disrupted a Mormon meeting.[126]

Having secured a foothold in Bedford the new church made rapid progress. By the spring of 1838 the Bedford branch was reporting forty members and by 1841 the crowds attending their public lectures in the town were so great that the venue had to be changed to a hall on Castle Hill that could hold a thousand people. Preaching had also spread beyond the town and was now carried on in at least ten other places.[127] By 1843 ten local branches had been formed into the Bedfordshire conference, a preaching circuit whose boundaries bore an uncanny resemblance to the original Wesleyan Bedfordshire circuit; and by 1851 their number had swollen to twenty-six. Even this figure may understate the number of Mormon congregations as some branches appear to have had several meeting places.[128] Eaton Bray was a centre of particular strength. Some 230 people from the village, or neighbouring Edlesborough, were baptised between 1846 and 1851. When Job Smith preached there in 1850 he found ninety members in good standing under the leadership of William Johnson's son, Benjamin. Smith, who was a travelling elder on the Bedfordshire conference from 1850 to 1853, also records in his diary a large congregation meeting in the Oddfellows Hall in Bedford and about three hundred people attending a public lecture in Luton (although there were only about twenty saints in the branch).[129] Nowhere else in southern England did Mormonism find such a warm response. Although largely overlooked by the census of religious worship, in 1851 the Bedfordshire conference reported a total of 908 members, but by then seven thousand British Mormons had already crossed the Atlantic to join their co-religionists in far-off Utah, including a significant number from local branches.[130] One newspaper report alone, from October 1850, records how:

> Lately a hundred persons arrived in Liverpool from Bedfordshire and the neighbourhood, on their way to the Salt Lake Valley, North America, the adopted country of the singular sect, the Mormons. The party consisted of small farmers, market gardeners, mechanics and labourers, with their wives and children.[131]

The Wesleyan Reform Movement

Despite the strength of Wesleyanism in Bedfordshire, Free Methodism (the generic term for the breakaway Methodist groups that allowed laymen a greater say in running their connexions) seems to have found the county infertile ground. There had been two local secessions, at Eaton Bray in 1803 and at Hemel Hempstead in

---

[126] *Robert Hodgert: a pioneer ancestor*, 9–11; Diary and autobiography of Job Smith, 5 March 1851, Brigham Young University, Harold B. Lee Library, MSS 881.

[127] *Millennial Star*, vol. 2, no. 3 (July 1841), 34. North Crawley (Bucks), Kempston, Maulden, Graveley (Hunts), Honeydon, Thorncote, Wyboston, Whaddon (Cambs), Wellingborough, Northampton 'and other places too numerous to mention' (Ibid., 37).

[128] The Thorncote branch, for instance, appears to have had sub-meetings at Upper Caldecote, Biggleswade and Sandy.

[129] Diary and autobiography of Job Smith, Brigham Young University, Harold B. Lee Library MSS 881.

[130] *Millennial Star*, vol. 4, no. 3 (July 1843), 35–6 and vol. 13, no. 1 (January, 1851), 15.

[131] *Cambridge Chronicle* 7 October 1850. This may well have been the party led by Christopher Layton from Thorncote (Cannon, *Autobiography of Christopher Layton*, 108). Of the 163 names mentioned in the records of the Edlesborough branch between 1846 and 1849, seventy-seven can be identified as people who subsequently emigrated (Bartholomew, 'Pattern of missionary work and emigration in Buckinghamshire, 112).

1836. In the latter the leader, James Price, was able to take advantage of the fact that the barn-chapel was not settled on the conference trust to declare independence and appoint himself minister.[132] There is no record of any local participation in the wider disputes which led to the formation of the Methodist New Connexion or the Protestant Methodists or the Wesleyan Methodist Association, although it is evident that local Wesleyans were aware of them.[133] It was not until the Reform agitation of 1849, that the local circuits were seriously troubled by tensions in the national connexion. The crisis was prompted by the decision of the Wesleyan conference in 1849 to expel three ministers, Everett, Dunn and Griffith, who were suspected of writing a series of pamphlets (the 'Fly-sheets') attacking the dominance of a small cabal of London preachers led by the four-times president, Jabez Bunting.[134] The first local references to the civil war that subsequently broke out across the Wesleyan connexion occur in the minutes of the Bedford circuit's quarterly meeting. On 1 October 1849 the minutes record that:

> It was moved by Mr Twitchell, seconded by Mr Stimson – Circuit Stewards … that this meeting, aware that efforts are being made to create disaffection amongst the members of the Wesleyan Body by certain parties on whom the recent Conference deemed it incumbent to exercise discipline, feels itself called upon, under the peculiar circumstances of the case, to express its cordial approval of the general system of Wesleyan discipline and its unabated confidence in the general executive of the Connexion and pledges itself to cultivate amongst its members and the several societies with which they are now immediately connected, an increased spirit of prayer, unity and fraternal love and that the above resolution be advertised in the 'Watchman' newspaper.[135]

The resolution was adopted unanimously and there does not appear to have been any suggestion at this stage that the agitation was anything other than distant thunder. What was happening in other circuits certainly seems to have been a source of grave concern, however, for three months later the same meeting felt it necessary to adopt a second resolution:

> that this meeting, thoroughly convinced of the impracticability and danger of any organic changes in the constitution of Wesleyan Methodism and deeming the system of Lay Delegation and other innovations now importunately urged upon the Connexion, not only undesirable but legally inadmissible, rejoices in the assurance that the interests of Methodism are, under the Divine blessing, perfectly safe in the hands to which they have hitherto been so satisfactorily and prosperously entrusted.'[136]

Again, it was agreed that the motion would be advertised in *The Watchman* and again the meeting was unanimous.

No one from the Bedford circuit is listed as having attended the national Wesleyan

[132]   Greaves, *Wesleyan Methodism in the St Albans Circuit*, 68–9.
[133]   A resolution in support of the conference's action against Dr Warren was adopted by the Bedford circuit and published in *The Watchman* on 21 January 1835. A specially printed issue of the Warrenite *Christian Advocate* was distributed in the Biggleswade circuit (*The Watchman*, March 1836). An Association chapel was opened in neighbouring Northampton (Ward, *Religious census of Northamptonshire*, 103).
[134]   Beckerlegge, *United Methodist Free Churches*, 30–9.
[135]   Bedford Wesleyan circuit, minutes of quarterly meeting 1 October 1849, BLARS, MB 6.
[136]   Bedford Wesleyan circuit, minutes of quarterly meeting 31 December 1849, BLARS, MB 6.

delegate meeting held by the three expelled ministers in Albion Street Independent chapel in London in March 1850 but there were men present from the Hitchin, Luton and Leighton Buzzard circuits.[137] It was in the last of these circuits that the trouble broke out soon after. At a tumultuous Leaders' meeting Thomas Bradbury, a local preacher and teacher at Leighton Buzzard British School, was expelled from the Leighton Buzzard society for attending the reform meeting.[138] He took his case to the district meeting, but his appeal was dismissed, the meeting ruling that he had forfeited his right to be heard as his 'behaviour when conducting the case was extremely unbecoming and insolent.' At the close of the day the circuit stewards from Bedford and Biggleswade proposed a loyal address to the conference:

> ... at the same time, while they express their regret that in some circuits of the District the minds of some of our people have been unsettled by gross and plausible misrepresentations, they feel themselves called upon to express their lively gratitude to God that the greater number of the societies are favoured with so much peace.[139]

James Isitt, a steward from Bedford, and William Charter, a steward from Wellingborough, further proposed that the motion be published in *The Watchman*. Their relief was to prove premature.

On 4 June 1850 Bradbury organised a reform meeting in Leighton Buzzard, Ebenezer Baptist chapel having been lent for the occasion. William Gandy, Esq. of London, took the chair but the other speakers were all local men: William Higgins and James Darley from Luton, a Mr Wood from Aspley Guise, William Woodstock and John Robinson from Leighton Buzzard and Bradbury himself.[140] 'The meeting was a good one, and well attended, and we have no doubt that the cause of reform was greatly advanced by the Christian spirit which ran throughout the whole of the speech delivered by the worthy Chairman,' the *Bucks Advertiser* reported.[141] A month later, on Thursday 4 July, Samuel Dunn and William Griffith themselves, were in Leighton Buzzard. A poster for the visit announced that the local reform committee would be holding a service in the afternoon at Ebenezer chapel, followed by a tea and a public meeting in the evening. Tickets for the tea were 8d and for the meeting 6d or 3d, depending on the location of the seat.[142] According to the *Bucks Advertiser* Griffith preached at the service with 'great ability and rich powers' to a 'pretty numerous assembly.' A large number of people attended the tea, 'chiefly Wesleyans, from all parts of the circuit.' In the evening, the meeting was held in a tent, the 200-seater Ebenezer chapel having, presumably, been judged too small. The chair was taken by the Revd James Price, leader of the breakaway Methodist society in Hemel Hempstead. Dunn spoke first, for nearly an hour and a half, and sat down amid much applause. Griffith then spoke for about the same length of time

---

137 They were Joseph Little from Hitchin; W. H. Higgins and John Jordan from Luton; and Richard Price and Thomas Walters from Leighton Buzzard (*Wesleyan Delegate Takings 1850*, 182, 186, 184).
138 *The Watchman*, 10 April 1850.
139 Bedford and Northampton Wesleyan district, minutes of district meeting 1850, MARC. According to the 1851 census, Bradbury, aged 29, was a native of Huddersfield (TNA, HO 107/1756 fol. 150).
140 It has not been possible to identify a Mr Wood at Aspley Guise with Wesleyan links and it may be that the gentleman in question was Charles *Inwood*.
141 *Bucks Advertiser* 15 June 1850, p. 7, col. 2. See also *Bucks Chronicle* 8 June 1850, p. 3, col. 4.
142 Poster found among papers of the Aylesbury Wesleyan circuit, CBS, NM 100/9/4.

but in a much more demagogic tone: 'Was it fair? ("No, no") A little louder, was it fair? (Loud cries of "No, no").' At the end of his speech a resolution 'expressing sympathy with the deeply-injured men, and disapprobation of the cruel and tyrannical proceedings of the Conference' was passed unanimously. [143]

It all appeared to have gone very well for the reformers, until the questions began. Several prominent radicals were present and endeavoured at this point to have their say. One suggested that 'a hired, paid priesthood was the secret of all this despotism which had been exposed', to which Griffith took exception. Another asked Dunn and Griffith if they had written the flysheets, which they refused to answer. An attempt was then made to close the meeting but the radicals claimed that the reformers were stifling debate in exactly the same way as the Wesleyan conference and the meeting broke up in disarray; Dunn complaining that 'in the one hundred and fifty meetings which had been held throughout the country, they had never been so badly treated as in Leighton Buzzard.'

Shortly after this, according to one account, the majority of the members at Ivinghoe were expelled and the village was dropped from the circuit preaching plan. The local steward, Richard Price, had been a delegate at the meeting in Albion chapel and was the brother of James Price of Hemel Hempstead. He opened a new preaching-room on his own premises and the society continued to operate as Independent Wesleyans until 1864 when they joined the Wesleyan Reform Union.[144]

Reform sentiment was certainly not confined to one village. In July 1851 another reform meeting was held in Leighton Buzzard, the first public meeting to be held in the new town hall. The *Bedford Times* reported that reformers mustered in large numbers for the occasion and that 'Reform principles are gaining a fair hold upon the societies in this circuit.'[145] Circuit membership dipped only slightly, falling from 1,144 at the conference of 1849 to 1,026 by the conference of 1851, suggesting that, Ivinghoe aside, most reformers remained in membership, at least for the duration of the agitation. Relations within local congregations, however, were extremely strained. Loyalists organised a boycott of reformers' businesses and reformers described the junior minister as an 'unchristian slanderer' and the superintendent, John Wevill, as 'Cardinal Wevill'.[146] At Hudnall, where loyalists from Hemel Hempstead and reformers from Ivinghoe preached in the same barn on alternate Sundays, the reformers are said to have removed all the pews one Saturday night hours before the loyalists were due to hold their service.[147] Fifty years later the intensity of the bad feeling was still a painful memory to those who had lived through it.[148] Circuit membership began to decline rapidly and by 1855 was down to 792. It is hard to avoid the conclusion that those who were lost were not principally reformers but simply people exhausted by the acrimony.

Events took a different course in the Higham Ferrers circuit. At a local preachers' meeting in June 1850 four preachers were admonished for 'affording public counte-

---

143   *Bucks Advertiser* 6 July 1850, p. 4, col. 2.
144   *Wesleyan Reform Union Magazine* (1865), 107–8; Legg, *Buckinghamshire returns of the census of religious worship*, 68.
145   *Bedford Times* 26 July 1851, p. 3, col. 2.
146   *Bedford Times* 26 July 1851, p. 3, col. 2.
147   Brewin, *The story of the exploits of the Methodist saints and heroes of Hudnall*.
148   *WMM* (1901), 316.

nance to the agitation by which our Connexion is now disturbed' and the following quarter they were given an ultimatum, either they pledge to desist from agitation or cease to be preachers.[149] They refused to give the required assurance and over the next twelve months nine of the twenty-nine local preachers on the circuit either withdrew or were expelled. A similar proportion of the ordinary members went with them.[150] A reform committee, covering both the Higham Ferrers and Wellingborough circuits, began to organise alternative services.[151] At Finedon loyalists and reformers were worshipping separately by March 1851 and at Wellingborough perhaps even earlier.[152] At Wymington official services were suspended in April 1851, because the owner of the house in which they were held had allowed the reformers to preach there, and the whole society went over to the reform cause. The societies at Rushden and Bozeat followed suit. In fact, reform congregations sprang up across Northamptonshire creating schisms in the Northampton, Peterborough, Towcester, Brackley and Kettering circuits.[153]

The ripples spread and Northamptonshire reformers were prominent in the platform party when a reform meeting was held at Bedford in April 1851. Samuel Dunn was again the main speaker, invited by a local committee who had booked the Assembly Rooms, paid for posters to be published and raised subscriptions. Hundreds attended the two Sunday services and an even greater crowd gathered on the Monday evening for the public meeting, chaired by a Mr Brown from London.[154] The only person from Bedford to speak was James Howard, and he spoke to defend the conference. In the days that followed, one of the committee, a young local preacher called Thomas Lovewell, was tried before the circuit's local preachers for his part in organising the meeting; he was found 'unworthy to have his name continued on the Plan.'[155] But the storm passed, there was no significant fall in the circuit's membership and even Lovewell, despite strong family links with the Wesleyan Methodist Association and his treatment at the hands of the local preachers' meeting, appears to have continued to worship at the Bedford Wesleyan chapel.[156]

---

[149] Higham Ferrers Wesleyan circuit, minutes of local preachers' meeting 24 June 1850, Northants RO, HFMC/5.

[150] The combined membership of the Higham Ferrers and Wellingborough circuits fell from 939 in 1850 to 641 in 1851.

[151] Wesleyan Reform Minute Book of the Wellingborough and Higham Circuits, 1851–71, held by Alma Street Wesleyan Reform Church, Wellingborough. A reform committee appears to have existed in Wellingborough as early as 1849 (*Alma Street Church, Wellingborough - centenary souvenir*).

[152] Ward, *Religious census of Northamptonshire*, 144–7.

[153] Circuits based on Wellingborough, Northampton, Green's Norton and Deddington (in Oxfordshire) eventually joined the Wesleyan Reform Union. A circuit based on Peterborough joined the United Methodist Free Churches.

[154] *Bedford Times* 26 April 1851, p. 1, col. 7.

[155] Bedford Wesleyan circuit, minutes of local preachers' meeting 28 April 1851, BLARS, MB 29. A pamphlet, entitled *Bedford Fly Sheets* and giving details of the case together with Dunn's sermons and an account of the public meeting, was advertised in the local press but no copy appears to have survived (*Bedford Times* 26 April 1851).

[156] His brother, Wesley, was briefly a Wesleyan Methodist Association minister (1841 census and Beckerlegge, *United Methodist ministers and their circuits*, 148). Lovewell had children baptised by the Wesleyan minister in Bedford in September 1851 and November 1852 (Bedford Wesleyan circuit baptism register, BLARS, MB 3).

The evidence in respect of events in the Luton circuit is much more fragmentary. The minutes of the circuit's quarterly meeting make no reference to reform agitation and the minutes of the local preachers' meeting have not survived. It is known, however, that there were people sympathetic to reform in the town. Two local men, William Higgins and John Jordan, were among those who attended the Albion Street meeting in 1850, and three, Higgins, James Darley and William Tranter, spoke at the first Leighton Buzzard meeting.[157] There is also a passing reference in the records of the Luton Primitive Methodist circuit. In the circuit schedule for 1859 it was noted that Thomas James Smith, a class leader, had resigned: 'he was first a Wesleyan, then a Reformer, he then united with us and has now returned to the Wesleyans.'[158] One reading of this would be that there was, at least for a time, a separate congregation of reformers, and it is known that the town society lost seventy members between the conferences of 1850 and 1851, but in the absence of any corroboration it should probably be seen as a possibility rather than an established fact.[159]

All the circuits seem to have been affected eventually. In the Newport Pagnell circuit, where fourteen office-holders signed a pro-reform declaration in January 1852, circuit membership had fallen by 20% during the previous year.[160] The Hitchin circuit reported losses of the same order in 1851/2 and Dunstable of nearly 15% (about 150 members, including two local preachers) in 1852/3.[161] Even then, the crisis was not over and as late as January 1854 reformers were organising a public meeting at St Neots.[162] In the next two years the St Neots circuit lost more than 100 members, 18% of its total, and the neighbouring Biggleswade circuit at least 12%. When the crisis had run its course, the Free Methodist presence in Bedfordshire was tiny, with one society at Wymington and a handful of others close by in Buckinghamshire and Northamptonshire, but the damage done to the Wesleyan circuits had clearly been substantial.[163]

1851: A Last Snapshot

Nowhere is the scale of Methodism's success in early nineteenth-century Bedfordshire more clearly evident than in the returns of the census of religious worship held on Sunday 30 March 1851. For all its limitations (and these are discussed

---

[157] *Wesleyan Delegate Takings 1850*, 182.

[158] Luton Primitive Methodist circuit annual report 1859, BLARS, MB 518.

[159] The schedules of the Luton Primitive Methodist circuit also appear to refer to the existence of another Methodist congregation in the town. A member is described as having joined the 'Bryanites', a reference to William O'Bryan the founder of the Bible Christians, a Methodist grouping largely confined to the West country (Luton Primitive Methodist circuit annual report 1855, BLARS, MB 518). Four years earlier the education census of 1851 records a Bible Christian Sunday school with almost 100 pupils (Bushby, *Bedfordshire schoolchild*, 123).

[160] *Declaration of Wesleyan Methodist officers and members on the state of the connexion* (1852), pp. 8 and 10 (CBS, NM 100/9/3).

[161] One of the local preachers subsequently asked for re-admission, explaining that 'his views on Methodism have undergone a change' (Dunstable Wesleyan circuit, minutes of local preachers meeting 23 December 1852, BLARS, MB 342).

[162] *Cambridge Chronicle* 4 February 1854.

[163] It is intriguing to note, but beyond the scope of this study to explore, the fact that the early Victorian period was to witness considerable dissension within Bedfordshire's Baptist community and that this produced secessionist congregations at Sharnbrook (1827), Leighton Buzzard (1833), Woburn (1835), Luton (1836), Stotfold (1841), Blunham (1842), Biggleswade (1843), Cranfield (1849), and Bedford (1851).

Table 10. Church attendance in Bedfordshire, 1851

Denomination	Places of worship	Estimated attendance	
		numbers	as a % of Bedfordshire's population (124,478)
Church of England	137	36,832	29.6%
Dissenters:			
Baptists	52	16,762	13.5%
Independents	18	5,477	4.4%
Union	13	4,410	3.5%
Total Dissenters	83	26,649	21.4%
Quakers	3	152	0.1%
Methodists:			
Moravians	6	1,324	1%
Wesleyans	87	20,647	16.6%
Matthewsites	2	173	0.1%
Latter Day Saints	6	510	0.4%
Primitive Methodists	38	4,715	3.8%
Temperance Christians	1	43 }	
Wesleyan Reformers	1?	50? }	0.2%
Bible Christians	1?	150? }	
Total Methodists	142	27,612	22.2%
Catholic Apostolic	1	120	0.1%
Roman Catholic	1	60	>0.1%
TOTAL	367	91,425	73.4%

The table is based on the returns to the religious census of 1851, with allowances for the 5 Church of England, 11 Wesleyan, 20 Primitive Methodist, 3 Moravian, 2 Mormon, 1 Wesleyan Reform, 1 Bible Christian and 3 Union places of worship for which there are no returns. Attendance at the ten missing Wesleyan cottage meetings has been estimated on the basis of the mean average for the eight Wesleyan cottage meetings for which there are returns. Attendance at the Wesleyan chapel at Tebworth has been estimated on the basis of the mean average of two other Wesleyan chapels in the same area with similar sized societies and buildings, Toddington and Harpenden. Estimates for the other groups are based on a similar process.

Source: Bushby, 'Ecclesiastical census, Bedfordshire', as amended from manuscript sources.

in Appendix A), the census provides a unique snapshot of church attendance and reveals the extraordinary level of popular support which Methodism enjoyed even after a decade or more of significant decline. Something like 17% of the total population attended a Wesleyan service on census day, and perhaps 5%, the services of other Methodist groups. The total Methodist community was, of course, even larger, for there would inevitably be some people who were unable for a variety of reasons to attend that day. The size of this wider community can be gauged from the census return for Luton Primitive Methodist chapel. On the Sunday of the census, whether by good fortune or design, they were celebrating their Sunday school anniversary with the result that attendance at the three services that day was about twice what it was normally. Some of this may be explained by those who usually only came once or twice on a Sunday coming to a second or third service; and some of it by people who generally went to another church coming to join in the special occasion, though the returns for other churches in the town leave little evidence of this. Most of it, however, seems to be accounted for simply by a higher than average proportion of the chapel's total community making the effort to be present on a particular Sunday for a big occasion.[164] Interestingly, a comparison of the figures for Wesleyan Sunday school scholars recorded by the census and the connexional returns of children enrolled in those Sunday schools also suggests that turnout on any given Sunday was as little as half of its full potential.[165] On this basis some 30% to 40% of the county's total population may have been at least occasional attendants at Methodist worship and, given the high turnover of membership, the percentage who had attended Methodist worship at some stage in their life may have been higher still.[166]

The census also highlights subtleties in the geography of Methodism, which is depicted on Maps 1 and 2. It was weakest in the north and east of the county. In the seventy-two towns and villages covered by the Bedford, Biggleswade, St Neots and Wellingborough census registration districts there were only 24 Wesleyan chapels and 11 preaching places. This was an area with a strong tradition of Dissent and it appears to have been extremely difficult for Methodism to gain a foothold in the villages which already had an established meeting-house.[167] With many of the larger villages occupied by the Baptists and Independents, the Wesleyans were effectively

---

[164] The same does not seem to have been true of Dissenting chapels. Union Chapel, Luton held its Sunday school anniversary on the same day as the Luton Primitive Methodists but recorded congregations only marginally larger than its average.

[165] In the Newport Pagnell circuit the total number of scholars enrolled was 808 but the religious census found only 408 at worship on 30 March 1851 (Newport Pagnell Wesleyan circuit, education schedule 1851, CBS, NM 500/7/20). A register for Toddington Wesleyan Sunday school confirms this picture with only half the children present on any one Sunday and only one in ten attending both morning and afternoon sessions (Toddington Wesleyan Sunday school roll book 1846–7, BLARS, MB 1446). In the Ampthill section of the Bedford circuit, the situation was slightly better with the census schedule suggesting that about two-thirds of the children enrolled in Sunday school where at worship (536 out of 766) (Bedford Wesleyan circuit, education schedule 1851, BLARS, MB107).

[166] Horace Mann, who wrote the original report on the census, estimated that to allow for irregular attendants Nonconformists figures should be increased by 66% and Church of England by 100% (Thompson, 'Religious census of 1851', 252).

[167] Ten villages had Dissenting churches founded before 1800: Blunham, Carlton, Eastcotts, Goldington, Keysoe, Little Staughton, Roxton, Sharnbrook, Stevington and Southill. The Wesleyans failed to gain a foothold in any of them.

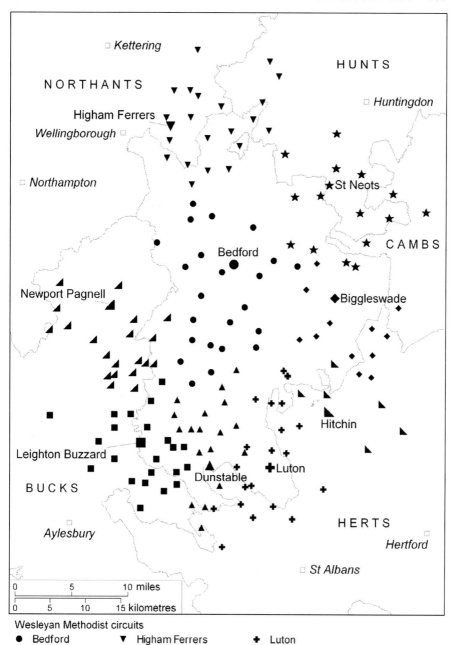

Wesleyan Methodist circuits

●	Bedford	▼	Higham Ferrers	✚	Luton
◆	Biggleswade	◣	Hitchin	◢	Newport Pagnell
▲	Dunstable	■	Leighton Buzzard	★	St Neots

Map 1. Distribution of societies in Wesleyan Methodist circuits in March 1851

confined to the less populous parishes and to outlying settlements.[168] Methodism was stronger in mid-Bedfordshire, where Dissent was comparatively weak, and the Wesleyans were able to attract congregations in 25 of the 35 parishes. The real stronghold, however, lay in the south of the county. In the Luton and Leighton Buzzard registration districts there was a Wesleyan congregation in all but one of the 17 parishes and they generally attracted a larger proportion of their local community than Wesleyan congregations elsewhere in the county.[169] At Stanbridge over 50% of the population probably attended a Wesleyan service on the day of the census of religious worship, at Heath it was 43% and at Sundon 41%. Here Methodist strength appears to have been principally at the expense of the Church of England which attracted only a fraction of the support it commanded further north.[170]

Differences can be detected not only between north and south but also between town and country. About 36% of Bedfordshire's population lived in towns in 1851, but the town congregations accounted for only 29% of Wesleyan attendants, even though overall church attendance in the towns was generally higher than in the villages and town chapels often drew members from neighbouring parishes.[171] The picture was not uniform and the true extent of Wesleyan Methodism's weakness in the towns of Bedfordshire is to some extent masked by its extraordinary success in Dunstable, where it formed the largest religious community and drew nearly 40% of the population to its Sunday services. This pattern of rural strength and urban weakness echoes the situation in the Church of England in 1851 but contrasts strikingly with that of Dissent, whose following was disproportionately urban.[172] If the Wesleyan congregations in Bedford and Luton were relatively small, however, their society membership was relatively large. In village societies members appear, on average, to have constituted about 18% of attending adults (indeed at Shefford it was as low as 5%) but in the towns it was nearly 40%. One possibility is that this discrepancy simply reflects the ability of a larger proportion of town-dwellers to afford the financial cost of membership but, as has already been suggested, another is that it points to a significant decline in the attendance of non-members, tempted back to the parish church by the introduction of evening services or to new, more convenient places of worship being built in the developing residential districts.

[168]   Examples of Wesleyan chapels built in outlying settlements include: Beeston (in Sandy), Upper Caldecote (in Northill), Moggerhanger (in Blunham), Langford End (in Tempsford), Brook End (in Stotfold), and Radwell (in Felmersham).

[169]   Taking the population of the villages in which Wesleyan services were held, in the Bedford registration district attendance at those services was equivalent to 22% of the population; in the Bedfordshire villages of the Biggleswade district it was 21%; in those of the Luton district, 25%; and in those of the Leighton Buzzard district, 39%.

[170]   In the Bedfordshire villages of the Leighton Buzzard district, about 16% of the population attended Church of England services; in the Bedford district it was 36% and in the Bedfordshire villages of the Wellingborough district, 48%.

[171]   The towns in question being Ampthill, Bedford, Biggleswade, Dunstable, Leighton Buzzard and Luton. The Howard family travelled to Bedford Wesleyan chapel from Biddenham and the Inskips from Harrowden. Charles Smith similarly walked to Biggleswade every Sunday from Potton, even when a Wesleyan chapel had been opened in his home village (Williams, *The veteran school-superintendent*, 20).

[172]   Attendance at the Dissenting chapels in Bedford, Luton, Dunstable, Biggleswade, Ampthill and Woburn accounted for 39% of the total attendance at Dissenting worship in Bedfordshire. Attendance at the parish churches of those towns accounted for only 24% of the total attendance at Church of England services.

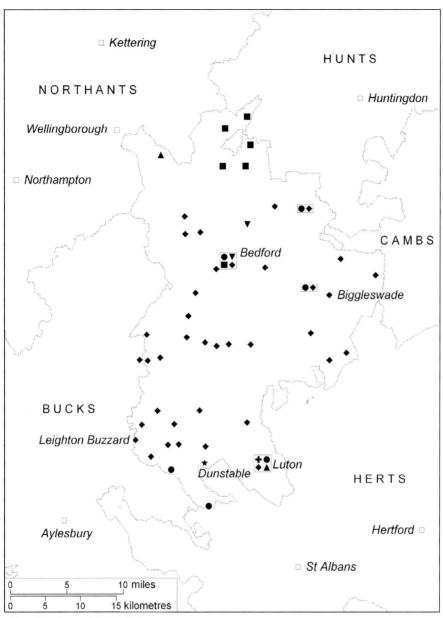

Non-Wesleyan Methodist groups

+ Bible Christians   ■ Moravians   ▲ Wesleyan Reformers
● Latter Day Saints   ◆ Primitive Methodists
▼ Matthewsites   ★ Temperance Christians

Map 2. Distribution of non-Wesleyan Methodist groups in 1851

Table 11. Membership of Wesleyan societies as a percentage of the total adult attendance at Wesleyan worship

Villages	percentage
Biggleswade circuit	13%
St Neots circuit	15%
Bedford circuit	18%
Newport Pagnell circuit	21%
Luton circuit	21%
Towns	
Ampthill	20%
Biggleswade	22%
Bedford	39%
Luton	39%

Details of the membership of individual societies are not available for the Higham Ferrers, Dunstable and Leighton Buzzard circuits. For the Luton, Newport Pagnell, Biggleswade and St Neots circuits the figures apply only to societies in Bedfordshire.

Source: Membership is taken from the schedules of the Bedford, Biggleswade, Luton, St Neots and Newport Pagnell circuits (BLARS, MB 107, MB 834, MB 403, MB 1000; CBS, NM 500/7/4Q). Attendance is based on Watts' calculation.

The geography of the Primitive Methodists closely mirrored that of the Wesleyans, with more societies and generally higher attendance at their services in the south and west than in the north and east. Twenty-seven of the thirty-eight Primitive Methodist congregations were in towns and villages with a Wesleyan society, and one of their strongest congregations was in that most Wesleyan of villages, Stanbridge.[173] Despite its reputation as a rural denomination, however, Primitive Methodism, drew a disproportionate share of its support in Bedfordshire from the towns. Bedford and Luton accounted for only 18% of the county's population in 1851 but their chapels accounted for 27% of adult attendance at Primitive Methodist services. Perhaps not unexpectedly, members seem to have formed a significantly smaller proportion of Primitive Methodist congregations than they did among the Wesleyans.[174] The Latter Day Saints too were found predominantly in the south-west, their strongest branch, Eaton Bray, being only two miles from Stanbridge.

A second census, of educational provision, gives a glimpse of another area of religious life in 1851, Sunday schools. By 1851 there were, it appears, at least fifty-seven Wesleyan Sunday schools in Bedfordshire, twice the number there had been in 1833. That still meant that about a third of Wesleyan congregations had no school

---

[173] The Stanbridge Primitive Methodist congregation represented 36% of the village's population.
[174] The Wesleyans had c.3,850 members in Bedfordshire and by Watts' calculation a total of 16,786 adult attendants on census day, making the membership about 23% of the adult attendance. The Primitive Methodists had c.600 members and by Watts' calculation a total of 4,220 adult attendants making the membership only 14% of the adult attendance.

attached to them, which by national standards was quite a high proportion.[175] The bulk of the societies without Sunday schools were relatively recently formed, within the previous ten years, and this would seem to suggest that such schools were not, at this point, seen as a means of beginning work in a new area but rather as a venture for societies that were already well-established. Altogether, some 5,380 children were enrolled in the schools, representing a market share of nearly 22%, roughly in line with the denomination's share of adult church attendance.[176] The Primitive Methodist societies in Bedfordshire, by contrast, supported six Sunday schools in 1851 with 499 scholars.[177] Expense, as ever with the Primitive Methodists, may have been a factor but a lack of volunteers with sufficient literacy to teach may well have been another.

Table 12. Sunday school attendance, 1851

Denomination	Congregations	Percentage of adult church attendance	Sunday schools	Percentage of Sunday school enrolment
Church of England	137	37.9%	121	48.2%
Baptists	52	21.1%	33	13.7%
Independents	18	6.5%	14	6.2%
Union	13	3.7%	8	7.1%
Moravian	6	1.4%	3	0.7%
Wesleyans	87	23.7%	57	21.7%
Primitive Methodists	38	4.5%	6	2.0%
Bible Christian	1?		1	0.3%
Other	15	1.2%		
Totals	367	100%	243	99.9%

Source: Adult attendance is based on the returns to the census of religious worship of 1851 interpreted using Watts' formula. Sunday schools figures are from the summary table of the 1851 education census for Bedfordshire as reproduced in Bushby, *Bedfordshire Schoolchild*, 122–3.

[175] Nearly 75% of nonconformist congregations in England as a whole had a Sunday school (Watts, *Dissenters*, II, 290).

[176] It is not entirely clear whether the figures for Sunday school scholars given in the returns for the census of religious worship represent the number of children who attended the Sunday school itself or the number of Sunday school children attending public worship. It certainly appears to have been common practice for scholars to be taken to morning and afternoon services *en bloc* and the question about numbers of Sunday scholars seems to have been generally interpreted in that light. The return for Heath Baptist chapel, for instance, includes the note 'afternoon congregation including 24 children of the Sunday school. Children instructed on morning of Lord's day', while Heath Wesleyan chapel's return was careful to point out that in the evening scholars were simply included in the general congregation. Other returns refer to the special seating for scholars: at Luton parish church there was a gallery for the Sunday school boys and at Eggington 'the sittings are for adults, some of the scholars sit on forms in the chancel.' At Union chapel, Luton 'large numbers connected with the Sabbath School are adults who after teaching are mixed with the general congregation' but by inference the children were kept together.

[177] Bushby, *Bedfordshire schoolchild*, 123. Only four were picked up by the census of religious worship (Bedford, Luton, Stanbridge and Toddington) but circuit records confirm that there were also schools at Houghton Regis and Oakley (Luton Primitive Methodist circuit annual report 1851, BLARS, MB 518; Hull Primitive Methodist district property schedule 1850, Hull History Centre).

Part 2 About the People

Labouring men: Wesleyan recruits in the 1830s and 1840s
Nothing highlights more starkly the difference between the surge in Wesleyan membership in the early 1830s and the growth spurts that preceded it than the fact that on this occasion the recruits were neither predominantly female nor generally young. The overwhelming majority were middle-aged, and men may well have been in the majority. Of the 14 people who joined the Eaton Socon society in 1831, 10 were over thirty years of age at the time, 2 others were over twenty-three and the age of the remaining two cannot be ascertained. It was the same story at Woburn Sands where, of the 17 recruits whose age can be ascertained, none were under twenty-nine at the time of joining.

Men were also more prominently represented in this wave of recruits. At Aspley Guise, Cranfield, Salford and Woburn Sands, all in the Newport Pagnell circuit, they had formed only 31% of the membership in 1830 but by 1835 the wave of new converts had taken that to 48%. At Tempsford and Great Barford, in the St Neots circuit, 40% of the members had been men in 1824 but by 1831, the last year for which membership lists are available, that had risen to 45%. In the Bedfordshire societies of the Leighton Buzzard circuit the rise was from 35% in 1828 to 40% in 1834.

Particularly interesting is the number of couples who joined together. At Eaton Socon eight of the 14 recruits joined with their spouse and at Woburn Sands it was eighteen out of 28. Whole families, it seems, not only individuals, were throwing in their lot with the Wesleyans and this may, in part, explain the significant rise in the number of baptisms which Wesleyan preachers were asked to perform in the 1830s. The records of these baptisms are themselves an important glimpse into the social mix of Wesleyan congregations at this period and suggest a dramatic reversal in the trend of recruitment. Between 1815 and 1828, 48% of the fathers presenting their children for baptism in the Biggleswade circuit had been labouring men, but between 1828 and 1836 that soared to 64% as large numbers of poorer families crowded into Wesleyan meetings.

Few of these recruits remained members for very long but their retention rate was not markedly different from that of those who had joined back in the war years. At Cranfield, Salford, Aspley Guise and Woburn Sands, of the 50 people who joined between 1828 and 1832 at least 50% had ceased to meet by 1834; while a class book for Tempsford in the St Neots circuit shows that 7 of the 13 people who joined between 1833 and 1836 were members for less than three years. The cumulative effect of this low retention rate was that new members formed a higher proportion of the total membership than might appear at first sight. In the Bedfordshire societies of the Newport Pagnell circuit, for instance, the total membership rose from 64 in 1830 to 84 in 1835, which might superficially suggest that there were twenty new members. In reality, however, of the 84 members in 1835 only 29 had belonged in 1830 and the overwhelming majority had joined in the previous five years.[178]

---

[178] Newport Pagnell Wesleyan circuit book 1814–38, CBS, NM 500/7/1. In the Leighton Buzzard circuit, where membership of the Bedfordshire societies rose from 293 in 1828 to 549 in 1834, only

Turnover remained high throughout the 1830s and 1840s. Between 1849 and 1852 the total membership of the Bedford circuit fell by eighty, from 1,135 to 1,053, but the circuit schedule records that no fewer than 396 of the members in 1849 (over a third) were no longer members in 1852.[179]

The Wesleyan cousinhood

There continued, of course, to be a core of long-term members and it was from among them that the leadership of the local societies and circuits were drawn. One of them was Ezra Labrum, from Battlesden, who joined in 1832 and continued in member-ship, serving as both a class leader and a local preacher, until his death in 1863.[180] Like most of the post-1830 recruits who went on to merit an obituary, he was the child of a Methodist home and joined the society when he was still young. Indeed, considerable pressure was often brought to bear on children as they approached adulthood. Daniel Pressland made it clear to his children that they would cause him much grief if they did not enter membership and Ezra's own parents 'were most diligent and prayerful in their efforts to induce him to seek a personal and saving interest in the precious blood of Jesus.'[181] Revivals among the children attending Wesleyan Sunday schools, such as the one recorded at Salford, near Battlesden, in 1838, helped to provide the necessary rite of passage.[182] In an age of large families, the cumulative effect of this biological evangelism was not insignificant. By the time of his death in 1849, Thomas Hawkes boasted seventy-two descendants and delighted in seeing many of them join him at worship in Luton's Wesleyan chapel: 'it shows the deferent effect the conduct of the head of a large family will have on the following generations.'[183]

The growth of a Wesleyan cousinry was reinforced by the expectation that serious Wesleyans would find their marriage partners from within the denomina-tion. Ezra probably married his partner, 'an excellent lady, whose religious views were in harmony with his own', in a parish church but with the passage of the Marriage Act in 1836 it became possible for such weddings to be conducted by a Wesleyan minister in a Wesleyan chapel. At first, it was not clear that Wesleyans would take advantage of this legislation. Several leading ministers argued that it was not part of the ministerial function to conduct weddings – 'The Apostles did not marry people' – and it appears that there was a concern that religious weddings in some way encouraged the Popish superstition that marriage was a sacrament. When the Bedford circuit asked the annual conference in 1837 for advice on whether to licence chapels under the act, the conference refused to offer any guidance. Such was the demand for Wesleyan weddings, however, that other local circuits pressed ahead without waiting for sanction. Biggleswade chapel was licensed in July 1837

---

175 of those 549 people had been members six years earlier (Leighton Buzzard Wesleyan circuit book 1828–36, BLARS, MB 1534).
[179] One hundred and forty-three had removed to other circuits, 25 had died and 228 had been struck off as backsliders.
[180] *WMM* (1865), 188–90.
[181] *WMM* (1845), 844.
[182] *WMM* (1845), 501; Hempton, *Religion of the people*, 19 and 40.
[183] Letter from Thomas Hawkes to Joseph Hawkes, 29 June 1846, quoted in Hawkes, *Rise of Wesleyan Sunday schools*, 9.

with the first wedding taking place that November. Leighton Buzzard followed in January 1838, Luton and Dunstable in 1845, and Ampthill in 1848.[184]

By the 1830s many of the county's leading Wesleyans were linked not only by blood and marriage but by business. Thomas Twitchell, a Wesleyan farmer at Willington, hired the rams that tupped his sheep from the circuit steward, Samuel Bennett.[185] Ezra Labrum, as a grocer, probably owed much of his custom to co-religionists. Certainly when Samuel Claridge, a young Wesleyan from Leighton Buzzard, established a similar business in Hemel Hempstead a few years later, and then thought of joining another religious community:

> Methodist friends talked with me and cautioned me about the step I was going to take saying You are young and just started out in life, and it might ruin me financially, as many of my customers were Methodist.[186]

The launch of *The Watchman,* a national weekly newspaper for Wesleyans, in 1835, vastly extended the opportunities for this kind of preferential purchasing. Its classified advertisements made it possible for Wesleyans to patronise a whole range of Wesleyan businesses, including schools, insurance companies, asylums, publishers, medical services and a restorer of silver-plated cutlery! Even the businesses themselves were sold through the paper, helping to keep them within the economy of the denomination.[187]

The Watchman may also have contributed to the creation of a Wesleyan investment market. The trustees of the Luton, Leighton Buzzard and St Neots chapels all advertised for investors in the paper's columns, offering a healthy 4½% return.[188] Thomas Ward of Hitchin bought shares in the Wesleyan Proprietary Grammar School at Sheffield but he also invested in his local chapel, effectively using it as a pension fund by giving the trustees land in return for an annuity.[189]

The columns of *The Watchman* certainly provided an employment exchange, taking to a new level the old preference for employing other members of the society. Fifty-one local jobs were advertised between 1835 and 1851, of which the two vacancies in Joseph Flemons' drapery shop were typical:

> TO DRAPERS' ASSISTANTS
> WANTED, immediately, an active YOUNG MAN, of obliging manners, who understands the general trade. A Wesleyan preferred. Also an APPRENTICE who will be treated as one of the family.
> Apply to T. Flemons, Leighton Buzzard[190]

---

[184] Gregory, *Side lights on the conflicts of Methodism,* 236–7.

[185] *The Watchman* 13 December 1843.

[186] Ellsworth, *Samuel Claridge,* 12. The Wesleyans were not unique in this respect. See also William Hale White's reference to there being 'generally two shops of each trade; one which was patronised by the Church and Tories, and another by Dissenters and Whigs' (Rutherford, *Autobiography,* 26).

[187] Five local businesses were advertised for sale between 1835 and 1851 including a builder's yard, a chemist's, a baker's, a school and a draper's.

[188] *The Watchman* 25 January 1837, 16 June 1841, p. 185, col. 4; and 22 June 1842.

[189] *The Watchman* 13 July 1836 and 30 December 1835. For another local example of a chapel providing an annuity investment see Wilson, *A history of the Methodist churches in the Rugby and Daventry circuit,* 8–9.

[190] *The Watchman* 15 October 1845.

By the same token, twenty-four individuals from local circuits, mostly young men, placed advertisements looking for posts. These often expressed a preference for being placed with Wesleyan families, one explaining that he did not wish to be in a position where he was compelled to break the Sabbath. A young chemist from Biggleswade looked for an employer who would accommodate his work as a local preacher.

> WANTED, by a Young Man, who is a Wesleyan Local Preacher, a SITUATION as a CHEMIST and DRUGGIST. He is competent to undertake every part of the Business; and his object is not so much a salary, as a comfortable home, where he might have a little leisure for the duties of the Ministry.
> Letters, (pre-paid,) addressed to J. S. at the Rev. Thomas Staton's, Biggleswade, Beds.[191]

The relationship between this largely self-contained, middle-class, Wesleyan cousinhood and the bulk of the membership appears to have been quite distant. In a lengthy obituary for Thomas Hine, in 1858, the *Wesleyan Methodist Magazine* painted an idyllic picture of Bedfordshire as verdant pasturage and smiling cornfields dotted with respectable farmhouses and farmed by substantial Wesleyan farmers:

> Many of the occupants of these comfortable dwellings are Wesleyan Methodists; and not a few of the hardy sons of toil, by whom the lands are cultivated, belong to the same communion. The writer has known instances in which the master, cultivating his own estate, called his labourers together in the fields, and, before an ear of corn was cut, held a prayer-meeting under the canopy of heaven.[192]

This was hardly an accurate description of the great bulk of the Wesleyan members in Bedfordshire but it is, perhaps, a clue as to how those who held office, headed the subscription lists and sat in the rented pews, liked to think of themselves and how they viewed their relationship with the ordinary folk who sat in the chapel's free seats.

Disillusioned Wesleyans: Primitives, Mormons and Reformers

No membership lists for the Primitive Methodist societies in Bedfordshire survive but there are baptism registers for all the circuits, except the Baldock mission, and given the very small percentage of the Primitive Methodist community in formal membership these may, in any case, provide a better impression of its overall make-up. What they show is an overwhelmingly plebeian constituency. Some 85% of the village children baptised were from labouring families and most of the fathers who were tradesmen were small-scale plait dealers, who went from door to door buying straw plait to take to market, rather than shopkeepers. The poverty of the members seems to have surprised even the travelling preachers. John Parrott, stationed at Bedford in 1850, wrote to the magazine that 'The farm-labourers are getting no more than about 7s or 8s per week! and with this small wage many a member has to support a wife and five or six children. How he manages to live on such a sum

---

[191] *The Watchman* 7 October 1840.
[192] *WMM* (1858), 769.

is to me a painful mystery.'[193] In most of the villages of the Bedford mission none of the members could afford to offer the travelling preachers hospitality and mid-week services had to be held at 5.00pm (rather than the usual hour of 7.00pm) so that the preachers would be able to walk back to town afterwards.[194] Even in Luton, unskilled manual workers predominated. Only in Bedford did the congregation have a more mixed background, including a surprising number of small tradesmen and clerical workers.

Table 13. Primitive Methodist baptisms 1836–1851: occupation of father

Occupation	Villages		Luton		Bedford		Total	
	no.	%	no.	%	no.	%	no.	%
Farmer	0		0		0		0	
Tradesman	12	6	4	9	5	10	21	8
Clerical worker	0		0		5	10	5	2
Artisan	16	9	5	11	22	45	43	15
Labourer	155	85	36	80	17	35	208	75
Total	183	100%	45	100%	49	100%	277	100%

The figures represent all the baptisms that took place in the Bedford mission and the Luton circuit before 1852 and all the baptisms in the Bedfordshire parts of the Aylesbury circuit, the Newport Pagnell and Buckden missions before that year.

Sources: Bedford Primitive Methodist mission baptism register (held by Park Road Methodist church, Bedford); Luton Primitive Methodist circuit baptism register (BLARS, MB 522); Newport Pagnell Primitive Methodist mission baptism register (BLARS, MB 1552); Buckden Primitive Methodist mission baptism register (Cambs RO, MRF/4/1); and Aylesbury Primitive Methodist circuit baptism register (CBS, NMP 100/10/1).

The registers suggest that, as with the Wesleyans, most of these people were connected with Primitive Methodism for quite a short time. Of the 99 families recorded in the Bedford register, 72 appear in connection with a single occasion and, presumably, had ceased to be attached to Primitive Methodism by the time their next child was born. This may at first sight seem an extraordinarily high rate of turnover but it is not far off the situation revealed in the annual report of the Luton circuit for 1844. There had been 190 members in the circuit in 1843 and at the end of the year there were 183, but during those twelve months, 76 members had been lost and 69 recruited.[195] As always, the financial cost of membership was one reason for dropping out. The annual report for the Bedford mission in 1847 noted that some 'have left us in consequence of not being able to assist the cause.'[196] More common, however, seems to have been a simple tailing away of interest after the first rush of enthusiasm. Six women and a man who left the society at North Marston, in the Aylesbury circuit, in 1842 'gave no reason, save [having] lost the good feeling they

---

[193] *PMM* (1850), 120–1.
[194] Bedford Primitive Methodist mission, minutes of preparatory quarterly board 15 December 1840, BLARS, MB 182.
[195] Three had died, 2 had moved away, 37 had 'fallen' (i.e. had been expelled) and 34 had left the society of their own volition (Luton Primitive Methodist circuit annual report 1844, BLARS, MB 518).
[196] Bedford Primitive Methodist mission annual report 1847, BLARS, MB 1671.

had.'[197] There may also have been seasonal factors at work. The same report from Aylesbury describes recent recruits as having fallen away 'when summer and the feasts came on' and the minutes of the Bedford mission described the impossibility of attracting village congregations during the harvest, 'Our country friends will not, *cannot* attend preaching on a week night in Harvest.'[198] Religion, for some people at least, was an activity for the long, dark winter nights.

In Bedford and Luton a substantial majority of the families listed in the baptism registers lived in streets immediately adjacent to the chapels, which were erected in new residential districts on the outskirts of the towns.[199] Convenience rather than any distinctiveness in worship or ethos appears to have been the draw for them, a consideration also mentioned in several obituaries. At Bedford, for instance, Eliza Kent 'coming to reside near our chapel, and being in a very delicate state of health … thought it best to cast in her lot amongst us'; while Matilda Gostling 'having a small family, and this chapel being near … was induced to attend it.'[200]

The fact that many of the children baptized were not infants (in the Bedford mission about a fifth were over the age of two) and the fact that often groups of siblings were baptized together, may suggest that a significant proportion of the recruits to Primitive Methodism had not previously had any kind of church affiliation. This would certainly fit with the claims which Primitive Methodists made about their work. When William Harvey preached on the Aylesbury circuit, in 1836, he noted in his journal that most of those who attended his open-air services were 'persons who frequent no place of worship' and added the comment, 'these are they we are in pursuit of.' Eleven years later John Guy would make the same point to a man in Biggleswade who observed that he had seen 'many people attend our preaching who had not usually attended places of worship anywhere. I told him these were the persons whom we sought to bring to the Saviour's fold.'[201]

It is clear, however, that this was not the whole story. Primitive Methodist societies were formed not where religious provision was weak, but where the Wesleyans were already strong. Of the 38 Primitive Methodist societies that are known for certain to have existed in Bedfordshire in 1851, no fewer than 29 co-existed with older Wesleyan societies and, of the remaining nine, 2 were formed as a direct result of Wesleyan societies closing and 5 co-existed with some other branch of evangelical Dissent.[202] Some Wesleyans clearly suspected that the Primitive Methodists

---

[197] Aylesbury Primitive Methodist circuit annual report 1842, CBS, NMP 100/7/1.

[198] Bedford Primitive Methodist mission, minutes of preparatory quarterly board 29 September 1842, BLARS, MB 182.

[199] In Bedford 28 out of the 42 families whose addresses can be identified lived in adjacent streets. The Bedford chapel is described in contemporary sources as being in the New Town, an area developed in the 1830s. The Luton chapel was in Donkey Hall (later known as Hightown) an area that was developed from the 1820s onwards.

[200] *PMM* (1853), 701 and (1854), 516.

[201] *PMM* (1837), 307; (1847), 739.

[202] Primitive Methodist societies were formed alongside existing Wesleyan societies in Ampthill, Arlesey, Aspley Guise, Battlesden, Bedford, Biggleswade, Billington, Caldecote, Clifton, Clophill, Cranfield, Everton, Houghton Regis, Kempston, Langford, Leighton Buzzard, Leighton Heath, Lidlington, Luton, Marston Moretaine, Millbrook, Pavenham, Salford, Stanbridge, Stotfold, Tilsworth, Toddington, Woburn Sands and Wootton. At Colmworth and Sharpenhoe the Primitive Methodists moved in when the Wesleyans pulled out. At Cople, Oakley, Potsgrove, Stevington and Wrestlingworth they established themselves in villages with existing congregations of Dissenters.

deliberately targeted their congregations. An anonymous historian of Totternhoe Wesleyan chapel in 1863 recorded that

> Before the year 1840 the Totternhoe Wesleyans belonged to the Eaton Bray Society, but about that time the Primitives came to Totternhoe and tried to establish a cause by getting the members belonging to the Wesleyan society to join them.[203]

Even the Primitive Methodist registers, when compared with those of the Wesleyan circuits, show that about one in ten of the families asking a Primitive preacher to baptize a child had previously had children baptized by Wesleyan preachers.

The recruits from Wesleyanism may have been particularly important in providing the core membership of the new societies. Among the individuals who merited an obituary in the *Primitive Methodist Magazine* more than half had belonged to other evangelical communities before joining and of these the overwhelming majority had been Wesleyans.[204] Another distinction between the core membership and the majority of recruits appears to have been one of age. Many of the converts were apparently young. The annual report of the Aylesbury circuit for 1842 records that the success of their revival meetings had been 'principally among the young people.'[205] A protrated meeting at Wavendon in 1847 likewise produced 20 converts, 5 of them young men and 11 children – 'most of whom were above 14 years of age.'[206] By contrast, more than 50% of those prominent enough to be memorialised in the magazine were over thirty years of age when they joined and more than 30% were over forty.

The success of the Primitive Methodists in drawing away support from existing Wesleyan communities seems to have had several causes. One was that the Wesleyan circuits were too stretched to meet the demand for Methodist religion, particularly in the new districts of Bedford and Luton but also in some of the smaller villages. At Streatley, the Wesleyans ceased to preach in William Clarke's house once a chapel had been opened in the neighbouring village of Barton; in response Clarke 'readily offered the loan of his house to our missionaries … and he, his wife and his daughter, became members of our society.'[207] Colmworth was taken up in the same way and an attempt at something similar was clearly made at Totternhoe.[208] Another reason for the success of Primitive Methodist recruitment among Wesleyans must surely have been division and disillusionment in the Wesleyan ranks.[209] Some of this may have had personal and local roots and some may have been a response to

---

[203]   From a handwritten history of Totternhoe Wesleyan chapel, dated 1863 quoted in Bourne, *Dunstable Methodist Circuit*, 147.

[204]   There are obituaries for 36 Bedfordshire residents who joined the Primitive Methodists before 1851 and the religious background of 29 are known. Twelve are described as having been sinners, or 'strangers to experimental religion'; 13 as having previously been Wesleyans; 3 as having been Baptists; and 1 as having been 'pious.'

[205]   Aylesbury Primitive Methodist circuit annual report 1842, CBS, NMP 100/7/1; *PMM* (1840), 95.

[206]   *PMM* (1848), 49.

[207]   *PMM* (1844), 239.

[208]   Bedford Wesleyan circuit, minutes of local preachers' meeting 27 December 1841, BLARS, MB 9; Bedford Primitive Methodist mission, minutes of preparatory quarterly meeting 22 March 1842, BLARS, MB 182.

[209]   For the way in which the smaller Methodist bodies have been categorised as either 'offshoots' or 'secessions', see Currie, *Methodism divided*, 54–71.

the direction of the changes taking place in the Wesleyan community. Jane Jefford, one of the very first people to join the Primitive Methodist society in Luton in 1839, had left the Wesleyans after 'a little unpleasantness occurred and she dismembered herself.'[210] Eleven years later, during the rather greater unpleasantness of the reform crisis within Wesleyan Methodism, the membership of the Primitive Methodist circuits in Bedfordshire would grow by more than 25% in three years.[211]

It is possible to build up a slightly fuller picture of the Primitive Methodist leadership from the surviving preaching plans and the minutes of the quarterly boards. An astonishing proportion of members were involved in leading worship, whether as local preachers, exhorters or prayer leaders. In the Buckden mission thirty-eight names are listed on the preaching plan for the summer of 1852, in a circuit that had barely two hundred members.[212] Given that the overwhelming majority of the names were those of men, and that men were almost certainly in a minority among the membership, it may be that anything up to half of the male membership were preachers of one kind or another. The majority of these preachers were often labouring men but there was still a disproportionate representation of the better off. Of the 16 accredited local preachers on the plan of the Baldock mission in 1853, 6 were labourers but the other 10 included a master bricklayer employing five men, a market gardener who employed four men, and the son of a farmer who employed twenty-one men.[213] Not that all the preachers were men. One of the names on the Baldock plan is definitely that of a woman, and three of those on the Buckden plan might be. There are references to a number of female local preachers in the minutes of the Bedford and Luton quarterly boards during the 1840s and at least one female travelling preacher was stationed on the Aylesbury circuit during the early part of that decade.[214] Even among this inner circle of preachers the turnover of personnel was extraordinary. In its annual reports between 1843 and 1851 the Luton circuit consistently reported about 17 local preachers but in those nine years no fewer than 31 individuals either resigned or were struck off the plan.[215]

Looking at the congregation of Timothy Matthews' chapel in Bedford in 1844, Edward FitzGerald characterised them as all poor people but his observation is not born out by the only surviving record of the Bedford Primitive Methodist Episcopal Church, the baptism register. The register shows a constituency that was broadly

---

[210] *PMM* (1854), 445.

[211] Between 1850 and 1853 membership of the Primitive Methodists circuits in Bedfordshire increased by 167. Among the new recruits were Thomas James Smith, whose case was detailed above (see p. 156), and Mr Pickering, a local preacher in the Dunstable Wesleyan circuit.

[212] Buckden Primitive Methodist mission, preaching plan July-October 1852, BLARS, MB 1049.

[213] Baldock Primitive Methodist mission, preaching plan January-April 1853, Society of Cirplanologists.

[214] Bedford Primitive Methodist mission, minutes of preparatory quarterly board 10 June 1841, BLARS, MB 182; Luton Primitive Methodist circuit, minutes of quarterly board 18 March 1844, BLARS, MB520. Ann Goodwin was certainly appointed to the Aylesbury circuit and a Miss Anscombe may also have been (Graham, *Chosen by God*, 29–30 and 7–8).

[215] Luton Primitive Methodist circuit, minutes of quarterly board 1848–58, BLARS, MB 520. Many of the preachers seem to have simply lost interest and the first that the circuit authorities often knew about it seems to have been when a string of congregations reported that they had not turned up to preach. The prevalence of this problem can perhaps be judged by the praise given to Thomas Quarterman of Weedon in his obituary: 'his strict attention to his appointments never left the people in suspense as to whether he would take them up' (*PMM* (1841), 169–70).

based and rather less representative of the labouring class than either the Primitive or Wesleyan Methodists. Of the 129 fathers who brought their offspring to Matthews for baptism, 55% were labourers, 36% were artisans, 8% were tradesmen and 1% were farmers. Besides which, as the occasional presence of the FitzGerald brothers in the congregation testifies, Matthews enjoyed the personal support of a number of admirers from social cycles quite unknown to mainstream Methodism.

Mormon growth in Bedfordshire appears to have followed essentially the same pattern as across Britain as a whole. Most of the recruits had a religious background with the initial foothold being gained at the expense of one of the smaller Methodist bodies, in this case the Primitive Episcopal Church, and subsequent expansion chiefly at the expense of the Wesleyans.[216] Indeed, Samuel Claridge, a former Wesleyan class leader at Hemel Hempstead, baptised in 1851 as a Mormon, at one stage 'thought I could convert all my old Methodist friends.'[217] The Wesleyans were not the only community to suffer loses to the Latter Day Saints. The Baptist church at Northall, which had begun life as an independent Methodist congregation, suffered a number of defections including the son of the minister. Luton's Primitive Methodist circuit experienced quite a serious disruption in 1844 which resulted in two local preachers, Thomas Squires and Thomas Day, being expelled for attempting to 'make a division in the circuit' and talking of 'establishing a new connexion' and was still losing members to the 'Mormonites' a decade later.[218] At Bishop's Stortford it was the temperance society that provided the recruiting ground and a congregation of teetotallers, who had withdrawn from their churches because of the use of alcohol at the Lord's Supper, went over *en masse*.[219] The records of the Eaton Bray branch of the Latter Day Saints suggest that Mormonism was unusually attractive to men, who accounted for 44% of the baptisms and who, in reversal of the usual pattern amongst Methodists, often joined before their wives.[220] The converts were generally young, about a third were under twenty and well over half were under thirty. Above all they appear to have been poor. Samuel Claridge, who was a successful baker and grocer, reflected that 'It was quite a test for human nature to give up my respectable Methodist folk with their fine new meeting-house, to go with the very poor, despised Mormons.'[221]

About forty local people can be identified as supporters of the Wesleyan reform movement, all of them men and at least twenty-six of them local preachers. David Gowland's study of the origins of Free Methodism in Lancashire found that the movement fed on existing tensions within the Wesleyan community about politics, loss of status or local rivalries and there are some hints that similar issues may have been at work in Bedfordshire.[222] Three of the leading Bedfordshire reformers were

216   Thorp, 'The religious background of Mormon converts in Britain,' 60.
217   Ellsworth, *Samuel Claridge*, 14. Christopher and Mary Layton were also Wesleyans (Cannon, *Autobiography of Christopher Layton*, 3).
218   Luton Primitive Methodist circuit annual report 1844, BLARS, MB 518; Luton Primitive Methodist circuit annual report 1855, BLARS, MB 518. Squires appears to have been baptised a Mormon in 1844 and Day was elder of the Latter Day Saints at Flamstead by 1851.
219   *Robert Hodgert: a pioneer ancestor*, 13.
220   Bartholomew, 'Babylon and Zion: Buckinghamshire and the Mormons in the nineteenth century', 235.
221   Ellsworth, *Samuel Claridge*, 12.
222   Gowland, *Methodist secessions*, 65.

incomers, Thomas Bradbury from Huddersfield, Thomas Lovewell from Ipswich and John Jordan from Devon and it is possible that this was an obstacle to their attaining the position in their local society or circuit which they felt their talents merited. At Higham Ferrers and Wellingborough, where the reformers gained their greatest success, Wesleyanism was already in decline and leading members may well have felt that their status in the wider community was being undermined as a result.[223] What can be said with rather more certainty is that, unlike any of the other minor Methodist bodies, reform appealed to middle-aged shopkeepers and artisans rather than to the young and the poor; and that while disenchantment with the Wesleyan connexion among the young and the poor was sufficient to support several alternative Methodist communities, among the more middle-class members it was not.

Postscript: Stotfold, 1860

If there is little evidence from the 1840s which gives an insight into the way in which the social make-up of Methodism evolved in the decade leading up to 1851, a document from a few years later provides a valuable glimpse of where the trajectory would lead. Nine years after the close of the period under examination, the Revd Joseph Fenn, a Church of England clergyman at Stotfold in the east of Bedfordshire, prepared detailed notes on the churchgoing habits of the inhabitants of the village for his successor.[224] A large parish, with a population of 2,071, Stotfold boasted, in addition to its parish church, two Baptist meetings and both Wesleyan and Primitive Methodist chapels. Berridge had preached here and the Wesleyan society dated back to the Napoleonic wars. The village had also been at the centre of some of the worst disturbances in 1830 and there had been strong feeling against the Church of England for the part played by the then curate in having two men transported. Thirty years later, Fenn's notes record the head of each household, their occupation and religious affiliation, as well as some personal observations (see Table 14).[225]

The document suggests that the social make-up of both the Church of England and Wesleyan congregations in the village mirrored fairly accurately the social make-up of the community as a whole; that the Baptists were disproportionately strong among the village's tradesmen but weak among the labourers; and that almost all the Primitive Methodists were from labouring families.

The glimpse which Fenn's notes offer of Methodism in Stotfold in 1860 supports the view that the Wesleyans soon lost the very high levels of support which they enjoyed among the rural poor in the 1830s. Between 1830 and 1839, 88% of the fathers who presented their children for Wesleyan baptism in the village had been unskilled workers, a far higher proportion than in the population as a whole. By the early 1850s that had fallen to 76% and by 1860 labouring households comprised only 70% of the Wesleyan community, about the same proportion as in the village generally. Even more telling are Fenn's observations on who constituted the leading

---

[223] According to Benjamin Gregory, Wellingborough was 'very low' in the mid-1840s and the same description is given by another observer to the society at Thrapston in the Higham Ferrers circuit (*WMM* (1893) 939; *The Watchman*, 29 January 1845).

[224] List of inhabitants of Stotfold 1 March 1860, BLARS, P 83/28/2.

[225] These include such comments as 'beware of her begging habits' and 'saucy!'

members of the Wesleyan society. In 1838 the steward and the class leaders at Stotfold had all been labourers but by 1860 the principal Wesleyans were nearly all farmers. There were still many poor Wesleyans but Wesleyan Methodism was no longer a religion of the poor.

Table 14. Religious affiliation of households in Stotfold, 1860

	Wesleyan		Prim. Meth.		C of E		Baptist		None		Total	
	no.	%	no.	%	no.	%	no.	%	no.	%	no.	%
Independent	-	-	-	-	1	1	-	-	-	-	1	
Farmers	6	8	-	-	6	7	2	3	3	3	17	5
Tradesmen	8	11	-	-	13	14	13	22	11	10	45	13
Clerical	-	-	-	-	2	2	1	2	2	2	5	2
Artisans	7	10	1	12	7	8	8	14	11	10	34	10
Labourers	50	70	7	88	61	67	35	59	79	75	232	69
Not known	1	1									1	
Total no.	72		8		90		59		106		335	
Affiliation as % of all households	21%		2%		27%		18%		32%			

Twenty-three families had divided loyalties and they have been counted as a half for each of the appropriate denominations. Totals and percentages have been rounded to the nearest whole number.

Source: List of inhabitants of Stotfold 1 March 1860, BLARS, P 83/28/2.

Fenn's notes provide more than simply the opportunity to look at the social make-up of two Methodist congregations, they also show them in the context of the whole village. They reveal that not only were labouring families becoming a smaller proportion of the Wesleyan community, but that declining church attendances meant that Wesleyans were becoming a smaller proportion of the labouring community. Even in 1851, when the Wesleyans may already have been in decline for a decade, some 27% of the population of Stotfold were probably attending their chapel and 83%, were attending some place of worship.[226] By 1860 Fenn identified only 21% of households as Wesleyan and only 67% as having a church affiliation of any kind. In other words, by 1860 more labouring and artisan families attended no place of worship at all than attended the Wesleyan chapel; and while it is true that the Primitive Methodist chapel continued to offer the kind of plebeian religious community, which had once been the attraction of Wesleyan Methodism, it enjoyed the support of only a tiny minority of the village's labouring families.

   Of all the myths that late nineteenth-century Methodists would weave around their history perhaps the most powerful is that first fostered by John Wesley, namely that Methodism began by winning the support of the humble poor and then, by encouraging habits of industry and thrift, set them on the path to social betterment. It is clear, however, that, if the Wesleyan congregations of Bedfordshire looked

[226] Based on Watts' calculation, for an explanation of which see Appendix A.

rather more prosperous in 1851 than they had in 1831, it owed more to the fact that Methodism was losing the support of the poor than that large numbers of Methodists were moving up the social scale.

Part 3 Being a Methodist

The Evolution of Wesleyan Worship
Superficially at least, the convulsion of rapid growth which seized the Wesleyan societies in Bedfordshire in the early 1830s gave a sudden and fresh dynamic to the same evolutionary process that had begun during the boom of the war years and then stalled in the downturn that followed. Attendance at Methodist services soared, chapels were built in unprecedented numbers and Sunday schools sprang up on every side.[227] By the mid-1830s the old-style, closed societies had virtually disappeared and almost everywhere Wesleyan communities now conformed to the more open model which had become a feature of the local towns twenty or so years earlier. At another level, what emerged in the villages of Bedfordshire during the early 1830s was a quite new variant of Methodism. The town congregations had been gathered by professional preachers bent on a deliberate policy of expansion using music and preaching, novelty and entertainment to attract the young and aspiring. There is little evidence that the professional preachers played much part in the gathering of these new village congregations. Indeed the circuit preaching plans show that they were still spending the overwhelming majority of their Sundays in a small minority of chapels.[228] This growth spurt was demand-led rather than supply-led, spontaneous rather than planned. In 1814 the chapel in Luton had been built in the hope of attracting a congregation; now circuit meetings were forced to build chapels to house congregations that had already mushroomed.[229] Moreover, these new congregations performed a quite different function in village society from that which Wesleyan congregations played in the local towns.

The most detailed insight into the experience of being a village Methodist during these years comes from John Buckmaster. Interestingly, although he mentions the music, 'which made the service attractive', for Buckmaster the heart of the Methodist experience was not the Sunday preaching service but rather the prayer meetings. Such meetings were certainly not new. George Coles refers to prayer meetings being held three nights a week at Stewkley in 1804, and they were clearly part of Methodist life at Raunds at about the same time.[230] Of all the Methodist meetings this was perhaps the most open and inclusive: an itinerant preacher recalled that 'the

---

[227] Between 1830 and 1835 nineteen Wesleyan chapels were built in Bedfordshire. By 1833 there were at least twenty-eight Wesleyan Sunday schools (Bushby, *Bedfordshire schoolchild*, 61–81).
[228] The three itinerant preachers on the Biggleswade circuit did not take any of the Sunday services at 11 of the 23 places on their plan in the six months from November 1836 to April 1837. On the Leighton Buzzard circuit, 9 out of 20 congregations did not see a professional preacher on a Sunday between November 1831 and April 1832.
[229] At Ashwell, in the Biggleswade circuit the society 'was greatly increased and a spirit of hearing prevailed to such an extent that the old barn was filled, while others were glad to catch a word at the windows or the door' (*WMM* (1834), 217).
[230] Coles, *Youthful days*, 82; *MM* (1816), 47.

leadership was arranged impromptu' in a very 'free and easy yet patriarchal way.'[231] It was a meeting in which anyone could have their say, and it is evident that they did.

In old age Buckmaster could still remember how 'they talked familiarly about Jesus Christ, as if he were a farm labourer keeping a family on nine shillings a week.' The idea of a God who listened and cared was a source of comfort to men and women who were stressed and anxious. Buckmaster recalled how Methodism 'gave these poor men … comfort in time of want and suffering; it was to them the only thing which made this life tolerable, with the hope of a better.'[232] He was particularly struck by a ploughman who, as he worked

> used to give out verses of hymns, such as … 'And am I born to die?' … 'Come on, my partners in distress' and then to sing them in a low tone of voice, and appeared happy, although his singing was far from being cheerful or musical.[233]

The intense small meetings of Methodism, which had once helped to keep the world at bay, now, it seems, came into their own as a cathartic outlet for fears, worries and grievances.

> The trials and temptations to which such men were exposed found relief in the weekly prayer meeting or class meeting and hymns, and their earnest appeals to the Lord for strength …[234]

Praying together both affirmed their faith and created a community of consolation. Many years later Benjamin Gregory could still remember how such meetings had 'a deep undertone of plaintiveness and pathos.'[235]

There was more than comfort in such meetings, there was also an opportunity to rage and protest:

> The landlords and some of the farmers were prayed for by name. 'Cursed is he who removeth his neighbour's landmark, and oppresseth the poor and needy, and joineth land to land,' and stoppeth footpaths; these sentences always met with hearty amens.[236]

For people to whom the existence of God was at least as real as the existence of parliament, and to whom the former probably seemed vastly more approachable than the latter, this was a means of petitioning for redress that offered a better prospect of success than signing a petition or attending a political meeting. It was also a form of protest which, unlike setting fire to hayricks or attempting to organise collective action against low wages, enjoyed a measure of both legal and cultural protection from reprisal. Circuit preaching plans make no reference to these prayer meetings but they do confirm the increasing popularity of another meeting in which the ordinary members also had a chance to speak up, the love-feast. In the Biggleswade circuit, the plan for November 1824 to April 1825 provided for only three love-

---

[231] In the Bedford Wesleyan circuit only 3 societies out of 15 held such services during a seven-month period in 1825, but 11 out of 24 held them during four months in 1839. Plans from the Leighton Buzzard and Biggleswade circuit tell the same story.
[232] Buckmaster, *Village politician*, 39–40.
[233] Buckmaster, *Village politician*, 24.
[234] Buckmaster, *Village politician*, 40.
[235] Gregory, *Autobiographical recollections*, 11. Gregory had been the junior preacher on the Kettering circuit for the year 1843–4.
[236] Buckmaster, *Village politician*, 40.

feasts, but the plan for November 1836 to April 1837 provided for nineteen. Such was the draw, and possibly the power, of these meetings that it was sometimes thought necessary to attempt to restrict attendance. The notice for one love-feast in the Aylesbury circuit warned 'No one to be admitted but regular members of the Methodist Society, and those who receive notes of admittance.'[237]

Buckmaster's account also suggests that, in one respect at least, the village Methodist chapel acted as something more than a simple pressure valve and provided a means by which people could dramatically change their circumstances. It facilitated emigration.

> One of the farmers who had emigrated some years ago to America wrote a glowing account of the country and its prospects, urging all who could to come over to Iowa. The letter was read in almost every cottage. It was read at the village inn and at the Methodist chapel every Sunday until it was nearly worn out. The Lord had now opened a door of escape. Special prayer meetings were held to know the Lord's will, which was that they should go. … A farewell service was held in the Methodist chapel, which was crowded, and the services lasted through the night till daybreak. The following evening, in the glorious springtime of May, some thirty-three men, women and children knelt down in the street, and after a short prayer meeting, marched through the village singing hymns. The whole village turned out, and many accompanied them for miles. … Prayers in the Methodist chapel were regularly offered up for the exiles until news came of their safe arrival and settlement. This induced others, in batches of threes and fours, to follow for several years.[238]

There is evidence of Methodists from a number of villages emigrating at much the same time.[239] It is impossible to say whether Methodists were more likely to emigrate than their neighbours but there can be little doubt that denominational networks made emigration easier for Methodists, offering a crucial point of initial contact at their chosen destination. When George Coles had left for America in 1818 he had taken with him not just a letter of commendation from his employer but 'heaps of quarterly membership tickets … and printed plans of different circuits on which I had laboured as a local preacher.' When he arrived in America his first call was on the local Methodist church and his first night was spent as a guest of the Methodist pastor.[240] Even those who did not go as far as to cross the Atlantic, but looked for new opportunities closer to home in local towns or even London, may still have found that Methodism was an important source of connections with the world beyond their own village.

The appropriation of Methodist structures, as a vehicle for expressing popular unrest, was to prove only a temporary phenomenon. The huge effort made in housing the mushrooming congregations in purpose-built chapels had the effect of containing them in spaces over which the preachers and more affluent members had

---

[237] Durley, *Centenary annals*, 21.

[238] Buckmaster, *Village politician*, 48–9.

[239] Three of the Fieldings left Honeydon for Canada between 1832 and 1834. Abraham Briggs left Bromham for Tasmania in 1833. Thomas Turner went from Milton Ernest to Nova Scotia in about 1831. Joseph Swannell from Radwell and James Dixon from Bedford both went to America at some point between 1825 and 1837.

[240] Coles, *Youthful days*, 213–14 and 253.

ultimate control, and they moved quickly to curtail much of the freedom of expression in Wesleyan worship.

At Pavenham, in 1832, the congregation was censured for holding a fellowship meeting 'contrary to our Rules'.[241] At Kettering some kind of controls appear to have been introduced around who could contribute to the prayer meeting and one working-man complained that it had become 'a *Qualification* prayer-meeting'. Tellingly, perhaps, he decided to attend a political club instead.[242] Love-feasts too were reined in, their number being dramatically cut back and leadership of them taken out of the hands of the local preachers.[243]

Changes in Wesleyan music-making from the late 1830s onwards were also reducing the opportunities for the popular voice to be heard in worship. When congregational singing was led by instrumental bands, the choice of hymns was often largely in the hands of the musicians, rather than the preacher, not least because the musicians may have had a limited repertoire of tunes.[244] At Stotfold, it was later recalled, the musicians had 'very complete control' of the hymn-singing.[245] All of that, however, began to change as communal orchestras in larger chapels were displaced by a solo instrument, the organ. The trustees of Ampthill chapel were given permission to install the first organ in a Bedfordshire Wesleyan chapel in 1835 but other trusts soon followed suit.[246] There was an organ at Bedford by 1846 and a group of wealthy members presented one to the St Neots chapel in 1848.[247] With the organs came a new style of hymn tune, promoted in several semi-official tune-books published in the 1840s. Slower and more sedate, the new tunes marched steadily from chord to chord without any of the runs, repeats and embellishments that had been a feature of Methodist music over the previous forty years.[248] Of the nine tunes specifically listed by George Coles as typical of local hymn singing in about 1814, only one was included in the tune-book prepared for the Bedford chapel in 1862.[249] The method of giving out the words of the hymns changed also, with preachers reading out whole verses rather than two lines at a time, again reducing opportunities for fugues and repeats. The cumulative effect was to make hymn-singing more measured, less emotional, and more self-consciously dignified or, as the expression at the time seems to have been, more 'harmonious'.[250] Not everyone was impressed and at Stotfold, the first time a preacher gave out a whole verse of a hymn, the choir walked out.[251]

In place of love-feasts and gallery bands, forms of worship were promoted that emphasised order, self-control and hierarchy, and which deliberately harkened back to an earlier form of Methodism. Quarterly fast-days, theoretically part of Wesleyan

---

241   Bedford Wesleyan circuit, minutes of local preachers' meeting 31 December 1832, BLARS, MB 9.
242   *WMM* (1893), 934–5.
243   By 1849 the preaching plan of the Biggleswade circuit provided for only two congregations to hold a love-feast in the quarter August to October.
244   *Companion to the Wesleyan hymn-book* (1847), iii.
245   Phillips, *Wesleyan Methodist church, Biggleswade circuit*, 37.
246   Bedford Wesleyan district minutes 1835, MARC.
247   Notes on St Paul's Wesleyan chapel, BLARS, X302/9/2; *The Watchman* 19 December 1848.
248   *The Wesleyan Psalmist* provided tunes specifically for the organ.
249   Coles, *Youthful days*, 92; Bedford Wesleyan chapel MS tune-book, 1862, BLARS, X 302/4.
250   See Davies, *History of the Methodist church*, IV, 491–2.
251   Phillips, *Wesleyan Methodist church, Biggleswade circuit*, 37.

discipline from the outset but not previously mentioned in local records, began to be routinely published on circuit plans from the late 1830s.[252] Covenant services are likewise reported for the first time in the Biggleswade circuit in 1846 and the Dunstable circuit in 1848.[253] Most significant, however, was perhaps the revival of interest in communion services. After several decades in which the sacrament was celebrated with decreasing frequency by a dwindling proportion of societies, there was a dramatic reversal. By 1847, 16 of the eighteen societies in the Dunstable circuit were holding communion services at least once a quarter and 16 out of nineteen on the Luton circuit.[254] There is evidence too that communion practice was changing. When a new chapel was opened at Stewkley in 1840, it was noted that it included 'a convenient communion rail, the want of which is much felt in most of our village chapels in this neighbourhood.'[255] A similar addition, together with a font, was installed in the Ampthill chapel later the same year.[256] Prior to this, chapels either had no communion table at all (the bread and wine being blessed from the pulpit and then taken to the congregation in their pews) or had a table that was surrounded on three sides by a special communion pew (in which communicants sat to receive the bread and wine).[257] Now, it would seem, members were expected to come forward and kneel before the preacher to receive communion, highlighting both the privilege of admission to such a sacred moment and also the status and authority of the preachers who led the service.

A concerted attempt was also made to raise the tone of the spoken element of Sunday preaching services. In 1837 the district meeting passed a resolution recommending that readings from the Bible be more frequently included in services and circuit preaching plans began to carry a lectionary of appropriate passages.[258] Leighton Buzzard had already led the way as early as 1831 but Bedford followed suit by 1839 and the other circuits by 1850. Most plans gave details of two lessons to be read at the morning service but a Hitchin circuit plan offered an evening lesson as well and a Luton plan, both an afternoon and an evening lesson. The selection of lessons appears to have been based on the calendars in the Book of Common Prayer but it is evident that this was simply a practical convenience rather than an expression of loyalty to the state church for in 1843 the district meeting recommended that the conference produce a new lectionary adapted to the needs of the connexion.[259] The introduction of Bible readings was only gradually accepted, not least because some local preachers were unable to read, and as late as 1851 a note was still necessary on the St Neots circuit preaching plan to remind preachers that they

252   The first occasion is on the Biggleswade Wesleyan circuit preaching plan November 1836-April 1837, MARC. By 1851 all the local circuits, except Luton, were carrying such notices on their plans.
253   *WMM* (1858) 777; Dunstable Wesleyan circuit preaching plan, November 1847-January 1848, MARC.
254   Dunstable Wesleyan circuit preaching plan November 1847-January 1848, MARC; Luton Wesleyan circuit preaching plan February-May 1846, MARC.
255   *The Watchman*, 12 February 1840.
256   *The Watchman*, 11 November 1840.
257   Plans in the 1820s and 1830s of the interior layout of two chapels in the Aylesbury circuit preserved in the account books of the chapel stewards, Bierton Wesleyan Chapel steward's account 1827–60, CBS, NM 102/3/1; Whitchurch Wesleyan chapel steward's accounts 1808–87, CBS, NM 114/3/6.
258   Bedford and Northampton Wesleyan district minutes, 1837, MARC.
259   Bedford and Northampton Wesleyan district minutes, 1843, MARC.

were 'expected to read a portion of God's word at each service.' [260] Where it was adopted, the reading of a lengthy passage from the Authorised Version introduced a new solemnity to the occasion, counter-balancing the colloquial tone of many of the prayers and sermons and giving the service a more respectable feel.

One or two chapels may even have introduced liturgical services. When the Wesleyan chapel at Aylesbury was re-opened after renovation in 1844, the local Tory newspaper reported a rumour that 'this faithful congregation intend shortly to use the excellent Church Liturgy, instead of extempore prayers, in the same manner that is done in the Methodist Chapels at Oxford, Bedford, London and many other places.'[261] At Biggleswade, the chapel opened in 1834 had boards behind the pulpit bearing the words of the Lord's prayer, the ten commandments and the apostles' creed, raising the possibility at least that these may have been recited during services.[262] Several of the other chapels built in this period seem to point to a new tone in worship, if not to any specific new practices. Older chapels, like Leighton Buzzard, originally built in 1803, were plain affairs (see Plate 16):

> the walls [were] a dingy white colour, the straight-backed pews uncomfortable, the gallery-front painted a sombre drab; and the pulpit, a tub like construction, and standing upon a pedestal, painted a miserable imitation of mahogany. The free seats were immediately in front of the pulpit, and were of considerably less elaborate construction than the pews.[263]

The new chapel at Luton, built in 1852 to seat 1,800 people, was a rather different beast (see Plate 22). The ground glass of its windows gave the whole chapel a 'soft light' and the pulpit, built of 'solid mahogany, polished, large and handsome', cost £70 by itself. Downstairs, the central block of seating was now reserved for the most expensive pews 'all lined with blue cloth, cushioned, and carpeted.'[264] At Tebworth the chapel, erected in 1842, was in a gothic style (see Plate 20) and at Bedford the ceiling of the chapel was 'prepared with light blue paper with little white clouds floating about all over it, to represent the sky.'[265] There was also a move towards making the chapel a space solely for worship by providing ancillary rooms for the Sunday school, business meetings and social gatherings. A Sunday school room was included in the building works at Biggleswade in 1834 and was quickly copied by the societies at Harpenden, Leighton Buzzard, Stewkley and Toddington among others.[266]

---

[260] St Neots Wesleyan circuit preaching plan, September 1851-January 1852, copy in the author's possession.

[261] *Bucks Herald*, 3 February 1844, p. 4, col. 2.

[262] The new Luton chapel, built in 1852, also had commandment boards (Tearle, *Our heritage*, 6).

[263] Brigg, *Methodism in the Leighton Buzzard circuit*.

[264] Davis, *History of Luton*, 66–7. The pulpit, rather unusually, stood against the front wall of the chapel so that the congregation entered by doors either side of it in full sight of those who were already seated; a disincentive, perhaps, to lateness. Subsequent chapels at Aley Green (1856), Edlesborough (1858), Markyate (1859) and Kimpton (1871) adopted the same arrangement.

[265] Notes on St Paul's Wesleyan chapel, BLARS, X302/9/2; *The Watchman* 30 November 1842. The chapels at Toseland and Potton, both in the St Neots circuit, were also described as being in a Gothic style (*The Watchman* 17 October 1849 and 1 October 1851).

[266] *The Watchman* 27 March 1839, p. 106, col. 3; 23 September 1840, p. 310, col. 4; and 4 November 1846, p. 524, col. 2; *WMM* (1835), 214.

Efforts were also clearly made to bring the local preachers under tighter supervision. In the Bedford circuit new rules were adopted in 1832 governing the selection and admission of new preachers and steps were taken against local preachers who had allowed young men to share in leading services without the superintendent's permission.[267] A few years later, in what appears to have been a clamp down on preachers with radical political sympathies, the same circuit banned from its pulpits anyone who belonged to the Oddfellows club.[268] In the Leighton Buzzard circuit one local preacher was even given an involuntary make-over. William Arnold of Stanbridge:

> Used to wear a coloured neck handkerchief, a yellow waistcoat, and knee breeches in the pulpit, so someone sent him three white handkerchiefs and a black waistcoat. When he came home at night, and his wife told him, he said, 'Oh, Sal! I can never wear them.' But his friends prevailed on him.[269]

Over the next fifteen years the body of preachers became older and more respectable. There had never been many labouring men among them but by the 1840s there appear to have been none at all in most circuits.[270] Classes and libraries were established to inculcate doctrinal orthodoxy and preachers were encouraged to script their sermons and memorise them rather than to preach extempore.[271] Despite the progress made in increasing their respectability and orthodoxy the status of local preachers was increasingly downplayed. On many circuit preaching plans the names of the itinerants, which had always been placed at the head of the list of preachers, were now also marked out by capital letters; and the heading changed from 'the plan of the Wesleyan preachers' to 'the plan of the Wesleyan ministers and local preachers.' It is perhaps not to be wondered that local preachers were so prominent among the ranks of the reformers.

The status of the ministers, as they were now beginning to be called, was correspondingly enhanced. James Rigg, a young local preacher in the Biggleswade circuit, has left a detailed account of the various stages of the selection process operating in the 1840s, beginning with a trial sermon and interrogation before the ministers of the district and then a trip to London to be interviewed by a committee of the connexion's leading ministers.[272] Like many of the candidates for the ministry by this date, Rigg was himself the son of a minister and was warned by his father that the requirements for acceptance were becoming progressively more demanding: 'many things which will be tolerated in one now in the ministry will close the door for ever against one who wishes to enter it.'[273] From 1835 some of the successful candidates were even being sent to the newly created Wesleyan Theological Institution for a residential course of study. With greater status came greater rewards. By 1843 the superintendent of the Dunstable circuit was receiving £126 a year, with

---

[267]   Bedford Wesleyan circuit, minutes of local preachers' meeting 31 December 1832 and 5 April 1836, BLARS, MB 9.
[268]   Bedford Wesleyan circuit minutes of local preachers' meeting 28 September 1840, BLARS, MB 9.
[269]   *Our own magazine* (July, 1896).
[270]   Token working class preachers like Charles Richardson remained popular for special occasions.
[271]   Bedford Wesleyan circuit minutes of local preachers' meeting 25 September 1843, BLARS, MB 9; Hawkes, *Rise of Wesleyan Sunday schools*, 3; Rigg, *Wesleyan Methodist reminiscences*, 13.
[272]   Rigg, *Wesleyan Methodist reminiscences*, 6–9.
[273]   Telford, *Rigg*, 26.

free housing, no responsibility for rates or property tax, and an additional allowance for each child.[274] Gone were the days of trudging round the circuit for it was becoming standard for circuits to provide a horse and gig.[275] Underpinning this elevation of the minister was a new doctrine of the ministry. Locally, it was set out in a sermon preached before the district meeting in 1842 and subsequently published at their request:

> If you account Ministers as appointed by Christ, you will regard them with reverence, you will venerate their character, you will treat them with kindness and affection, you will provide that which is necessary for their comfort and the comfort of their families; you will seldom oppose them ... the same regard you would pay to Christ, if he were present, you will, in a due degree, pay to the Ministers who you believe he has sent.[276]

Although ministers played a leading role in the drive to confirm Wesleyan Methodism as a respectable religious community, they were only able to achieve what they did with the support of the leading members. In several initiatives, including the creation of Methodist day schools, lay people appear to have been the primary instigators. David Hempton has argued that the motivation behind the creation of such schools was to win back support among the working classes but the evidence from Bedfordshire suggests that day schools had more to do with the drive to buttress Wesleyanism's middle class identity.[277] It is certainly interesting that the first Methodist educational venture in Bedfordshire, beyond a handful of Sunday schools, was not a charity school for the children of the poor but a private boarding school for the sons of well-to-do Wesleyan families. John Conquest's academy, established at Biggleswade in 1834 and catering for boys between the ages of 5 and 15, was 'where most of the scions of our best families in the neighbouring towns were trained.'[278]

The second Methodist school to appear in the county was also a private venture but on a rather different model. Ridgmont Wesleyan day school was founded in 1846 and largely underwritten by Samuel Bennett. Bennett, who farmed 400 acres on the Duke of Bedford's estate and won fame for his progressive agricultural methods, was a second generation Wesleyan, a local preacher, trustee, circuit steward and district treasurer. He had been one of the laymen invited to attend a special meeting of 'ministers and lay-gentlemen' in London in 1843 to discuss Wesleyan day school provision and this may have prompted his initiative.[279] His vision for the school unquestionably included a missionary function, as argued by

---

274   Phillips, *Dunstable Methodist circuit*, 10.
275   Bushby, *Two hundred years of Methodism*, 16.
276   Bacon, *Christian Ministry*, 14.
277   Hempton, *Methodism and politics*, 150.
278   *WMM* (1892), 718. Although not large, there were 33 pupils resident in 1841 and 26 in 1851. It not only met the needs of middle-class Methodism in the surrounding counties but was an important precursor to other more substantial Methodist educational initiatives. James Rigg, who would be principal of the Westminster training college for more than thirty-five years, began his own teaching career as Conquest's assistant; as did William Moulton, later the first headmaster of The Leys school, Cambridge, the pinnacle of Wesleyan middle class educational provision (Telford, *Rigg*, 23). Miss Gale's Ladies' Seminary at Neots also appears to have had Wesleyan links and there seems to have been an attempt to establish a small Wesleyan boarding school near Leighton Buzzard (*The Watchman* 6 January 1841 and 9 April 1846).
279   *The Watchman* 8 November 1843, p. 365, col. 2.

Hempton, for he believed that 'the well-being of Methodism depends much upon impressing the minds of the rising generation with the great truths of our holy religion', although it is not clear that it was aimed at working class children in particular.[280] It also seems to have been born out of a desire on Bennett's part to make a statement about his social status and the status of the religious community to which he and his family belonged: he was as rich as any local squire and his church as good as the Church of England. It was clearly a matter of considerable significance that the Wesleyan school was judged superior to its Church of England rival, Bennett's obituary recording that:

> This school excited great interest in the neighbourhood; and it was affirmed by the Government Inspector to be one of the most efficient and best-conducted in the district. Lord Charles Russell on one occasion came to visit the National school at Ridgmount, and, after spending a short time there, stepped into the Wesleyan school, where his attention was so powerfully arrested by what he saw and heard that he remained nearly two hours.[281]

By 1851 the school boasted 72 boys and 48 girls on its roll and over the following decade it would be imitated in Dunstable (1853), Eaton Bray (1860), Luton (1853), Tebworth (1862) and Toddington (1854).[282]

The capital expenditure on chapels and school rooms saddled the local Wesleyan circuits with a heavy burden of debt. In 1846 the chapel trusts of the Luton circuit owed £3,377 and the following year the quarterly meeting of the Bedford circuit was discussing how they might reduce their trust debts to £5,000.[283] Some of these loans had been made, interest free, by local members but many were raised at commercial rates. Meeting the mortgage payments on these loans was a major commitment and one that was not always fulfilled. At Newport Pagnell the chapel steward was almost bankrupted by having to carry an accumulated deficit on the trust of £968.[284] With pew rents wholly insufficient to finance these loans, fundraising became a major feature of chapel life. Collections taken at anniversary services had been an important source of income from the turn of the century but in the 1830s and 1840s a variety of innovations appear to have been introduced to increase their appeal and thereby maximise attendance.

The efforts of the Bedford congregation to provide the latest music were noted by the local paper:

> It has long been a matter of notoriety throughout the county, that the performances at the Wesleyan chapel were as lively as those at concerts. Indeed to such an extent have they carried out their musical taste … that one or two gentlemen have been in the habit of making annual visitations to the metropolis in order that they might get the 'new tunes' (neat and fresh as imported) before any of

---

280   *WMM* (1857), 200–1.

281   *WMM* (1857), 200. Inspectors' reports on the school can be found in Bushby, *Bedfordshire schoolchild*, 108–11. There is also an account of the school in *The Christian Miscellany and Family Visiter* (1849), 289–91.

282   Later there would also be Wesleyan schools at Ampthill, Eaton Socon and Potton. Wesleyan schools were opened over the county boundary at St Neots (1849), Raunds (in the Higham Ferrers circuit) (1848) and Whitchurch (in the Aylesbury circuit) (1846).

283   Luton Wesleyan circuit schedule book 1844–61, BLARS, MB 403; Bedford Wesleyan circuit minutes of quarterly meetings 1841–54, BLARS, MB 6.

284   Bedford and Northampton Wesleyan district minutes 1847, MARC.

the other congregations obtained them. These they performed in concerto, and I have heard in that chapel, airs which have made one's very feet twinkle.[285]

The main act, however, in these popular entertainments was a new kind of celebrity preacher. Leading ministers of the connexion had always been prime choices for chapel openings and there are many references to visits by Joseph Beaumont, Robert Newton, Theophilus Lessey and Jabez Bunting. From the 1830s, these names are mixed with those of lay preachers such as Billy Dawson, 'the Yorkshire Farmer'; Charles Richardson, 'the Lincolnshire Thrasher'; and Joseph Marshall, 'the Blind Preacher.' The pulling power of these men extended far beyond the Methodist community itself.[286] When Dawson was due to preach at Bedford in 1837, 'long before the service commenced the place within and without was crowded to an almost suffocating excess'; while Richardson's appearance at St Neots in 1844 drew 'such a crowd as the people never saw.'[287] Both these preachers appear to have delighted and amused congregations with their rustic appearance and quaint expressions; and the irony of their popularity, just at the moment when the voices of local labourers were being muffled in those same chapels, seems to have gone unnoticed. The *Cambridge Independent Press* raved about the Wesleyan missionary anniversary at Biggleswade in 1830 when 'The friends who came from the country to enjoy this "religious frolic"' were treated to 'a profusion of oratory, gigantic strides of eloquence and depth of mind' and rounded off the day with loud bursts of applause.[288] Little wonder that such occasions were viewed as 'welcomed festivals' in otherwise 'equable and quiet lives.'[289]

For a time the success of this religious music hall was so great that it became difficult to manage. In the Luton circuit the quarterly meeting agreed that:

> All the preachers in the circuit be recommended not to publish any anniversary services to be holden on the Lord's Day in any other town or village than that in which the announcement is made and that all Sunday school societies in the circuit be recommended to hold their anniversary services upon the weekday instead of the Sabbath.[290]

Novelty, of course, by its nature, is hard to maintain and one of the problems faced by Wesleyans in the 1840s may well have been that this form of religious entertainment was losing its draw. George Adams, one of the early Latter Day Saint missionaries to Bedfordshire, certainly detected that 'there is great dissatisfaction about religion ... people are tired of their old ways, and are looking for something new.'[291]

---

[285] *Bedford Mercury* 3 June 1837, p. 3, col. 5. The preface to a tune-book published by the Wesleyan Bookroom in 1847 complained about 'those who expect much novelty' and 'the constant introduction of new tunes' (*Companion to the Wesleyan hymn-book*, v).

[286] When the Bedford Wesleyans announced in the local paper that Newton, Lessey and Dawson were all to preach at the opening of the new chapel in 1832, the editor congratulated 'the trustees in having succeeded in procuring such efficient aid' (*Huntingdon, Bedford and Peterborough Gazette*, 29 September 1832, p. 3, col. 1).

[287] Coulson, *Peasant preacher*, 124.

[288] *Cambridge Independent Press* 24 July 1830.

[289] *WMM* (1893), 936.

[290] Luton Wesleyan circuit minutes of quarterly meeting 29 September 1841, BLARS, MB 498a.

[291] *Millennial Star*, vol. 1, no. 4 (August 1840), 93.

Fresh sources of income were desperately needed and the same urge for respectability that had driven the building spree and produced the debts now created new money-raising activities. In this endeavour women took the lead. In March 1837 the ladies of the Leighton Buzzard congregation demonstrated both their generosity and their domestic accomplishments by 'furnishing gratuitously' a tea for three hundred people, tickets for which were sold at a shilling each, with 'poorer friends' being admitted the following evening for sixpence and some free. The whole event raised £16 for the chapel trustees.[292] Methodists had often eaten together, most commonly at quarterly meetings, but this is the first local instance of it being a source of income and it would quickly become a staple of Methodist life. Another solution, at once both respectable and profitable, was to be the ladies' sewing circle and their annual bazaar. The handicrafts produced for these occasions showcased the refinement, industry and leisure of the ladies of a congregation and the events themselves attracted a well-to-do clientele (see Plate 31). At St Neots, in 1850:

> The taste and tact displayed by the ladies in the arrangement and management of their stalls, and the variety and excellency of the articles for sale, elicited the warmest expressions of approbation from the numerous visitors who favoured the bazaar with their presence …[293]

The proceeds amounted to an impressive £107 even though, as the local paper noted, 'some of the articles were fixed at a price too high for the visitors, respectable though they were; [and] consequently a large portion of the goods remain unsold.'[294] The idea was taken up at Bedford the following year where a two-day bazaar held in the Assembly Rooms brought the 'highest credit to the ladies who had superintendence of the affair' and raised more than £100.[295] Ladies' committees almost certainly also took the lead in organising the concerts of sacred music, such as the performances of Handel's *Messiah* and *Saul* that were staged by the Aylesbury Wesleyans in 1850.[296] More mundane forms of fundraising, by collections and subscriptions also multiplied. In 1837 six leading members of the Luton Wesleyan circuit were asked to 'wait upon the friends for subscriptions' and in 1841 the class leaders made 'personal application to each of their members requesting them to contribute their quota weekly, and to increase it, where they think there is the ability.'[297] Even the Sunday school children were recruited as juvenile missionary collectors.[298] Being a Methodist had always involved a financial commitment but the number of times a Wesleyan was expected to put his hand into his pocket was undoubtedly increasing.

The Model Methodist
Given the debt burden created by the chapel building boom of the 1830s it is not altogether surprising that generosity comes to figure largely during this period in the model Methodist lives celebrated in the obituary columns of the denominational

---

292 *The Watchman*, 8 March 1837, p. 78, col. 3.
293 *The Watchman*, 5 June 1850, p. 182, col. 4.
294 *Cambridge Chronicle*, 1 June 1850.
295 *Bedford Mercury*, 12 July 1851, p. 3, col. 1.
296 Aylesbury Wesleyan circuit collection of posters, CBS, NM 114/9/1.
297 Luton Wesleyan circuit minutes of quarterly meetings, BLARS, MB 498a.
298 *The Watchman*, 22 January 1851.

magazines. John Hudson of Hitchin 'took a part in supporting various institutions, to which piety and benevolence have given rise'; and Mrs Wilkinson of Bedford:

> was a woman of great benevolence. Few persons ever did so much good with the same means. She practised much self-denial, and was very economical in all expenses relating to herself. She literally 'saved all she could,' that she might 'give all she could'.[299]

In Eaton Bray chapel, a monument to Margaret Battams informed the congregation that she 'died April 15, 1839, aged 69 years, and bequeathed 200 Pounds to this Chapel. Reader! Consider.'[300] Financial contributions to the connexion were also regularly celebrated in the pages of *The Watchman* which printed long lists of subscribers to funds for missionary work, education, the Theological Institution, a new painting of John Wesley, famine relief in Ireland and Scotland, and the orphaned family of a preacher – all recording the size of each donation.

Positive references to the worldly success of some members also begin to be seen. Thomas Marlow achieved 'considerable worldly prosperity'; William Iredale of Markyate's 'diligence in his temporal affairs' was crowned with success and Edward Smith of Bedford was 'diligent in business'.[301] Such men were clearly valuable assets to the Methodist community and not only because of what they could put into the collection plate. Their affluence gave them social standing and that standing gave Methodism respectability, another recurring theme in the official hagiographies. Ann Fairey of St Neots was 'highly respected by all classes'; Edward Gibbard of Flamstead 'had a good report of all men'; and John Higgins' funeral was attended by half the population of Luton, 'so great was the respect in which he was held.'[302]

It was not only to the connexion that the ideal Methodist was now generous. Elizabeth Linnell of Fenny Stratford was kind to the poor as well as liberal to the cause; Mrs Pheasant of Bedford was ready 'to relieve every case of distress'; and Rachel Fielding of Honeydon held to the maxim:

> That whatever is given to relieve the necessities of the poor, is, if given in a right spirit, lent to the Lord; and that He can easily take that from us which is withheld from those who are perishing in want.[303]

Visiting the sick again became a laudable habit and the circuit schedules show that societies were beginning to appoint poor stewards to distribute alms.[304] In the winter of 1830 members of the Biggleswade congregation

---

[299]   *WMM* (1842), 71; (1845), 290; (1847), 429. Of the 73 obituaries relating to people from Bedfordshire circuits published between 1830 and 1851, 23 refer in some way to the generosity of the departed towards Methodism.

[300]   Brigg, *Methodism in the Leighton Buzzard circuit.*

[301]   *WMM* (1845), 187; (1841), 247; (1830), 211.

[302]   *WMM* (1832), 903; (1836), 238 and 967.

[303]   *WMM* (1845), 188; (1834), 557; (1830), 517.

[304]   Twenty-one out of the seventy-three obituaries mention sick visiting. The Newport Pagnell circuit was slow to appoint poor stewards. Where the circuit schedule provided space to record their names, the superintendent wrote in 1839 'our people being all poor, each one is his own steward' and in 1842 'everyone who has money to give' (Newport Pagnell Wesleyan circuit schedule book, CBS, NM 500/7/2). At Luton the poor steward went round the sick members on Sunday afternoons with a gift from the poor fund (Hawkes, *Rise of Wesleyan Sunday schools*, 11).

entered into a weekly subscription privately among themselves (so long as the weather continues so severe) further to alleviate the wants of the many families who are almost freezing, having entirely to depend on the cold hand of charity for support.[305]

Barton Sunday school even formed a clothing club, although it was warned not to collect subscriptions on the Sabbath.[306]

At first glance it might seem strange that such a concern for the poor was growing among middle class Methodists, given that they were busily engaged in disenfranchising the poorer members of their congregations. One motive may have been fear that the Church of England was beginning to use its charities to reward attendance at the parish church and was drawing sheep from the Wesleyan fold. At Brixworth, in Northamptonshire, the steward noted that:

> The poor boys in the parish [are] not allowed to go to the free school on the week days except they go to the Church [Sunday] school on the Sunday, which takes most of the boys from the Wesleyan [Sunday] school.[307]

Perhaps the best way to understand this new enthusiasm for almsgiving and good works, however, is to see it as a means by which the affluent, aspirational and respectable element of Wesleyanism could publicly distance themselves from the poor, asserting their higher status by their acts of visible generosity. Almsgiving was certainly not an expression of solidarity with the downtrodden. On the contrary it appears to have been mixed with a certain disdain for the poor and a tendency to hold them responsible for their own plight. Samuel Bennett gave temporal aid to those 'whose circumstances exposed them to difficulty and want' but,

> At the same time, he never gave any countenance to opinions and measures which went to exonerate the poor from what he regarded as the privilege as well as the duty of contributing towards the expenses of that part of the church with which he and they were connected. He would often say, in homely but very significant language, that it was a poor religion which did not enable even the poor man to save, by abstinence from worldly customs, more than it cost him; and that, in giving up the often expensive and even ruinous worldly amusements to which many are addicted, they obtained higher and richer pleasures, which, instead of interfering with their domestic comforts, heightened them, and enabled them to enjoy life in a manner unknown before.[308]

The solution to poverty was not higher wages or cheaper bread but more frugal and diligent labourers and it was in that spirit that many members of the local Wesleyan leadership enthusiastically sponsored the early temperance movement. Bedford Wesleyan chapel provided the venue for the town's very first temperance meeting in 1838 and a Wesleyan minister took the chair at the second, held in a public hall. The local newspaper's account of this gathering seems particularly

---

[305] *Cambridge Independent Press,* February 1830.

[306] Luton Wesleyan circuit minutes of quarterly meetings 25 June 1840, BLARS, MB 498a.

[307] Ward, *Religious census of Northamptonshire,* 132. At Oakley, the Primitive Methodists complained that 'sundry gratuities and privileges, which are at the disposal of the parliamentary church agents, become a great snare to the poor in these parts ... several of the children have been discharged from the national day-school, and deprived of the church's 'benefit club', because they entered our school' (*PMM* (1850), 120).

[308] *WMM* (1841), 720.

telling, for it describes how the hall was 'crowded to the doors with the labouring classes' and watched over by 'several well-dressed females'.[309] Not everyone in the Wesleyan community greeted the new movement with such enthusiasm. Jonathan Turner, superintendent of the Biggleswade circuit 1834–36, was a determined opponent. For Turner, the arguments of the temperance advocates were a dangerous and radical innovation that challenged the absolute authority of the Bible by creating moral standards for which there was no Biblical justification.[310] The Wesleyan conference agreed and in 1841 passed a resolution prohibiting temperance meetings from being held on any Wesleyan premises.[311] The decision did little to diminish support for the cause and would eventually be overturned, in large measure due to the work of the Revd Charles Garret, who entered the ministry from the Hitchin circuit in 1849.[312]

Another antidote to poverty actively sponsored by local Wesleyans was the formation of friendly societies to provide insurance against the breadwinner in a family falling ill or dying. The rules of the Bedford Wesleyan Friendly Society were enrolled at the Quarter Sessions in 1835 and at Luton a Men's Wesleyan Benefit Club held a service in the chapel every Whit Tuesday before retiring to the Black Swan for its annual meeting and feast.[313] By the early 1850s these local initiatives were to some extent being overtaken by ventures on a larger scale. William Underwood was acting as the local agent of the Wesleyan Provident Friendly Society in Luton by 1851 and a branch of the Wesleyan Local Preachers' Mutual Aid Association was active in Leighton Buzzard by 1853.[314]

If habits of prudence, temperance and hard-work were not sufficient to earn financial security, or if illness, injury or bereavement struck, the model Wesleyan was expected to submit to the burden with stoical courage. Elizabeth Hudson's obituary, in 1844, recorded that

> The grace of God was especially manifested in the submission she constantly evinced to the divine will, and the calmness with which she sustained her distressing malady. Her mental faculties were unclouded to the end; and her last words breathed forth the praises of God.[315]

It is a theme that recurs in almost every obituary and by its pervasiveness highlights the degree to which fear of disease and sudden death was a constant shadow in early Victorian life. This, rather than despair about poverty, was the anxiety which official Methodism offered to comfort. In a sermon entitled *An invitation to Christian fellowship*, printed at the request of the Biggleswade society, the Revd Wright Shovelton set out the main purpose of Methodist membership:

---

309   *Bedford Mercury*, 7 April 1838, p. 4, col. 2.
310   Turner, *Teetotalism illustrated* (1842). The same argument would be used by Methodists in the Southern United States against the abolitionist movement (Owen, *The sacred flame of love*).
311   Edwards, 'Teetotal Wesleyan Methodists', 63–70.
312   Brake, *Drink: ups and downs of Methodist attitudes to temperance*, 11–16.
313   Wigfield, 'Recusancy and Nonconformity in Bedfordshire', 225; Hawkes, *Rise of Wesleyan Sunday schools*, 9. A Wesleyan Benefit society owned land at Ampthill in 1862 (BLARS, HN 10/274/Amp1).
314   *The Watchman*, 4 June 1851, p 1, col. 4; *Bucks Chronicle* 26 November 1853. The Wesleyan Local Preachers Mutual Aid Association was suspected of having sympathy with the reformers and use of Leighton Buzzard chapel for its meeting was refused. The meeting went ahead in Lake Street Baptist chapel with the Wesleyan choir leading the singing and the Baptist minister, the devotions.
315   *WMM* (1844), 57.

O live with those with whom you wish to die. Be associated with those who would surround your death bed, even accompany you to the swellings of Jordan, and then be heard soliciting your Divine Joshua, to afford his timely aid, and to bring you into his promised rest.[316]

Being a Methodist was itself an insurance policy against the darkest uncertainty of all.

Another theme that begins to recur in the obituaries during this period is that of loyalty to the connexion. In 1829 Richard Hudson was described as having been 'strongly attached to the doctrines and discipline of the Methodists' and his esteem for the preachers as 'great and undeviating'.[317] Similarly, in 1836 it was written of Edward Gibbard that he 'was cordially attached to the ministers, doctrines and discipline of the body.'[318] Susan King of St Neots was said to have 'loved the connexion' and Samuel Bennett to have been 'very affectionately attached to the Wesleyan Ministers.'[319] Jemima Tite of Wavendon was 'warmly attached to the constitution of Methodism' and George Parker of Higham Ferrers 'to the doctrines and principles of Wesleyan Methodism.'[320] It is hard to know precisely what prompted the preachers who wrote these obituaries to underline the warm attachment that a model Methodist should cherish for the connexion but it seems almost certain that it reflects a growing concern about a lack of loyalty. It was a concern that was clearly not baseless, for quite apart from the Reform agitation, the district minutes record ten complaints brought against ministers between 1835 and 1851.

Defections and moaning may not have been the only loyalty issues facing Wesleyanism after 1835. The numerous references in obituaries to regular and diligent attendance 'at all the means of grace', 'in all weathers, summer and winter', strongly suggest that many people were irregular in their attendance and particularly in relation to the class meeting. Classes certainly continued to meet and continued to be conducted in the traditional manner. Mary Cooper's diary makes frequent mention of class meetings, including an occasion in 1849 at Dunstable where she 'had a gracious season at the class. I felt truly humbled, but greatly encouraged by the testimony of the members.'[321] Two years earlier Hannah Hillson had experienced a less successful evening, but her complaint suggests that expectations could still be high:

> Another class-night has passed, but I do not feel my mind fully relieved. I could not say what I wished, and dear Mr. --- did not take up my broken language, nor did he enter into my experience as my dear leader would have done had he been present. I bless God, however, I am not wholly destitute of consolation.[322]

The surviving class books from this period confirm, however, that attendance at class meetings was now quite patchy. Of the 26 members of John Cope's class at Tempsford in the autumn of 1835 only 10 attended at least once a fortnight and

---

[316] Shovelton, *Invitation to Christian fellowship*, 16–17. Shovelton was superintendent of the Biggleswade circuit 1848–51.
[317] *WMM* (1829), 289
[318] *WMM* (1836), 238.
[319] *WMM* (1841), 147 and 705
[320] *WMM* (1846), 308; and (1848), 341.
[321] Quoted in Fish, *Memorials of Mary Sarson Cooper*, 178.
[322] *Memoirs of Miss Hannah Hillson*, 19.

5 never appeared at all. Explanations for the decline of the class meeting have usually made much of how its peculiar intimacy was out of step with Victorian sensibilities but, in fact, all kinds of meetings were now thinly attended. Benjamin Gregory records that the traditional mid-week preaching services attracted only small congregations by the 1840s.[323] The register of the Bedford leaders' meeting shows that in 1847 there was never more than half the leaders present and the minutes of the Dunstable circuit local preachers' meeting for 1849 reveal that about two-thirds of the preachers failed to turn up for their quarterly meeting.[324] It was also getting harder to find people to fill some church offices. By the late 1840s there was no longer anyone at Knotting willing to act as class leader and it was left to the local preachers to meet the members after the service, while at Aley Green, Cockernhoe, Stopsley and Kinsbourne Green the Sunday schools could only be sustained by volunteers walking out from Luton.

Primitive Methodism
The very name of the *Primitive* Methodists clearly represented a deliberate and conscious claim to be the guardians of an older tradition of Methodist faith and practice than that practiced by the Wesleyan connexion. It was a claim that held good in Bedfordshire, in one respect at least, for just at the point when the life of many Wesleyan societies was moving into purpose-built chapels and schoolrooms, Primitive Methodism did represent a return to an older pattern of religious life centred on cottage meetings. Even in this, however, there was something new. Primitive Methodist preachers spent an unprecedented amount of time visiting people in their homes. Every circuit, in its annual report, was required to give an account of the average number of families that their preachers visited in a week. No target figure is given but when Henry Pope, a preacher on the Luton circuit, only averaged five visits a day he clearly felt under pressure to give a detailed explanation of why that had been the case.[325] In fact, the local area was thought to be peculiarly receptive to such work. George Price, a preacher on the Aylesbury circuit, reckoned the local area 'to be one of the best countries I ever was in for visiting; for if we knock at any door, they generally pay us this compliment, "Please to walk in".'[326] A particular advantage was the local custom by which women would gather in a neighbour's house during the day so that they could chat as they worked on lace or straw plait. The preachers would apparently read passages from the connexional magazine to these ready-made congregations, chat with them about religion, and lead them in singing and prayer. It was then a small step from such conversations to the love-feasts and watch-nights which were a mainstay of Primitive Methodist worship.

The central disciplines of early Methodism, however, were not observed by the Primitive Methodists with any greater devotion than their Wesleyan contemporaries. The mid-week preaching services seem to have been poorly attended. At Bedford, in 1852, a society of 72 members with a Sunday congregation of 250 could muster an

[323]   *WMM* (1893), 934.
[324]   Register of Bedford Wesleyan society leaders' meeting 1847, BLARS, MB 34; Dunstable Wesleyan circuit minutes of local preachers' meetings 1849, BLARS, MB 342.
[325]   Luton Primitive Methodist circuit annual report 1848, BLARS, MB 518.
[326]   *PMM* (1837), 307.

average of only 30 people to its weeknight service and it was the same story again in Luton, although the turn-out in some of the villages may have been rather better.[327] Class meetings, too, appear to have been largely neglected. In the Baldock Mission 9 of the 11 societies did not have a class leader in 1853 and in the Luton circuit even the local preachers appear to have had a poor attendance record.[328]

There was a nod towards the old standards of plain dress, and when the first Primitive Methodist preachers reached Luton in 1839 they were apparently 'dressed in an uncommon style, wearing hats of the Quaker type, coats of the flitch of bacon pattern, and boots with thick soles.'[329] Circuits would continue to be asked to confirm that their travelling preachers observed the connexional dress code (including a stipulation on hairstyle) well into the 1850s but there is no evidence that it was observed any more widely among the general membership than similar expectations were among the Wesleyans.[330] Indeed, it was thought noteworthy that Sarah Keadle, one of the first members at Sharpenhoe, was faithful in 'her deadness to the vain fashions of the world.'[331]

Even the hymns that the Primitive Methodists sang were not the traditional Wesleyan canon, but an entirely new collection partly drawn from American sources and partly consisting of verses composed by Hugh Bourne and William Sanders, two of the movement's early leaders.[332]

In fact, one of the distinguishing features of Primitive Methodism was its susceptibility to American innovations. One crucial influence was the American camp meeting, an open-air religious festival that had become hugely popular on the western frontier of the United States at the turn of the nineteenth century. Stories of

---

[327] Luton Primitive Methodist circuit, chapel schedules 1848, BLARS, MB 519; Bedford Primitive Methodist mission, chapel schedules 1852, Hull History Centre.

[328] Baldock Primitive Methodist mission, preaching plan 1853, Society of Cirplanologists. In the Bedford mission 6 out of 9 places had no class leader and in the Buckden mission 8 out of 14. The quarterly meeting of the Luton circuit resolved in 1846 that 'the Local Preachers shall meet in Class according to the rule or come off the Plan' and had to dismiss at least 3 preachers over the next fifteen months for breaking the rule (Luton Primitive Methodist circuit, minutes of quarterly meeting 1843–58, BLARS, MB 520).

[329] *Introduction of Primitive Methodism into Luton 1839*, 5.

[330] Some have argued that the plain dress code was influenced by Hugh Bourne's early involvement with Quakerism (Milburn, *Primitive Methodism*, 3). Examples of the approved haircut, broad-brimmed hat and bonnet can be found in Kendall, *Origin and history of the Primitive Methodist church*, I, 155, 171 and 245. For plain dress among contemporary Wesleyans see the story of Patty Tompkins, who commented on some of the children at her chapel 'They are very nice but they don't look a bit like Methodist children' (Pope, *Finedon Methodism*, 11) and Coley, *Life of Thomas Collins*, 252–4.

[331] *PMM* (1850), 521. See also *PMM* (1858), 292.

[332] During this period the Primitive Methodists used two hymn-books usually published together in one binding: the 'Small' hymn-book, first published in 1821, and the 'Large' hymn-book, first published in 1824. The American hymns were drawn from a hymn-book published in Liverpool in 1806 by the visiting American revivalist, Lorenzo Dow (Mankin, *Our hymns*; Kent, *Holding the fort*, 63–70). Very little is known about the tunes to which the hymns were sung. The names of a handful are mentioned in the hymn-book, including *Dying Pilgrim* and *Redemption*, which appear to be of American origin. There is also evidence that popular tunes of the day were simply pressed into service. Henry Higginson, the first preacher in Luton, on one occasion 'heard a lad singing a song which attracted him. "Here, my lad, sing that again and I'll give thee a penny." The lad did as he was told, more than once. "Here you are, my man," said Higginson, throwing him the penny; "I've got the tune, and the devil may take the words"' (Kendall, *Origin and history of the Primitive Methodist church*, II, 32; see also Farndale, *Secrets of Mow Cop*, 51–2). At this period Primitive Methodist congregations appear to have sung unaccompanied, the introduction to their hymn-book specifically denouncing 'cat-gut scraping'.

the extraordinary revivals sparked by these gatherings had been brought to Britain by the American Methodist revivalist Lorenzo 'Crazy' Dow in 1806 and the desire to emulate such an occasion, by holding a day of prayer on Mow Cop in Staffordshire, had played a significant part in the creation of Primitive Methodism. Indeed, camp meetings remained the movement's signature activity for much of the nineteenth century. Such meetings generally began at about 9.00am with a procession through the village and then proceeded to a field where a farmer's cart would provide a makeshift platform for the preachers. After a day of preaching, praying and singing, the gathering concluded in the evening with a love-feast. The first recorded camp meeting in Bedfordshire was held at Stanbridge in May 1839 and lasted three days:

> On the first day the seed of life was plentifully sown, nine short sermons were delivered. In the lovefeast several were in distress, one got converted, and one sanctified. On the second day, after farmer Tapping had given a short exhortation, from Acts iii. 19, 'Repent ye, therefore, and be converted' etc, the work broke out, and continued until we broke up for dinner. Several were brought into gospel liberty on the Camp ground, and a mighty flow of Divine power was felt through the day. In the lovefeast, two obtained the blessing of sanctification.[333]

Most societies would have hosted one such festival a year, more usually for a single day, but they would also have held many other services outdoors. Every spring, as the weather improved and the days lengthened, local circuits routinely arranged not only to extend preaching into villages where they had yet to secure the use of a cottage but to take some of the services outdoors even where they had already established themselves.[334]

Although inspired by an American model, these events also had local resonances which may have contributed to their popularity. Just a few years before the love-feast at Stanbridge John Buckmaster had witnessed a strikingly similar event a few miles away on the Dunstable Downs:

> Early one May morning I started with two or three others in an old farm-cart for the Downs. On the road there passed other carts and waggons crowded with passengers; some had flags and music. As we drew near to the Downs the procession and excitement increased. On a slight elevation you could see a number of wagons. This was the centre of the gathering. ... The flags and banners had on sentences, such as, 'No pensions for royal concubines!' ... 'More pigs and fewer parsons!' 'He saw the people were oppressed and He smote their oppressors!'[335]

There was certainly a note of defiance in meeting on the village green rather than behind closed doors. When a preacher was arrested at St Albans for holding an open-air service and required by the local magistrate to give an assurance, before being released, that there would be no repetition of this breach of the peace, he 'told the policeman I should not accept illegal liberty, and that he must tell the magistrate I should consider myself a prisoner till properly set at liberty.'[336] The preacher was eventually released without bond and went on, with help from local Baptists, to prosecute the police for common assault.

---

[333] *PMM* (1840), 391; see also the account of a camp meeting at Graveley in the Buckden mission, *PMM* (1845), 497.
[334] Luton Primitive Methodist circuit minutes of quarterly meeting 14 March 1853, BLARS, MB 520.
[335] Buckmaster, *Village politician*, 54.
[336] Church, *Gospel victories*, 141–5.

The noisy atmosphere of Primitive Methodist meetings, while echoing the early Methodist services at Everton, was also probably influenced by accounts of American camp meetings. At Luton, 'cries for mercy were heard in various parts of the chapel' during services and according to the *Cambridge Chronicle*, one Primitive Methodist chapel

> was occasionally not closed till 12 or 1 o'clock in the morning ... [and] what I have seen there you would scarcely believe if you were to see it – I have seen people jumping about, and the women lying down on their backs and their bellies, sometimes kicking up one leg, and then the other, with their clothes flying up.[337]

American influence is certainly detectable in Primitive Methodist conversion narratives which celebrate instantaneous transformations rather than the gradual reformation described in earlier Methodist writing and associated with regular attendance at class meeting. The account of a conversion at Biggleswade, under John Guy's preaching, is typical:

> At one meeting I spoke to a man in distress, pressing him to come to Jesus. He said '*Not now.*' I said '*Come now!*' Again he said, '*Not now.*' I continued urging him to come now, and after meeting his 'not now' with my 'come now', about twenty times, he yielded, bowed his knees, prayed, believed, and found peace; and now he is going on his way rejoicing.[338]

Primitive Methodists were also keen advocates of sanctification, a second conversion experience to which believers could aspire and in which they would be freed from the impulse to sin. Although inspired in part by John Wesley's teaching on Christian Perfection, the emphasis on sanctification among Primitive Methodists owed much to another American influence, the Holiness movement, which began to take shape in the 1830s. Holiness teaching would have a significant impact on Wesleyan Methodism in the second half of the nineteenth century, but as early as 1839 a Primitive Methodist local preacher came to the camp meeting at Stanbridge 'with the intention to be sanctified' and there was a sermon on 'entire sanctification' during a protracted meeting at Luton in 1845.[339]

An early advocate of this 'second blessing' was the American revivalist James Caughey who visited Britain in 1841.[340] Caughey introduced British Methodism to a number of new techniques for orchestrating revivals, including the protracted meeting. Although the use of protracted meetings was by no means confined to Primitive Methodism (indeed, a number of local Wesleyans societies held them by

---

337   *Cambridge Chronicle* 16 February 1850. Watch-nights were often held on 31 December but were not confined to that occasion. There was a watch-night at Bedford during the summer of 1840 (Bedford Primitive Methodist mission, minute book 1840–3, minutes of the Bedford preparatory board of 9 June 1840, Hull circuit quarter day board, BLARS, MB 182). Communion was not widely celebrated. In the Bedford mission in 1840, 8 societies generally held love-feasts each quarter but only 2, Bedford and Ampthill, held communion services.
338   The writer was the travelling preacher John Guy and the event took place at Biggleswade (*PMM* (1848), 309).
339   *PMM* (1840), 390 and (1845), 224.
340   James Caughey (1810–91) was born in Ireland but brought up in the United States. Ordained as a minister of the Methodist Episcopal Church, he visited Britain from 1841 to 1847 and again in the 1850s and 60s. Also among the innovations which he introduced were the 'anxious bench' and the practice of allowing women to pray aloud in mixed gender prayer meetings.

1851), the Primitive Methodists were certainly amongst the first and the most enthusiastic exponents of Caughey's methods.[341] The Bedford congregation held their first protracted meeting within months of Caughey's arrival and the Luton circuit followed their lead three years later:

> The Protracted meeting commenced on Sunday, November 17, 1844, and was continued the fourteen following days. Every day's services of the first week commenced at five o'clock in the morning, when a sermon was preached, followed by a prayer-meeting, which usually continued till about seven. At this hour of the evening, two sermons were preached, and were followed by a prayer-meeting. The second week's services were held in the evenings only. The subjects chiefly illustrated and enforced were the atonement of Christ, repentance, conversion, forgiveness of sins, and entire holiness of heart manifested in a corresponding life. The length of time allotted for each discourse was twenty minutes, and the praying and singing services were proportionately short and well supported. A penitent's form was generally used, whither the seekers of salvation resorted; and brethren who understood the nature of faith, joined with them in waiting on the Lord for the desired blessing. ... During the whole of the services, the Holy Spirit was copiously poured out, and corresponding effects followed.[342]

Twenty converts were reported at the conclusion of the fortnight and the place of such meetings in the winter calendar of local Primitive Methodist societies was assured.

The enthusiasm of Primitive Methodists for the newest revival techniques, the latest religious experiences, and the most recent songs was rooted in the same need that drove Wesleyan societies to develop novel and entertaining forms of worship, the need to raise money. For even though they were not burdened with the chapel debts of the Wesleyans, the Primitive Methodists were still pressed to cover their costs. There was a clear and unsentimental understanding of the close relationship between drawing crowds, making converts and balancing the books. The minutes of the Luton circuit record how

> At our last September Quarterly meeting, having read the report of the circuit for the time being, we discovered real cause to deplore the low state of our financial and spiritual concerns; consequently, a free conversation was proposed on the nature and causes of revival. On this delightful subject the brethren present conversed freely for about an hour.[343]

At Biggleswade they succeeded in drawing hundreds of listeners by the innovation of holding outdoor services in the weeks leading up to Christmas, 'Sometimes by moonlight, sometimes by lamp.'[344] One of the motives behind the willingness of the Primitive Methodists to allow women to preach may also have been the novelty which their appearance created. The visit of a Miss Clarke to Bedford in 1837 was noteworthy enough to be recorded by the *Cambridge Independent Press,* and the sermons of the dozen or so local preachers who can be identified as women would undoubtedly have been a talking point in the villages they visited.[345] Youth,

---

341   Coley, *Life of Thomas Collins,* 258; *Finedon Methodism,* 19–20; *The Watchman* 18 April 1849.
342   *PMM* (1845), 27.
343   *PMM* (1845), 27.
344   *PMM* (1848), 308. See also Stevens, *Cornish women preachers.*
345   *Cambridge Independent Press* 2 December 1837.

as well as gender, were marketable qualities in a preacher and Danzy Sheen, 'the boy preacher' was, for a season, much in demand for special occasions.[346]

One of the most important fundraising events was the annual missionary meeting. Unlike the Wesleyan missionary anniversary this was not an occasion to raise money for spreading the gospel in foreign lands but rather to garner support for the work of Primitive Methodist preachers in Britain.[347] By marketing themselves as a specialist mission to the labouring classes (rather as the Salvation Army would do half a century later) the Primitive Methodists achieved some success in soliciting contributions from the wider evangelical public. William Higgins, a wealthy Wesleyan, regularly chaired the Luton missionary meetings and Robert Robinson, the minister of Union chapel, was often the main speaker.[348]

Although the constituency of Primitive Methodism was drawn predominantly from poorer occupational groups it would be a mistake to imagine that they were somehow immune to the desire for respectability which worked so powerfully on Wesleyan Methodism. When the Primitive Methodist chapel in Bedford was re-built, in 1849 (see Plate 21), the object was to provide much more than a functional preaching box:

> The windows are circular headed, and blue slate covers the erection, which is entered from a front street by stone steps, and through a portico. The preacher's house has a recess of eight feet, fenced from the street by a brick wall, and entered by an iron gate. This recess is planted with a row of poplar trees and shrubs, rendering the property conspicuous and ornamental to the locality.[349]

Inside the chapel the rentable pews occupied the middle of the floor while the free seats were confined to the 'other parts'. Indeed, the proportion of free seats in the new chapel was lower than in almost any other nonconformist chapel in the town.[350]

Attempts to express the respectability of the connexion were by no means confined to bricks and mortar. The arrangements for the Luton Sunday school anniversary seem to have been designed to demonstrate exactly the message:

> About 200 children processioned to each of the services four-a-breast, in the most orderly manner, from our chapel in High Town to the town-hall, – attended by their superintendent and twenty-seven teachers. It was an interesting sight, and there was much in the appearance of the children which reflected considerable credit upon their parents and friends.[351]

At Toddington a similar anniversary included recitations of 'some pieces of poetry and a dialogue'.[352] Even in the villages where there was no chapel and no

---

346   Danzy Sheen (1844–1926). 'Master Danzy Sheen' from Clyro in Wales, then 17 years old, preached in aid of the projected new chapel in Dunstable in 1862 (*Luton News* 16 August 1862).
347   Primitive Methodist work overseas was confined at this stage to British emigrants and the local fundraising to support these missions in Australia and New Zealand was restricted to a collection among the Sunday school children and their teachers (*PMM* (1846), 435).
348   Luton Primitive Methodist circuit minutes of quarterly meeting 1843–58, BLARS, MB 520; *PMM* (1846), 311. Independent ministers also spoke at the missionary meetings in Bedford (*PMM* (1850), 115).
349   *PMM* (1849), 749.
350   According to the 1851 census of religious worship 25% of the seating was free. Only the Strict Baptists, at 10%, offered less. The figures for the others were: Matthewsites 29%, Baptists 31%, Wesleyans 34%, Old Meeting 38%, New Meeting 46%.
351   *PMM* (1852), 365.
352   *PMM* (1851), 445.

Sunday school, by 1850 tea meetings were becoming as much a part of Primitive Methodist programmes as revival meetings. At Colmworth they held 'an excellent tea-meeting ... in an orchard; and upwards of 90 persons enjoyed the social repast, beneath the agreeable shade of the spreading apple trees.'[353] Some societies began to hold services to mark traditional holy days, such as Good Friday and Christmas. In the Luton circuit there was even a weekly meeting to improve the standard of the local preachers.[354]

The desire to assert a moral and spiritual distinction between the chapel community and the wider working-class community from which it was drawn may also explain the enthusiasm of Primitive Methodists for temperance. The early progress of Primitive Methodism in Bedfordshire was often inextricably entwined with the advance of the temperance campaign. At Ampthill and Houghton Regis makeshift chapels were shared by Primitive Methodist and temperance societies, while at Buckingham and Dunstable the Primitive Methodists rented the temperance hall for their services.[355] Officially, the connexion held back from endorsing the new, more radical, creed of total abstinence and when an application was made to use the Luton chapel for a teetotal meeting in 1850 it was declined as being contrary to 'our general rules'.[356] This may have been a source of discontent among the membership and have lain behind the decision of the Dunstable society to withdraw from the Luton circuit in 1847. Denominating themselves Temperance Christians, they continued to meet in the temperance hall and only rejoined the circuit in December 1851, shortly after the arrival of a superintendent who was himself a zealous advocate of total abstinence.[357] By 1856 all hesitation had been swept aside and the Luton circuit were petitioning the connexion to include articles on teetotalism in every issue of the *Primitive Methodist Magazine*.[358]

If novelty and respectability were themes in the life of Primitive Methodism every bit as much as of Wesleyan Methodism, there was still something distinctive about the dynamics of the community. Reading the records of local Methodist circuits, the Primitive Methodist documents are instantly identifiable by their blunt honesty. Brother Lowe's sodomy, Brother Clarke's adultery, Brother Rose's drunkenness and Brother Odell's debt are all set down in plain, uncompromising terms.[359] Even the obituaries of those who endured, faithful to the end, admit no flattery or gloss. There was no covering up that Hannah Pakes, in the delirium of a fatal fever, had 'uttered some expressions which, though excusable in her case would have been reprovable to a sane Christian'; or that Joseph Males' abilities as a preacher were

353   *PMM* (1850), 565.
354   Luton Primitive Methodist circuit minutes of quarterly meeting 1843–58, BLARS, MB 520.
355   Luton Primitive Methodist circuit annual report 1844 and 1845, BLARS, MB 518; *PMM* (1844), 485.
356   Luton Primitive Methodist circuit minutes of quarterly meeting 1843–58, BLARS, MB 520.
357   The same superintendent, Henry Sharman, was given permission in 1852 to form a temperance society in the old Primitive Methodist chapel in Luton (Luton Primitive Methodist circuit minutes of quarterly meeting 1843–58, BLARS, MB 520)
358   Primitive Methodism was also hostile to smoking, the annual report asking circuits to confirm that their preachers did not use tobacco. Calvinistic Methodist congregations, by contrast, provided their preachers with tobacco (Rees, *The golden age of religion in Anglesey*, 17)
359   Luton Primitive Methodist circuit annual reports 1844–59, BLARS, MB 518; Aylesbury Primitive Methodist circuit annual reports 1842–48, CBS, NMP 100/7/1.

'but feeble'; or that Isaac Whetstone's 'previous intemperate habits had weakened his constitution.'[360] The obituaries also reveal different preoccupations and ideals from those evident in Wesleyan death notices. There is much about the emotional transformation wrought by conversion and above all about the power of faith to help men and women endure everything that life and death could throw at them. The story told of James Burgess' life was archetypal. He lived as a 'wicked sinner' for sixty years but under the influence of Primitive Methodist preachers underwent 'a great moral change' and eventually 'entered clearly into the blessed liberty of God's dear children' during a protracted meeting. One day he said in class 'if I can but prove faithful two or three days longer I shall get to glory' and that night his spirit took flight 'without having caused the now stiffened body one convulsive struggle!'[361] By the 1840s the ideal Wesleyan was expected to achieve something in life, the ideal Primitive Methodist, by contrast, was lauded for having simply endured it.

Matthews and the Latter Day Saints

The importance of novelty and showmanship in the popular religious life of early Victorian Bedfordshire is perhaps nowhere more obvious than in the career of Timothy Matthews. From his habit of summoning congregations with blasts from a silver trumpet to his huge frame, impeccably turned out in Geneva gown and bands, everything about Matthews promised drama and his sermons, by all accounts, did not disappoint (see Plate 13). On one occasion, it is said that he 'held up from the pulpit a bunch of keys, exclaiming, "Such things would not be necessary if everyone was honest."'[362] The poet Edward FitzGerald was entranced by his performance in the summer of 1842 and commended him to a friend as he might have done the latest play: 'If you are here on a Friday or a Sunday, go and hear him.'[363] From 1838 Matthews became an advocate of total immersion as the only proper method of baptism and these ceremonies, performed in local rivers, became huge crowd-pullers. His own account of one such occasion, in 1843, records how:

> On the Friday morning we had a baptism at a lake of water belonging to the Fitzgerald family, about one hundred acres of the reservoir of the [Grand Junction] Canal, situated a little to the west of Naseby. There were about a thousand persons present. Nine were baptised, five of whom were women all dressed in white[364]

Five years earlier, according to a local newspaper, hundreds had gathered on the banks of the Ouse at Biddenham to watch him baptise Charlotte Beeby by moonlight.[365]

---

360   *PMM* (1845), 358, 475 and 535.
361   *PMM* (1851), 253.
362   Wright, *Life of Matthews*, 90.
363   Wright, *Letters of Edward FitzGerald*, I, 122.
364   Wright, *Life of Matthews*, 87–8. Matthews appears to have come to this position on baptism as a result of his discussions with the Latter Day Saints (Adams, *A few plain facts shewing the folly, wickedness and imposition of the Rev. T. R. Matthews*, 10). Unlike the Latter Day Saints (and Baptists), he not only immersed adult converts but the infant children of believers (Wright, *Life of Matthews*, 80).
365   *Bedford Mercury*, 17 March 1838.

Perhaps because, as a Cambridge-educated clergyman of the Church of England, he already possessed social-standing, the desire for respectability appears to have had no sway over Matthews and the services he led seem to have evolved in a direction quite contrary to that pursued by the Wesleyans. By the mid-1840s he had almost completely abandoned liturgical prayers and was offering more emotionally engaging patterns of worship instead. Edward FitzGerald, joining the Bedford congregation for Good Friday 1844, observed how:

> he called at the end of his grand sermon on some of the people to say merely this, that they believed Christ had redeemed them: and first one got up and in sobs declared she believed it: … and then another – I was quite overset.[366]

It was not the only occasion on which Matthews broke with convention and allowed women to speak during worship. He recognised one young woman, Mary White of Moulsoe, as having a special dispensation to exhort in public and

> The powerful and fervent manner in which she addressed herself to those who heard her will never be forgotten. The Second Advent of the Lord was her favourite topic. The Millennial Reign and the Judgments that must precede it, were subjects with which she was most familiar.[367]

Indeed, Matthews seems sometimes to have courted controversy, particularly with his open-air preaching. In November 1837 he is recorded as having taken his stand on St Peter's Green as the congregation were leaving the parish church and to have caused such offence by the 'party and personal nature of his remarks' that the incensed churchgoers threw stones at him.[368]

The Mormons were no less confrontational, although it was rare for them to preach in the open air.[369] More typical was the approach which Job Smith took when trying to open his mission to Huntingdon. Having first secured a room in which to meet, he 'walked about among the people getting conversations with such as appeared favorable to the cause of truth and giving notices of our meetings and distributing tracts.'[370] At Bedford the bell-man was paid to go around the town announcing the meetings and at Luton bills were printed.[371] These public meetings, often described as lectures and sometimes structured as debates, could be tumultuous affairs. At Bedford a packed audience in the Castle Hill rooms, numbering perhaps as many as a thousand, soon got out of hand. William White, a member of the Old Meeting, managed to interrupt the speaker and denounce the Latter Day Saints as money-digging fortune-tellers with the result that 'Some cried one thing, and some another' and 'the Devil … succeeded in throwing the meeting into confusion.'[372]

The weekly round of church life was generally quieter and followed the broader Methodist pattern, with the travelling elders constantly moving around a circuit of branches holding mid-week services and local elders leading the majority of the

---

366   Wright, *Letters of Edward FitzGerald*, I, 160.
367   Quoted in Wright, *Life of Matthews*, 72.
368   *Bedford Mercury* 18 November 1837, p. 4, col. 3.
369   *Millennial Star* vol. 17, no. 29 (21 July 1855), 462.
370   Diary and autobiography of Job Smith, 12 January 1851, Brigham Young University, Harold B. Lee Library, MSS 881, 112.
371   *Millennial Star* 1840, vol. 2, no. 3 (July 1841), 37; Diary and autobiography of Job Smith, 16 June 1851, Brigham Young University, Harold B. Lee Library, MSS 881, 129.
372   *Millennial Star* vol. 2, no. 3 (July 1841), 34–5.

Sunday worship. In the larger branches there were choirs and Sabbath schools, testimony and prayer meetings, tea parties and communion services (described as the sacrament in line with Methodist practice).[373] As with all Methodists there was 'lively and animating' singing and there was the odd flourish of the kind of American revivalism that was popular among the Primitive Methodists. On one occasion the congregation at New Mill End, near Luton, were invited to stand in a circle around a fire and each given a bottle of wine, the preacher 'telling them to throw it on the floor as soon as he gave the word of command. This they did – and then followed a wild dance, accompanied with shouts of "Glory be to God! Hallelujah!"'[374] With baptism, confirmation and ordination to a variety of offices – deacon, teacher, priest and elder – there were a range of rites to confer status and dignity on converts; and ascent through the ranks could be quite swift. Samuel Claridge of Hemel Hempstead was ordained a priest within six weeks of his baptism and within five months of that was raised to the eldership.[375]

The American ties of Mormonism were clearly very important. The Latter Day Saints in Great Staughton struggled to make progress until they were able to announce 'that a man from Great Salt Lake City, who was personally acquainted with the prophet Joseph was to be there to address them ... [which] drew out a large number that otherwise would not have come.'[376] Curiosity, no doubt, played a part in this but there was a very practical element to it as well. Mormonism's transatlantic link offered not just a brush with the exotic but an explicit invitation to emigration and it is clear that that invitation was one of the central elements in the appeal of the movement. Elder Robert Wolcott found local members refusing to pay their dues in 1855 on the grounds that 'We were promised emigration by so and so. He is gone, and we are left and forgotten.'[377]

Emigration was only one of the ways in which Mormonism promised to improve the daily lives of its members. Much was also made of the supernatural powers which restoration to the faith of the apostles could unlock. A report on the progress of the Bedford conference in 1842 claimed that 'the gifts and blessings of the spirit of God [are] extensively enjoyed by the Saints, particularly the gifts of healing, tongues and interpretations.'[378] Various members are recorded as having experienced visionary dreams and Robert Wolcott found that he was 'called on almost every day some weeks to administer to the sick ... *many of whom have been perfectly restored.*'[379]

---

[373] *Millennial Star* vol. 9, no 16 (August 1847), 247; vol. 17, no. 19 (May 1855), 299; Diary and autobiography of Job Smith, 7 February 1851, 17 March 1851 and 28 April 1851, Brigham Young University, Harold B. Lee Library, MSS 881, 113, 118 and 123.

[374] Collings, *History of Union Chapel, Luton*. Compare this episode with one at Yelling in the Buckden mission recorded in the *PMM*: 'a penitents ring was formed; and the seekers of salvation being invited to enter it, several obeyed and soon received the spirit of adoption ... My soul praise the Lord!' (*PMM* (1845), 497).

[375] Ellsworth, *Samuel Claridge*, p 13–14.

[376] Diary and autobiography of Job Smith, 23 March 1851, Brigham Young University, Harold B. Lee Library, MSS 881, 119

[377] *Millennial Star,* vol. 17, no. 19 (12 May 1855), 299.

[378] *Millennial Star*, vol. 2, no. 10 (February 1842), 143.

[379] *Millennial Star*, vol. 17, no. 19 (12 May 1855), 298–9. For examples of visionary dreams see Cannon, *Autobiography of Christopher Layton*, 3, and Diary and autobiography of Job Smith, 28 April 1851, Brigham Young University, Harold B. Lee Library, MSS 881, 124.

Such beliefs and practices had, of course, long been a feature of Methodist spirituality and even at this point were certainly not unique to Mormonism. Timothy Matthews anointed the sick with oil and claimed to have effected remarkable cures by this means. More famously, he was credited with the miraculous healing of a paralytic who, having been immersed in the river Ouse, 'Immediately said, "Leave me go, I can walk," and walked out of the water, and ran some distance up a hill till she was exhausted.'[380]

The Primitive Methodists too told the story of how a strange dream had foretold their coming to Luton and even among the Wesleyans, as late as 1855 the *Christian Miscellany*, an official publication of the connexion, carried the story of a miracle healing in Bedfordshire affected by the prayers of a Wesleyan preacher.[381]

Perhaps the most revealing incident, recorded in Job Smith's journal, comes from Northampton in 1851 when Smith

> was called to administer to the younger of Br Gibson's boys, a boy of about 12 years. He was under the influence of an evil spirit, and as I was called to rebuke it, I did not like to leave him until he was better. It was more than his father could do to hold him. I rebuked the spirit but it would not come out of him. I determined not to leave him until he was better. As no elders were near I called for some teachers who were near to assist me in praying for him, which they did. But his father had not a clear idea that it was the influence of an evil spirit, but thought that it must be some physical disease. About 12 o'clock at night, after remaining with him some 5 or 6 hours the spirit left him and he was humble and sensible, 'as a little child'. During the time I staid with him the spirit spoke in tongues within him, and spit in my face and exhibited many signs of wicked revenge that I never witnessed before.[382]

In many ways this exorcism almost exactly mirrors the way in which the Wesleyans at Waddesdon had struggled with a 'demon-possessed' child in 1808 but there are clues in the story that over the intervening forty years the context had changed. The boy's father was inclined to interpret the symptoms in medical rather than supernatural terms and when, in a further intervention, it was decided to baptise the child in the river, it was felt that it had to be done at night with 'much care to avoid the police and the public.' Supernaturalism of this kind was clearly no longer acceptable in the public sphere but old beliefs and old ways had not yet lost their hold on everyone and Methodist communities of all shades continued to provide a space in which they could be legitimised.[383]

Part 4 Methodists and Politics

The Election of 1830

If the early 1830s witnessed a transformation in the scale of Methodist support in Bedfordshire, the change in the movement's political profile was nothing short of

---

380   *Bedford Mercury*, 17 March 1838.
381   *Introduction of Primitive Methodism into Luton*, 5; *Christian Miscellany* 1855, 60.
382   Diary and autobiography of Job Smith, 12 April 1851, Brigham Young University, Harold B. Lee Library, MSS 881, 121–2; Account of a diabolical possession at Waddesdon, CBS, NM 100/9/2.
383   See also Obelkevich, *Religion and rural society*, chapter 6; and Clark, *Between pulpit and pew*, who found traces of this tradition among Methodists of the 1970s.

revolutionary. Having eschewed politics since the 1780s, at the general election of 1830 the Methodists of Bedford strode out into the very centre of the national stage, humbling one of the foremost Whig politicians in the country, Lord John Russell, just as his party was sweeping to power. In retrospect the story probably begins the previous year when Parliament was debating the Roman Catholic Relief Bill. At first sight this was not a measure that might have been expected to arouse much interest in Bedfordshire, after all there were probably no more than fifty Catholics in the whole county at the time. Furthermore local Dissenters supported the measure, which they saw as inseparable from their own fight for religious equality, and the influence of the great Whig landowners ensured that the clergy of the established church were quiescent on the subject. There was, however, intense popular opposition to the measure and some of the Wesleyans apparently considered taking the lead in organising a petition. 'An official personage of the Wesleyan Society' wrote to the president of the Wesleyan conference, the Revd Jabez Bunting, for his support but was told that as the bill was brought forward by the King's ministers 'it was impolitic for them to oppose'.[384] There the matter was left, but news of the correspondence was picked up by the *Bedford Gazette* and the potential of the Methodists as an anti-reformist political force seems to have been noted by local Tories. When a general election was called in June 1830, one of the opening gambits of the Tory candidate's campaign was to put up posters around Bedford proclaiming 'Lord John Russell's Opinion of the Methodists' and carrying a quotation from his *Memoirs of the Affairs of Europe*, published the previous year. The Methodists, Russell had written,

> multiply miracles, far beyond the regular and limited practice of the Romish Church. If a Methodist preacher wants a dinner, a suit of clothes, or a few pence to pay a turnpike, he puts up a prayer, and his want is immediately supplied. Thus between forgery, fanaticism, and cunning, genuine Christianity is utterly lost.[385]

The posters went on to ask

> Methodist electors! Can you, will you, vote for the man whose opinion of you is recorded above? ... prove that you are sincere enough to detest duplicity, firm enough to spurn an insult, and united enough to make him feel it.[386]

The local Methodist leadership, seeking advice on how best to respond, turned once again to Jabez Bunting (although in this particular year he was neither president nor secretary of the conference). The letter they received from Bunting does not appear to have survived but it is clear that on this occasion he gave his sanction to them entering the political fray and actually encouraged them to take an active role in opposing Russell's election.[387] By 13 July *The Times* was already scenting a political upset:

---

[384] *Huntingdon, Bedford and Peterborough Gazette*, 14 March 1829, p. 3, col. 1. For the bigger picture of Methodist opposition to Catholic emancipation see Hempton, *Methodism and politics*, 134–42.
[385] Muggeridge, *History of the late contest*, 13.
[386] Muggeridge, *History of the late contest*, 13.
[387] Gregory, *Side lights on the conflicts of Methodism*, 202 and 224. After Russell's defeat in the Bedford election he was hastily nominated for Tavistock, another seat in which the Duke of Bedford

> Captain Polhill, it is expected, will disappoint the expectations of Lord John Russell, who offers himself for Bedford ... his Lordship having grievously offended the Methodists, who are very numerous, by some severe strictures in one of his publications.[388]

For the next month Russell and his agents worked flat out to win back the lost ground. In his printed election address Lord John claimed that he had been 'unfairly quoted to create great prejudice against me' and argued that 'the rights and feelings of the Methodists have ever been an object of my respect.'[389] Writing directly to one Wesleyan, Russell confessed that several of his comments had been misjudged and promised to revise any future editions of his book accordingly:

> The passage concerning Miracles, reprinted in a handbill at Bedford, should have been restricted to certain sects of small numbers, and not applied to the general body of Methodist Preachers. ... The passages in which Methodism is *(en passant)* compared to a quack medicine, &c., as they are naturally offensive to a large and respectable body of men, ought to be expunged.

He would not withdraw, however, his comments on Methodist intolerance, commenting that 'a man ought to be as free to give his opinion of Methodism, as the Methodists are in giving theirs, of the Roman Catholic Church.'[390] The Methodist voters more generally were addressed by a second wave of posters, which announced:

> Methodist electors! – some of you have resented deeply an error in the writings of Lord John Russell but are you prepared to give your aid to the work of brutal intoxication by which it is expected to carry an election in your town?[391]

Polhill responded swiftly with another poster of his own, asking Methodist electors to compare Russell's appeal to their morality with his published opinion that 'another defect of Methodism is, that by the confession of Wesley himself; it borders close on doctrines destructive of all morality.'[392]

At the close of the poll Russell was beaten into third place by a single vote and it was universally agreed by contemporary observers that it was the Methodists who had put him there. *The Times* reported that 'it is said by many that the return of Lord John Russell was lost by an artful working upon the prejudices of the Methodists, with which sect the town abounds.' The newspaper went on to note that their opposition arose from a belief that 'the religious liberty which his lordship so zealously advocated was of too lax and latitudinarian a nature, embracing within its protection Atheists and Deists.'[393] Bedford's jubilant Tories even produced a victory song mocking Russell's discomfiture:

> O dear, what can the matter be!
> Dear, dear, how they laugh at and batter me,

---

exercised great influence. On this occasion the Revd Robert Newton, a close ally of Bunting's, actually travelled down to the town to encourage the Methodists in their opposition to his candidature.

388 *The Times* 13 July 1830, p. 3, col. 3.
389 Muggeridge, *History of the late contest*, 14.
390 *Huntingdon, Bedford and Peterborough Gazette* 28 August 1830, p. 2, col. 5.
391 Muggeridge, *History of the late contest*, 16.
392 Collection of election posters 1830, BLARS, AD 1081.
393 *The Times* 6 August 1830, p. 4, col. 1.

Oh how I wish I had ne'er come that Saturday
To hear all the Methodists scoff![394]

Phillip Hunt, a local Whig clergyman, was drawn to the same conclusion. When he wrote to inform Lord William Russell of the disaster he explained that, 'intolerant High Church feelings actuated the Moravians, and even the Methodists, who still talk about their loyalty [i.e. to the Protestant constitution], and their dread of Latitudinarian principles in religion.'[395]

On the face of it the result was a psephological phenomenon. A leading aristocratic family had lost a seat which for the past forty-two years they had not even needed to contest and all because of the influence of a Methodist chapel. What is more, this was not the story of some northern manufacturing town undergoing the revolutionary transformation of rapid population growth and industrialisation but of a small, rural, southern borough. The poll-book, however, reveals a very different story and suggests that the impact of Methodist voters on the election was, in fact, a psephological red herring.

There were some 250 Methodist members in the Bedford society in 1830 and about 500 regular hearers, altogether the equivalent of about one in ten of the borough's population. Of these 750 people, however, a significant number were children, two-thirds of the adults were probably women, and many of the men did not meet the qualification to vote.[396] Taking all that into account, it may well be that the thirty voters who can be identified from minute books, chapel deeds and baptism registers as being connected with the Wesleyan chapel represent a near full complement of the much sought after Methodist electors of Bedford.[397] Between them those thirty men constituted a mere 4% of the total resident electorate of the borough. Although hardly 'numerous', in a closely fought race those thirty men could still have represented a decisive force if they had acted together as a voting block, but the poll-book shows that they did not. In fact, Frederick Polhill secured 14 Methodist votes compared with Russell's 18 and William Whitbread (his running-mate)'s 22 votes. Had the electorate as a whole voted in the same proportions Russell would have romped home ahead of Polhill with a majority of 150. Russell's lead over Polhill among the Wesleyan voters is all the more striking because among the resident voters generally (that is, putting aside the non-resident freemen) he lost heavily to Polhill.[398]

The impression that the Methodists voted against Russell was almost certainly created by the actions of two men, John Howard and Maximilian Wilson. At the nomination of candidates, Howard, a circuit steward, ironmonger by trade and consistent Tory voter, had insisted on his right to address the voters and made a bitter attack on Lord John for the 'totally unfounded and calumnious attack, so unblushingly made upon the Wesleyan Methodists.'[399] It was he who condemned

[394] *The Bedford Chronicle and Independent Truth Teller*, BLARS, BorBG10/1/27.
[395] *Letters to Lord G. William Russell*, II, 263.
[396] Bedford Wesleyan district minutes 1832, MARC.
[397] *A Copy of the poll for the borough of Bedford 1830*; Bedford Wesleyan circuit minutes of local preachers' meetings 1829–53, schedules 1837–43 and baptism register 1810–37, BLARS, MB 9, 105 and 115. Methodists formed an even smaller proportion of the county electorate, perhaps no more than 2%.
[398] Flick, 'Bedford election of 1830', 167–8.
[399] Muggeridge, *History of the late contest*, 40.

Russell's views on religious liberty as being of 'far too great a latitude for me, in as much as it opens, as it were, a sluice gate, not only for the admission of Papists, but sceptics, Deists and infidels.' His speech roused the crowd to such agitation that Russell's attempt to reply was apparently completely inaudible. Wilson, for his part, was the superintendent minister of the Bedford Wesleyan circuit. He was later accused of having suppressed a letter in which a group of leading Wesleyan preachers had sought to advise local members that 'every methodist should be satisfied with Lord Russell's honourable concessions of error and promise of future correction. Nor ought any feelings of resentment to influence their votes at the approaching election.'[400]

Wilson was in Leeds, at the annual conference when polling began. However, the Revd William Dixon, a supernumerary preacher living in Bedford, took a two-horse chaise up to Yorkshire to fetch him back for the vote (breaking the Sabbath in the process, as a critic pointed out). According to one account they arrived only just in time: 'five minutes before the poll closed a big cheer was raised by the Conservatives and Mr Wilson was hustled into the room and had just time to sign his paper when the clock struck.'[401]

The Legacy of 1830
There was, of course, a reckoning to pay for such an affront to the county's most powerful family. The Duke of Bedford was not a subscriber to Bedford's new Wesleyan chapel in 1832 and an application to use the Sessions House for services during the building work was denied, although a similar request from the Old Meeting had previously been granted.[402] Applications to the duke for land on which to build village chapels met similar disappointment and in 1836 the circuit was sufficiently concerned to seek the advice of the conference. In a reversal of their usual roles, on this occasion it was Bunting's opponents who championed the 'no politics' rule, William Atherton commenting dryly, 'I think we should learn a lesson from this not to take a forward part in electioneering matters.'[403]

The lesson which local politicians, of all hues, learnt from the election, however, was that the Methodist vote was a key battleground. Polhill and William Stuart, the Tory MP for Bedfordshire, both gave £20 towards the cost of the new chapel in 1832 but so too did the Whig, William Whitbread.[404] Three years later Samuel Crawley, the radical who defeated Polhill in the general election of 1832, contributed £5 to Bedford's new Primitive Methodist chapel and across the county boundary the ultra-Tory Marquis of Chandos not only leased the Wesleyans of Aylesbury land for a chapel and gave them ten guineas towards their building fund but even promised to attend the opening.[405] There was more to the courting of Methodism, however,

---

400 *Huntingdon, Bedford and Peterborough Gazette*, 28 August 1830, p. 2, col. 5. The letter was signed by Humphrey Sandwith, but drafted in consultation with Adam Clarke and Richard Watson, among others.
401 Nichols and Woods, 'Memoirs of Jane and William Inskip', 102.
402 Bedford Wesleyan chapel, stewards' accounts, 1832–46, BLARS, MB 25; Wigfield, 'Recusancy and Nonconformity in Bedfordshire', 223–4; Tibbutt, *Bunyan Meeting Bedford*, 44–5.
403 Gregory, *Side lights on the conflicts of Methodism*, 224.
404 Bedford Wesleyan chapel, stewards' accounts, 1832–46, BLARS, MB 25.
405 *Huntingdon, Bedford and Peterborough* Gazette, 6 June 1835, p. 3, col. 1; *Bedford Mercury*, 2 December 1837, p. 4, col. 4.

than a few well-publicised subscriptions. At the borough election in 1832, Samuel Crawley, the radical candidate, having been accused of inconsistency and of previously supporting both a Tory and a Whig candidate, chose the Methodist chapel as the sacred ground on which to make his public declaration: 'As I am a living Man, and in the Place that I am, so help me God, I never Voted till 1826, when I gave a Plumper for Lord Tavistock.'[406]

Five years later Crawley again made a bid for the Methodist vote when he opened his campaign to retain his seat with a front-page advertisement in the *Bedford Mercury* headed 'The High Church Tories and the Wesleyan Methodists.' In it he detailed 'the atrocious calumnies circulated by the Tories against the Wesleyan Methodists' and warned the Methodists of Bedford that behind their friendly words the Tories were really planning 'a revival of the infamous bill of the Tory Lord Sidmouth.'[407] Even though not specifically named, the Bedford Methodists may well also have been at least part of the intended audience for Crawley's anti-slavery pronouncements during the election campaign in 1832 and 1837, and even more so for Polhill's repeated tub-thumping about the Catholic threat.[408]

Given this attention, it is perhaps not surprising that, despite earning the duke's displeasure and being warned not to take a prominent part in electioneering matters, Methodists in Bedfordshire became progressively more assertive during the 1830s about the status and recognition owed to their community in local public life. In 1835 the Biggleswade circuit launched a successful legal action against the toll collector of the Henlow turnpike, claiming for Wesleyan preachers travelling to Sunday appointments the same right to exemption from tolls granted by the General Turnpike Act of 1773 to those attending 'their normal place of worship'. This was a battle subsequently taken up by the Bedford and Luton circuits. The Bedford circuit also went to court to protect their interest in the Hurst charity, and the Luton circuit mounted a public campaign to secure the right to hold services in the workhouse.[409] Local mayors were now invited to chair annual missionary meetings and local town halls were booked as the venue.[410] By the early 1840s local Wesleyans were even involved in pressing for proper recognition of their community's importance at a national level. When, in 1843, Sir James Graham failed to consult the Wesleyan

---

[406] Election poster, 1832, BLARS, BorBG10/1/50.

[407] The calumnies included the accusation that 'illegitimacy, drunkenness and defrauding of creditors are as notorious among them as the light of noon-day' and that the Wesleyan conference had a secret fund amounting to millions of pounds which it used to influence elections (*Bedford Mercury* 15 July 1837, p. 1, col. 3).

[408] Collection of election posters 1832, BLARS, AD 1734; *Bedford Mercury* 15 July 1837, 22 July 1837 and 29 July 1837; see also Floyd, *Church, chapel and party*, 89–105. Floyd argues that candidates studiously avoided appealing to religious divisions but his focus on Church and Dissent misses the role of the Methodists as the perceived middle ground.

[409] Under the will of Anna Frances Hurst, dated 1782, £100 was left in trust for the benefit of the Bedford Wesleyan circuit. In about 1840 payments ceased to be made and in 1843 the circuit launched legal proceedings to obtain their resumption. The case was finally settled in 1848 by both sides agreeing to meet their own costs (Anderson, *Early Methodism in Bedford*, 22; Bedford Wesleyan circuit, minutes of quarterly meetings 27 June 1842, 25 September 1843, 26 December 1844, 25 June 1845, 29 December 1846, 28 June 1847, 27 September 1847, 11 March 1848, 27 December 1848 (BLARS, MB 6); *Bedford Mercury*, 18 November 1837).

[410] The mayor of St Albans chaired a Wesleyan missionary meeting in the town hall in 1835 and the mayor of Higham Ferrers did likewise in 1841 (*The Watchman* 8 July 1835, p. 213, col. 4; 17 November 1841, p. 366, col. 5).

leadership on his proposals for the publicly-funded education of children working in factories, the Bedford circuit was one of many that were quick to take offence. The minutes of the circuit quarterly meeting record thanks

> to Messrs. Dunn, Baker and Stimson for preparing and forwarding the numerous petitions to parliament against the educational clauses of the Factory Bill and to Mr Biggs for his very efficient and successful correspondence with the members of Parliament for this Borough and County upon the same important measures.[411]

Nationally and locally, Wesleyans were beginning to engage with politics in a new way. Two years after their petition on Graham's Factory Bill, the Bedford quarterly meeting spent 40 shillings (equivalent to the total weekly earnings of four working men) on another petition, this time against government proposals to increase the annual grant to Maynooth College, a Catholic seminary in Ireland.[412] The 'no politics' rule had effectively collapsed and Robert Peel's 'Romanizing Government' was denounced from local Wesleyan pulpits as Ahab and the prophets of Baal.[413]

Venturing into national politics had, in turn, the effect of drawing the Wesleyans even more deeply into local politics. When, having opposed the Maynooth grant, the Bedford circuit sought a government grant for their new day school at Ridgmont, they were publicly condemned for hypocrisy at a meeting of the Bedfordshire Union of Christians. The fierce interchange of letters which this provoked in the local newspapers displayed a degree of 'political excitement' that would have horrified an earlier generation of Methodists, who had actively cultivated a happy detachment from the world 'when any thing of a public nature was going forward.'[414] James Rigg, a young local preacher in the Biggleswade circuit, would later look back on these years as the time when what had been a religious society was transformed into 'an energetic, social, and more or less indirectly political … organisation.'[415] Perhaps the most striking testimony to Wesleyan Methodism's increasing entry into political life, however, is the fact that some chapel trustees were now using their ownership of a chapel as qualification to vote.[416] By the 1850s Wesleyans were even beginning to seek elected public office again. When Luton elected its first representative body in 1850, a board of health, John Waller, a leading Wesleyan, headed the poll and became its chairman.[417] Six years later, in 1856, Bedford would see its first Wesleyan mayor in over seventy years, with the election of John Howard.

'Dominant Toryism' and 'underlying liberalism'[418]

The fact that most of the Methodist voters in the Bedford borough election of 1830 did not support the Tory candidate is not, of course, evidence that they were in any

---

[411] Bedford Wesleyan circuit, minutes of quarterly meeting 26 June 1843, BLARS, MB 6.
[412] Bedford Wesleyan circuit, minutes of quarterly meeting 25 June 1845, BLARS, MB 6.
[413] Coley, *Life of Thomas Collins*, 273.
[414] *Bedfordshire Times* 5 June 1847, 12 June 1847, 26 June 1847 and 31 July 1847; Greeves, *Memorials of Wm Cumberland*, 52.
[415] Rigg, *Wesleyan Methodist reminiscences*, v–vi.
[416] The chapel in question was at Eaton Bray (Register of electors for the Shire of Bedford, 1841, BLARS, R4/903).
[417] Waller had opposed the creation of the board and was one of a slate of candidates pledged to minimise its work and cost.
[418] Edwards, *After Wesley*, 7.

way political radicals. Many of those who voted for Russell and Whitbread, representatives of two of the county's most powerful families, will certainly have done so for the essentially conservative reason that their landlord, employer or customers expected it of them. Lord John, for instance, we are told did not need to canvas the men who worked for a Mr Green, 'their master having kindly satisfied his Lordship on their behalf.'[419] There is evidence, however, of radical sentiment among some Wesleyans. John Turner, a member of the Wesleyan society at Milton Ernest, thought the Tories 'wicked' and 'self-interested' for opposing the Reform Act and believed that the Church of England 'must lick the dust for her arrogance and insolence.'[420] At Slapton, John Buckmaster remembered that a Methodist shoemaker 'used to make uncivil remarks about the landlords and House of Lords, the House of Commons, the new poor law, bishops, parsons, Corn Laws, the church, and class legislation.'[421]

Indeed, although Wesleyans were entirely absent from the platform of the great anti-church rate meeting held at Bedford in 1837, Buckmaster describes Methodists as leading the grassroots protest in the villages. The shoemaker, he recalled,

> counted out one-and-sixpence in pence and placed it on the table, and said: 'Give me a receipt. I pay this under protest; it is a robbery. Tithes were abolished by order of Melchisedec.' There were faint manifestations of applause. Mr. Tapper [the curate] said this disaffection in the parish was due to the spread of Methodism, … Mr Tapper made a speech about the growing disregard of the Church and resistance to constitutional authority among the labouring classes, refusing to render unto Caesar the things which belonged to Caesar. The shoemaker had great difficulty in keeping quiet.[422]

Buckmaster himself became a paid lecturer for the Anti-Corn Law Association, travelling from village to village using the networks of Wesleyan and Primitive Methodism to find local contacts who might provide a venue. Mixing hymns, prayers and politics the meetings he held were 'like a great camp meeting of Methodists' and occasionally were even held in Methodist chapels.[423] The element of anti-establishment protest which accompanied the upsurge of attendance at Methodist services in the villages of Bedfordshire during the late 1820s and early 1830s was still evident in the mid-1840s when Benjamin Gregory found the poorer element of local congregations 'much inclined to levelling theories'.[424]

Contemporaries seem to have been aware of this political division within the Wesleyan community, between an essentially conservative leadership and a potentially radical following. When the *Bedford Mercury* carried a story in 1838 that William Biggs, a Wesleyan trustee and local preacher, had told a meeting of local Tories that they 'had the support of nineteen-twentieths of the Wesleyan body', he was swift to correct them. What he had said was that 'nineteen-twentieths of the wealth, respectability, and all that was worth having of the Wesleyans supported the

---

[419] Muggeridge, *History of the late contest*, 12.
[420] Letters from John Turner to his brother Thomas, 19 November 1833, BLARS, Z 629/4 and 629/5.
[421] Buckmaster, *Village politician*, 41.
[422] *Bedford Mercury* 1 April 1837, p. 2, col. 5 and p. 3, col. 2–4. Buckmaster, *Village politician*, 42–3.
[423] Buckmaster, V*illage politician*, 180–1 and 193. William Bennett, a third generation Wesleyan and substantial tenant farmer, by contrast, denounced Cobden (*The Watchman* 10 May 1843, p. 149, col. 2.)
[424] *WMM* (1893), 934. This undercurrent of social rebellion has been noted by several writers in relation to Primitive Methodism. See Obelkevich, *Religion and rural society*, 257 and Scotland, *Methodism and the revolt of the field*, 22.

Conservatives.'[425] The poll-book for the Bedford borough election in 1837 appears to confirm his arithmetic. Of the 12 Wesleyan office-holders who can be identified among the voters, 11 backed the Tory candidates and only 1 the Whig. Among those who did not hold office, however, the political sympathies were almost exactly reversed, 16 of them voting for the Whig and only 1 for the Tory. How well the Bedford congregation coped with these political divisions is unclear but it is evident that other Wesleyan chapels found them hard to manage. A by-election for the borough of St Albans in 1846 caused serious divisions among the Wesleyan community in the town and the general election the following year left a legacy of ill-feeling 'which it will take years to amend'.[426]

During the 1840s the proportion of Wesleyans voting Conservative grew larger. At the election of 1841 a majority of both office-holders and non-office-holders supported the Conservative candidates, and with the exception of 1847, when the Whig candidate was the sabbatarian evangelical Sir Harry Verney, this continued to be true in every borough election thereafter until the late 1860s.[427] One of the factors in this may have been an exodus of disappointed Whigs and radicals but there is some evidence that it was also the result of a migration of Tories to the Wesleyan chapel from the Dissenting meeting-houses. William Day, a member of the New Meeting, and an unswerving Tory voter, seceded to the Wesleyans in the late 1830s and in Mark Rutherford's 'Cowfold', it was well known that the Methodist chapel was 'supported mainly by the brewer, who was drawn thither for many reasons one of which was political.'[428]

Nor was it only the Wesleyans who showed a conservative bias in politics. Timothy Matthews, although he observed the old Methodist way by abstaining from voting, preached sermons that Edward FitzGerald thought 'would do very well for Manchester in opposition to Chartists, etc.'[429]

More surprising, perhaps, are the Primitive Methodists, who officially boasted that they rejected 'as irrational and unscriptural, the senseless doctrines of passive obedience and non-resistance; doctrines which none but fools ever believed, and none but slaves ever obeyed.'[430] Seven of them had the vote in 1841, and 5 of them voted for the two Conservative candidates; six years later the number of voters in the congregation had increased to 9, but there were still only 3 who did not vote Conservative.

Part 5 Contemporary Responses to Methodism

Bishop Allen's Visitation Charge
In May 1837, as part of a package of measures to improve the efficiency of the Church of England, the parishes of Bedfordshire were transferred from the sprawling

---

425   *Bedford Mercury* 1 December 1838, p. 4, col. 5.
426   Coley, *Life of Thomas Collins*, 266 and 275
427   In the borough election of 1854 the Conservatives took three Wesleyan votes for every two that went to the Liberals, an advantage they maintained until the late 1860s.
428   Rutherford, *Tanner's Lane*, 196.
429   Quoted in Wright, *Life of Matthews*, 69.
430   Church, *Sketches of Primitive Methodism*, 53.

Lincoln diocese into the care of the diocese of Ely. Four years later, Joseph Allen, their new bishop, conducted his first visitation of the county. In his charge to the clergy Allen avoided any direct reference to Methodism but the shadow of the movement hung over almost every sentence of his address. Exhorting his clergy to 'do their duty,' Allen set out a series of measures which he believed would bring those who currently attended 'conventicles' back to the church. He wished to see two full services performed in every parish each Sunday, to be held at regular times and conducted in a dignified manner; he wanted greater care to be taken in sermon preparation; and he asked every incumbent to 'influence' the children attending the National school in his parish 'by every means in his power, as well as by application to the scholar's friends, to attend the Sunday School.' He was confident, he assured his clergy, that 'the additional labour entailed will be amply repaid by the religious and moral improvement of the parishioners, and by the check, which will thereby be given to dissent.'[431]

Behind such advice, of course, lay a widely held, but no less painful, presumption that it was exactly because the clergy had not conscientiously 'done their duty' that Dissent had mushroomed. Many clergymen saw the building of a chapel in their parish as a judgement upon their own labours, and attendance at it as a personal snub. The vicar of Emberton described the Methodist congregation in his village as 'a few of the poor people who for one cause or another have taken offence at me.'[432] At Houghton Conquest, the building of a Wesleyan chapel in 1832 'almost broke' Thomas Barber's heart and he was convinced that 'it was built and endowed, out of mere spite.'[433] Professional morale, clearly, was badly dented by the popularity of Methodism and, as was pointed out to the Bishop of Lincoln, 'Many of our divines ... feel themselves sinking in the scale of importance.'[434] The bitterness of the humiliation can perhaps best be judged in the scorn which was poured on Methodist preachers:

> He was tall and thin, almost to deformity. His countenance, that index of the inner man, was so wrapped and twisted, that I could read it ... a certain cunning, sinister expression ... his mouth was pursed up and drawn down at the corners, and had an expression of inordinate self-esteem; ... his little narrow, white cravat, drawn around his neck with tightness which threatened strangulation, convinced me at the first glance, that my companion was a Methodist preacher.[435]

Many of the old aspersions thrown against Methodists were dusted off for a fresh outing. Bishop Allen himself drew upon an eighteenth-century tradition of anti-Methodist writings when he raised the warning spectre of the Great Rebellion:

> That anything approaching to Puritanism should ever again gain ground in this country, notwithstanding the bitter fruits produced by it in former ages, would be quite incredible, did we not see such proof of it that we cannot be mistaken.[436]

---

431   Allen, *A charge delivered to the clergy of the Diocese of Ely 1841*, 31.
432   Returns of the clergy for Bucks, 1829, CBS, Q/W/G.
433   Quoted in Houfe, *Bedfordshire*, 193.
434   *A warning voice to the Church*, 9.
435   *Cambridge Chronicle*, 27 June 1846.
436   Allen, *A charge delivered to the clergy of the Isle of Ely, 1837*, 18–19.

Others repeated the old charge that the emphasis on justification by faith in Methodist preaching undermined morality:

> The effect wrought upon the character of servants ... by their conversion and regeneration, is usually a subject of serious regret to their employers ... [and among businessmen] duplicity lurking under the profession of Methodism is a theme of ordinary discourse.[437]

Even the accusation that Methodism was a form of Popery, in 'the great weight attached to death-bed repentance' was resurrected.[438]

To these antique insults, however, were added new, more sophisticated critiques that showed real insight into the nature of contemporary Methodism and bit all the more deeply as a result. Modern Methodism was not the admirable, if rather austere, community of fifty years before:

> The stern but simple features which it wore in the days of Wesley, have undergone wonderful changes to suit the fashion of the times and to perpetuate the charm of novelty. In the dress of its votaries, in the structure of its sanctuaries, in the auxiliaries to its devotional services, there is a strange departure from the conceptions of its pious founder.[439]

It was no longer the religion of those who were truly serious about being Christians but simply 'piety at a cheap rate', for its members were not required to 'become really good' but only 'to profess their faith, to attend the prayer meetings, to contribute freely.'[440] The innumerable meetings encouraged parents to neglect their children, the constant appeals for money kept the people poor, the 'avowed contempt of human learning' encouraged superstition, and the 'exciting exhibitions' at lovefeasts and band-meetings actively provided opportunities for immorality. By trying to counteract the spread of Methodism, the Church of England was not acting out of narrow self-interest but in the best interests of the nation.

In the face of such a challenge many of the Bedfordshire clergy seem to have come to the same conclusion as their bishop and to have begun to put greater energy into their duties even before his visitation. Only 25 parishes (out of 133) had no resident clergyman, and in 16 of these he lived in an adjacent village. Only 15 parishes had no singing and the number enjoying two full services every Sunday (that is where not only morning and evening prayers were read but a sermon was preached on each occasion) had already risen from 18 in 1837 to 45 in 1841.[441] Influence, of various kinds, was also being brought to bear, not just on children but adults as well, to provide additional reasons, if not to come to church then at least to stay away from any chapels. At Ampthill, in 1829, the rector reduced the rations of one resident of the parish poorhouse, an orphaned 14-year-old, to bread and water for going to the Wesleyan chapel and subsequently expelled him when he continued to attend. At Shefford the clergyman successfully delayed the building of another Wesleyan chapel by the simple device of buying every piece of land that

---

[437] *A warning voice to the Church*, 10.
[438] *A warning voice to the Church*, 12.
[439] *A warning voice to the Church*, 15.
[440] *A warning voice to the Church*, 10.
[441] Diocese of Ely, episcopal visitation returns 1837 and 1841, Cambridge University Library, C/3/19, 22, 23.

came on the market.[442] The creation of burial grounds next to a number of Wesleyan chapels, including Bedford (1825), Luton (probably 1830), Newport Pagnell (1836), Biggleswade (1836), Bierton (mid-1840s), North Marston (1844), Dunstable (1845) and Toddington (1846), strongly suggests that control of the parish graveyard was another influence being brought to bear.[443]

Nor were the clergy acting alone. A number of the landowners made attendance at the parish church a condition of farm tenancies.[444] J. T. Brooks, the Tory squire of Flitwick, 'Made all our people attend so that the Church was filled with labourers' and entirely concurred with the bishop that the reason why 'vile dissenters of all sorts have sadly gained ground' was owing to 'the sad neglect of the old Foxhunting parsons.'[445] Even the Whig Duke of Bedford made a concerted attempt to drive nonconformity out of Oakley: purchasing the cottage in which a congregation of Independents met and demolishing it; refusing the Primitive Methodists access to a plot of land that they had purchased; and letting it be known he would not tolerate open-air preaching.[446] But it was another incident at Ampthill that became the most infamous. In 1837 Joseph Morris, a local brewer, egged on by the curate, announced that every man in his service would have to attend the parish church. Three Methodists and two Dissenters, all of whom had been in his employment for more than twelve years, refused and were summarily dismissed.[447]

'Excluding, of course, the Wesleyan Methodists'

Not all churchmen shared the perspective of the parish clergy. For those whose loyalty to the Church of England was essentially political, part of a commitment to the established order and the Protestant constitution, the popularity of Methodism was not wholly bad news. Shaken by the Duke of Wellington's conversion to Catholic emancipation and by the reforming agenda of the Whig government that replaced him, some ultra-Tories began to look on the Wesleyan connexion as a potential ally. By 1834 the Tory-supporting *Bucks Herald* felt confident enough in the Wesleyans' loyalist sympathies to place them in the Church of England's camp when it published a comparison of the numerical strength of the Church and Dissent.[448] Ten years later it was still obviously eager to report evidence of the essential conservatism of the Wesleyans. Noting that the congregation at the re-opening of the Wesleyan chapel in Aylesbury was both very numerous and 'highly respectable', the paper informed its readers that the preacher 'spoke with kindness of the Church and her Ministers, with whose doctrines in a great degree the congregation coincide, and the advantages derived to all classes by having an establishment in the

---

[442] Phillips, *Wesleyan Methodist church, Biggleswade circuit*, 33.
[443] The right of the clergyman to insist on conducting any burial in the churchyard and to deny burial to the 'unbaptised' (which might include those baptised by Wesleyan preachers) was regularly maintained in the local Tory press (*Cambridge Chronicle* 8 October 1835, 15 August 1840, 7 November 1840). At Southill, the clergyman refused to say the burial prayers over a member of the Baptist church or to allow anyone else to say prayers and took the opportunity to harangue the mourners on the evils of nonconformity (*WMM* (1830), 484).
[444] Nichols and Woods, 'Memoirs of Jane and William Inskip', 93.
[445] Morgan, *Diary of a Bedfordshire squire*, 167.
[446] *PMM* (1850), 50.
[447] *A short account of the cruelties inflicted on Dissenters by the High Church Party*, 1.
[448] *Bucks Herald*, 8 February 1834, p. 3, col. 5–6.

country.'[449] A few months later, reporting on the opening of a new Wesleyan chapel at Whitchurch, the editor similarly reassured them that

> All the preachers spoke with warmth and love of 'their parent', *the Church of England*, and it is probable that the numerous chapels in the Wesleyan connexion were erected to receive the surplus congregations which the parish churches could not contain.[450]

The *Cambridge Chronicle,* another Tory-leaning newspaper with a local circulation, adopted much the same line, apprising its readers in 1835 of 'the startling fact everywhere starting to view, that the Wesleyans consider themselves as in strict communion with the established church.'[451] Throughout the rest of the 1830s the *Chronicle* was careful to qualify many of its virulent attacks on Dissent with the provisory clause, 'excluding, of course, the Wesleyan Methodists.'[452] In 1839, in particular, the paper heaped praise on the Wesleyans for their staunch opposition to Lord John Russell's proposals for a system of state-controlled education and rejoiced to know that they could be counted upon in the fight against 'the infidel and the revolutionary schemes' of the Whig government.[453] It even carried articles that year about local celebrations of the centenary of Methodism, a chapel opening and the proceedings of the Wesleyan conference.[454]

With the collapse of the Whig administration in 1841, the threat to the established position of the Church of England receded. Buoyed up by the efforts of Sir Robert Peel's Conservative government actively to revive the fortunes of the Church, within a few short years the self-confidence of churchmen soared. By 1844 the *Bucks Herald* was trumpeting the unassailable strength of the state church:

> Nothing was ever more marked out for political destruction; nothing seemed more devoid of resources, wherewith to avert the danger. ... [but] the Church of England only spoke, and the spell which was supposed to be around her vanished.[455]

With the need for Methodist support removed, sympathetic references to the Wesleyans evaporated. As early as 1840 there were calls for 'no more compromise, no more tampering with leaders of Methodism ... [no] alliance of ignorance and fanaticism with the chaste and liberal institutions of the Church.'[456]

The *Cambridge Chronicle* was especially quick to change its tune, describing a service the following year, led by the popular Wesleyan preacher William Dawson, as 'revolting to a pious mind.'[457] Ignorance of the affairs of 'these mushroom sects' was now deliberately cultivated and when the *Chronicle* did take condescending notice of a piece of Wesleyan news it made a point of providing its genteel readers with a glossary to such obscure events:

---

449   *Bucks Herald,* 3 February 1844, p. 4, col. 2.
450   *Bucks Herald,* 2 November 1844, p. 4, col. 4.
451   *Cambridge Chronicle* 14 August 1835. The revelation may have owed something to the launch of *The Watchman* earlier that same year.
452   *Cambridge Chronicle,* 8 June 1839, 22 February 1840, 31 October 1840.
453   *Cambridge Chronicle*, 31 August 1839; and see Hempton, *Methodism and politics*, 158–64.
454   *Cambridge Chronicle*, 2 February 1839, 29 June 1839, 17 August 1839 and 31 August 1839.
455   *Bucks Herald* 24 August 1844, p. 6, col. 2.
456   *A warning voice to the Church,* 23.
457   *Cambridge Chronicle* 2 January 1841.

The Wesleyans [at Upwell] have had what is termed 'a revival' (i.e. converting of the soul through importunate prayers, used with irritable spirit) progressing at a rapid rate. ... It is principally among the juveniles that this sad and mistaken excitement exists.[458]

There was always room, however, in its columns for a chapel scandal and the heated meetings of the Wesleyan reform controversy were reported in detail.

At the meeting held in Lincoln the lights were put out, and blows harder than words were resorted to by way of argument. It is stated by one of the sufferers that some of the 'fair' sex were quite as anxious to use their finger nails as their tongues.[459]

Respectable churchmen were presumably suitably shocked but not at all surprised!

'Mark Rutherford'

William Hale White, born in 1831, was brought up among the élite of Bedfordshire's Dissenting community, his father being one of the deacons of Bedford Old Meeting. In his fifties, while working in London as a civil servant, he conjured up the town of his youth in a series of novels which he wrote under the pseudonym of Mark Rutherford. White clearly remembered the physicality of the Bedford Wesleyan chapel quite well, accurately describing it in *The Revolution in Tanner's Lane* as 'new, stuccoed, with grained doors and cast-iron railing' (see Plate 18) but on another occasion, in *The Autobiography of Mark Rutherford*, seems to have allowed himself some artistic license in order to make a deeper point, consigning the Wesleyans to 'a new red-brick chapel in the outskirts'.[460] To those among whom White grew up, the Wesleyans, for all their popularity, were a novelty of little significance: 'With regard to the Wesleyan Chapel, nothing much need be said. Its creed was imported, and it had no roots in the town. The Church disliked it because it was Dissenting, and the Dissenters disliked it because it was half-Church and above all, Tory.'[461]

There was some communication between the two communities. In 1837 the Wesleyan chapel in Bedford was lent to the local branch of the London Missionary Society for their annual meeting and Corbett Cooke, the superintendent preacher on the Luton circuit, preached one of the sermons at the opening of the town's Union chapel. In the 1840s Richard Fish, a local preacher in the Kettering circuit, was apparently much in demand among the neighbouring Independent churches.[462] White's sense of the distance between the Wesleyans and Dissenters, however, seems to have been well observed. When Thomas Street withdrew from Cotton End Meeting, in about 1849, it astonished his family that he suggested attending a Wesleyan chapel. In fact their inexperience of Methodism was such that they were even more surprised to find a large chapel, well filled and a good choir and organ.[463] Various factors may have contributed to this lack of awareness. Connexional rules

---

[458] *Cambridge Chronicle* 4 March 1843.
[459] *Cambridge Chronicle* 5 January 1850. Another scandal covered by the *Chronicle* was the story of a 'ranting parson' from Buckden who left his children without food believing that the Lord would provide (5 June 1841).
[460] Rutherford, *Tanner's Lane*, 195 and Rutherford, *Autobiography*, 27.
[461] Rutherford, *Tanner's Lane*, 196.
[462] *WMM* (1893), 934.
[463] Nichols and Woods, 'Memoirs of Jane and William Inskip', 95.

prohibited Wesleyan chapels from inviting Dissenting ministers into their pulpits and the preference for denominational ventures in education, missions and even relief funds kept Wesleyans out of many local cross-denominational ventures. Politics, however, as White pointed out, was certainly an important gulf between the two communities. Few occasions can have demonstrated this more graphically than the meeting calling for the abolition of church rates, held in April 1837, when the platform was packed with Dissenting ministers but which not a single Wesleyan is recorded as having attended. Not all Dissenters were Whigs, let alone radicals, but the poll-books show that a very substantial majority were and in an age when political loyalties could be costly (William White's windows were smashed during the election of 1832), the Tory sympathies of the leading Wesleyans can hardly have endeared them to many at the meeting-house.[464]

Some Dissenters were willing to acknowledge the religious good done by Wesleyans, and particularly their usefulness in evangelising the rural poor. At Rickmansworth, in the St Albans circuit, a member of the Society of Friends provided the Wesleyans with a 'commodious chapel free from all incumbrance' on the condition that they ran a Sunday school.[465] Evan Lewis, minister of Rothwell Independent church in Northamptonshire, was prepared to congratulate the connexion for the work they did among

> those classes of society which had been too much neglected by the Established Church and Congregational Dissenters. ... They have caused the Gospel of Salvation to be preached in the darkest hamlets of their native country, and by their self-denying local preachers, have kept open a House of God where no stated minister could have been sustained.[466]

He had deep misgivings, however, about the Wesleyan's church polity:

> All Methodists know, and most – if not all – of them confess, that Wesleyan Methodism is really a system of hierarchical despotism, to which, however, they submit, not because it is in harmony with reason, or proved ... by the teaching of Scripture: but because it is a mighty machinery for the accomplishment of good.[467]

For all its strengths, Methodism was in reality a form of Popery that deprived the ordinary people of any rights except to pay their dues and obey the preachers. Instead of providing, as did the Independent churches, a model for democratic reform, it brought into the religious world the corruptions of Britain's existing constitution: 'I believe it to be a great idol, and the sooner it is destroyed the better.'[468] Just how widely these reservations, about the profoundly anti-democratic constitution of Wesleyan Methodism, were felt among Dissenters can perhaps be judged by the support which they lent to the Wesleyan reform movement. At Leighton Buzzard, Ebenezer Baptist chapel hosted several reform meetings; at Bedford many Dissenters attended the services led by Samuel Dunn in the Assembly Room; and at Cambridge

---

464 Rutherford, *Early life*, 39.
465 *The Watchman* 8 July 1835, p. 214, col. 4.
466 Lewis, *Independency*, 83.
467 Lewis, *Independency*, 82.
468 Lewis, *Rev. H. Fish*, 29.

the minister of Downing Street Independent chapel told a public meeting that he had 'no hesitation in expressing [his] sympathy with the present movement'.[469]

Subtler, but no less significant, differences also added to the mutual incomprehension, including matters relating to class and culture. A bizarre incident in 1837 provides a curious example of this tangled knot of prejudices. It all began when some members of the Bedford Wesleyan chapel choir appeared in a concert of the town's newly formed Harmonic Society. One of the songs included in the programme contained the words 'snowy bosom' which proved 'sufficient to sink a concert into the "deepest depths" of Wesleyan hatred.' Thomas Staton, the superintendent preacher, who was already of the opinion that 'concerts are abominations', took summary action and expelled the offending singers from membership of the Wesleyan society. The *Bedford Mercury*, mouthpiece of the local Dissenting élite, was predictably quick to denounce Staton's tyranny. The condemnation of Staton, however, was not restricted to the lack of due process in Wesleyan discipline. The Wesleyans as a whole were accused of 'Agnewism', of being opposed to every kind of pleasure that was not strictly religious, but at the same time of allowing musical performances in their worship that were virtually 'Popish'.[470] Wesleyan worship was too fancy for those brought up in the plain traditions of the meeting-house but the lives of Wesleyans were too narrow for those middle-class Dissenters who were fully engaged in contemporary culture; men like James Raban, the minister of Eggington and Hockliffe Independent church, who published poetry, or Robert Robinson of Union chapel, Luton, who gave lectures on British history and animal instinct, or William Stowell, who combined his role as minister of Maulden Meeting with the assistant editorship of the *Bedford Mercury*.[471]

The Common People

Not everyone, of course, took religious distinctions that seriously. As early as 1829, the clergyman at Ravenstone in Buckinghamshire had observed that a common evangelical culture united many churchgoers: 'dissenters of different denominations and church people are in this neighbourhood so mixed and united and so many of them approximate so near to each other that it is impossible to discriminate.'[472]

When a clerical magistrate attempted to secure the acquittal of a young man accused of disturbing a Wesleyan congregation, on the grounds that the evidence of members of the congregation was unreliable, the jury would have none of it and instantly returned a guilty verdict.[473] Even at Ampthill, the curate's attempts to bring pressure to bear on nonconformists in 1837 simply underscored how unacceptable such behaviour had become. It was the curate himself who was denounced as a reformer and disturber of the peace, and Lord Holland, the town's largest landowner,

---

[469] *Cambridge Independent Press*, 20 July 1850, p. 1, col. 3.
[470] From Sir Andrew Agnew, MP (1793–1849), a leading spokesman for the Lord's Day Observance Society.
[471] Tibbutt, *Hockliffe & Eggington Congregational Church*, 27; Collings, *History of Union Chapel, Luton*, 9; Peer, *Ampthill Union Church*, 22.
[472] Returns of the clergy for Bucks 1829, CBS, Q/W/G.
[473] *Huntingdon, Bedford and Peterborough Gazette*, 30 January 1829. The original incident had taken place in the village of Bradfield Combust in the Bury St Edmunds circuit.

made it clear that he would continue to employ without reference to religion.[474] If most people no longer found Wesleyan Methodism dangerous or subversive, however, nor did they find it especially exciting. When Benjamin Gregory tried to mission the Northamptonshire village of Geddington, in the 1840s, he found that his efforts were met with polite indifference: 'the sturdy men-folks gave me gruff, curt thanks as I shook hands with them but we could get no foothold.'[475]

While the overwhelming majority of people in Bedfordshire attended one kind of church or another, there was still, of course, a significant minority who chose not to do so. Thomas Street's landlord did not 'care a rap for the Parsons' and William Hale White recalled that although the thoroughfares of Bedford were deserted during service times on a Sunday, plenty of people could have been found, out of sight, quietly tending their gardens or getting on with other things.[476] The views of these non-churchgoers are hard to capture and can only be surmised from odd episodes. Many, including those who, while not attending services themselves, sent their children to Sunday school, probably went along with the general recognition of Wesleyan Methodism as a respectable body. Some, however, will have shared the flippancy expressed by a man arraigned in 1834 for being drunk at Cranfield:

> In extenuation he said he did not know a man who did not at times get drunk; he knew several Methodist parsons who had a peculiar method of their own in that way; he however could not pay the same compliment to Church parsons ... but, he dare say, they did at times.[477]

Others openly espoused a militant secularism. At Luton there was even a public debate, in 1852, between the secularist Robert Cooper (author of *The Holy Scriptures analyzed: showing its contradictions, absurdities and immoralities*) and John Bowes, a former colleague of Timothy Matthews.[478]

As Wesleyans became bolder, and sought not simply to impose their code of respectability on themselves but on the community at large, opposition among working-class men became more vocal and more serious. When a public meeting in support of total abstinence, held in Eaton Bray Wesleyan chapel in 1839, was told that 'the drunkard was a more wicked and more mischievous animal than a mad dog' some of the audience (poetically described as 'the friends of Sir John Barleycorn') took such offence that the parish constable had to be called.[479] The following year, a large temperance demonstration at Newport Pagnell was subject to a sustained assault. As reported in *The Watchman*,

> A mob ... collected, some of whom took deep offence at a black banner, bearing the inscription, 'Because of drunkenness the land mourneth,' and the procession was assailed with yells and hisses. ... A drunken fellow went up to the bearer of

474 Peer, *Ampthill Union Church*, 20.
475 *WMM* (1893), 935.
476 Nichols and Woods, 'Memoirs of Jane and William Inskip', 93–4; Rutherford, *Tanner's Lane*, 196.
477 *Hertford Mercury and Reformer*, 16 December 1834, p. 3, col. 6. Some Methodist preachers certainly did get drunk. In 1831 Donald McPherson, the junior preacher on the Biggleswade circuit, was found to have been intoxicated in the pulpit at Hitchin. It was recommended that he be 'dropped from the work' and given £50 to set himself up in business (Bedford Wesleyan district minutes of special district meeting 27 January 1831, MARC).
478 Bowes, *Autobiography*, 510.
479 *Stamford Mercury* 26 July 1839, p. 4, col. 4.

the flag, and, having deliberately felled him to the ground, he and his companions tore the offending trophy to ribands. The teetotallers behaved with great forbearance, but their assailants were not to be conciliated; other violent and brutal attacks were made, and some of the teetotallers received severe injuries. The mob afterwards broke the windows of a house, in which we believe the teetotal committee were sitting, and an attempt was made to cut the supporting ropes of a large tent erected on the green, and beneath which the teetotallers were taking refreshments. If the attempt had succeeded, it is impossible to calculate the serious loss of life which must have followed.[480]

In the early 1830s many labouring men had looked on Wesleyan Methodism as a vehicle through which they might challenge respectable society. By the late 1830s it appeared to be the means by which respectable society would challenge the culture and habits of the working-man.

'Fallacious and Dangerous': Attitudes to the Revivalist Sects

If most people were willing to accept that the Wesleyans had a place in local society by the 1830s and 1840s, they did not extend that acceptance to the new Methodist groups that sprang up in these decades. Opposition to the Primitive Methodists, to the Matthewsites and to the Latter Day Saints was widespread and intense. Matthews was stoned by churchgoers in Bedford in 1837, and at Hitchin a group of Primitive Methodists trying to hold an open-air service in a poor quarter of the town in 1846 'were roughly treated, being beaten with a dead cat, and abused with diverse missiles.'[481] The Primitive Methodist societies at Norton, Arlesey, Clifton, Croydon and East Hatley, in the Baldock mission, all collapsed within weeks of each other when local landlords forbade their tenants to hold meetings in their cottages.[482] In the Buckden mission 'the new converts were deprived of work on account of having joined our society'; an experience shared by Christopher Layton of Northill when he became a Mormon.[483]

The loud and emotional meetings of all these groups, with their 'hysterical fits, groaning, and screaming for conversions', was certainly one cause of the antagonism they provoked. The *Cambridge Chronicle* undoubtedly spoke for a far wider section of the community than just its own high Tory readership when it denounced such proceedings as 'disgraceful, disorderly and revolting'.[484] Some observers were clearly concerned about the political consequences of this religious excitement and several local newspapers drew parallels between Timothy Matthews and the millenarian insurrectionist John Thom, whose announcement that the year of jubilee was at hand led to an armed rising in Kent and the deaths of ten men.[485] Others found cause for concern in the levity which revivalist meetings encouraged rather than the intensity. Rumours of the antics to be witnessed at such gatherings often drew 'the

480 *The Watchman* 21 October 1840, p. 341, col. 3.
481 *PMM* (1846), 27.
482 *PMM* (1849), 368.
483 *PMM* (1845), 222; Cannon, *Autobiography of Christopher Layton*, 3.
484 *Cambridge Chronicle* 18 February 1845.
485 *The Reformer; or Herts, Beds, Bucks, Essex, Cambridge, and Middlesex Advertiser,* 15 September 1838. The story also appeared in the *Huntingdon, Bedford and Peterborough Gazette*. Thom had been killed at the 'battle of Bosenden Wood' a few months previously on 31 May 1838. It was reported at the time that many of his followers were Methodists (Reay, *Last rising of the agricultural labourers*, 132).

idle and the curious' undermining the proper respect in which worship should be held. In one incident, at Saxon Street in Suffolk, a number of young men attended the Primitive Methodist chapel 'for the sake of fun and diversion' and one, 'for the amusement of his companions, caused it [his dog] to stand erect upon a seat with a short pipe in its mouth.'[486] Memories of the collapse of the United Revivalists, leaving a trail of unpaid debts, re-enforced the suspicion that the Primitive Methodists, and others like them, were 'street spouters' who would 'not be here long' and made a 'trade of religion by selling tracts and books'.[487] These were not legitimate denominations but 'disgraceful imposters in religion [who] ought to be suppressed by some legal enactment, and turned out of all respectable society as a common nuisance.'[488]

George Price, one of the first Primitive Methodist missionaries in the Aylesbury circuit, felt that the opposition from 'some who profess to be Christians' was rooted in a concern that he and his brethren had come to the area 'for the purpose of drawing away members of other communities.'[489] Competition may have been a concern, especially to the Wesleyans, but both they and the Dissenters may also have felt the need to establish clear lines of distinction between themselves and the new groups in order to avoid being tarred with the same brush. The Wesleyan authorities permitted no interchange with Matthews's society and Dissenters led the charge in ridiculing his miraculous healing of Charlotte Beeby:

> in all modern miracles we may take it for granted that one or both of the parties concerned, that is the performer or the patient, or both, are imposters … the cold water of the river Ouse at midnight in the month of April would make any one jump who had legs to use; and we may well suppose when she was lifted from the bank into the water, that she cried out, perhaps, before she touched the water, 'that she was quite cured' … it is sadly to be deplored that one who calls himself a Minister should thus make a mockery of Almighty power and delude poor benighted ignorant people.[490]

Wesleyans and Dissenters were likewise to the fore in disrupting Mormon meetings, organising anti-Mormon lectures, and circulating stories that the Latter Day Saints were guilty of 'heresy, slavery, blasphemy and treason'.[491]

Not everyone took quite such a negative view, at least of the Primitive Methodists. Some radical Dissenters argued that the principle of religious freedom was indivisible. The *Cambridge Independent Press* defended the right of Primitive Methodists to worship undisturbed using whatever forms they pleased 'their tenets might be reasonable or unreasonable, orthodox or heterodox; with that the magistrates had no concern.'[492]

A more positive kind of support came from evangelicals of various backgrounds who saw in Primitive Methodism a vehicle to spread Christianity among the working

---

486   *Cambridge Independent Press*, 15 June 1850, p. 2, col. 8.
487   *PMM* (1837), 307.
488   *Bucks Herald*, 17 August 1844.
489   *PMM* (1837), 307.
490   *Bedford Mercury*, 21 April 1838, p. 3, col. 1.
491   *Millennial Star*, vol. 2, no. 3 (July 1841), 37. The fact that Mormons practised polygamy was not revealed until 1852.
492   *Cambridge Chronicle*, 13 July 1850.

classes. 'A Member of the Established Church', writing in the *Cambridge Chronicle*, was particularly impressed that, in Weston Colville, under Primitive Methodist influence 'men formerly drunkards, have become sober; and the majority of the labouring population are becoming respectable members of society.'[493] At Luton, William Higgins, a trustee of the Wesleyan chapel, provided the Primitive Methodist preachers with their first home in the town and was one of the two trustees of their first chapel. Samuel Francis, another Wesleyan, paid the rent for a Primitive Methodist preaching room at Ampthill.[494] When the Primitive Methodist preacher, John Parrott, was taken ill with typhus in 1850, Professor Frost, minister of Cotton End Meeting,

> deputed two of his students to beg that I would keep my mind at rest relative to my preaching appointments, as either himself or his students would supply my pulpit in Bedford until I should be able to resume my labours; and this service they kindly performed from February till June 16th.[495]

In fact, several leading Independent and Baptist ministers were willing to preach for the Primitive Methodists by the late 1840s as their behaviour became more respectable and their focus on work among the labouring classes established their reputation as a useful adjunct to those communities who would come to see their 'special mission' as being to the middle classes.[496] The Wesleyan preachers, however, who still harboured missionary ambitions of their own amongst the labouring classes, would remain aloof for some years to come.

Part 6 Early Victorian Methodism

Many of the forms and structures of eighteenth-century Methodism were still evident among Bedfordshire's Wesleyans in 1851. Classes still met, membership tickets were still distributed, and the itinerant preachers still made their rounds of week night preaching. In the circuit book of the Hitchin Wesleyan circuit an outgoing superintendent left careful instructions for his successor on the routine to be followed:

1st Week
Sabbath day, as on plan.
Monday, preach at Hitchin. Leaders, Teachers or Collectors meeting as may be.
Tuesday, go to Walkern. Tea at Mr. Aldridges's, sleep at Mr Cock's.
Wednesday, Dine at Mr. Christy's at Weston, tea & sleep at Mr Farr's.
Thursday, Dine once a fortnight at Mr. Hornett's, Stevenage, once at Mrs. Lawrence's. Preach & return to Hitchin.

2nd Week
Sabbath, as on plan.
Monday, as before.
Tuesday, go to Pirton return after preaching.

---

[493] *Cambridge Independent Press*, 18 May 1850, p.1 col. 1.
[494] *Introduction of Primitive Methodism into Luton,* 6; Bedford Primitive Methodist mission preparatory quarterly meeting minutes 14 December 1841, BLARS, MB 250.
[495] *PMM* (1850), 566–7.
[496] Thorne, *Congregational missions*, 53–89.

> Wednesday, go to Ickleford preach and return
> Thursday, go to Arlesey and return after preaching.
> On Friday meet classes and hold prayer meeting.[497]

There was still talk of divine interventions in everyday life (the *Christian Miscellany* reported a miraculous healing at Leagrave as late as 1855), still a deep antipathy towards Catholics (Thomas Collins preached at St Albans that the Irish famine was a judgement on the nation's papists), and the Wesleyans, at least, still sang the same hymns.[498]

The old hymns, however, were now being sung to different tunes and beneath a rather thin veneer of continuity Methodism had been transformed. Large, impressive chapels now occupied prominent sites in all of Bedfordshire's towns and neat, smaller versions of these were evident in many of the villages. A myriad of social, educational and business meetings provided the rhythm to the Methodist week and a series of popular festivals punctuated the year.[499] It was a movement that was now confident in its own strength and assertive in its own interest, as the curate of Hemel Hempstead, among others, discovered to his cost.[500]

This was the consummation of an evolutionary process that had been evident among the local Wesleyans since the 1790s, but as a snapshot it obscures the fact that in the intervening years it had been far from clear that Methodism would continue to pursue this path of aspiring to respectability. In the early 1830s it had seemed for a time as if Methodism might become instead a vehicle for popular protest, its prayer meetings and love-feasts providing an opportunity for ordinary people to vocalise their grievances in a way that was protected to some extent by a cloak of religion. This had been the moment when membership and attendance had soared and the Methodist community, as a percentage of the total population, had reached its high water mark. But by the late 1830s Wesleyan Methodism in Bedfordshire had turned its face against radicalism, just as the Wesleyans of Yorkshire and Lancashire had done twenty years earlier.[501]

Rival Methodist bodies had also appeared in the county offering millenarian visions and much greater opportunities for working class people to assume positions of leadership. But despite some initial successes they had never come close to displacing the Wesleyans and the largest of them, the Primitive Methodists, were every bit as committed to respectability as the Wesleyan élite.

If a picture paints a thousand words, the print of the new Wesleyan chapel opened in Luton in 1852 speaks volumes about the self-image of local Wesleyans by the mid-nineteenth century (see Plate 22). For there, in front of the chapel, they stand, improbably dressed in crinolines and top hats, the very image of prosperous respectability. The second half of the nineteenth century would bring that aspiration for respectability and influence closer to fulfilment, both for Wesleyan and Primitive Methodism, but the social base of the movement would be much narrower in future.

---

497   Hitchin Wesleyan circuit book, 1842–64, HALS, NM 4/37.
498   *Christian Miscellany* (1855), 60–2; Coley, *Life of Thomas Collins*, 271–2.
499   Thomas Shaw suggested an interesting parallel between these Methodist festivals and the *pardon* in Breton villages (Shaw, *Gwennap Pit*).
500   Collins, *A letter to the curate of Hemel Hempstead, Herts.*.
501   Hempton, *Methodism and politics*, 104–10.

The days when Methodism was the religion of the people in Bedfordshire were coming to an end.

There is very little physical evidence remaining of the heyday of Methodism in Bedfordshire. The great Wesleyan cathedrals in Chapel Street, Luton and Harpur Street, Bedford have long since been demolished. In fact, only a handful of the chapels built before 1851 are still standing, and none of them preserves its original interior. Looking at the shell of what was once the Wesleyan chapel in Leighton Buzzard (see Plate 16), it is hard to credit the story of one local woman who, on being asked what heaven was like, 'said it was like our chapel'.[502] Yet these walls did once echo with life and excitement, generated by an astonishing number of local people who, whether for a lifetime or, more often, for a season, came here week by week. An historian can only go so far in resurrecting such spirits, but the imagination of a poet can perhaps breathe life back into even so unpromising a scene. Reflecting on an equally forlorn chapel in his native Wales, R. S. Thomas wrote:

> ... here once on an evening like this,
> in the darkness that was about
> his hearers, a preacher caught fire
> and burned steadily before them
> with a strange light, so that they saw
> the splendour of the barren mountains
> about them and sang their amens
> fiercely, narrow but saved
> in a way that men are not now.[503]

---

[502] *Bedford Mercury* 25 May 1838.
[503] Thomas, *Collected Poems 1945–90*, 276.

Chapter Four

Re-visiting the rise of Methodism: Bedfordshire and the historiography of Methodist growth

Explaining the appeal of Methodism

This study of Methodism in one particular English county has been an attempt to meet a need, identified by several writers, to get beneath the national statistics and official reports, the pamphlets and correspondence of connexional leaders, and to reconstruct a bottom-up view of Methodism from the perspective of ordinary members and adherents. It aims to offer a response both to E. P. Thompson's call to 'know more about, not the years of revivalism, but the months; not the counties, but the towns and villages', and to David Hempton's for 'more sophisticated local studies showing what the Methodist message was and how it was heard and appropriated.'[1]

So how does an understanding of the rise of Methodism in Bedfordshire add to the understanding of the rise of Methodism more generally? Two questions have dominated the historical study of Methodism: why did it grow in the way that it did, and what was the impact of its growth on society? Answers to the first of those questions have generally focussed on the social and economic background to the rise of Methodism. Changes in society, it is argued, created a need that Methodism met. In his first book, *Religion and Society in Industrial England* (1976), Alan Gilbert argued that that need was for new communities in a society where traditional communities were being disrupted both by population movement and by changing economic relationships:

> Why then did people value the benefits of participation in chapel communities highly enough to accept the stringency of a sectarian discipline? ... perhaps the most important of the latent functions of Methodism and New Dissent involved the capacity for satisfying the profound associational and communal needs of people experiencing anomie and social insecurity in a period of rapid social change and dislocation.[2]

In a refinement to this idea Gilbert later wrote about the appeal of Methodism for a class of people who felt themselves at odds with the existing establishment:

> The labourers, artisans and tradespeople, the school teachers and other minor professionals, and even (albeit to a much lesser extent) the merchant and manufacturing groups who became Methodists in early industrial England, were the kinds of people who, in matters of politics, industrial relations or social status,

---

[1] Thompson, *Making of the English working class*, 429; Hempton, *Religion of the people*, 28.
[2] Gilbert, *Religion and society*, 89.

often found themselves at odds, in one way or another, with the norms, values and institutions of the ruling classes.[3]

His ideas have been echoed by several others. James Obelkevich's *Religion and Rural Society: South Lindsey 1825–75* (1976), for instance, found the growth of Wesleyan Methodism in Lincolnshire to be the product of a nostalgic impulse, an attempt to preserve a traditional village community that was fast disappearing in the wake of enclosure and the commercialisation of agriculture:

> For those who were reluctant to give up the sociability of the old village community, Methodism created a new, artificial community. Farmers and labourers could unite in the same congregation and in the same class meeting when they were being separated from each other in the wider society.[4]

Deborah Valenze's *Prophetic sons and daughters: female preaching and popular religion in industrial England* (1985) reached similar conclusions:

> sectarian Methodism conferred official status upon informal associations and elevated everyday features of English laboring life that were under assault by changes in the agrarian economy. The attempts of marginal people to preserve domestic and personal relations in their work gained cosmic significance.[5]

All of this would seem to fit with Thompson's observation that Methodism thrived when working class communities were under economic pressure:

> whenever hope revived, religious revivalism was set aside, only to reappear with renewed fervour upon the ruins of the political messianism which had been overthrown. In this sense the great Methodist recruitment between 1790 and 1830 may be seen as the chiliasm of despair.[6]

Others have focused on the needs met by the message of Methodism rather than by the communities it created. Analysing the imagery of Methodist hymns, Thompson wrote of the movement's role in facilitating the psychological adaptation necessitated by industrialisation. The message of Methodist preaching, tracts and, above all, Sunday schools, represented a dramatic break with traditional popular culture and indoctrinated the working classes in 'a pitiless ideology of work' that made them useful operatives in the new factory system.[7] While taking up Thompson's interest in the impact of Methodist ideas, a later generation of writers has reached a diametrically contrary conclusion. Owen Davies's article on 'Methodism, the clergy, and the popular belief in witchcraft and magic' (1997) is one of several to point out that Methodism's emphasis on divine intervention and spiritual experiences created a considerable cultural congruence with traditional superstitions and folk religion, giving renewed legitimacy to beliefs from which the established church was increasingly distancing itself.[8]

Looking at the rise of Methodism in Bedfordshire it is clear that any attempt to comprehend the appeal of the movement has to take more seriously the warning

---

3 Gilbert, 'Religion and political stability', 89.
4 Obelkevich, *Religion and rural society*, 217.
5 Valenze, *Prophetic sons and daughters*, 32.
6 Thompson, *Making of the English working class*, 427.
7 Thompson, *Making of the English working class*, 405.
8 Davies, 'Methodism, the clergy, and the popular belief in witchcraft and magic', 252–65.

that there were 'many Methodisms, in many places, at many times.'[9] Each of the three local surges in Methodist support drew a body of recruits that exhibited a quite distinct profile and suggest that different motives were at work at different moments. With a largely rural and settled population, Bedfordshire experienced little of the urban anomie of which Gilbert wrote but there is local evidence that links the third phase of Methodist growth, in the early 1830s, to the dislocation of rural communities in economically hard times. Twenty years earlier, however, the second phase of Methodist growth appears to have been bound up with an economic boom and to have been brought to an end by the onset of a recession. Economics clearly influenced the narrative of Methodist expansion but the links were neither simple nor mechanistic and the movement benefited from various phases in the economic cycle.

The strength of Calvinistic Methodism in the eighteenth century must cast doubt on the claims made for the importance of Wesley's Arminianism in the appeal of Methodism. The easy way in which individuals and societies moved between connexions of different theological persuasions suggests that these debates were marginal to grass roots Methodism. What emerges from the Bedfordshire records as being far more central to ordinary Methodists is the emphasis in Methodist teaching on the miraculous. Stories of dreams, healings, answers to prayer and the sudden deaths of opponents litter early Methodist literature, linking the new movement to traditions of magic and superstition that were disappearing from public discourse. Such stories continued to be a feature of local Methodist life well into the nineteenth century, as indeed did a far deeper enthusiasm for an imminent apocalypse than has been generally acknowledged.[10]

The Geography of Methodist Growth
The success of Methodism was far from uniform across England and the geography of Methodist growth has attracted considerable attention. John Walsh in many ways opened the field with his observation that 'The spread of Methodism as a popular movement was decidedly uneven, and its geographical density was deeply conditioned by various social and economic factors which affected men's receptivity to its message.'[11]

Through the 1960s and 70s a number of articles and books by various authors endeavoured to identify and catalogue those 'social and economic factors'. Robert Currie's 'Micro-theory of Methodist growth' argued that Methodism grew where the Church of England and the old Dissenting denominations were weak and that this was principally north of the Wash-Severn line.[12] John Gay's *The Geography of Religion in England* (1971) focused on northern districts where the Church of England was slow to respond to large increases in population and where it was slow to commute tithes.[13] The most influential contribution has been Alan Everitt's *The Pattern of Rural Dissent* (1972), a study based on four counties. Everitt produced

9   A phrase originally coined by Alun Howkins in a seminar led by John Walsh and recorded by Robert Coll in Samuel, *People's history and social theory*, 357.
10   David Hempton's view, for example, is that 'English Methodists in the mass never surrendered to the millenarian speculations of the Reformed churches' (Hempton, *Methodism and politics*, 77).
11   Walsh, 'Origins of the Evangelical movement', 160.
12   Currie, 'A micro-theory of Methodist growth', 65–73.
13   Gay, *Geography of religion*, 144–8.

an impressive list of communities susceptible to all kinds of religious Dissent, including Methodism: parishes that were large and where settlement was dispersed, parishes where landownership was in many hands, settlements on the boundaries between parishes, parishes with non-resident clergy, settlements on canals and railways, industrial villages and decayed market towns.[14] As time has gone on and more studies have been produced, the idea of establishing a neat, scientific explanation for the pattern of Methodist growth has become progressively less sustainable. Gay's findings have been contradicted by Keith Snell and Paul Ell who found that far from being areas of Methodist strength, areas of high and rapidly expanding population were commonly areas of Methodist weakness.[15] In the same way, David Hempton has cast doubt on Robert Currie's 'Micro-theory' by drawing attention to the degree to which Methodism was parasitical upon an existing Anglican culture.[16]

Looking at local sources what quickly becomes apparent is how partial and distorted a picture of the spread of Methodism many of these views are based upon. An over-reliance on Wesleyan sources has obscured the strength and importance of a variety of other Methodist groupings and a failure to acknowledge the shortcomings of the 1851 census of religious worship, particularly in regard to cottage-meetings, has created a misleading impression of the extent of Methodist penetration into rural communities. The scale of Methodist support in Bedfordshire, a rural county where Church and old Dissent were both strong, appears to be at odds with Currie and Gay's observations and its success was so widespread (there were Methodist congregations in 70% of Bedfordshire parishes) that it raises a question about the importance of the kind of factors identified by Everitt.

In Bedfordshire, rather than ask what made some communities susceptible to Methodism, the more relevant question would seem to be what was special about the thirty-eight parishes where Methodism failed to gain a foothold? Three things stand out. The first is the prior existence of some form of evangelical Dissent. In fifteen of the parishes with no Methodist presence in 1851 Baptist or Independent congregations were already established by 1818 and where subsequent attempts were made to establish Methodist congregations they quickly failed.[17] The second limitation appears to have related to the size of population. Thirteen of the parishes which had neither a Methodist nor a Dissenting meeting were each inhabited by fewer than two hundred people. Only three parishes of this size had any nonconformist presence in 1851.[18] There had been attempts to form congregations in at least another four of these villages but they seem to have been simply too small to provide enough people to sustain a viable meeting.[19] The third limitation appears to have been hostility from landowners. Of the ten remaining parishes, eight stand

---

[14] Everitt, *Pattern of rural dissent*. The four counties considered were Kent, Leicestershire, Lincolnshire and Northamptonshire.

[15] Snell and Ell, *Rival Jerusalems*, 126.

[16] Hempton, *Methodism: empire of the spirit*, 18–23.

[17] In four of these villages, Carlton, Keysoe, Sharnbrook and Southill, the Dissenting congregations pre-dated 1715. At Dunton Dissenting preaching dated from the 1750s. At Little Staughton the church was formed in 1766. At Goldington and Roxton preaching began in 1797, at Harrold in 1802, Wilden in 1806, Thurleigh in 1808, Elstow in 1812, Wrestlingworth in 1814 and Bolnhurst in 1818.

[18] The three parishes were Battlesden, Knotting and Whipsnade, all of which had Wesleyan preaching.

[19] Little Barford, Eyeworth, Holwell and Shelton (Welch, *Bedfordshire chapels*, 24, 76, 87 and 152–3).

out as being in the domains of the county's most prominent Tory landowners.[20] It is hard to avoid the conclusion that in all of these villages nonconformity was kept at bay by a mix of deference, obstruction and occasional intimidation. Not that any of these considerations was insuperable. Wesleyan societies were established, and chapels eventually built, at both Knotting (population 187) and Whipsnade (population 183); forty-three villages supported at least one Methodist and one Dissenting congregation; and in a county where half the land was owned by just fifty people, many congregations were formed in villages with a resident Tory squire.

The most important influence in the local geography of Methodist success appears to have been the level of female employment. By 1851 southern Bedfordshire had the highest rate of adult females economically active anywhere in England, many of them employed in the straw plait industry.[21] This margin of economic independence appears to have allowed larger numbers of women to take on the financial commitment of Methodist membership, not only boosting Methodist numbers but also giving local Methodist congregations an even greater female bias than was usual.[22] As late as the early 1870s a visitor to Dunstable Wesleyan chapel still found:

> the Sunday congregation very large, and to an obvious extent composed of young women, whose clear voices gave a melodious fullness to the singing, and the week-night prayer-meeting numerously attended, with the same proportion of fair girls engaged in the light and elegant trade of the town.[23]

By 1851 Methodism had established itself in virtually every community in southern Bedfordshire. It was in the north and east of the county, where female employment levels were lower, that Methodism was not always able to surmount the hurdles to viability created by competition from Dissent, hostile landlords and small populations.

Supply and Demand

In his earlier writings on the geography of Methodist growth, W. R. Ward maintained an argument close to Alan Everitt's. In David Hempton's words:

> With all due attention to Methodist theology, organization and personal motivation, he nevertheless views Methodism's great age of expansion in English society as part of much wider structural changes in the generation overshadowed by the French Revolution. In this period a complex of social tensions caused by population growth, subsistence crises and the commercialization of agriculture, and further exacerbated by prolonged warfare, sharpened class conflict and undermined the old denominational order. ... Methodism thus made its fastest gains in areas least amenable to paternalistic influence, including free-

---

[20] Much of the land in Silsoe, Pulloxhill and Henlow was part of the de Grey estate. Bletsoe and Melchbourne were likewise dominated by the estate of Lord St John. Sutton was the home of Sir John Burgoyne, Podington of the Orlebars, and Old Warden was the seat of Lord Ongley.

[21] Shaw-Taylor and Wrigley, *Occupational structure of England c.1750–1871.*

[22] The proportion of women members in the Leighton Buzzard circuit was consistently higher than in other parts of the county. The last available figures are for 1834, at the height of the growth spurt that involved a disproportionate number of male recruits. Even then women formed 60% of the membership.

[23] Hare, *Ministry and character of Robert Henry Hare*, 395.

hold parishes, industrial villages, mining communities, market towns, canal- and sea-ports and other centres of migratory population.[24]

Towards the end of his career, however, Ward seems to have changed his mind. In an introductory essay to a collection of eighteenth-century episcopal visitation returns, he confessed to grave doubts about the accepted orthodoxy:

> Much of the writing (including much of my own) about the geographical distribution of the mature Methodist movement assumes that its rooting was demand-led, and has sought social explanations of the great variations in success which it experienced. These may be regional (e.g. hostility to enclosures where the movement to enclose was most intense) or local (e.g. the difference between landlord parishes where the squire could, were he so minded, keep deviant movements out, and open parishes where no such authority existed). All these factors were no doubt of importance, but the Surrey material raises the question whether factors of a different, more entrepreneurial kind, ought not to be given more weight.[25]

In other words, passionate preachers and the availability of the resources to support them were one of the keys to Methodist success. More recently Snell and Ell's survey of the returns to the 1851 census of religious worship has found that in many areas where Methodism was weak Methodist chapels were actually very full, suggesting that there may have been greater demand but that insufficient provision had been made to cater for it.[26]

Investment in both preachers and chapels certainly seems to have played a major part in the growth surge experienced in Bedfordshire between 1790 and 1815. The relationship between supply and demand appears, however, to have been subtle and complex. Methodist missionary preachers, who are often characterised as the agents of religious awakening, appear rather to have gathered into the Wesleyan fold a religious enthusiasm that pre-dated their coming, while the new chapels, which might be seen as simply the consolidation of Methodist success, seem to have been the stimulus for fresh forms of religious activity and to have broadened Methodism's appeal. What is undoubtedly the case is that when staffing levels were cut back after 1815 and chapel building ground to a halt, the growth of Wesleyan Methodism in Bedfordshire faltered while the appetite for Methodism, as reflected in the rapid expansion of the United Revivalists, remained voracious. It would be wrong to extrapolate from this particular episode to an explanation for Methodist growth more generally, for when local Wesleyan fortunes revived at the end of the 1820s they did so without any significant increase in the staffing of circuits and prior to the great wave of chapel building.

The Political Impact of Methodism
Turning to the question of Methodism's impact on society, it is impossible to venture very far into the debate without acknowledging the contribution of Elie Halévy.[27]

---

24 Hempton, *Religion of the people*, 7.
25 Ward, *Parson and parish in eighteenth-century Surrey*, xii.
26 Snell and Ell, *Rival Jerusalems*, 127.
27 Halévy, *Birth of Methodism in England*, English translation by Bernard Semmel (Chicago, 1971), first published in *La Révue de Paris*, 1906, and *History of the English People in 1815*, English translation by E. I. Watkins and D. A. Barker (London, 1924–47), 4 vols.

Although far from being the first person to write about the history of Methodism, Halévy was arguably the first non-Methodist to write about the movement as if its history had significance for anyone but Methodists. Looking at the history of England from a Gallic perspective, Halévy was struck by the contrast between the political upheaval which France had endured during the eighteenth and nineteenth centuries and the stability which seemed to have attended English society:

> Why was it that of all the countries of Europe England has been the most free from revolutions, violent crises, and sudden changes? We have sought in vain to find the explanation by an analysis of her political institutions and economic organisation.[28]

He took up the claim, made for many years by Methodist writers, that Methodism had not only 'saved' individuals from sin but England from violent revolution and argued that the rise of evangelical religion had been a decisive factor in facilitating Britain's peaceful transition from an hierarchical to a democratic society.[29] His analysis of the movement's influence was much subtler than many subsequent writers have allowed, for although he noted that 'the statutes of the Wesleyan body expressly demanded from their members loyalty and obedience to the King and his Government', he saw the real significance of the Methodist movement as lying not in its conservative teaching but in the new social structures that it created:

> The religious bodies whose freedom was respected by the State were societies which, because they lacked the power of legal coercion, were obliged to direct their efforts to the establishment of a powerful moral authority alike over their own members and over society as a whole. ... the free organization of the sects was the foundation of social order in England. 'England is a free country': this means at bottom that England is a country of voluntary obedience, of an organisation freely initiated and freely accepted.[30]

While some of the detail of Halévy's work has not survived subsequent scrutiny, his underlying thesis, that Methodism in some way played midwife to the birth of a society in England that was both free and ordered, has echoed through the works of many later writers, albeit with a number of twists and variations.[31] Perhaps the most enthusiastic supporter of Halévy's work has been Robert Wearmouth, for whom 'most authorities acknowledge the truth of the claim and there is no need to enlarge upon it.' Playing down the conservative theology of the movement, he catalogued the way in which the creation of opportunities to be local preachers, stewards and trustees in the various Methodist connexions taught ordinary men, and to some extent women, the skills to make themselves heard: 'When no other example of collective endeavour presented itself to the working classes, Methodism became a pattern and parent for their democratic exercises and idealism.'[32] It would be easy to see Wearmouth's version of Methodist history as the wishful projection of a man who was himself both a committed Methodist and a socialist but several local

---

[28] Halévy, *History of the English people*, I, 371.
[29] Jackson, *Centenary of Wesleyan Methodism*, 286; Townsend, Workman and Eayrs, *New history of Methodism*, I, 370–1.
[30] Halévy, *History of the English people*, I, 514.
[31] For an exposure of some of Halévy's mistakes, see Kent, *The age of disunity*, 86–102 and Walsh, 'Elie Halévy and the birth of Methodism', 1–20.
[32] Wearmouth, *Methodism and the working-class movements of England*, 273.

studies have provided solid evidence in its support. Nigel Scotland's *Methodism and the Revolt of the Field* (1981) established the debt which agricultural trade unionism in East Anglia owed to Methodism in terms of personnel, language and structures, while Robert Colls, in *The Pitmen of the Northern Coalfield* (1987), similarly placed Methodism at the heart of the vigorous culture that developed in mining communities of the north-east during the 1820s and 1830s.[33]

Others, of course, have taken a different view and have emphasised the conservative nature of Methodism, parting company with Halévy in seeing its influence as malignant rather than providential. Two years before the publication of Wearmouth's *Methodism and the Working-class Movements of England*, Maldwyn Edwards, like Wearmouth a Methodist minister, had written that:

> One cannot easily exaggerate the help Methodism gave to the Government in the early nineteenth century by this attitude of uncritical admiration and unswerving loyalty. Its ultimate effect was to strengthen in a dangerous fashion the forces of reaction and conservatism, but its immediate effect was to enable the Government to prosecute the war abroad, without any feeling of insecurity or half-heartedness at home.[34]

Thirty years later E. P. Thompson, the son and grandson of Wesleyan ministers, recast Halévy's thesis even more boldly, arguing that Methodism had not saved England from revolution but had condemned the English working classes to lives of hardship and repression that a political upheaval might have transformed. For Thompson the movement was 'a component of the psychic processes of counter-revolution.' It fed off the hunger, hardship and anomie of the migrants to the expanding industrial towns, draining them of energy and spirit: 'The box-like, blackening chapels stood in the industrial districts like great traps for the human psyche.'[35]

Neither Wearmouth's nor Thompson's view can be dismissed out of hand and various attempts have been made to reconcile them. In *The Methodist Revolution* (1973) Bernard Semmel attempted to draw a distinction between the impact which the spread of Methodist ideas made, which amounted to 'a spiritual Revolution of a progressive and liberal character', and the impact of Wesleyan Methodism as an organisation, which was to control and divert social pressures. Within this broad thesis, he specifically highlighted the founding of the Wesleyan Methodist Missionary Society in 1813 as a *coup d'état* within the movement by a group of Wesleyan Tories whose stated purpose was to channel the energy of the ordinary members away from dangerous bread and butter issues and into harmless foreign adventures.[36]

W. R. Ward's *Religion and Society in England 1790–1850* (1972), which came out the year before Semmel's book, offered an alternative view that was both more firmly rooted in the primary evidence, which had become more accessible with the opening of the Methodist archives centre, and more nuanced. In his own way, Ward

---

[33] See also Horn, 'Methodism and agricultural trade unionism in Oxfordshire', 67–71 and Griffin, 'Methodism and trade unionism in the Nottinghamshire-Derbyshire coalfield', 2–9.
[34] Edwards, *After Wesley*, 152.
[35] Thompson, *Making of the English working class*, 419 and 404.
[36] Semmel, *Methodist revolution*, 4–5 and 169.

too argued that there had been a Methodist revolution in England but not, as Semmel had imagined, of 'progressive' Arminian ideas, rather of cottage prayer meetings and lay preaching. The upsurge of popular religion inflicted a death blow to the old structures of the state church and constituted the beginnings of a pluralistic society. Acknowledging, while not accepting, Thompson's work, he also saw evangelical nonconformity as having defused some of the class tensions in English society by internalising them, an argument that formed the basis for David Gowland's study of Free Methodism in Lancashire.[37]

More recently, Ward's line of thinking has been developed and extended in the works of David Hempton. Ward had written primarily about Methodism in the northern industrial towns and, while generally concurring with his findings, Hempton has been at pains to do justice to the fact that Methodism took root in other parts of Britain and of the world. In his first book, *Methodism and politics in British society* (1984), Methodism emerges not as a monolith but as a movement that was in many ways self-contradictory, a fact which partly explains why the movement was so fissiparous in the early nineteenth century. Twelve years later, in *The Religion of the People: Methodism and Popular Religion* (1996), Hempton went further and provided a collection of essays that offered a panoramic view of a subject that was 'complex, ambiguous, multifaceted and unamenable to a single narrative.'[38] His conclusions about the social impact of Methodism included a tempered version of the Halévy thesis:

> Methodism not only contributed more than any other movement to that process [the growth of pluralism in British religion and politics], but also helped make the transition more ordered and more peaceful than otherwise might have been the case.[39]

He also restated Ward's view that Methodism provided an alternative world in which social and political conflicts could be played out:

> It is vital to see not only that religious deviance and political radicalism could inform one another, but also that the same contentious issues could be fought out as vigorously *within* the Methodist polity as they were *between* Methodism and other established interests.[40]

The importance of Methodism was that it allowed ordinary people to make a protest against the establishment while remaining within the law:

> Popular evangelicalism did not create the free-born Englishman, nor did it single-handedly create the English capacity for disciplined protest, but through Methodism and the connexional system it offered a vibrant religious vehicle for both to operate outside the confines of the Established Church without seriously destabilizing the British state in the era of the French Revolution.[41]

The religious space created by Methodism in Bedfordshire was always, in reality, a political space semi-detached from the local establishment of squire and parson,

37 Ward, *Religion and society in England*, 266; Gowland, *Methodist secessions*.
38 Hempton, *Religion of the people*, 173.
39 Hempton, *Religion of the people*, 173.
40 Hempton, *Religion of the people*, 176–7.
41 Hempton, *Religion of the people*, 8–9.

although the degree to which that space was used varied considerably over time and between groups. Borough politics played a significant role in the earliest years of both the Moravian and Wesleyan congregations in Bedford but there is no evidence of a political edge to John Berridge's work in the east of the county. Although concerns were expressed by some observers about the potential political significance of Methodism in Bedfordshire during the war with revolutionary France, locally at least the movement's professions of undying loyalty to crown and constitution seem to have been taken at face value. It was not until the 1830s that the political possibilities of Methodism became apparent and even then they were paradoxical. For while many cottage meetings and village chapels were providing what Nigel Scotland has described as 'an act of open rebellion against parson, squire, and farmers', the Methodist shopkeepers of Bedford were giving the Wesleyan connexion a national reputation as Tory die-hards.[42]

The Social Impact of Methodism

Claims for the social significance of early Methodism have ranged far beyond the question of social stability and class conflict. Despite Thompson's attempt to bury the idea that the movement made any significant contribution to education, it still appears as a self-evident fact in many books.[43] According to Vicki Tolar Burton:

> Because of Wesley's welcoming of the poor to Methodism and the high value he placed on literacy, Wesley's followers were to be among the most energetic proponents of establishing schools on Sunday for working-class children, which had a widespread impact on spiritual literacy.[44]

The interest in Methodist Sunday schools has been completely overshadowed by the multiplicity of books, mostly by American writers, claiming that Methodism created new social space, roles and opportunities for women. For Paul Chilcote the early British 'Methodist societies provided an environment which was conducive to the empowerment of women.'[45] Phyllis Mack has likewise written of eighteenth-century Methodism increasing women's energy and self-confidence:

> Methodist women [behaved] in highly radical ways: writing sermons, establishing primary emotional ties with other women, and attempting to create domestic arrangements that would enhance their opportunities for female companionship and their financial independence.[46]

There has been particular interest in the existence of women preachers among the early Methodists:

> It is clear that Methodist women in Mr. Wesley's Methodism often did not conform to the stereotypical patterns which have often been seen as limitations on female leadership in religious affairs. Detailed examination reveals that the ministries exercised by women in early Methodism were remarkable both in kind and quality.[47]

---

[42] Scotland, *Methodism and the revolt of the field*, 22.
[43] Thompson, *Making of the English working class*, 414–15.
[44] Tolar Burton, *Spiritual literacy in John Wesley's Methodism*, 266.
[45] Chilcote, *John Wesley and the women preachers of early Methodism*, 239.
[46] Mack, *Heart religion in the British Enlightenment*, 167.
[47] Brown, *Women of Mr. Wesley's Methodism*, 15.

Most of this, it has to be said, has been based on the letters, journals and writings of the same handful of individuals – principally Mary Fletcher (*née* Bosanquet), Sarah Crosby and Hester Rogers. British historians have been far less interested and a cursory flick through the index of most recent books on English social history will quickly reveal a dearth of references to Methodism.

Although there were some local educational initiatives sponsored by Methodists in the eighteenth-century – a boarding-school formed part of the Moravian settlement at Bedford, Elizabeth Harvey ran a school at Hinxworth and Abraham Andrews at Hertford – they could not be described as adding up to a significant contribution to the expansion of educational provision. The Bedford Wesleyan congregation was not a partner in the town's non-denominational Sunday school and the half dozen Wesleyan Sunday schools that were formed by 1818 were completely overshadowed by the sixty-four Sunday schools sponsored by the Church of England.[48] Even by 1851, most Methodist congregations in Bedfordshire did not support a Sunday school and levels of illiteracy, in this Methodist stronghold, were the highest in the country.[49] The written word appears to have played a small part in local Methodist life. Among the 649 members of the Biggleswade Wesleyan circuit in 1840 there were only 14 subscribers to the *Wesleyan Methodist Magazine* and 6 to the sixpenny digest. The accounts of the Bedford Primitive Methodist mission record a similar picture with only a handful of members subscribing to magazines and almost the only other publication sold being the denominational hymn-book.[50] Indeed, the fact that Methodism was a primarily oral culture may have been part of its appeal.

The case for seeing early Methodism as an emancipatory movement for women is likewise only very partially supported by the evidence from grassroots Methodist life in the south Midlands. Women certainly formed a significant majority among local Methodists at almost every stage between 1736 and 1851, and some, like Ann Okely and Elizabeth Harvey, gave the movement important financial support. Among the early Moravians there were distinct opportunities for women to meet and live together, and women even played some part in decision making, but this was not mirrored locally among other Methodist groups.[51] Although the office of class leader among the Wesleyans was theoretically open to both sexes, men exercised an almost exclusive hold even on this office, accounting for twenty-three of the twenty-six class leaders in the Bedfordshire circuit in 1781.[52] There is certainly no evidence of women preaching or exhorting among any of the early Methodist communities in the area and it is interesting that the great female religious writer of the district, Anne Dutton, was not a Methodist but a Particular Baptist.[53] Part of the argument put forward by Mack and others is that after an initial moment of gender liberation:

[48] Tibbutt, *Bunyan Meeting Bedford*, 67–70; Bushby, *Bedfordshire schoolchild*, 37–59.
[49] Horn, *Joseph Arch: the farm workers' leader*, 31; Stephens, *Education, literacy and society*, 322.
[50] Biggleswade Wesleyan circuit schedules 1838–52, BLARS, MB 834; Bedford Primitive Methodist mission book stock and accounts 1840–42, BLARS, MB 1669. There was, apparently, a library attached to Markyate Wesleyan chapel in 1847 (Burg, *Religion in Hertfordshire*, 29).
[51] There were 'choirs' (devotional meetings) for single and married sisters, and there were female members of the labourers' conference. It was not acceptable, however, for women to exhort, even in all female meetings (Welch, *Bedford Moravian Church*, 37).
[52] Bedfordshire Wesleyan circuit book, BLARS, MB 1.
[53] Whitebrook, *Anne Dutton*.

Methodism was transformed from a renewal movement within Anglicanism into an autonomous organized church. The loose Wesleyan system of conferences and circuit preaching was buttressed by an elite group of preachers and stewards, and a network of chapels was built in the industrializing counties of Yorkshire, Lancashire, and other strongholds of Methodist worship. ... Men of substance assumed the mantle of church leadership, while women were told to stop preaching and devote themselves to domestic and charitable activities.[54]

What emerges from the local records, however, is that it was precisely with the building of chapels and the burgeoning of denominational structures that opportunities for women increased. By the 1820s women were busy collecting missionary subscriptions, distributing tracts and running Sunday school classes, and by the 1850s they were organising a significant element of the fundraising effort necessary to meet the burden of chapel debts. Indeed, the first record of a woman preaching, for the Bedford Primitive Methodists in 1837, appears to have been for just such a purpose. At Eversholt, in 1849, the young Hannah Toombs found herself not only the class leader of the Wesleyan society and superintendent of its Sunday school but its steward as well, responsible for both the finances and the recently erected premises.[55]

Varieties of Methodism

Most of what has been written about Methodism has been focussed on Wesleyan Methodism. Of all the other varieties of Methodism only Primitive Methodism has attracted any significant academic interest. In Obelkevich's *Religion and rural society*, Valenze's *Prophetic sons and daughters* and Julia Werner's *The Primitive Methodist connexion* (1984) the Primitive Methodists are cast in the role of radical, working-class sect to Wesleyan Methodism's respectable, middle-class denomination.

Primitive Methodism in Bedfordshire certainly attracted an overwhelmingly working-class following (although it is worth remembering that many more working-class people attended Wesleyan chapels) but far from rejecting respectability Primitive Methodists appear to have set great store by it. By creating a space in which working people had opportunities for office-holding and status, that were the preserve of the well-to-do in larger and more established denominations, Primitive Methodism was a vehicle for precisely the respectability that it is often represented as challenging.

Epilogue

The evidence from Bedfordshire requires then a reconsideration of the rise of Methodism in England. It adds fresh colours to the already kaleidoscopic picture of the movement and underlines the need for a sensitive appreciation for the range of its manifestations and a much keener recognition of the speed and degree of its evolution. Wesley's was not the only, nor even the principal, form of eighteenth-century Methodism and there was a world of difference between it and the Methodism that existed in 1815. Even within a small, fairly homogenous geographic area there

---

[54] Mack, *Heart religion*, 261.
[55] *City Road Magazine* (1874), 50.

were major differences between the Methodism that took root in the villages and that which flourished in the principal market towns. The rise of Methodism was, in short, not a single process, but a series of cumulative developments by which a wide range of people at different times and in different settings appropriated its flexible organisation and resonant language as vehicles for the expression of quite distinct aspirations, concerns and goals. The result was a movement that was complex and contradictory, clinging to the past and helping to facilitate change, loyal and subversive. It may not, however, have been a movement that exercised anything like the influence that some have imagined. Although there was always a core of life-long members, people for whom the society, circuit and connexion were their primary loyalties, as Methodism grew such members were very much the exception rather than the rule. The career of most members was short, beginning while still in their late teens and over within five years, and becoming a member was not so much about a 'dramatic characterological change' as a rite of passage.[56] The real impact of Methodism was not that it saved England from revolution, or subjugated the English working-classes to the demands of the factory system, but something on an altogether more human scale. It provided respectable people with something to do on long winters' evenings, it seasoned their calendars with high days and festivals, and it gave generations of young people opportunities to mix with the opposite sex that were beyond the reproach of their elders. As William Hale White explained:

> These services were not interesting to me for their own sake. I thought they were, but what I really liked was clanship and the satisfaction of belonging to a society marked off from the great world. It must also be added that the evening meetings afforded us many opportunities for walking home with certain young women, who, I am sorry to say, were a more powerful attraction, not to me only but to others, than the prospect of hearing brother Holderness, the travelling draper.[57]

---

[56] Haartman, *Watching and praying*, 6.
[57] Rutherford, *Autobiography*, 11.

Appendix A
Evaluating the sources for Methodist history

Facts and Figures: the Reliability of Methodist Membership Returns
Almost from the outset, Methodists of various kinds meticulously recorded a bewildering array of detailed information about their connexions. A considerable body of that material survives for several Methodist groups in Bedfordshire but it is worth considering the nature of these documents and to ask, how reliable are they?

The earliest surviving local register is a list of the members of Okely's society in December 1744 which gives not only their names, but their marital status and place of residence. A second document lists those formally admitted to the Moravian congregation between 1744 and 1812, their date and place of birth, marital status, place of residence and previous religious affiliation. Formal admission was decided by lot and some people had to wait several years to be admitted which means that the timing of those admissions bears no clear relation to the timing of the recruitment of the individuals concerned. There are no comparable records for any of the Calvinistic Methodist groups who were active in the county.

The first Wesleyan statistics come from a book, begun in July 1781, which lists the members of each class in the Bedfordshire circuit, their marital status, occupation and place of residence. The list was probably drawn up by the senior preacher before he set off for that year's conference, with the intention of providing some kind of handover notes for his successor and perhaps to help him calculate the number of members he should report.[1] Gradually the information recorded each year increased. In 1792 there is, for the first time, a note of the money being taken to conference, the proceeds of the Yearly collection, the Kingswood collection and subscriptions to the Preachers' fund. The entry for 1799 begins the practice of listing the stewards and local preachers and from 1802 the accounts show how much each society had collected for the 'West India Mission'.

Circuit books of this kind seem to have been a standard feature of Wesleyan circuit life until 1836, when they were replaced by an officially produced volume setting out a number of schedules to be completed quarterly.[2] The schedules required each society in the circuit to be listed, their class leaders named and the number meeting in their classes (see Plate 26). It also required the names of the circuit stewards and of the trustees, the society, chapel and poor stewards for each place in

---

[1] Bedfordshire Wesleyan circuit book 1781–1806, BLARS, MB 1. The idea that the book was intended to form handover notes from one assistant to the next is supported by the note at the end of the list for 1784 from Joseph Pescod, 'I earnestly pray that whoever come into this Circuet next year, may have more comfort than I have ...' (see Plate 23). The entry for 1797 likewise passes on details about what collections to make around the circuit and that of 1799 suggests where to hold the quarterly meetings.
[2] A second Bedford circuit book, covering the years 1807–36, was apparently still extant in 1948 but had disappeared when the circuit records were deposited at the county archives in 1959. A circuit book for the St Neots Wesleyan circuit 1793–1812 similarly went missing in the 1940s but a photocopy of a second book, covering the years 1813–31, is held at BLARS. Two circuit books for the Leighton Buzzard Wesleyan circuit survive, covering the years 1812–27 and 1828–36 (BLARS, MB 1533 and 1534); one for the Newport Pagnell Wesleyan circuit, 1814–38 (CBS, NM 500/7/1); and one for the Higham Ferrers Wesleyan circuit, 1794–1804 (Northants RO, HFMC 13).

the circuit; the amount each society had given to the various connexional funds; and even the number of people who subscribed to each of the connexional magazines.

Nor were these the only official lists and records being kept by then. The accounts of the Bedford circuit stewards from 1817, the Clophill chapel trustees from 1823 and the Biggleswade missionary society from 1827 all survive. The only surviving class register from a Bedfordshire circuit was not commenced until 1833, but the records of the Aylesbury circuit, in neighbouring Buckinghamshire, contain examples from as early as 1804. By 1851 circuit superintendents were also expected to complete annual schedules for property – how many people did the chapel seat, what was its value, what was the mortgage – and for Sunday schools – how many scholars, how many teachers, what was the annual cost?[3]

Primitive Methodist records have not survived in Bedfordshire as well as those of the Wesleyans, probably because so many of the Primitive Methodist chapels in the county were closed before any organised attempt was made to preserve their history. Enough survive, however, to show that the Primitive Methodists were every bit as keen on statistics. In particular, from at least 1842 onwards, each circuit was required to fill in an annual report in March. The report detailed the number of members in the circuit, the places of worship, the number of children in each Sunday school, the extent of the circuit's debt and a whole series of questions about the conduct of the 'travelling preachers' (as ministers were called) and circuit officials.[4] The Mormons also kept detailed registers, recording 'the Names, Births, Baptisms, Confirmations, Marriages and Ordinations of the Saints.'

Despite such extensive records, it is far from easy to establish an accurate picture of Methodism's development in Bedfordshire. For these innumerable reports and endless numerical returns were originally compiled not for analytical reasons but theological ones, and they often pose grave problems of interpretation for the historian. Methodism's apologists, beginning with John Wesley, claimed it to be a movement providentially raised up by God in order to 'spread scriptural holiness throughout the land'. Its *raison d'être* was neither a peculiar point of doctrine nor of church government but, rather, its achievements as 'a mighty machinery for the accomplishment of good'.[5] The annual membership returns were the proof of its usefulness and the sign that God was continuing to use Methodism as an agent of his salvation. Increasing membership was the justification for the denomination's existence.

On a local level the statistics took on even greater importance for they reflected not on Methodism in the abstract, but on the labours and faithfulness of particular preachers, class leaders and members. Where the form for a Primitive Methodist circuit's annual report asked 'If the circuit be prosperous, say in what respects', spiritual prosperity was almost always measured by membership. So the Luton circuit

---

3   Luton Wesleyan baptism register 1803–37, TNA, RG8/1; Bedford Wesleyan baptism register 1810–37, Bedford Wesleyan circuit stewards' account book 1817–37, Clophill Wesleyan account book, and Biggleswade Wesleyan circuit missionary society accounts 1823–47 are all held at BLARS with the respective references: MB 32, MB 12, MB 76 and MB 862; Durley, *Centenary annals*, 4.
4   Luton Primitive Methodist circuit, annual reports 1844–59, BLARS, MB 518. There is an annual report from the Aylesbury circuit for 1842 (CBS, NMP 100/7/1).
5   Lewis, *Independency*, 83.

in 1845 responded 'spiritually – our congregations are good and we have increased 37 in the number of members'.[6]

A decrease in membership, on the other hand, was a sign of divine displeasure. Faced in 1844 with a loss of seven members, the Luton Primitive Methodist circuit was badly shaken. The quarterly meeting suppressed the annual report because 'it would neither be beneficial to ourselves or others' and a long conversation was held on the state of the circuit. Members were called upon to join in daily prayers for a revival, special services were arranged and, perhaps most significantly, it was determined to take steps for 'the increased purity of the Church'.[7]

It was, however, on the itinerant preachers, the paid professionals, that the membership returns reflected the most unforgiving light. One of the opening shots in the Reform agitation, which shook Wesleyan Methodism in the late 1840s, was a book called *Wesleyan Takings* which detailed the total increase or decrease in members that various prominent preachers had reported during their careers, and the average per annum.[8] The Primitive Methodist annual report officially recorded what increase in membership a preacher had witnessed in his previous station. Clearly, losses seriously undermined a preacher's credibility.

The significance attached to growth influenced Methodist record-keeping in several ways. At the crudest level it encouraged deceit and fraud. On numerous occasions preachers arrived in their new circuits to discover that the roll of members left by their predecessors bore little relation to the number of people actually meeting in class. At Luton, in 1855, almost a third of the membership of the Primitive Methodist circuit was written off at a stroke. Samuel Wilshaw, the incoming circuit superintendent, found that some of his supposed members 'had left the country, others seldom or ever attended any of our places of worship, some … had gone to the Established Church, Wesleyans, Baptists and Mormonites, some … were grossly immoral and others ... could not be found at all'. On one class-book the signature of the class leader had been forged, on others the previous superintendent had simply signed in their place. Asked to explain the incorrect returns, the junior preacher replied that the previous superintendent had told him that if they did not cover up the decline that had taken place in the circuit during their stay 'while the decrease would not be injurious to himself it would injure him [the junior minister] and cause almost endless trouble in reference to his application for admission into the "Annual List" and full membership to the Preachers' Friendly Society.'[9]

A subtler effect of the pressure to record ever greater numbers was a relaxation over time of the requirements of membership. In the eighteenth century, and the early nineteenth century, membership of a Methodist society required weekly attendance at a class meeting with only distance or sickness being accepted as a legitimate reason for absence. By the 1840s, however, even some of the local preachers were becoming neglectful: Brother Kent, a Wesleyan, had 'not met in class more than

---

6   Luton Primitive Methodist circuit, annual report 1845, BLARS, MB 518.
7   Luton Primitive Methodist circuit, minutes of quarterly meeting 23 September 1884, BLARS, MB 520.
8   Everett, *Wesleyan takings* (1840).
9   Luton Primitive Methodist circuit, annual report 1855, BLARS, MB 518.

twice in the last twelve months' and only ended up in trouble even then because he had not turned up for a preaching appointment.[10]

It would be wrong to conclude, however, that the real membership figures were always somewhat less than the official returns. From the very outset membership statistics played a part in assessing how much each society should contribute to circuit funds and each circuit to the connexion; it was a powerful incentive to count conservatively. In 1792 the Bedford circuit book shows 594 members but records that the number reported to the Conference was only 550.[11] In 1849 the Newport Pagnell Primitive Methodist mission actually discussed in their quarterly meeting how many members they would report and how many were 'to be kept in reserve.'[12]

Still further difficulties arise from the fact that the very choice of statistics to be collected was itself governed by largely theological considerations. Membership was assiduously recorded because it was generally believed to be a good indication of the number of people who had been brought to salvation by Methodist preachers. Redemption and membership were not seen as wholly synonymous, but it was certainly felt that anyone who had been saved would want to join a class and that anyone unconverted who attended this 'means of grace' would soon be saved. In the first decades of the nineteenth century, however, the Methodist community came to include a much wider range of people than simply those attending class meetings. Many who regularly attended the Sunday services, rented pews, contributed to the funds, perhaps even taught in the Sunday school, never met in class and thus were not members at all but only adherents. Clearly, from an historical perspective the number of a chapel's adherents is a vital consideration in assessing the influence of Methodism in a town or village, and statistically it is an essential accessory to the membership returns. Without information about the size of congregations it is very difficult to judge whether an increase in membership represents genuine growth or merely the regularisation of the status of some adherents. Yet the schedules rarely make any reference to this extensive class of Methodists. They had made no profession of faith and, to the evangelical mind, the profession of faith was all important.

One document that sometimes gives a glimpse of that wider Methodist community is the baptism register. The first local registers, those for St Neots and Biggleswade, date from 1797 and 1799 respectively. From 1812 Wesleyan preachers were permitted to baptise not only the children of members but 'of our regular hearers' as well and it is clear that locally they did so almost immediately.[13] Some of the registers provided a column in which to record the father's occupation and it is these that allow an insight into the social and economic make-up of Methodist communities.[14] In all, the occupations of 695 men who presented their children to Wesleyan preachers for baptism in Bedfordshire between 1797 and 1839 are

[10] Bedford Wesleyan circuit, minutes of local preachers' meeting 29 December 1845, BLARS, MB 9.

[11] Bedfordshire Wesleyan circuit book 1781–1806, BLARS, MB 1.

[12] Newport Pagnell Primitive Methodist mission, minutes of quarterly meeting 13 March 1849, BLARS, MB 1551.

[13] Mumford, 'The administration of the sacrament of baptism in the Methodist Church', 115.

[14] The baptismal registers which contain details of the father's occupation are: Ampthill Wesleyan circuit 1815–37, Higham Ferrers Wesleyan circuit 1828–37, and Biggleswade Wesleyan circuit 1799–1837 TNA, RG4/1272, RG4/307 and RG4/310; Bedford Wesleyan circuit 1810–37 and 1838–42, BLARS, MB 2 and MB 840; and Newport Pagnell Wesleyan Circuit 1834–37, CBS, M12/3.

known (by which time the officially-produced baptism register no longer contained a column for father's occupation). Michael Watts has argued that: 'We can ... be confident that the occupations listed in the Nonconformist baptismal registers are a reasonably accurate guide to the social structure of those congregations.'[15] However, it is necessary to be aware that this evidence does have limitations. It is clearly a very small sample of the total Methodist community; it excludes those who were single, childless or past childbearing age; and it is not actually clear to what extent it was distorted by some Wesleyans continuing to have their children baptised in their parish church.[16]

The end result of these various and unquantifiable considerations is that the superficially concrete evidence of the circuit books, schedules and annual reports may or may not be accurate for any given year. Surges and troughs may or may not represent fluctuations in religious activity and long term trends may simply reflect changing definitions rather than changing realities. That is not to say that the schedules are worthless; far from it. They are easily the richest source of information about the pattern of Methodist growth and decline, but to establish some corroboration, the information needs to be constantly tested against other sources such as the records of pew rents, passing comments by observers and the returns of the 1851 census of religious worship.

The 1851 Census of Religious Worship
The returns of the census of religious worship held on Sunday 30 March 1851 are another rich vein of statistical data which need to be handled with care.[17] In the first place, the tables in the published summary of the census often reveal a number of discrepancies when compared with the original individual returns. These inaccuracies seem to have had several causes: the misidentification of congregations' denominational allegiances; the failure to spot duplicate returns; and simple arithmetical error. Generally, these inaccuracies have been thought to be statistically insignificant but the Bedfordshire returns suggest that they were not always so.[18] A comparison of the published tables and the original individual returns shows that the number of Baptist, Independent, Wesleyan Methodist, Plymouth Brethren and isolated congregations are all incorrect.[19] A comparison of the published attendance figures and the individual returns unearths similar mistakes in relation to the attendance figures for the Church of England, Baptists, Independents, Wesleyans and Primitive Methodists.[20]

---

[15] Watts, *Dissenters*, II, 681.
[16] Holland, *Baptism in early Methodism*, 104–15.
[17] Interest in the census emerged with Inglis's article, 'Patterns of religious worship in 1851', 74–86, but debate about its historical value was provoked by Thompson's 'The Religious Census of 1851', 241–68. Field has provided a select bibliography of the literature in *PWHS* 41 (1977–8), 53–60 and *The Local Historian* 27 (1997), 194–217. By far the most substantial treatment of the subject, however, is Snell and Ell, *Rival Jerusalems*.
[18] David Robinson found that a comparison of the printed report and the original returns for Surrey revealed numerous minor discrepancies but concluded that the published returns for registration districts were still generally reliable (Robinson, *The 1851 religious census: Surrey*, p, lxiii).
[19] Fourteen congregations were misidentified, two duplicate returns were counted by mistake and the total number of congregations given in the report exceeds the total number of returns, including duplicates, by five.
[20] *Census of Great Britain, 1851: Religious Worship, England and Wales, Report and Tables*, cxcv.

Even the original returns, of course, may contain errors. In the archive of the Newport Pagnell Wesleyan circuit is a record of the returns prepared by the super-intendent.[21] In the event, however, the forms were mostly completed by others and with quite different figures.[22] There is no way of knowing how such discrepancies arose, nor how common they were. It can only be noted that these figures are inevi-tably rough estimates not exact statistics.

A second difficulty, and one that has been far more widely acknowledged, is that the census returns record attendances at services rather than at churches. Ninety-six people attended the afternoon service at Greenfield Wesleyan chapel on the day of the census and 106 people the evening service, but it is not clear from those returns whether the chapel had 106 supporters, all but ten of whom attended twice, or 202 supporters, all of whom attended only once. Horace Mann, the Home Office official who oversaw the census, recognised this problem at the time and proposed that a rough estimate of the number of individuals attached to particular denominations could be achieved by adding together their total number of morning attendances, half the number of afternoon attendances (on the basis that half those attending in the afternoon had already attended in the morning) and one-third of evening attend-ances. This crude calculation almost certainly worked against the Methodist denom-inations whose highest attendance figures were for evening services and in favour of the Church of England whose services were mostly held in the morning and afternoon. Historians have subsequently offered a variety of alternative approaches. The most conservative is that put forward by W. S. F. Pickering who argued that the best attended service of the day should be taken as an indication of the minimum number of individual attendants.[23] K. S. Inglis, by contrast, seems to have accepted that the true number of individual attendants cannot be recovered and proposed instead an 'index of attendances', a measurement for comparing levels of religious activity between districts and denominations, produced by adding together the attendances at all the services during the day and expressing them as a percentage of the population.[24] More recently, Michael Watts has suggested that an estimate of the strength of each local congregation can be produced by adding together the adult attendance at the best attended service of the day, the highest attendance of Sunday school scholars in the day, and one-third of the number of adults attending any other services.[25] Evidence to support Watts' approach can be found in the return made by the vicar of Cople. Having recorded an average of 65 in the general congregation in the morning, together with 75 Sunday school scholars, and 130 in the afternoon, he went on to explain that 'as the greater part of the morning congregation do not

---

21 Newport Pagnell Wesleyan circuit returns of chapels and Sunday schools 1851, CBS, NM 500/7/20.
22 For Salford, for instance, the superintendent recorded 102 adults in the general congregation and thirty Sunday school scholars in the afternoon and 120 in the general congregation in the evening but the official return, signed by 'T. Summerford, Occasional Preacher', has 20 in the general congregation and fifteen Sunday school scholars at morning and afternoon services and 65 in the general congregation in the evening. In fact, of the 17 places listed in the circuit document, in only 2 cases do the figures correspond with the official census return.
23 Pickering, 'The 1851 religious census – a useless experiment?', 382–407.
24 Inglis, 'Patterns of religious worship', 79.
25 Watts, *Dissenters*, II, 671–3.

attend in the afternoon ... the average number of those who attend at one or other services may be reckoned at 240 or 250 distinct individuals.'[26]

Although the census was extensive, it inevitably fell short of being complete.[27] Nonconformists complained at the time that a significant number of their preaching places had been overlooked and, although some historians have tended to dismiss that claim, a close examination of the Bedfordshire returns seems partially to justify their concern.[28] Only 2 Church of England parishes in the county failed to make any return (in 3 other instances the returns were incomplete) and only 5 Dissenting congregations seem to have been missed.[29] The Methodist returns, however, show some serious deficiencies. The census found 76 Wesleyan congregations in Bedfordshire but it is clear from circuit records that another 11 were missed by the registrars.[30] In the same way, the census found 18 Primitive Methodist congregations but denominational records reveal that at least another 20 may have been overlooked.[31] Only 3 congregations of Moravians and 3 of Latter Day Saints were found but there were actually 6 of each.[32] No Wesleyan Reformers were reported in the county but there is evidence to suggest that some may have existed, not to mention a congregation of Bible Christians. Matthewsite congregations too may have been overlooked but the paucity of records makes it very difficult to know. Most of these missing places of worship were cottage meetings but they included at least one purpose built Wesleyan chapel, at Tebworth, that could seat more than three hundred people.[33]

Magazines and Myths

Not all the surviving evidence, of course, is statistical. Denominational magazines, and later newspapers, preserve a great number of contemporary accounts of chapel openings, missionary meetings, and especially faithful lives. Obituaries were published for more than 250 members of Bedfordshire Wesleyan societies alone.[34] These stories tell us a great deal, but more often about the values and aspirations of

---

[26] Bushby, 'Ecclesiastical census, Bedfordshire', 134–5.

[27] See Maps 1 and 2 for the distribution of Wesleyan Methodist and non-Wesleyan Methodist societies.

[28] 'This problem is not as prominent as it may seem' (Snell and Ell, *Rival Jerusalems*, 37).

[29] The Church of England parishes of Chellington and Southill made no return at all; Felmersham and Pavenham gave no numbers for attendance at worship; and Stevington gave no numbers for an evening service held in the schoolroom. The Dissenting congregations overlooked were an outpost of Luton Old Meeting at Pepperstock, one of Markyate Baptist Church at Brick Kiln and three places linked with the Bedfordshire Union of Christians, at Milton Ernest, Clifton and Langford (Bedfordshire Union of Christians treasurer's account book 1838–97, BLARS, Z 206/17).

[30] The Wesleyan societies overlooked by the census were at Battlesden, Bromham, Everton, Knotting, Millbrook, Milton Bryan, Souldrop, Tebworth, Tilbrook, Woodside and Wymington.

[31] The Primitive Methodist congregations overlooked certainly included: Ampthill, Aspley Guise, Arlesey, Battlesden, Biggleswade, Caldecote, Clifton, Cranfield, Everton, Leighton Buzzard, Kempston, Langford, Millbrook, Pavenham, Salford, Sharpenhoe, Tilsworth, Wootton, Wrestlingworth and Wyboston. They may also have included Clapham, Holme, Maulden, Odell, Renhold, Ridgmont, Silsoe and Willington.

[32] The missing Moravian congregations were at Dean, Keysoe and Tilbrook. The missing Mormon congregations were those at Bedford, Eaton Bray and Luton.

[33] It was not only in Bedfordshire that Methodist congregations were overlooked. In Suffolk, 82 Wesleyan congregations were recorded and thirteen missed, with 68 Primitive Methodist congregations recorded and twenty missed (Timmins, *Suffolk returns from the census of religious worship*, 175–81). In Shropshire 80 Wesleyan congregations were recorded and fifty-eight missed, with 161 Primitive Methodist congregations recorded and 113 missed (Field, *Church and chapel in early Victorian Shropshire*, li–liii).

[34] A list of both Wesleyan and Primitive Methodist obituaries is presented on BHRS's website.

their writers (and editors) than about the actual lives of the individuals concerned. The idea that Methodist preaching reached the 'outcasts of men'[35] untouched by other religious agencies was an important and powerful myth among the various Methodist communities from the very earliest days. When men like John Wynn in 1785, or Richard Crosby and Samuel Rhodes in 1795, were converted in the condemned cell of Bedford gaol by Wesleyan preaching, their stories were recorded in considerable detail and given national publicity.[36] Fifty years later Primitive Methodist missionaries would use similar stories to justify their own intrusion into communities that already enjoyed established Wesleyan congregations.[37] It would be wrong, however, to infer from the recurrence of such narratives that they tell us anything about the average recruit to Methodism. A mission to the humble poor was, in any case, only one of the ways in which Methodists liked to view and present their communities. The idea that the Lord blessed those who were faithful also had wide currency and there was a strong desire to assert the respectability, prosperity and success of both Methodists and Methodism.[38] It is interesting that the death of Samuel Bennett, who founded the Wesleyan society at Tempsford and became a prosperous farmer, was marked with a lengthy obituary in the *Wesleyan Methodist Magazine* but that the passing of William Emmerton, the farm labourer who founded societies at Stanbridge and Tilsworth and laid the foundations for the extraordinary strength of Wesleyanism in south-west Bedfordshire, was not.[39] Wealthy supporters, of course, not only evidenced a connexion's divine sanction and social respectability, but they also paid many of its bills. Inevitably their generosity was often recognised by their appointment to leading roles but their prominence in the records does not make them any more of a typical Methodist than the condemned men in Bedford gaol.

Memoirs

The influence of John Wesley's published *Journal* in shaping accounts of early Methodism has been inestimable. Easily accessible, eminently readable and packed with what appear to be factual details about the spread and strength of the Methodist movement, the *Journal* has been the primary source of countless local histories and many more substantial works. It is a mistake, however, to imagine that it is a candid and straightforward record of the progress of early Methodism. Wesley carefully prepared these volumes for publication and used them to project a very particular vision of the movement and of his own role within it. The account gleaned from the *Journal* of his societies in Bedfordshire is a point in case, obscuring the work of other Methodist groups and the extent to which the Wesleyan circuit was built on rustling sheep from other men's flocks.

---

[35] 'Outcasts of men, to you I call,/ Harlots, and publicans, and thieves!' – from Charles Wesley's hymn 'Where shall my wond'ring soul begin' (*Works of Wesley* VII, 117).

[36] *AM* (1788), 69–71, 124–7 and *AM* (1795), 390–5.

[37] See the account of the Primitive Methodist missioning of Biggleswade, *PMM* (1847), 739–41.

[38] John Wesley himself claimed, in the face of allegations that Methodism impoverished its members, that people materially benefited from being Methodists: 'Abundance of those in Cork, Bandon, Limerick, Dublin, as well as in parts of England, who, a few years ago, either through sloth or profuseness, had not bread to eat, or raiment to put on, have now, by means of the preachers called Methodists, a sufficiency of both' quoted in Jennings, *Good news to the poor*, 171.

[39] *WMM* (1841), 705–21.

An important source for this account of Methodism in Bedfordshire has been the autobiography of John Buckmaster, *A Village Politician*. Writing in the 1890s, and following a convention of the day, Buckmaster cloaked the identity of many of the places and people in his memoirs beneath pseudonyms but as the introduction to a modern edition concluded:

> In fact, it is an accurate autobiography, and most of the places and background events can be readily identified from Buckmaster's descriptions. More than this, a copy of 'A Village Politician' has survived which was lavishly annotated by a local antiquarian, Frederick G. Gurney, who knew the Buckmasters well and also researched their ancestry. From his notes it is possible not only to corroborate Buckmaster's account, but to add details of his background and family history.[40]

There are some details where either his memory was confused or he allowed himself artistic licence: the opening of the Methodist chapel took place more than ten years earlier than he seems to suggest. Although his description of the close links between Methodism and rural unrest in the 1830s is not corroborated by Methodist records there is, however, no reason to doubt it. Methodist records, both local and national, were equally, and quite deliberately, silent about events at Tolpuddle in Dorset in 1834, when five Methodists, perhaps as many as three of them local preachers, were arrested and transported for trying to form a trade union.[41]

---

[40] Introduction by John Burnett to Buckmaster, *Village politician*, x. Buckmaster's account of local agitation also receives some corroboration from Gibbs' *Buckinghamshire: a record of local occurrences*. The reform meeting on the Dunstable Downs, in particular, appears to be recorded in volume III, 234.
[41] Rodell, 'Methodism and social justice', 478–9, 489.

Appendix B

The sub-division of the Bedfordshire Wesleyan circuit 1763–1851

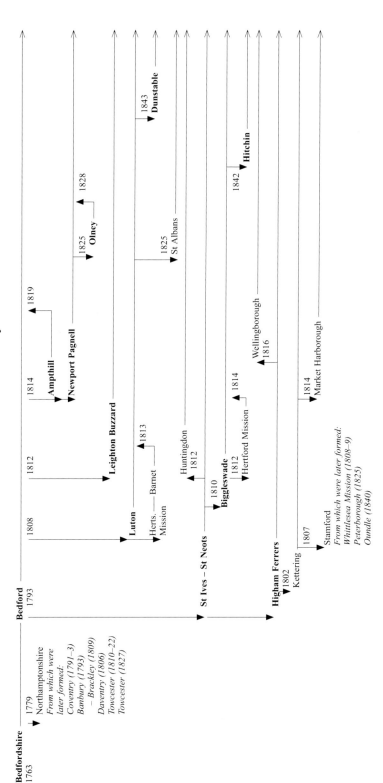

Note: the Newport Pagnell circuit appears to have been created principally from the Bedford circuit but to have received societies from both the Leighton Buzzard and the Northampton circuits. The St Ives circuit, re-designated the St Neots circuit in 1800, contained one Bedfordshire society. Eaton Socon, when it was created and received the Great Barford society from the Bedford circuit in 1802. From 1798 to 1802 the Higham Ferrers circuit was re-designated the Kettering circuit. From 1810 to 1816 it was re-designated the Wellingborough circuit.

Table 15. Comparison of membership changes between the English and the Bedfordshire Wesleyan circuits, 1767–1851

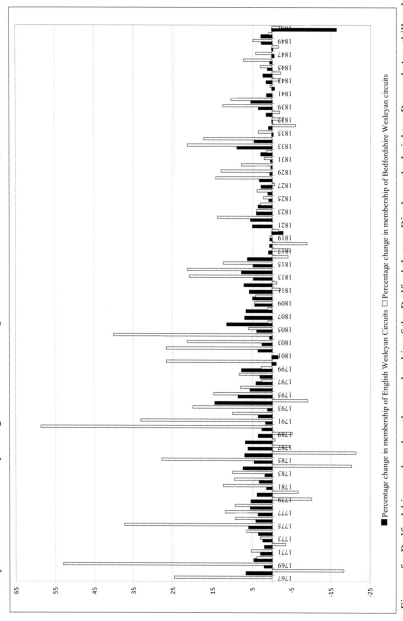

Sources: Figures for Bedfordshire are based on the membership of the Bedford, Luton, Biggleswade, Leighton Buzzard, Ampthill and Dunstable Wesleyan circuits and calculated from the returns published in the annual *Minutes of Conference*. Figures for England are taken from Currie, *Churches and churchgoers*, 139–41.

Table 16. Membership of the Bedford, St Ives and Higham Ferrers Wesleyan circuits (including their offshoots), 1794–1851

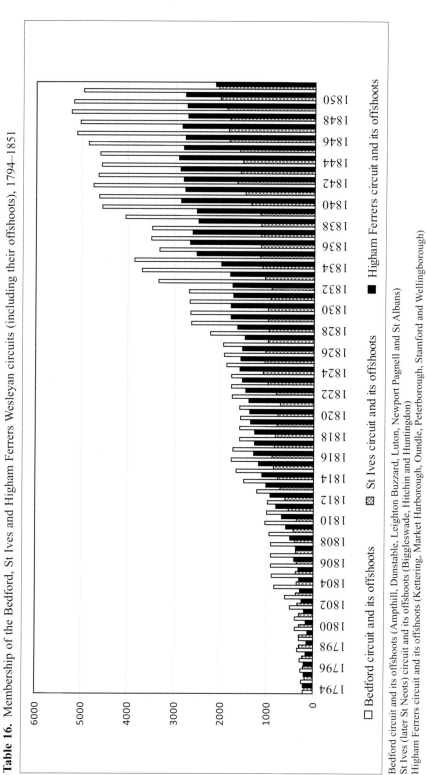

Bedford circuit and its offshoots (Ampthill, Dunstable, Leighton Buzzard, Luton, Newport Pagnell and St Albans)
St Ives (later St Neots) circuit and its offshoots (Biggleswade, Hitchin and Huntingdon)
Higham Ferrers circuit and its offshoots (Kettering, Market Harborough, Oundle, Peterborough, Stamford and Wellingborough)

☐ Bedford circuit and its offshoots   ⊠ St Ives circuit and its offshoots   ■ Higham Ferrers circuit and its offshoots

Sources: Figures are from the official returns published in the annual *Minutes of Conference*. See pp. 235–9 for the discussion on statistics.

Glossary

For a full explanation of Methodist terminology readers are referred to the online edition of John Vicker's *A Dictionary of Methodism in Britain and Ireland* which can be found at http://www.wesleyhistoricalsociety.org.uk/dmbi/ The following notes, however, may be helpful to some.

Adherent – A term in use from the 1830s onwards to describe people who were involved in a chapel community without entering into formal membership, including adults who attended services and children who attended the Sunday school. *See also* **Hearer**

Bands – In Moravian communities as well as meeting for worship all together, men and women, married and single, met together in sub-groups known as bands (or choirs). In Wesleyan Methodism the term came to apply to a weekly gathering of three or four people all of the same gender, for prayer and mutual encouragement. It constituted a voluntary additional commitment above and beyond attendance at the class meeting. *See also* **Class meeting**

Choirs *see* **Bands**

Circuit – A group of Methodist societies in a particular locality and served by the same team of preachers.

Class meeting – A weekly meeting, attendance at which was the pre-eminent condition of membership for Wesleyan and Primitive Methodist societies. In the meeting each member was quizzed by the leader on their spiritual state and advised how to improve it.

Class money – A weekly subscription of 1d paid by members of Wesleyan and Primitive Methodist societies.

Conference – George Whitefield chaired a conference of Methodist preachers as early as January 1743 to discuss practicalities, not least who would preach where, and points of doctrine. John Wesley began to hold annual conferences from the following year. Held in August, this gathering of senior preachers from across Britain (a separate conference was held in Ireland) agreed the rules governing the community and allocated the preachers to their respective spheres for the forthcoming year. The Primitive Methodists met in similar fashion in July but membership of their conference was not restricted to preachers. Among the Latter Day Saints the term was used to describe both national gatherings on the Wesleyan model and a regional level of organisation more akin to a Wesleyan circuit.

Congregation *see* **Society**

Congregation diary – Each Moravian congregation kept a diary of its life and transcribed copies were regularly sent to other congregations where they were read aloud at meetings convened for the purpose on designated Letter Days.

Dissenter – A term used by contemporaries to describe members of the religious communities that had been formed by opponents of the state church created in

1662. These included not only the Particular Baptists, Independents and Presbyterians (sometimes described as the Three Denominations) but the General
Baptists, Quakers and, by the nineteenth century, the Unitarians.

District – From 1791 Wesleyan circuits were grouped into geographical districts.
The Bedfordshire circuits were originally part of the London district but subsequently formed the basis for a Bedford, and later Bedford and Northampton,
district. A meeting of the preachers in the district acted on behalf of the conference in selecting and disciplining preachers and in granting permission to build
chapels. The Primitive Methodists also organised their circuits into districts. In
the period covered by this volume, however, these were not primarily geographical units but rather represented the sometimes scattered offspring of a powerful
mother circuit.

Exhorter – Someone who was authorised to lead Methodist meetings and to give
short addresses but not to preach full sermons.

Hearer – A term used, particularly before the 1830s, to describe someone who
attended Methodist preaching without being in formal membership. *See also*
Adherent

Home missionaries – A term used by Wesleyan Methodists in the early years of
the 19th century to describe professional preachers supported from central funds
rather than local funds and who were sent to preach in areas where the denomination had not yet established itself.

Itinerant preacher – A term used by Wesleyan Methodists to describe their paid,
full-time preachers. By the 1840s it was beginning to be superseded by the term
Minister. *See also* **Labourer** *and* **Travelling preacher**

Kingswood collection – An annual collection made in Wesleyan societies, usually
in November, to meet the costs of a boarding school maintained for the sons of
itinerant preachers.

Labourer – A term used by eighteenth century Moravians to describe their paid,
full-time preachers. *See also* **Itinerant preacher** *and* **Travelling preacher**

Letter day *see* **Congregation diary**

Local preacher – A term used by Wesleyan and Primitive Methodists to denote
formally accredited amateur preachers who supplied Sunday services in their
local circuit under the direction of the professional preachers.

Love-feast – An act of worship practised by the Moravians, and subsequently by
both the Wesleyan and Primitive Methodists, in which hymns were interspersed
with opportunities for members of the congregation to speak about their spiritual
experience. During the service plates of biscuits or cake and a large two-handled
cup of water were passed among those present.

Membership – Most Methodist groupings (John Berridge's circuit being an exception) operated as organisations with a formally defined membership. Those
admitted into that membership submitted themselves to the oversight and discipline of the group's leadership. They were required to attend specified meetings,
contribute to specified funds and maintain specified standards of behaviour. Failure
to do so resulted in expulsion. Among the Moravians distinctions were drawn
between those admitted to society membership and those who were admitted
to full membership of the Moravian church. (See Congregation). Many groups,

including the Wesleyan and Primitive Methodists, issued tickets of membership each quarter to those in good standing.

Mission – A term used, at various stages, by both the Wesleyans and the Primitive Methodists to denote a circuit that was dependent on external financial support. Or, from the 1840s, a series of special services held with the object of creating religious excitement and conversions.

Preachers' fund – A fund maintained by the Wesleyan conference to support 'worn-out' preachers. There were no public collections for the fund but private subscriptions were solicited from wealthier members.

Preaching shops – A term used by John Berridge to describe the cottages and barns where he and his assistants preached.

Protracted meeting – A series of prayer meetings and preaching services held every morning and evening for a week or more and designed to create a level of religious excitement that would yield emotional conversions. Based on American revivalist techniques they began to form part of Methodist practice from the early 1840s.

Society – The term was widely used in the 18th century in a number of religious settings. Even before the advent of Methodism there were local societies in many Church of England parishes that met for prayer and to listen to religious readings. Outside the established church the Quakers constituted a Religious Society of Friends and other Dissenters used the term in relation to their local church. The initial policy of the Moravian leadership was not to establish churches in Britain but to create societies through which members of existing denominations could access Moravian teaching. Even when full Moravian congregations were established in some places, society membership was still offered as a less onerous alternative to being a member of the congregation. Among most Methodist communities, by contrast, it was the society that constituted the body of people in full membership and a member of the congregation was someone who simply attended public preaching services. *See also* **Adherent** *and* **Hearer**

Stationing – Unlike their Dissenting colleagues who were called (that is invited) by a local church to become their minister, Methodist preachers were stationed (that is sent) to local circuits usually by the annual conference of their denomination.

Steward – A term used among the Wesleyans and Primitive Methodists to describe a number of officeholders (circuit stewards, society stewards, chapel stewards and poor stewards) who were responsible for financial and practical matters.

Ticket money – A quarterly subscription of 1s paid by members of Wesleyan and Primitive Methodist societies when the itinerant preacher renewed their membership tickets.

Travelling preacher – A term used by Primitive Methodists to describe their paid, full-time preachers. *See also* **Labourer** *and* **Itinerant preacher**

Watch-night – A late night meeting for singing and prayer, often planned on the full moon to make the journey home afterwards easier. The practice originated among the Moravians but was copied by other Methodist groups.

Yearly collection – A collection made among the members of Wesleyan societies each July towards clearing the deficit of the local circuit and the national conference.

Works cited

Manuscripts

Alma Street Wesleyan Reform Church, Wellingborough
Wesleyan Reform minute book of the Wellingborough and Higham Circuits, 1851–71

Bedfordshire and Luton Archives and Records Service (BLARS)
AD 1081   Collection of election posters 1830
AD 1734   Collection of election posters 1832
BorBG 10/1/27   *The Bedford Chronicle and Independent Truth Teller* Ch4/395
BorBG 10/1/50   Election poster 1832
CRPu 4/16   Woburn Congregational Church Book 1791–1837
CRT 180/183   Genealogical notes on Richard Partridge
HN 10   Records of Hobourn of Woburn, solicitors: original bundles
L 30/11/132   Lucas archive: letters from Lewis Harrison to Countess de Grey
MB 1–181   Records of Bedford and Ampthill Methodist Circuits
MB 182–190   Records of Bedford Primitive Methodist circuit
MB 191–308   Records of Leighton Buzzard Methodist circuit
MB 309–329   Deposit of registers by the Methodist Conference, August 1977
MB 335–371   Records of Dunstable Wesleyan Methodist circuit
MB 387–440   Records of Luton Wesleyan Methodist circuit
MB 497–833   Records of Luton (North) Methodist circuit
MB 834–998   Records of Biggleswade Methodist circuit
MB 999–1267   Records of St Neots Methodist circuit
MB 1346   Records of St Neots circuit
MB 1445–1446   Records of Dunstable (The Square) circuit
MB 1527–1627   Records of Leighton Buzzard circuit including the former Stewkley circuit
MB 1669   Bedford Primitive Methodist mission book stock and accounts 1840–2
MB 1671   Bedford Primitive Methodist mission annual report 1847
MB 1824/1   Luton Wesleyan circuit preaching plan July-October 1843
MO   Archives of the Bedford Moravian Congregation in Bedford St. Peter's 1728–2008
P83   Stotfold parish records
PO 66   *The Bedford Chronicle and Independent Truth Teller*
R 3   Russell Archive: Correspondence of the Russell Family and the Bedford Estate
R 4   Russell Archive: Papers of the estates of the Dukes of Bedford (Bedford Settled Estates), Miscellaneous estate papers 1739–1948
Typed transcript of the Church book of Carlton Baptist church made by F. W. P. Harris
X 37/42   Letter relating to teaching in Sunday School; six printed notices relating to Bible or Mission societies, including Wesleyan Methodist and Moravian; all but one local. 1811–1824
X 302   A collection of personal papers, including photographs and plans, from the Wesleyan, Moravian, Wesleyan Methodist and Primitive Methodist faiths, deposited by Dr Joan Anderson, 1758–1953
X 525/1   Church Book of Blunham Baptist Meeting 1724–1891

Z 206   Minutes, reports, financial and miscellaneous records of The Bedfordshire Union of
    Baptist and Congregationalist Churches 1797–1969
Z 629   Turner Archive
Z 1115/1   Hymns to be sung at the Methodist Chapel, Leighton Buzzard

Berkshire Record Office
D/MC2/5A/1   Shefford Primitive Methodist circuit preaching plans 1836–7

Brigham Young University, Harold B. Lee Library, Tom Perry Special Collections
MSS 881   Diary and autobiography of Job Smith for 1851

Cambridge University Library
Ely Diocesan Records
C1/6 Visitation returns 1825
C/3/19, 22, 23 Episcopal Visitation Returns 1837 and 1841

Cambridgeshire Record Office
MRF/4/1 Buckden Primitive Methodist mission baptism register

Centre for Buckinghamshire Studies (CBS)
DX 544/1   Notebooks of James Durley of Bierton (1758–1814)
DX 603/8   Petition to the House of Lords from the Protestant Dissenters of Wing
M12/3   Newport Pagnell Wesleyan Circuit baptismal registers 1834–1837
NM 100/1–11   Aylesbury Wesleyan Methodist circuit records
NM 102/1–9   Aylesbury Wesleyan Methodist circuit: Bierton
NM 114/1–9   Aylesbury Wesleyan Methodist circuit: Whitchurch
NM 500/1–11   Milton Keynes Wesleyan Methodist circuit: circuit records
NM 514   Milton Keynes Wesleyan Methodist circuit: Newport Pagnell
NMP 100   Aylesbury Primitive Methodist circuit
Q/W/G   Returns of the clergy 1829

Drew University, Madison, NJ, United Methodist Archives and History Center
Thomas Marriott Collection of British Wesleyan Circuit Plans
Survey of Wesleyan Property by Thomas Marriott: Collection of plans, bound together in a
    scrap book

Dr Williams's Library, London
Jones MS 39.B.24   Folder of papers concerning John Berridge prepared by Revd John
    Jones, vicar of Bolnurst, c.1760

East Sussex Record Office
NMA/4/1/1   Sussex Wesleyan circuit book

Hertfordshire Archives and Local Studies (HALS)
NM 4/37   Hitchin Wesleyan circuit book, 1842–64

Hull History Centre
Bedford Primitive Methodist mission, chapel schedule 1852
Hull Primitive Methodist district chapel schedule 1849
Hull Primitive Methodist district property schedule 1850

Lincolnshire Archives
DIOC/SPE/4   Returns of Bishop of Lincoln's Visitation, 1788

Methodist Archives and Research Centre, John Rylands University Library, Manchester (MARC)
Circuit Plan Collection
    Biggleswade Wesleyan circuit preaching plan November 1836–April 1837
    Dunstable Wesleyan circuit preaching plan, November 1847–January 1848
    Luton Wesleyan circuit preaching plan February–May 1846
DDCW/5/102   Charles Wesley to Sally Wesley, 5th July 1759
DDPr 1/9   Early Preachers' collection, letters to Charles Wesley: John Barham to Charles Wesley, 4 December 1781
DDSe 37 and 39 Letters of William Seward (21 and 24 April 1739)
Diaries Collection: John Murlin: (WM) (1722–99) Journal/sermon notes: John Murlin's Sermon Register
District collection: District papers (WM):
    Bedford and Northampton Wesleyan District minutes 1835–51
    Bedford Wesleyan District Minutes 1831–1847
    London (West) Wesleyan District Minutes 1822–31
George Spilsbury's Account of the beginnings of Methodism in Luton, 1839
MAM P11b   Benjamin Ingham, copy journals etc: William Batty 'Church history collected from the memoirs and journals of Reverend Benjamin Ingham and the labourers in connexion with him', 14 July 1779
MAW LHB 4.10   Service sheet for Bedford Wesleyan Sunday school anniversary 1825

Northall Baptist Church
Church book of Northall Baptist church

Northamptonshire Record Office
BBMC   Buckingham and Brackley Methodist circuit records 1810–2003
HFMC   Higham Ferrers Methodist circuit records 1814–2004

Park Road Methodist Church, Bedford
Bedford Primitive Methodist mission baptism register

Society of Cirplanologists
Baldock Primitive Methodist mission, preaching plan 1853

Southern Methodist University, Dallas, Bridwell Library
Letter: Anne Dutton to Philip Doddridge, n.d.
Letter: John Wesley to Abraham Andrews, 18 August 1767
Letter: George Whitefield to Charles Wesley 17 March 1763

The National Archives
HO 107   1851 census returns
PROB 11   PCC wills
RG 4   Registers of Births, Marriages and Deaths surrendered to the Non-parochial Registers Commissions of 1837 and 1857
RG 8   Registers of Births, Marriages and Deaths surrendered to the Non Parochial Registers Commission of 1857, and other registers and church records

Newspapers and magazines

Titles of local newspapers may vary.
Arminian Magazine (London)
Baptist Magazine (London)
Bedford Chronicle and Independent Truth Teller (Bedford)
Bedford Mercury and Huntingdon Express (Bedford)
Bedford Gazette (Bedford)
Bedford Methodist Monthly Magazine (Bedford)
Bedford Times (Bedford)
Bedfordshire Times (Bedford)
Bucks Advertiser & Aylesbury News (Aylesbury)
Bucks Chronicle & Bucks Gazette (Aylesbury)
Bucks Herald (Aylesbury)
Cambridge Chronicle and University Journal, Isle of Ely Herald and Huntingdonshire Gazette (Cambridge)
Cambridge Independent Press (Cambridge)
The Christian History (London)
Christian Miscellany and Family Visiter [sic] (London)
City Road Magazine (London)
Congregational Magazine (London)
English Presbyterian Messenger (London)
Evangelical Magazine (London)
Gentleman's Magazine (London)
Hertford Mercury and Reformer (Hertford)
Huntingdon, Bedford and Peterbro' Gazette and Cambridge and Hertford Independent Press (Huntingdon)
Lloyd's Evening Post and British Chronicle 1757–1763 (London)
Luton Reporter, and Bedfordshire and Hertfordshire News (Luton)
Methodist Magazine (London)
The Methodist Recorder and General Christian Chronicle (London)
Millennial Star (Latter Day Saints) (Liverpool)
Missionary Notices (relating principally to the Foreign Missions first established by the Rev. J. Wesley, the Rev. Dr. Coke and others; and now carried on under the direction of the Methodist Conference) (London) continued as *The Wesleyan Missionary notices*
Northampton Mercury (Northampton)
Our Own Magazine (The monthly magazine of the Leighton Buzzard circuit)
Primitive Methodist Magazine (London)
The Reformer; or Herts, Beds, Bucks, Essex, Cambridge, and Middlesex Advertiser (Hertford)
Spalding Free Press and Eastern Counties Advertiser (Spalding)
Stamford Mercury (Stamford)
The Times (London)
The Watchman (London)
The Weekly Miscellany (London)
Wesleyan Methodist Magazine (London)
Wesleyan Reform Union Magazine (London)

Journals, letters and writings of major contemporary preachers

Berridge, John, *The Christian world unmasked: pray come and peep* (London, 1773), 232p.

Berridge, John, *A Collection of Divine Songs, designed chiefly for the religious societies of churchmen in the neighbourhood of Everton, Bedfordshire* (London, 1760), xxiv, 384p.

Berridge, John, *Sion's Songs, or Hymns: Composed for the use of them that love and follow the Lord Jesus Christ in sincerity* (London, 1785), viii, 458, [8]pp.

Bowmer, John C. and John A. Vickers, eds, *The letters of John Pawson: Methodist Itinerant, 1762–1806* (Peterborough, 1994–1995) 3 vols.

The Experience of Several Eminent Methodist Preachers; with an Account of their Call, to and success in the ministry: in a series of Letters, written by themselves, to the Rev. John Wesley, A.M. (New York, 1837), 332p.

A fragment of the true religion: Being the substance of two letters from a Methodist-Preacher in Cambridgeshire, to a clergyman in Nottinghamshire (London, 1760), vi, 26p.

Gillies, John, ed., *The Works of the Reverend George Whitefield, M.A.: late of Pembroke-College, Oxford, and chaplain to the Rt. Hon. the Countess of Huntingdon containing all his sermons and tracts which have been already published: with a selection of letters, written to his most intimate friends, and persons of distinction, in England, Scotland, Ireland and America, from the year 1734 to 1770 ...* (London, 1771–2), 6 vols.

[Green, John], *The Principles and Practices of the Methodists Considered, in some Letters to the Leaders of that Sect. The First Addressed to the Reverend Mr. B-----e, wherein are some Remarks on his Two Letters to a Clergyman in Nottinghamshire, lately published* (London, 1760), 78p.

Grey, Zachary, ed., *The Quaker and Methodist compared, in an Abstract of George Fox's Journal with a copy of his Last Will and Testament, and of the Reverend Mr. George Whitefield's Journals, with Historical Notes* (London, 1740), 98p.

Houghton, S. M., ed., *Letters of George Whitefield for the period 1734–1742* (Edinburgh, 1976), xiii, 570p.

Murray, Iain, ed., *George Whitefield's Journals: a new edition containing fuller material than any hitherto published* (Edinburgh, 1960), 596p.

Oxenham, Thomas, *Fruits of the Bedfordshire Union: a Letter to the Rev. R. Whittingham, curate to the late Rev. John Berridge, of Everton, in Bedfordshire* (London, 1799), 61p.

Potts, J. M., ed., *The Journal and Letters of Francis Asbury* (London and Nashville, 1958), 3 vols.

Rowland, Thomas, *Memoirs of the Late Rev. Isaac Bradnack, Wesleyan Minister, and formerly a Missionary in the West Indies, with Extracts from his Diary and Letters* (London, 1835), 158p.

Telford, John, ed., *The Letters of the Rev. John Wesley, A. M.* (London, 1931), 8 vols.

Twenty six letters on religious subjects, to which are added hymns etc. by Omicron (London, 1774), iv, 224p. By John Newton but published anonymously.

Venn, John, *The Life and a Selection from the Letters of the late Rev. Henry Venn, MA* (London, 1834), xvi, 585p.

Wesley, John, *A letter to the Rev. Dr. Rutherforth* (Bristol, 1767), 24p.

Whittingham, Richard, *The Whole Works of the Rev. John Berridge with a Memoir of his Life*, 2nd ed. (London, 1864), 632p.

The Works of John Wesley: The Bicentennial Edition, editor in chief Frank Baker [and others] (Nashville: Abingdon), 1984–

I–IV   Albert C. Outler, ed., *The Works of John Wesley: Sermons* (Nashville, 1984–7) 4 vols.

VII   Franz Hilderbrandt and Oliver Beckerlegge, eds, *The Works of John Wesley: A*

Collection of Hymns for the use of the People called Methodists (Oxford and New York, 1983), 866p.

IX   Rupert Davies, ed., *The Works of John Wesley: The Methodist Societies: History, Nature and Design* (Oxford & Nashville, 1989), xvi, 607p.

X   Henry D. Rack, ed., *The Works of John Wesley: The Methodist Societies: the Minutes of Conference* (Oxford & Nashville, 2011), xxi, 1046p.

XVIII–XXIV   W. R. Ward and Richard P. Heitzenrater, eds, *The Works of John Wesley: Journal and Diaries* (Oxford and Nashville, 1988–2003), 7 vols.

XXV–XXXI   Frank Baker, ed., *The works of John Wesley: Letters* (Oxford, 1980–2), 2 vols to date.

Other books and articles

Abelove, Henry, *The Evangelist of Desire: John Wesley and the Methodists* (Stanford, 1990), xii, 136p.

Abstract of the answers and returns made pursuant to an Act, passed in the Eleventh Year of the Reign of His Majesty King George IV, intituled, an Act for taking an Account of the Population of Great Britain, and of the Increase or Diminution thereof, 1831 (London, 1833), 3 vols. HCP 1833 (149), HCPP Accounts and Papers, XXXVI.

Adams, George, J., *A few Plain Facts Shewing the Folly, Wickedness and Imposition of the Rev. T. R. Matthews: also a short sketch of the Rise, Faith, and Doctrine of the Church of Jesus Christ of Latter Day Saints* (Bedford, 1841), 16p.

Agar, Nigel E., *The Bedfordshire Farm Worker in the Nineteenth Century*, BHRS 60 (Bedford, 1981), ix, 213p.

Alleine, Joseph, *An alarme to unconverted sinners* (London, 1672), [46], 214p.

Allen, Joseph, *A Charge delivered to the Clergy of the Diocese of Ely at the second Quadrennial visitation of that part of the diocese comprising the Isle of Ely and the County of Cambridge; and at the Primary visitation of the other part of the diocese: held in June, July and August, 1841* (London, 1841), 32p.

Allen, Joseph, *A Charge delivered to the Clergy of the Isle of Ely, and the County of Cambridge at the Primary Visitation of that Part of the Diocese of Ely in September 1837* (London, 1837), 28p.

Alma Street Church, Wellingborough - centenary souvenir (np, 1951), pamphlet.

Anderson, Joan M., *Early Methodism in Bedford* (Bedford, 1953), 31p.

Andrews, C. B. ed., *The Torrington Diaries, containing the Tours through England and Wales of the Hon. John Byng (later Fifth Viscount Torrington) between the years 1781 and 1794* (New York, 1934–38) 4 vols.

Andrews, Stuart, *Methodism and Society* (London, 1970), x, 140p.

Atmore, Charles, *The Methodist Memorial; being an impartial sketch of the lives and characters, of the preachers, who have departed this life since the commencement of the work of God, among the people called Methodists late in connection with the Rev. John Wesley, deceased* (Bristol, 1801), 536p.

Atticus, *Our Churches and Chapels their Parsons, Priests and Congregations; being a critical account of every place of worship in Preston* (Preston, 1869), 214p.

Bacon, William, *The Christian ministry: a sermon; preached before the Bedford Wesleyan district meeting at Luton, on Wednesday, May 18th, 1842* (London, 1842), 19p.

Baker, David, ed., *The Inhabitants of Cardington in 1782,* BHRS 52 (Ampthill, 1973), viii, 242p.

Baker, Frank, 'The People Called Methodists: 3. Polity' in Rupert E. Davies, Raymond A.

George and Gordon E. Rupp, eds, *A History of the Methodist Church in Great Britain* (London, 1965–1988), I, 211–55.

Baker, Frank, *William Grimshaw 1708–63, Curate of Haworth* (London, 1963), 288p.

Baker, Reg, *For the generation following 1675–1975: a history of the Old Baptist Chapel Dunstable* (Dunstable, 1975), 24p.

Balch, A. E., *A Souvenir of a Century of Wesleyan Methodism in the town of Luton* (Luton, 1908), 39p.

Bartholomew, Ronald, '19th Century Missiology of the LDS Bedfordshire Conference and its Interrelationship with other Christian Denominations', *International Journal of Mormon Studies* 2 (2009), pp. 108–27.

Bartholomew, Ronald, 'Babylon and Zion: Buckinghamshire and the Mormons in the nineteenth century', *Records of Buckinghamshire* 48 (2008), pp. 231–545.

Bartholomew, Ronald, 'The Pattern of Missionary Work and Emigration in Nineteenth Century Buckinghamshire, England', *International Journal of Mormon Studies*, 1 (2008), pp. 99–136.

Baxter, J.,'The great Yorkshire revival, 1792–6: a study of mass revival among the Methodists', in M. Hill (ed.), *A Sociological Yearbook of Religion in Britain*, vol. 7 (London, 1974), xii, 158p.

Beckerlegge, Oliver, *The United Methodist Free Churches: A Study in Freedom* (London, 1957), 112p.

Beckerlegge, Oliver, comp., *United Methodist ministers and their circuits: being an arrangement in alphabetical order of the stations of ministers of the Methodist New Connection, Bible Christians, Arminian Methodists, Protestant Methodists, Wesleyan Methodist Association, Wesleyan Reformers, United Methodist Free Churches and the United Methodist Church, 1797–1932* (London, 1968), 268p.

Bell, Patricia, ed., *Episcopal Visitations in Bedfordshire 1706–1720,* BHRS 81 (Woodbridge, 2002), xvi, 256p.

Benham, Daniel, *Memoirs of James Hutton, comprising the annals of his life and connexion with the United Brethren* (London, 1856), iv, 639p.

Beynon, Tom, ed., *Howell Harris, Reformer and Soldier 1714–1773* (Caernarvon, 1958), 259p.

Beynon, Tom, ed., *Howell Harris's Visits to London* (Aberystwyth, 1960), x, 289p.

Bigmore, Peter, *The Bedfordshire and Huntingdonshire Landscape* (London, 1979), 240p.

Blaydes, F. A. ed., *Bedfordshire Notes and Queries* (Bedford, 1882–1893), 3 vols.

Boswell, James, *Boswell's Life of Johnson* (Oxford, 1904), 2 vols.

Bourne, Colin, *The Dunstable Methodist Circuit: one hundred and fifty years of witness 1843–1993* (Dunstable, 1993), viii, 190p.

Bowes, J, *The autobiography or history of the life of John Bowes* (Glasgow, 1872), [5], 595, [1] p.

Bowes, J, *The Truth Promoter* (London, Dundee, 1849–75), 10 vols. [Title varies.]

Bowles, A,. *One hundred and forty two years, being a History of the Wesleyan Methodist Chapel Gold Street Northampton* (Northampton, nd), 80p.

Brake, George, *Drink: ups and downs of Methodist attitudes to temperance* (London, 1974), xvi, 151p.

Brewin, George, *The story of the exploits of the Methodist saints and heroes of Hudnall* (np, nd), pamphlet.

Brigg, J., *Methodism in the Leighton Buzzard circuit with special reference to the Extinction of the Debt upon the Leighton Trust Property* (Leighton Buzzard, 1887), not paginated.

Brittain, Thomas, *The Theological Remembrancer* (Northampton, 1900), 42p.

Britton, John and Edward Brayley, *The Beauties of England and Wales, or, Delineations, Topographical Historical and Descriptive of each County,* (London, 1810–18), 18 vols.

Brown, Earl Kent, *Women of Mr Wesley's Methodism* (New York, 1983), xii, 261p.

Brown, John and David Prothero, *The History of the Bedfordshire Union of Christians: now known as the Bedfordshire Union of Baptist and Congregational Churches* (London, 1946), 131p.

Buckmaster, John, *A Village Politician: the Life-story of John Buckley* (Horsham, 1982), xxvii, 337p.

Bunney, David, *Bedford St Luke's: A bit of Church History* (Twickenham, 2010), 91p.

Bunting, Thomas Percival, *The Life of Jabez Bunting, D.D., with Notices of Contemporary Persons and Events* (London, 1859 and 1887), 2 vols.

Burdon, Adrian, *The Preaching Service – the Glory of the Methodists: A Study of the Piety, Ethos and Development of the Methodist Preaching Service* (Nottingham, 1991), 42p.

Burg, Judith, ed., *Religion in Hertfordshire 1847 to 1851*, Hertfordshire Record Publications 11 (Hertford, 1995), xxxviii, 226p.

Bushby, D. W., *The Bedfordshire Schoolchild: Elementary Education before 1902*, BHRS 67 (Bedford, 1988), ix, 260p.

Bushby, D. W., ed., 'The Ecclesiastical Census, Bedfordshire, March 1851', BHRS 54 (Bedford, 1975), pp. 109–200.

Bushby, D. W. *Two hundred years of Methodism in St Neots and District 1775–1975* (Eynesbury, 1975), 55p.

Butler, Jon, *New World Faiths: Religion in Colonial America* (Oxord, New York, 2008), xi, 183p.

Cannon, John, Q., ed., *Autobiography of Christopher Layton: with an Account of his Funeral, a Personal Sketch, etc., and Genealogical Appendix* (Salt Lake City, 1911), 317p.

Carnell, H. A., T. Booth and H. G. Tibbutt, ed., *Eight thousand years: a Kempston history* (Kempston, 1966), 118p.

Carter, Grayson, *Anglican Evangelicals: Protestant Secessions from the Via Media, c.1800–1850* (Oxford, 2001), xv, 470p.

Census of Great Britain, 1851: Religious Worship, England and Wales: Report and Tables (London, 1853), 1852–3 [1690]; HCPP Command Papers, Accounts and Papers, LXXXIX.

Ceylon Baptist Church, Wellington Street, Luton: Centenary Brochure 1846–1946 (?Luton, 1946).

Chalmers, Rev. William, 'Biographical Sketch of the Rev. T. R. Matthews, BA', *English Presbyterian Messenger*, new series, 2 (1849–50), pp. 257–63.

Champion, L. G., ed., *The General Baptist Church of Berkhamsted, Chesham and Tring 1712–1781*, English Baptist Records, 1 (London, 1985), xiv, 166p.

Chapman, David M., *Born in Song: Methodist Worship in Britain* (Warrington, 2006), x, 355p.

Chapman, E. V., *Rev. Robert Aitken,* Manx Methodist Historical Society, (Douglas?, 1982), 9p.

Chilcote, P., *John Wesley and the Women Preachers of Early Methodism* (Metuchen N. J., London, 1991), xii, 375p.

The Christian History; Or, a General Account of the Progress of the Gospel in England, Wales, Scotland, and America: so far as the Rev. Mr Whitefield, his Fellow-Labourers, and Assistants are concerned (London, 1747), 237p.

Church, Thomas, *Gospel Victories: or Missionary Anecdotes of Imprisonments, Labours and Persecutions endured by Primitive Methodist Preachers between the years 1812 and 1844* (London, 1851), 148p.

Church, Thomas, *Sketches of Primitive Methodism* (London, 1847), 127p.

Cirket, Alan. F., 'The 1830 Riots in Bedfordshire – Background and Events', in *Worthington George Smith and other Studies,* BHRS 57 (Bedford, 1978), pp. 75–112.

Cirket, Alan F., ed., *Samuel Whitbread's Notebooks 1810–11, 1813–14*, BHRS 50 (Bedford, 1971), 152p.

Clark, David, *Between Pulpit and Pew: Folk Religion in a North Yorkshire Fishing Village* (Cambridge, 1982), xii, 186p.

Cobbett, William, *Rural Rides*; edited with an introduction by George Woodcock (London, 1967), 532p.

Coles, George, *My Youthful Days* (New York, 1851), 267p.

Coles, William, *Opposition Opposed: or the Bedfordshire Minister's Reasons for not joining (at their Earnest Solicitation) with a society, at the New-York Coffee House London, in an Opposition to a Late Application to Parliament in Favour of Dissenting Ministers, Tutors, and Schoolmasters* (Bedford, 1773), 38, [2]p.

Coley, Samuel, *The life of the Rev. Thos Collins* (London, 1868), 488p.

Collett-White, James, ed., *How Bedfordshire Voted, 1735–1784: The Evidence of Local Documents and Poll Books*, BHRS 90 (Woodbridge, 2012), xvii, 305p.

Collings, Harry, *History of Union Chapel, Luton; being a Brief Record of Fifty Years of Christian Work* (Luton, 1887), 51p.

Collins, Thomas, *A letter to the curate of Hemel Hempstead, Herts.: in reply to a tract entitled "A country curate's protest against the interference of a Wesleyan preacher in his parish" with remarks upon the curate's conduct in taking away religious tracts from houses where they had been distributed*, 2nd ed. (London, 1852), 24p.

Colls, Robert, *The Pitmen of the Northern Coalfield: Work, Culture and Protest, 1790–1850* (Manchester, 1987), xv, 386p.

A Companion to the Wesleyan Hymn-Book: being a Selection of two hundred and twenty-eight Tunes ... Arranged in four parts, with accompaniments for the Organ and Piano Forte ... also a supplement of ... Chants, etc. (London, 1847), 252p.

A Copy of the Poll for the Election of two Burgesses to serve in Parliament for the Borough of Bedford taken before Sir William Long, Knight, Mayor, Thomas Woolridge Esquire, Thomas Abbott Green, Esquire, 1830 (Bedford, 1830), 31p.

Cooper, Robert, *The Holy Scriptures analyzed: or extracts from the Bible, showing its contradictions, absurdities and immoralities* (London, 1840), 64p.

Coulson, John, *The Peasant Preacher: Memorials of Mr Charles Richardson, a Wesleyan Evangelist, commonly known as the 'Lincolnshire Thrasher'* (London, 1867), xx, 398p.

Crookshank, C. H., *History of Methodism in Ireland* (London, Belfast, 1885–1960), 4 vols.

Crosland, J. Dayson, 'The Bedford Association: An Early Ecumenical Movement', *PWHS* 28 (1951–2), p. 95.

Crowe, J., *Some remarks on the address of the Rev. R. Exton to the Methodists in which the charges of falsehood, perversion etc. are answered and the Methodist ministry defended* (Towcester, 1830), 16p.

Crowther, Jonathan, *A portraiture of Methodism: or, the history of the Wesleyan Methodists, Shewing their rise, progress, and present state; biographical sketches of some of their most eminent ministers; the doctrines the Methodists believe and teach, fully and explicitly stated; with the whole plan of their discipline, including their original rules, and subsequent regulations. Also, a defence of Methodism, containing remarks on toleration*, 2nd ed. (London, 1815), xii, 512p.

Currie, Robert, Alan Gilbert and Lee Horsley, *Churches and Churchgoers: Patterns of Church Growth in the British Isles since 1700* (Oxford, 1977), xi, 244p.

Currie, Robert, *Methodism divided: a study in the sociology of ecumenicalism* (London, 1968), 348p.

Currie, Robert, 'A micro-theory of Methodist growth', *PWHS* 36 (1967–68), pp. 65–73.

Davies, O., 'Methodism, the Clergy, and the Popular Belief in Witchcraft and Magic', *History*, 82 (1997), pp. 252–65.

Davies, Rupert E., Raymond A. George and Gordon E. Rupp, eds, *A History of the Methodist Church in Great Britain* (London, 1965–1988), 4 vols.

Davies, W. P., *"A Brand Plucked out of the Fire!", or a Brief Account of Robert Kendall (including a Narrative, written by Himself), who was executed at Northampton, the 13th August, 1813: in a Letter to a Friend* (Northampton, 1813), 30p.

Davies, W. P., *A refutation of the charges alleged against the writer of Kendall's narrative* (Northampton, 1814), 23, [1]p.

Davis, Frederick, *The History of Luton, with its Hamlets etc.* (Luton, 1855), vii, 207p.

Davis, Richard, *Dissent in Politics 1780–1830: the Political Life of William Smith, MP* (London, 1971), xvii, 268p.

Davis, Richard, *Political Change and Continuity 1760–1885: a Buckinghamshire Study* (Newton Abbott, 1972), 262p.

Deacon, Malcolm, *Philip Doddridge of Northampton 1702–51* (Northampton, 1980), 212p.

Dearing, Trevor, *Wesleyan and Tractarian Worship: An Ecumenical Study* (London, 1966), xii, 166p.

Dixon, R. W., *A Century of Village Nonconformity at Bluntisham, Hunts* (London, 1887), viii, 311p.

Dolbey, George, *The Architectural Expression of Methodism: The First Hundred Years* (London, 1964), x, 195p.

Durley, Thomas, *Centenary Annals of the Birth and Growth of Wesleyan Methodism in Aylesbury and the Surrounding Villages* (Aylesbury, 1910), 32p. (Cover title: *Chronicles of Methodism in mid-Bucks*).

Dyer, James and John Dony, *The Story of Luton,* 3rd ed. (Luton, 1975), xv, 215p.

Edwards, Maldwyn, *After Wesley: A Study of the Social and Political Influence of Methodism in the middle period (1791–1849)* (London, 1935), 191p.

Edwards, Michael 'The teetotal Wesleyan Methodists', *PWHS* 33 (1961), pp. 63–70.

Ellsworth, George, S., *Samuel Claridge: Pioneering the outposts of Zion* (Logan, Utah, c.1987), xii, 339p.

Emmison, F. G., ed., 'John Pedley of Great Barford, 1773–95', in *Some Bedfordshire diaries*, BHRS, 40 (Luton, 1960), pp. 95–109.

Everett, James, *Wesleyan Takings, or, centenary sketches of ministerial character, as exhibited in the Wesleyan connexion, during the first hundred years of its existence* (London, 1840), x, 394p.

Everitt, Alan, *The Pattern of Rural Dissent: The Nineteenth Century* (Leicester, 1972), 90p. (University of Leicester. Department of English Local History Occasional papers, 2nd series 4).

Evers, Stan, *Potton Baptists, the Lord's faithfulness to a faithful people* (Potton, 2005), 80p.

'Extracts from the journal of Thomas Edman' *PWHS*, 18 (1931–2) pp. 46–53, 61–7, 99–106.

Farndale, W. E., *The Secrets of Mow Cop: A New Appraisal of the Origins of Primitive Methodism* (London, 1950), 76p.

Field, Clive, "The 1851 Religious Census of Great Britain: a Bibliographical Guide for Local and Regional Historians", *The Local Historian* 27 (1997), pp. 194–217.

Field, Clive, 'Adam and Eve: Gender in the English Free Church Constituency', *JEH* 44 (1993), pp. 67–79.

Field, Clive, 'Bibliography of Methodist Historical Literature, 1975', *PWHS* 41 (1977), pp. 53–60.

Field, Clive, ed., *Church and Chapel in Early Victorian Shropshire: Returns from the 1851 Census of Religious Worship*, Shropshire Record series 8, (Keele, 2004), lxiv, 171p.

Field, Clive, 'The Social Structure of English Methodism: Eighteenth-Twentieth Centuries', *BJSoc* 28 (1977), pp. 199–225.

Fish, Henry, *Memorials of Mrs Mary Sarson Cooper* (London, 1855), 195p.

Fisher, J. S., *People of the Meeting House: Tales of a Luton Church* (Luton, 1975), 98p.

Flick, Carlos T., 'The Bedford Election of 1830', in *Miscellanea*, BHRS 49 (Luton, 1970), 160–70.

Floyd, Richard, *Church, Chapel and Party: Religious Dissent and Political Modernization in Nineteenth-century England* (Basingstoke, 2007), xvi, 295p.

Franklin, Rev. Bernard G., *A Century and a Half – and More, at High Street Methodist Church, Leagrave, Luton* (?Luton, ?1976), 10p.

Fuller, Andrew, *The Gospel of Christ Worthy of all Acceptation: or the Obligations of Men fully to credit, and cordially to approve whatever God makes known* (Northampton, ?1785), xvi, 196p.

Gay, John D., *The Geography of Religion in England* (London, 1971), xviii, 334p.

Gibbs, Robert, *Buckinghamshire: a record of local occurrences and general events, chronologically arranged* (Aylesbury, 1878–82), 4 vols.

Gilbert, A. D., 'Religion and political stability in early industrial England', in P. K. O'Brien and R. E. Quinault, *The Industrial Revolution and British Society* (Cambridge, 1993), pp. 79–99.

Gilbert, A. D., *Religion and Society in Industrial England: Church, Chapel and Social Change, 1740–1914* (London, 1976), x, 251p.

Gilman, Richard G., *A Hundred Years at the Congregational Church in Potton* (Biggleswade, 1948), 23p.

Gilmore, G. D., 'Alderman Heaven, 1723–94', *Miscellanea*, BHRS 49 (Luton, 1970), pp. 135–46.

Godber, Joyce, *Friends in Bedfordshire and West Hertfordshire* (Willington, 1975), 100p.

Godber, Joyce, *History of Bedfordshire, 1066–1888* (Bedford, 1969), 592p.

Godber, Joyce, *The story of Bedford: an outline history* (Luton, 1978), 160p.

Gowland, David A., *Methodist Secessions: The Origins of Free Methodism in three Lancashire Towns: Manchester, Rochdale, Liverpool,* Chetham Society 26 (series 3) (Manchester, 1979), ix, 191p.

Graham, E. D., *Chosen by God: a list of the female travelling preachers of early Primitive Methodism* (Bunbury, 1989), iv, 31p.

Greaves, J. George, *Wesleyan Methodism in the City of the Proto-martyr and the St Albans Circuit with Reminiscences of Folk-lore* (St Albans, 1907), 152p.

Greeves, John, *Memorials of Wm Cumberland, of Bedford, upwards of forty years a Leader and Local Preacher amongst the Wesleyan Methodists* (London and Bedford, 1834), viii, 91p.

Gregory, Benjamin, *Benjamin Gregory: Autobiographical Recollections, edited with memorials of his later life,* by his eldest son J. R. Gregory (London, 1903), viii, 46p.

Gregory, Benjamin, *Side Lights on the Conflicts of Methodism during the second quarter of the Nineteenth Century 1827–1852* (London, 1898), 584p.

Griffin, Alan, 'Methodism and Trade Unionism in the Nottinghamshire-Derbyshire Coalfield, 1844–90', *PWHS* 37 (February 1969), pp. 2–9.

Griffin, Rev. Edward, *Strictures upon a publication entitled 'A brand plucked out of the fire', or a brief account of Robert Kendal, who was executed at Northampton, 13th August, 1813, by W. P. Davies* (Nottingham, 1813) 22p.

Haartman, K., *Watching and Praying: Personality Transformation in Eighteenth-century British Methodism* (New York, 2004), 241p.

Halévy, Elie, *The Birth of Methodism in England*, English translation by Bernard Semmel first published in *La Révue de Paris*, 1906 (Chicago, 1971) ix, 81p.

Halévy, Elie, *A History of the English People*, English translation by E. I. Watkins and D. A. Barker (London, 1924–47), 4 vols. Vol. 1 *England in 1815* (1924).

Hall, Joseph, *Memorials of Wesleyan Methodist Ministers: or, The Yearly Death Roll, from 1777–1840* (London, 1876), 312p.

Hall, Robert, *The Nature of Faith, considered in a Circular Letter from the Baptist Ministers and Messengers, Assembled at Kettering, in Northamptonshire, June 5, 6, and 7, 1781* (Northampton, 1781), 19p.

Hare, John, *The Ministry and Character of Robert Henry Hare, Wesleyan Minister* (London, 1874), vi, 480p.

Harris, Margaret, *To Serve the Present Age: Memories of Methodism in Riseley (Higham Ferrers Circuit)* (Riseley, 1967) 34p.

Harrison, J. F. C., *The Second Coming: Popular Millenarianism 1780–1850* (London, 1979), xvii, 277p.

Hartley , T. Galland, ed., *Hall's Circuits and Ministers: an alphabetical list of the circuits in Great Britain with the names of the ministers stationed in each circuit together with the appointments to departments and other offices from 1762 to 1912* (London, 1914), xix, 609p.

Hartley, Thomas, *Paradise Restored: or, a Testimony to the Doctrine of the Blessed Millennium: with some Considerations of its Approaching Advent from the Signs of the Times* (Leeds, 1799), xi, 275p.

Hawkes, Joseph. *The Rise and Progress of the Wesleyan Sunday Schools, Luton* (Luton, 1885), 24p.

Heitzenrater, Richard P., ed., *The Poor and the People called Methodists 1729–1999* (Nashville, 2002), 243p.

Hempton, David, *Methodism and Politics in British Society 1750–1850* (London, 1984), 276p.

Hempton, David, *Methodism: Empire of the Spirit* (New Haven, 2005), xiii, 278p.

Hempton, David, *The Religion of the People: Methodism and Popular Religion c. 1750–1900* (London, 1996), xiii, 239p.

Heslop, Luke, *Two Sermons and a Charge* (Newcastle, 1807), 60p.

Hews, Francis, *Spoils won in the day of battle* (Biggleswade, 1799), 108p.

Hindmarsh, D. Bruce, *John Newton and the English Evangelical Tradition between the Conversions of Wesley and Wilberforce,* Oxford Theological Monographs (Oxford, 1996), xvii, 366p.

Hobsbawm, E. J., 'Methodism and the threat of revolution in Britain' in E. J. Hobsbawm *Labouring men: studies in the History of Labour* (London, 1964), pp. 23–33.

Holland, Bernard, *Baptism in Early Methodism* (London, 1970), x, 200p.

Hollett, Calvin, *Shouting, Embracing, and Dancing with Ecstasy: the Growth of Methodism in Newfoundland, 1774–1874* (Montreal, 2010), xviii, 368p.

Hopkins, James K., *A Woman to Deliver Her People: Joanna Southcott and English Millenarianism in an Era of Revolution* (Austin, Texas, 1982), xxii, 304p.

Horn, Pamela, *Joseph Arch (1826–1919): The Farm Workers' Leader* (Kineton, 1971), x, 262p.

Horn, Pamela, 'Methodism and Agricultural Trade Unionism in Oxfordshire: the 1870s', *PWHS* 37(1969), pp. 67–71.

Horsley, Samuel, *The Charge of Samuel Lord Bishop of Rochester, to the Clergy of his Diocese, delivered at his Second General Visitation, in the year 1800* (London, 1800), 36p.

Houfe, Simon, *Bedfordshire* (London, 1995), xiii, 303p.

Inglis K. S., 'Patterns of Religious Worship in 1851', *JEH* 11 (1960), pp. 74–86.

The Introduction of Primitive Methodism into Luton, 1839 (Luton, 1889).

Jackson, Thomas, *The Centenary of Wesleyan Methodism: A Brief Sketch of the Rise,*

Progress, and Present State of the Wesleyan-Methodist Societies throughout the World (London, 1839), viii, 384p.

Jackson, Thomas, ed., *The Lives of Early Methodist Preachers: chiefly written by themselves* (London, 1878), 6 vols.

Jennings, Theodore W., *Good News to the Poor: John Wesley's Evangelical Economics* (Nashville, 1990), 234p.

Jensen, Richard and Malcolm Thorp, eds, *Mormons in Early Victorian Britain* (Salt Lake City, 1989), xiv, 282p.

Jones, D. C., *'A Glorious Work in the World': Welsh Methodism and the International Evangelical Revival 1735–1750* (Cardiff, 2004), xiv, 386p.

Jones, R. Tudur, *Congregationalism in England 1662–1962* (London, 1962), 504p.

Jones, Sarah Smith, *Memoir of the late Miss Susanna Row, of Cardington, Bedfordshire* (Hexham, 1867).

Kendall, H. B., *The Origin and History of the Primitive Methodist Church* (London, 1906), 2 vols.

Kent, John, *The Age of Disunity* (London, 1966), xii, 209p.

Kent, John, *Holding the Fort: Studies in Victorian Revivalism* (London, 1978), 381p.

King, James and Charles Ryskamp, eds, *The letters and prose writings of William Cowper* (Oxford 1979–86), 5 vols.

Kitson, Peter, 'The Male Occupational Structure of Bedfordshire, c.1700–1871: a Preliminary Report', University of Cambridge, Department of Geography http://www.geog.cam.ac.uk/research/projects/occupations/abstracts/paper11.pdf last accessed 3 May 2010.

Knight, Frances, *The Nineteenth-Century Church and English Society* (Cambridge, 1995), xiii, 230p.

Kussmaul, Ann, ed., *The Autobiography of Joseph Mayett of Quainton, 1783–1839,* Buckinghamshire RS 23 (Aylesbury, 1986), xxxii, 101p.

Laqueur, T. W., *Religion and Respectability: Sunday Schools and Working Class Culture, 1780–1850* (New Haven, 1976), xv, 293p.

Law, William, *A practical treatise upon Christian perfection* (London, 1726), [6], 535, 544–6, [2]p.

Lawton, George, 'Notes on early Methodism in Northampton', *PWHS* 25 (1945–6), pp. 88–94

Legg, Edward, ed., *Buckinghamshire Returns of the Census of Religious Worship 1851,* Buckinghamshire RS 27 (Aylesbury, 1991), 153p.

Letters to Lord G. William Russell from various writers 1817–1845 (London, 1915–19), 3 vols.

Lewis, Evan, *Independency: a deduction from the Laws of the Universe* (London, 1862), xii, 180p.

Lewis, Evan, *The Rev. H. Fish, M.A. and Wesleyan Methodism: a critique* (Kettering, 1863), 36p.

Lewis, Samuel, *A Topographical Dictionary of England: Comprising the Several Counties, Boroughs, Corporate and Market Towns, Parishes, Chapelries and Townships, and the islands of Guernsey, Jersey and Man ... with historical and statistical descriptions ...* (London, 1831), 4 vols.

Lightwood, James, T., *The Music of the Methodist Hymn-Book: being the Story of each Tune with Biographical Notices of the Composers* (London, 1935), xxiii, 549p.

Lovegrove, Deryck, *Established Church, Sectarian people: Itinerancy and the Transformation of English Dissent, 1780–1830* (Cambridge, 1988), 400p.

Luker, David, 'Revivalism in theory and practice: the Case of Cornish Methodism', *JEH,* 37 (1986), pp. 603–19.

Mack, P., *Heart Religion in the British Enlightenment: Gender and Emotion in Early Methodism* (Cambridge, 2008), xii, 328p.

Malmgreen, Gail, 'Domestic Discords: Women and the Family in East Cheshire Methodism, 1750–1830' in Jim Obelkevich, Lyndal Roper and Raphael Samuel, eds, *Disciplines of Faith: Studies in Religion, Politics and Patriarchy* (1987), pp. 55–70.

Mankin, Kenneth, *Our Hymns: a Commentary on Methodist Hymnody 1737–1988* (1988), 60p. (duplicated pamphlet).

Manning, F. J., ed., *The Williamson Letters 1748–1765*, BHRS 34 (Streatley, 1954), viii, 147p.

Mather, F. C. 'Georgian Churchmanship Reconsidered: Some Variations in Anglican Public Worship 1714–1830', *JEH* 36 (1985), pp. 255–83.

Memoir of the Rev. J. K. Martyn (London, 1850), 57p.

Memoirs of Miss Hannah Hillson of St Neots; consisting chiefly of extracts from her Journal (St Neots, 1848).

Methuen, Thomas Anthony, *A Memoir of the Rev. Robert P. Beachcroft, A.M., Rector of Blunham, Bedfordshire, and Chaplain to the Right Hon. Viscount Goderich* (London, 1832), xi, 286p.

Milburn, Geoffrey, *Primitive Methodism* (Peterborough, 2002), xi, 112p.

Milburn, Geoffrey and Margaret Batty, eds, *Workaday Preachers: The Story of Methodist Local Preaching* (Peterborough, 1995), xiv, 367p.

Millard, William, *The Branch, comprising Forty Psalm and Hymn Tunes* (London, 1810), musical score.

Morgan, Richard, ed., *The Diary of a Bedfordshire Squire*, BHRS 66 (Bedford, 1987), xiv, 246p.

Muggeridge, R. M., *A History of the Late Contest for the Representation of the Borough of Bedford* (London, 1830), 95p.

Mumford, Norman W., 'The Administration of the Sacrament of Baptism in the Methodist Church', *London and Holborn Quarterly Review* 172 (1947), pp. 113–19.

Namier, Lewis, and John Brooke, *The House of Commons 1754–90* (London, 1985), 3 vols. The History of Parliament Trust.

Nichols, Y. and S. Woods, eds., 'The Memoirs of Jane and William Inskip' in *Miscellanea*, BHRS 59 (Bedford, 1980), pp. 89–125.

Nuttall, Geoffrey, 'Baptists and Independents in Olney to the time of John Newton', *Baptist Quarterly* 30 (1983–4), pp. 26–37.

Obelkevich, James, *Religion and Rural Society: South Lindsey 1825–1875* (Oxford, 1976), xiii, 353p.

O'Connor, Bernard, *The History of St Mary's Church Everton cum Tetworth* (Everton? 2000), 28p.

Orr, J. E., *The Second Evangelical Awakening in Britain* (London, 1949), 302p.

Owen, Christopher, *The sacred flame of love: Methodism and society in nineteenth-century Georgia* (Athens, Georgia, 1998), xx, 290p.

Peer, A. H., *A History of Ampthill Union Church* (Ampthill, 1963), 46p.

Petty, John, *The History of the Primitive Methodist Connexion from its Origin to the Conference of 1860*, new ed. (London, 1864), xvi, 597p.

Phillips, Fred, *Wesleyan Methodist Church, Biggleswade Circuit: A brief history of each society in the circuit, from the formation to present time, with illustrations of each place of worship* (Biggleswade, 1905). Cover title: Souvenir: New Wesleyan Sunday Schools, Biggleswade.

Phillips, R. J., *Dunstable Methodist circuit, one hundred and fifty years of witness* (Dunstable Methodist circuit, 1993), 190p.

Pibworth, Nigel R., *The Gospel Pedlar: The Story of John Berridge and the Eighteenth-Century Revival* (Welwyn, 1987), vi, 313p.

Pickering, W. S. F., 'The 1851 Religious Census - a useless experiment?' *BJSoc* 18 (1967), pp. 382–407.

Pickles, H. M., *Benjamin Ingham, Preacher amongst the Dales of Yorkshire, the Forests of Lancashire, and the Fells of Cumbria* (Coventry, 1995), 152p.

Podmore, Colin, ed., *The Fetter Lane Moravian Congregation, London 1742–1992* (London, 1992) iv, 32p.

Podmore, Colin, *The Moravian Church in England, 1728–1760* (Oxford, 1998), xv, 332p.

Pope, Thomas, *The Story of Finedon Methodism: Its Founders and Its Progress: Lecture given at Finedon on March 5th 1914* (Wellingborough, 1914), 26p.

Powers, T., *A brief Memoir of the experience and happy death of Sarah Fisher, late scholar in the Methodist Sunday School, Bedford, who died May 29th, 1824* (Bedford, 1826), 12p.

Rack, Henry D., *Reasonable Enthusiast: John Wesley and the Rise of Methodism* (London, 1989), xvi, 656p.

Rack, Henry, 'Religious Societies and the Origins of Methodism', *JEH* 38 (1987), pp. 582–95

Rees, D. Ben, *The golden age of religion in Anglesey 1841–1885* (Llangoed, 2008), 64p.

Report from His Majesty's Commissioners for Inquiring into the Administration and Practical Operation of the Poor Laws (London, 1834), xiii, 362p. HCP 1834 (44); HCCP Reports of Commissioners, 1834 XXVII.

'Revival at Everton', *PWHS* 4 (1903/04), pp. 22–4.

Richey, Russell E., *Early American Methodism* (Bloomington, 1991), xix, 137p.

Richey, Russell E., *The Methodist Conference in America – A History* (Nashville, 1996), 304p.

Richmond, Rev. Legh, *The dairyman's daughter: an authentic and interesting narrative.* (London, 18–?), 5 parts. Many editions.

Rigg, James H., ed., *Sermons on special and ordinary occasions by the late Rev. Robert Newton, D.D.* (London, 1856), xii,372p.

Rigg, James H., *Wesleyan Methodist Reminiscences ... sixty years ago* (London, 1904), viii, 164p.

Roake, Margaret, ed., *Religious Worship in Kent: the Census of 1851,* Kent Records 27 (Maidstone, 1999), lii, 460p.

Robert Hodgert: A Pioneer Ancestor, ed. Lucile Thurman Buehler (np, nd), 101p.

Robinson, David, ed., *The 1851 Religious Census: Surrey*, Surrey Record Society 35 (Guildford, 1997), ccxxxvi, 164p.

Roddie, Robin, 'Keeping the Faith: Ireland's Primitive Methodism', *PWHS* 57 (2010), pp. 225–45.

Rodell, Jonathan, '"The best house by far in the town": John Wesley's Personal Circuit', *Bulletin of the John Rylands University Library of Manchester* 85 (2003), pp. 111–22.

Rodell, Jonathan, 'Francis Asbury's first circuit: Bedfordshire, 1767', *Methodist History* 42 (2004), pp. 110–21.

Rodell, Jonathan, 'Methodism and social justice' in W. Gibson, P. Forsaith and M. Welling, eds, *The Ashgate Research Companion to World Methodism* (Farnham, 2013), pp. 477–99.

Rodell, Jonathan, 'A new Wesley letter', *PWHS* 56 (2008), pp. 228–32.

Rowe, G. Stringer, *Memoir of Mary Calvert* (London, 1882), 58p.

Royle, Edward, 'When did Methodists stop attending their Parish Churches?', *PWHS* 56 (2008), pp. 275–96.

Rule, John, 'Explaining revivalism: the case of Cornish Methodism', *Southern History*, 20–21, (1998–9), pp. 168–88.

Russell, John, *Memoirs of the Affairs of Europe from the Peace of Utrecht* (London, 1824–29), 2 vols.

Rutherford, Mark [William Hale White], *The Autobiography of Mark Rutherford*, 13th ed. (London, nd), xii, 139p.

Rutherford, Mark [William Hale White] *The Early Life of Mark Rutherford* (London, 1913), 91p.

Rutherford, Mark [William Hale White], *The Revolution in Tanner's Lane* (London, 1984), 317p.

Samuel, Raphael, ed. *People's history and social theory* (London, 1981), History Workshop series, lvi, 417p.

Saul, G. Beamish, 'Methodism in Northants'. originally printed in an unidentified newspaper (probably *The Northamptonshire Methodist Monthly* or *Northampton Mercury*) around 1906 and preserved as a set of cuttings in the Wesley Historical Society Library, Oxford.

Scotland, Nigel, *Methodism and the Revolt of the Field: a Study of the Methodist Contribution to Agricultural Trade Unionism in East Anglia 1872–96* (Gloucester, 1981), 296p.

Semmel, Bernard, *The Methodist Revolution* (London, 1974), viii, 273p.

Seymour, Aaron Crossley Hobart, *Life and Times of Selina, Countess of Huntingdon; by a member of the houses of Shirley and Hastings* (London, 1840), 2 vols.

Sharp, J. Alfred, 'An eccentric Bedford Evangelist', *PWHS* 4 (1903–4) pp. 65–7.

Shaw, Thomas, *Gwennap Pit, John Wesley's amphitheatre: a Cornish pardon* (Busveal, 1992), 72p.

Shaw-Taylor, L. and E. A. Wrigley, 'The Occupational Structure of England c.1750–1871: Preliminary Report,' University of Cambridge, Department of Geography, http://www.geog.cam.ac.uk /research/projects/occupations/introduction/summary.pdf last accessed 2 May 2010.

Shepherd, Richard, *No false alarm; or, a sequel to Religious union, etc., being the result of a parochial visitation through the archdeaconry of Bedford* (London, Bedford, 1808), [4], 67, [1]p.

Short, Colin C., 'Robert Winfield and the Revivalists', *PWHS* 53 (2001), pp. 93–102.

A Short Account of the Cruelties inflicted on Dissenters by the High Church Party, occasioned by the Dismissal of five men from the service of Joseph Morris, Esq. upon their refusal to conform to a General Order "That EVERY man in Mr Morris's service should attend the Established Church" (Bedford, nd).

Short sketch of the work carried on by the Ancient Protestant Episcopal Moravian church in Northamptonshire (1886), 16p

Short Sketches of the Work Carried on by the Ancient Protestant Episcopal Moravian Church ... in Lancashire, Cheshire, The Midlands and Scotland, from 1740 (Leeds, 1888), 48p.

Shovelton, Wright, *An Invitation to Christian fellowship: A sermon preached in the Wesleyan Chapel, Biggleswade* (Biggleswade, 1850), 23p.

Sidney, Edwin, *The Life of the Rev. Rowland Hill, AM* (New York, 1848), 412p.

Simon, John S., 'The Repeal of the Conventicle Act', *PWHS* 11 (1917–18), pp. 103–8.

Simpson, Revd David, *A discourse on dreams and night-visions, with numerous examples ancient and modern* (Macclesfield, 1791), 148p.

Simpson, Revd David, *A Key to the Prophecies: or, a Concise View of the Predictions contained in the Old and New Testaments, which have been fulfilled, are now fulfilling, or are yet to be fulfilled in the Latter Ages of the World* (Macclesfield, 1795), xi, 462p.

Smith, George, *History of Wesleyan Methodism* (London, 1857–1861), 3 vols.

Smith, Henry, 'Early Methodism in Huntingdonshire and its immediate vicinity', *WMM* (1881), pp. 585–92, 745–92.

Snape, M. F., 'Anti-Methodism in Eighteenth-Century England: The Pendle Forest Riots of 1748', *JEH* 49 (1998), pp. 257–81.

Snell, K. D. M., *Parish and Belonging: Community, Identity and Welfare in England and Wales, 1700–1950* (Cambridge, 2006), xiv, 541p.

Snell, K. D. M. and Paul S. Ell, *Rival Jerusalems: The Geography of Victorian Religion* (New York, 2000), xvi, 499p.

Sorrell, Mark, *The Peculiar People* (Exeter, 1979), 168p.

Stead, Geoffrey and Margaret, *The Exotic Plant: A History of the Moravian Church in Britain 1742–2000* (Peterborough, 2003), xvi, 442p.

Stead, Geoffrey, *The Moravian Settlement at Fulneck, 1742–1790,* Thoresby Society, 2nd series, 9 (Leeds, 1998), viii, 127p.

Stelfox, James, 'Mr Wesley's Preface to the Hymn-Book' *WMM* (1876), pp. 529–34.

Stell, Christopher, ed., *An Inventory of Nonconformist Chapels and Meeting-houses in Central England* (London, 1986), xviii, 276p.

Stephens, W. B., *Education, Literacy and Society, 1830–1870: The Geography of Diversity in Provincial England* (Manchester, 1987), xii, 386p.

Stevens, Amanda, *Cornish women preachers 1750–1850: just 'novelty value'?* (Truro, 2007), 32p.

Stevenson, George J., *City Road Chapel, London, and its associations, historical, biographical, and memorial* (London, 1872), 624p.

Stokes, F. G., ed., *The Blecheley Diary of the Rev. William Cole, M.A. F.S.A. 1765–67* (London, 1931), lx, 392p.

The Story of Luton (DVD, Amazon Events, 2006).

Streather, G. T., *Memorials of the Independent Chapel at Rothwell* (Rothwell, 1994), 247p.

Supplement to the Short Sketch of the Work carried on by the Moravian Church in Northampton, issued in 1886 being accounts written by the Rev. Francis Okely B. A., respecting the erection of the chapel in that town in 1769/70 (Aylesbury, 1888), 14p.

Tattershall, Thomas, *An Account of Tobias Smith, a Gipsy, who was Executed at Bedford, April 3d, 1792* (np, 1792), 21p.

Taylor, E. R., *Methodism and Politics 1791–1851* (Cambridge, 1935), x, 226p.

Taylor, Thomas, *Ten Sermons on the Millennium: or, the Glory of the Latter Days: and Five Sermons on what Appears to Follow that Happy Aera* (Hull, 1789), 353p.

Tearle, J. D., *Our Heritage: Chapel Street Methodist Church, Luton 1852–1952* (Bedford, 1952), 40p.

Telford, John, *The Life of James Harrison Rigg: DD, 1821–1909* (London, 1909), ix, 423p.

Telford, John, *Two West-End Chapels: or Sketches of London Methodism from Wesley's Day 1740–1886* (London, 1886), viii, 292p.

Temperley, Nicholas, 'Methodist Church Music', in *New Grove Dictionary of Music and Musicians*, 2nd ed. (London, 2001), vol. 16 pp. 521–9.

Temperley, Nicholas and Stephen Banfield, eds, *Music and the Wesleys* (Urbana, Ill., 2010), 296p.

Thom, David, 'Liverpool Churches and Chapels; their destruction, removal or alteration: with notices of Clergymen, Ministers and others', *Proceedings and Papers of the Historic Society of Lancashire and Cheshire* 4 (1851–2), pp. 137–88; 5 (1852–3) pp. 3–56.

Thomas, Keith, *Religion and the decline of magic: studies in popular beliefs in sixteenth and seventeenth century England* (London, 1971), xviii, 716p.

Thomas, R. S., *Collected Poems 1945–90* (London, 2000), xi, 548p.

Thompson, D. M., 'The Religious Census of 1851' in R. Lawton, ed., *The Census and Social Structure: an Interpretative Guide to Nineteenth Century Censuses for England and Wales*, (London, 1978), pp. 241–68.

Thompson, E. P., *The Making of the English Working Class* (London, 1980), 958p.

Thorne, Susan, *Congregational missions and the making of an imperial culture in nineteenth-century England* (Stanford, CA, 1999), ix, 247p.

Thorp, Malcolm 'Popular Preaching and Millennial Expectations: the Reverend Robert Aitken and the Christian Society, 1836–40', in Malcolm Chase and Ian Dyck, eds, *Living and Learning: Essays in honour of J. F. C. Harrison* (Aldershot, Hants., 1996), pp. 103–17.

Thorp, Malcolm R., 'The Religious Background of Mormon Converts in Britain, 1837–52', *Journal of Mormon History* 4 (1977), pp. 51–65.

Tibbutt, H. G., *The Baptists of Leighton Buzzard* (Leighton Buzzard, 1963), 32p.

Tibbutt, H. G., *Bunyan Meeting Bedford 1650–1950* (Bedford, 1950?), 148p.

Tibbutt, H. G., *Cotton End Old Meeting 1776–1962* (Rushden, 1963), 47p.

Tibbutt, H. G., *Hockliffe & Eggington Congregational Church 1809–1959* (Bedford, 1959), 27p.

Tibbutt, H. G., *The Minutes of the First Independent Church (now Bunyan Meeting) at Bedford 1656–1766,* BHRS 55 (Bedford, 1976), 232p.

Tibbutt, H. G., *The Old Meeting, Blunham* (Blunham, 1951), 19p.

Tibbutt, H. G., *Some Early Nonconformist Church Books,* BHRS 51 (Bedford, 1972), 88p.

Tibbutt, H. G., *Stevington Baptist Meeting 1655–1955* (Stevington, 1955), 23p.

Tibbutt, H. G. and Robert P. Hart, *Keysoe Brook End and Keysoe Row Baptist Churches* (Keysoe, 1959), 32p.

Tice, F., *The History of Methodism in Cambridge* (London, 1966), vi, 143p.

Timmins, T. C. B., ed., *Suffolk Returns from the Census of Religious Worship of 1851*, Suffolk Records Society 39 (Woodbridge, 1997), lxxii, 230p.

Tindall, Edwin, *The Wesleyan Methodist atlas of England and Wales* (London, 1874), 46p.

Tolar Burton, Vicki, *Spiritual Literacy in John Wesley's Methodism: Reading, Writing and Speaking to Believe* (Waco, 2008), xix, 388p.

Townsend, W. J., H. B. Workman and G. Eayrs, eds. *A New History of Methodism* (London, 1909), 2 vols.

Turner, Jonathan, *Teetotalism illustrated by facts; including a brief view of teetotal sayings and doings in Saint Ives, and the west of Cornwall* (London, 1842), 42p.

Two sermons delivered at the Methodist chapel Luton, Beds: one by the Rev Max. Wilson and the other by the Rev. Thos. Rogerson (Dunstable, 1835), 34p.

Tyerman, Luke, *The Life and Times of the Rev. John Wesley, Founder of the Methodists* (London, 1870–71), 3 vols.

Tyerman, Luke, *The Life of George Whitefield, BA, of Pembroke College, Oxford* (London, 1876–7), 2 vols.

Tyerman, Luke, *Oxford Methodists: Memoirs of the Rev. Messrs. Clayton, Ingham, Gambold, Hervey, and Broughton, with biographical notices of others* (London, 1873), viii, 416p.

Urwick, William, *Nonconformity in Herts. Being lectures upon the non-conforming worthies of St. Albans, and memorials of Puritanism and Nonconformity in all the Parishes of the County of Hertford*, (London, 1884).

Valenze, D. 'Charity, custom and humanity: changing attitudes towards the Poor in eighteenth-century England' in J. Garnett and H. C. G. Matthew, eds, *Religion and revival since 1700: essays for John Walsh* (London, 1993), pp. 59–78.

Valenze, D., *Prophetic Sons and Daughters: Female Preaching and Popular Religion in Industrial England* (Princeton, 1985), xvi, 307p.

Varley, Joan, 'A Bedfordshire Clergyman of the Reform Era and his Bishop', in *Worthington George Smith and other Studies presented to Joyce Godber*, BHRS 57 (Bedford, 1978), pp. 113–40.

Vickers, John, *Thomas Coke: Apostle of Methodism* (London, 1969), xiv, 394p.

Victoria History of the Counties of England: Bedford, (Westminster, 1904–14), 4 vols.

Wallington, Arthur, 'Wesley and Anne Dutton' *PWHS* 11 (1917–18), pp. 43–8.

Walsh, John, 'The Cambridge Methodists' in Peter Brookes, ed., *Christian Spirituality: Essays in honour of Gordon Rupp* (London, 1975), pp. 251–83.

Walsh, John, 'Elie Halévy and the Birth of Methodism', *Transactions of the Royal Historical Society* 25 (1975), pp. 1–20.

Walsh, John, 'John Wesley and the Community of Goods' in Keith Robbins, ed., *Protes-*

tant Evangelicalism: Britain, Ireland, Germany and America, c.1750–c.1950: Essays in Honour of W. R. Ward, Studies in Church History, subsidia 7 (Oxford, 1990), pp. 25–50.

Walsh, John, 'Methodism and the Local Community in the Eighteenth Century' in *Vie ecclésiale: communauté et communautés* (Paris, 1989), pp. 141–53.

Walsh, John, 'Methodism and the Mob in the Eighteenth Century' in G. J. Cuming, and Derek Baker, eds, *Popular Belief and Practice: Papers read at the Ninth Summer Meeting and the Tenth Winter Meeting of the Ecclesiastical History Society,* Studies in Church History 8 (Cambridge, 1972), pp. 213–27.

Walsh, John, 'Origins of the Evangelical Movement', in Gareth Bennett and John Walsh, *Essays in Modern English Church History in Memory of Norman Sykes* (London, 1966), pp. 132–62.

Ward, Graham, ed., *The 1851 Religious Census of Northamptonshire,* Northamptonshire Record Society: Victor Hatley memorial volume (Northampton, 2007), 266p.

Ward, John, *A brief vindication of the Wesleyan Methodists in their doctrine and discipline, or what some would call their Church government with a view to condemn the inconsistent churchman, out of his own mouth: Being some strictures upon the writings of Mr. Exton, and his second. Wherien they have tried to defame the Methodists, and have brought reproach upon the true Church of England* (Northampton, 1820), 24p.

Ward, W. R., ed., *Early Victorian Methodism: the Correspondence of Jabez Bunting, 1830–1858* (Oxford, 1976), xxiii, 440p.

Ward, W. R., ed., *Parson and Parish in Eighteenth-century Surrey: Replies to Bishops' Visitations,* Surrey Record Society 34 (Guildford, 1994), xxvi, 198p.

Ward, W. R., *The Protestant Evangelical Awakening* (Cambridge, 1992), xviii, 370p.

Ward, W. R., *Religion and Society in England 1790–1850* (London, 1972), x, 339p.

Warner, Wellman J., *The Wesleyan Movement in the Industrial Revolution* (London, 1930), x, 299p.

A Warning Voice to the Church, being a letter addressed to the Bishop of Lincoln on the progress and tendencies of Methodism (Hull, 1840), 24p.

Watson, David Lowes, *The Early Methodist Class Meeting: its Origins and Significance* (Nashville, 1985), xiii, 273p.

Watson, JoAnn, ed., *Selected Spiritual Writings of Anne Dutton: Eighteenth-Century, British-Baptist, Woman Theologian* (Macon, GA, 2003–10), 6 vols.

Watts, Michael R., *The Dissenters* (Oxford, 1978–1995), 2 vols.

Wearmouth, Robert F., *Methodism and the Working-class Movements of England 1800–1850* (London, 1937), 289p.

Webb, B., *To Serve the Present Age: 150 years of Methodism in Lidlington* (np, 1962). Duplicated pamphlet.

Webster, Robert, *Methodism and the miraculous: John Wesley's idea of the supernatural and the identification of Methodists in the eighteenth century* (Lexington, Kentucky, 2013), xi, 273p.

Welch, Edwin, ed., *The Bedford Moravian Church in the Eighteenth Century*, BHRS 68 (Bedford, 1989), 283p.

Welch, Edwin, ed., *Bedfordshire Chapels and Meeting Houses: Official Registration 1672–1901*, BHRS 75 (Bedford, 1996), 231p.

Welch, Edwin, 'The Origins of the New Connexion of General Baptists in Leicestershire', *Transactions of the Leicestershire Archaeological and Historical Society* 69 (1995), pp. 59–70.

Welch, Edwin ed., *Two Calvinistic Methodist Chapels 1743–1811: the London Tabernacle and Spa Fields Chapel,* London Record Society 11 (London, 1975), xix, 108p.

Wellenreuther, Hermann, 'Politische Patronage von John, Fourth Duke of Bedford und die

Stellung der Herrnhuter Brüdergemeine in dem Borough of Bedford, 1745–1755', *Unitas Fratrum: Beiträge aus der Brüdergemeine*, 4 (1978), pp. 85–93.

Wesleyan Delegate Takings: or, short sketches of personal and intellectual character as exhibited in the Wesleyan Delegate Meeting, held in Albion Street Chapel, London, on the 12th, 13th, 14th, 15th March, 1850: together with an exposition and defence of the Resolutions passed at that meeting by some of them (Manchester, 1850), 190p.

The Wesleyan Psalmist: a collection of psalm and hymn tunes, by Edward Booth (London, 1843), 250p.

White, William Hale *see* Rutherford, Mark

Whitebrook, J. C., *Anne Dutton: a Life and Bibliography* (London, 1921), 20p.

Wigfield, W. M., ed., 'Recusancy and Nonconformity in Bedfordshire: illustrated by select documents between 1622 and 1842', in *Miscellanea*, BHRS 20 (Aspley Guise, 1938), pp. 145–249.

Wildman, Lilian M., 'Changes in Membership Recruitment and Social Composition in Ten Rural Old Dissent Churches in the South-East Midlands, 1715–1851', *Baptist Quarterly* 35 (1994), pp. 332–46.

Williams, H. W., *The Veteran school-superintendent: a Memoir of Mr Charles Smith of Potton, fifty years superintendent of the Wesleyan Sunday-school at Biggleswade* (London, 1861), 34p.

Wilson, R., ed., *A history of the Methodist churches in the Rugby and Daventry circuit* (Rugby and Daventry Circuit of the Methodist Church, 1993), iii, 44p.

Woodward, Robert, *A Candid Consideration of the Causes and Pretences for Separation from the Ancient Established Church* (Bedford, 1800), 94p.

Woodward, Robert, *Causes and pretences for separation from the Ancient Established Church considered and refuted* (London, 1802), viii, 220p.

Wright, Thomas, *The Life of the Rev. Timothy Richard Matthews, Friend of Edward Fitzgerald,* (London, 1934), xi, 218p.

Wright, W. A., *Letters of Edward FitzGerald* (London, 1894), 2 vols.

Wrigley, E. A., and R. S. Schofield, *The Population History of England 1541–1871: A Reconstruction* (London, 1981), xv, 779p.

Index

Places outside Bedfordshire and major towns are identified by county. Abbreviations used in the Index and not in the list on p. xv: